D1222048

The Victorian Mirror of History

The Victorian
Mirror of History

A. Dwight Culler

YALE UNIVERSITY PRESS
New Haven and London

Designed by Margaret E.B. Joyner
and set in Galliard type
by Brevis Press, Bethany, Ct.
Printed in the United States of America
by Vail-Ballou Press, Binghamton, N.Y.

Library of Congress Cataloging in Publication Data

Culler, A. Dwight (Arthur Dwight), 1917–
The Victorian mirror of history.

Includes bibliographical references and index.
1. Historians—Great Britain. 2. Historiography—
Great Britain—History—19th century. 3. Great Britain
Historiography. I. Title.
DA3.A1C85 1986 941'.0072 85–11985
ISBN 0–300–03452–0 (alk. paper)

10 9 8 7 6 5 4 3 2 1

Contents

Preface

By the Victorian mirror of history I mean the habit, which seems to have been pervasive among Victorian writers, of drawing analogies between their own age and various historical periods in the past and attempting to understand their problems, and their place in history, in terms of those analogies. An example would be the great interest in the Renaissance on the part of Browning, Pater, and others, which suggests, I believe, that in the latter part of the century there was a kind of "Victorian Renaissance," and that Carlyle, Newman, Arnold, and Ruskin constituted an oppressive "Middle Ages," from which Pater and others felt they were emerging. This is a simplified account of the matter, and indeed the interest of the topic is its complexity. Often the analogy was based upon a cyclical or undulatory conception of history, often on the supposed parallel between history and the course of human life. Sometimes, however, it was a mere affinity for some period in the past, and sometimes, as in Pugin's *Contrasts* and Carlyle's *Past and Present,* it was not an analogy at all but an opposition or contrast. In such cases the image of the mirror is strictly inappropriate, and I should emphasize that my interest is not primarily in the image but in the pragmatic or reflexive use of history. Nonetheless, because the mirror expresses that idea and because the image was widely used by the Victorians themselves, I have thought it worthwhile to retain it as a convenient symbol for a complex of ideas. The reader should understand, however, that there was not a single mirror of history but many different ones, and that some were distorting, magic, and even transparent. *Pace* Meyer Abrams, a few may even have been "lamps."

I begin with an introductory chapter on the Augustan Age, since that is the immediately preceding example of the analogical use of history, and then turn to Sir Walter Scott, who was primarily responsible for historicizing the imagination of the English people in the nineteenth century. I then proceed by major individual figures or groups of figures who were concerned either with a phase of the past or with a current problem in relation to the past. I wish I could say that a neat thesis concerning the use of the mirror of history had emerged, but in the Victorian Age that is seldom possible. The thesis of the book, if it has a thesis, is that the great Victorian debate about science, religion, art, and culture always had a historical dimension, always was concerned with the relation of the present to the past. Thus, in order to understand this debate we need to understand the elaborate web of interrelationships which the age wove between itself and the past.

I am very conscious that in my treatment I have been highly selective and that there are many other writers and subjects that might have been included. Tennyson will seem to many readers like a glaring example, but, apart from the fact that I have written on him elsewhere, he seems to me much more a poet of universal myth than of the particular temporal relationships of history. His Sir Bedivere and Ulysses are both determined to go forward, but the one does not do so in a peculiarly medieval and the other in a classical way; neither are Oenone, Mariana, and the Lady of Shalott so differentiated that they represent Greek, Renaissance, and medieval civilization. They are universal figures whose laments reverberate in cosmic, not historical, time. Apart from Tennyson, there are, of course, scores of historical novels, formal histories, and other writings that might have been treated. Perhaps the approach taken here will stimulate others to fill in and correct the outlines which I have suggested.

This study has been supported by grants from the John Simon Guggenheim Memorial Foundation, the National Endowment for the Humanities, and Yale University, and I am grateful to these benign institutions for their help. I am also most grateful to the staffs of the British Library, the Henry E. Huntington Library, and the Yale University Library for their courteous and efficient service. Among individuals, I am particularly indebted to my wife, Helen S. Culler, to my colleague, Frank Turner, and to the unidentified reader for the Yale University Press, all of whom read the manuscript in its entirety and made many helpful suggestions. Frank Brady, Maynard Mack, and Linda Peterson have also helped me in various ways. Diane Repak and Helen Westerfield typed the manuscript amid the press of many other duties. Ellen Graham has, as always, been a helpful and supportive editor.

Some sections of this work were originally tried out in lectures at the Graduate Center of the City University of New York, Hanover College, the University of Georgia, Vanderbilt University, and Yale University. I am grateful to my hosts and to the audiences at those institutions for the opportunity to address them. One of these lectures was published in the *Browning Institute Studies,* volume 10, and I wish to thank the editor and the Board of Directors of the Browning Institute for permission to reprint selected portions.

If it were appropriate to dedicate a book to an institution, I would dedicate this one to Yale University, and to Branford College within the University, which have, for nearly forty years, provided me with an ideal place to work.

The Victorian Mirror of History

Pompeii, by-the-by, was a thoroughly Victorian city.
Roger Fry

The thing that hath been tomorrow is that which shall be yesterday. *Günter Grass*

Human life occurs only once, and the reason we cannot determine which of our decisions are good and which bad is that in a given situation we can make only one decision; we are not granted a second, third, or fourth life in which to compare various decisions.

History is similar to individual lives in this respect. There is only one history of the Czechs. *Milan Kundera*

There will always be a connection between the way in which men contemplate the past and the way in which they contemplate the present. *H. T. Buckle*

History is what one age finds worthy of note in another. *Jacob Burckhardt*

To pay homage to our past is the only gesture that also includes the future. *Djuna Barnes*

No man can have in his mind a conception of the future, for the future is not yet. But of our conceptions of the past, we make a future. *Thomas Hobbes*

One would expect people to remember the past and imagine the future. But in fact, when discoursing or writing about history, they imagine it in terms of their own experience, and when trying to gauge the future they cite supposed analogies from the past; till, by a double process of repetition, they imagine the past and remember the future. *Sir Lewis Namier*

The one duty we owe to history is to rewrite it.
Oscar Wilde

Introduction

ONE OF THE MOST DRAMATIC MOMENTS in Victorian literature is that in the *Apologia pro vita sua* in which Newman first felt a doubt about the tenableness of his position in the Anglican Church. For half a dozen years he had been defending that position as a via media between Rome and extreme Protestantism, but now, in the summer of 1839, as he was reading in the history of the early church, he came upon an account of the Monophysites, a fifth-century sect which had played a similar mediatorial role between the Eutychians and the See of Rome. At first he was merely uneasy, but by the end of August he was seriously alarmed. "My stronghold," he wrote, "was Antiquity; now here, in the middle of the fifth century, I found, as it seemed to me, Christendom of the sixteenth and the nineteenth centuries reflected. I saw my face in that mirror, and I was a Monophysite." Newman's horror at being a Monophysite had nothing to do with the doctrinal controversy, which concerned the one or two natures of Christ, but simply with the relationship of the parties one to another and with the fact that, if an extreme version of a position is heretical, then a moderate version of that position is heretical also. "It was difficult," he wrote, "to make out how the Eutychians or Monophysites were heretics, unless Protestants and Anglicans were heretics also. . . . There was an awful similitude, more awful, because so silent and unimpassioned, between the dead records of the past and the feverish chronicle of the present. The shadow of the fifth century was on the sixteenth. It was like a spirit rising from the troubled waters of the old world, with the shape and lineaments of the new."[1]

A little later Newman received a second blow when a friend pointed out to him, in an article by Cardinal Wiseman, the palmary words of St. Augustine, "Securus judicat orbis terrarum"—"Untroubled the world passes its judgment." The words express simply the argument from catholicity, with which Newman had long been familiar; but "who can account," says Newman, "for the impressions which are made on him? . . . I had seen the shadow of a hand upon the wall. . . . He who has seen a ghost, cannot be as if he had never seen it."[2] It is clear from Newman's imagery that one reason these experiences were so impressive to him was their apparently providential character. In both cases he was simply going about his own business, not looking for trouble, when these awful admonitions were thrust upon him. But a second reason was their objective, historic character. The awful similitude was the more awful because so silent and unimpassioned. It was not the voice of some feverish controversialist that was speaking but the dead records of the past. It was a ghost, a spirit rising up from the troubled waters, the silent reflection in a mirror that simply looked at him and said, "You are a heretic!"

Three years before, this same mode of argument had been used against Newman by Thomas Arnold in an article in the *Edinburgh Review* entitled "The Oxford Malignants and Dr. Hampden." Renn Dickson Hampden was a liberal theologian who had been nominated by Lord Melbourne as Regius Professor of Divinity at Oxford, but the Tractarians, who considered him little more than a Socinian, had, by adroit campaigning and some misrepresentation, formed a cabal and got the appointment censured. Arnold was furious and, in what is certainly one of the most vitriolic attacks ever published in a reputable journal, he accused the Tractarians of being narrow-minded religious fanatics who, out of pure malignancy, were persecuting a good and religious man. After he had calmed down a little he made this philosophical reflection:

> The common language, which describes history to be philosophy teaching by examples, is an ambiguous expression of a great but ill-understood truth. No man would go to history for lessons of private morality: we have other far better and readier means of learning these. But what history does furnish, when read aright, is a mirror to reflect the true character of existing parties, and so, to determine our judgment in taking part with one or another. It gives us this true mirror when we have learned, in the parties and revolutions of past times, to separate what is accidental and particular from what is essential and universal.[3]

What the mirror had revealed in this instance is that the true antecedents of the Tractarians were to be found in that little group of diehard clergy whom Oliver Cromwell had called the "Oxford malignants"—in them and their descendants, the Non-Jurors of the late seventeenth century. They were also to be found in the persecutors of Huss at the Council of Constance and in the Jews and Judaizers of the New Testament.⁴ In other words, to Arnold there are bigots in every religion, and history helps us distinguish them from the forward-looking liberals. To Newman, on the other hand, "The principles and proceedings of the Church now, were those of the Church then; the principles and proceedings of heretics then, were those of Protestants now."⁵ Newman and Arnold looked into different mirrors and saw different things, but, as good Victorians, they agreed that the mirror of history provided a perspective glass which enabled one to see through contemporary controversy to more lasting truth.

Another well-known use of the Victorian mirror of history, in this case not to clarify the confusion among parties but rather to represent that confusion as it existed both in the past and the present, is to be found in the last lines of "Dover Beach":

> And we are here as on a darkling plain
> Swept with confused alarms of struggle and flight,
> Where ignorant armies clash by night.

The allusion is to Thucydides' account of the famous night battle between the Athenians and the Syracusans on the plains of Epipolae. The Athenians, new to the scene, became confused and in the moonlight could not distinguish friend from foe, so that they slew many of their own number and ultimately were thrown down from the cliffs and destroyed. This image evidently symbolized to many Victorians the intellectual confusion of their age, for it is so used by Carlyle at the end of "Characteristics," by Tennyson in "The Passing of Arthur," by Clough in the *Bothie of Tober-na-Vuolich,* and by Newman in his sermon "Faith and Reason, contrasted as Habits of Mind."⁶ "Controversy," says Newman, "at least in this age, does not lie between the hosts of heaven, Michael and his Angels on the one side, and the powers of evil on the other, but it is a sort of night battle, where each fights for himself, and friend and foe stand together." It has been suggested that the popularity of this image was due in large part to Thomas Arnold, the editor of Thucydides, who in his strong belief in the relevance of the classics would have impressed this meaning upon it as he taught Thucydides to his young men at Rugby. The suggestion is plausible, and yet it was clearly a habit of mind among the Victorians to perceive analogies between their own day and various historical epochs in the past and then to use these analogies in conducting their controversies. Their historical consciousness was a mode of self-consciousness, an awareness of the self by means of the other.

This is not to suggest that no one before the Victorian age ever drew a parallel between his own day and previous periods of history. Virtually every historian of antiquity and the Renaissance asserted the didactic function of history, and that function obviously implies some sort of analogy. Livy in the Preface to his work declared, "What chiefly makes the study of history wholesome and profitable is this, that you behold the lessons of every kind of experience set forth as on a conspicuous monument." Livy preferred the image of a monument, but the metaphor of the mirror, glass, or speculum was commonplace in the Elizabethan age, as in the popular *Mirror for Magistrates* (1559–87) or Richard Grafton's *Chronicle at Large* (1569), which offered "a glass to see things past, whereby to judge justly of things present and wisely of things to come." Most commonly, however, the focus during all this period was not on the great movements of history but on the individual actions of great men, which were thought to provide examples by which to inculcate morality in youth and political wisdom in statesmen. Leibnitz, for example, asserted, "The chief end of history, like that of poetry, is to teach prudence and virtue by examples, and to exhibit vice in such a way as to arouse aversion and lead to its avoidance."[7] This is the view of history as "philosophy teaching by examples" which was rejected by Thomas Arnold. The phrase originated with Dionysius of Halicarnassus, was repeated by Isaac Casaubon and others in the Renaissance, and was given wide currency by Lord Bolingbroke in his *Letters on the Study and Use of History* (1752).[8] It represented the standard view of the function of history from antiquity through the eighteenth century—that it provided a storehouse of examples for imitation and avoidance in the realms both of private and of public life.

The assumption on which this view was based is that of the uniformity of human nature. "It is universally acknowledged," wrote Hume, "that there is a great uniformity among the actions of men, in all nations and ages, and that human nature remains still the same, in its principles and operations. The same motives always produce the same actions: The same events follow from the same causes. . . . Would you know the sentiments, inclinations, and course of life of the Greeks and Romans? Study well the temper and actions of the French and English: You cannot be mistaken in transferring to the former *most* of the observations you have made with regard to the latter."[9] Students of Montesquieu, however, were aware that, although men might be similar in their reason and passions, the influence of climate, race, religion, customs, and manners in modifying these was very great. Even Bolingbroke admitted that there were two masters, history and experience, and that, of the two, experience was the more important. History was the ancient text, experience the modern language into which it had to be translated.[10] Thus, as interest shifted from the individual actions of great men to the larger movements of society, it also shifted from the exemplary anecdote to the broader cultural resemblances between societies. Henry Hallam, for example, in commenting upon the importance of cultural history, said that "without it, the statesman would form very erroneous estimates of events, and find himself constantly misled in any analogical application of them to present circumstances."[11] And Matthew Arnold, speaking of the problem of translating Homer, said: "Human nature under like circumstances is probably in all ages much the same; . . . but it is of little use to tell us this, because we know the human nature of other ages only through the representations of them which have come down to us, and the classical and the romantic modes of representation are so far from being 'one,' that they remain eternally distinct."[12] Change, in other words, rather than similarity, becomes the important feature when one turns from "human nature" to its modifications by culture.

It was on the continent in the work of Leibnitz, Lessing, Herder, and Goethe that the developmental conception of human culture arose which would transform the idea of history and hence of the use of history in interpreting the present. To this movement the name *historicism* has been given. Its essential elements, according to Friedrich Meinecke, are the ideas of individuality and development.[13] Human nature, far from being uniform in all countries and ages, manifests itself in an infinite variety of forms, each of which is constantly undergoing a process of development. These forms are to be understood not by bringing them before some universal bar of judgment but by seeing each in its own terms as a necessary phase in the sequence of which it is a part. Herder, whose *Reflections on the Philosophy of the History of Mankind* (1784–91) was the prime expression of this pluralistic vision of human culture, was not himself a catastrophist, but his vision seemed to culminate in and be confirmed by the French Revolution—"the greatest event," said Burke, "which the world has ever known." That event, as is usual with great calamities, turned men's attention to history. Barthold Niebuhr found he could not live through those soul-stirring days without imputing to his History of Rome the passion he found in the present. "Anyone," wrote Goethe, "who has lived through the Revolution feels impelled towards history. He sees the past in the present, and contemplates it with fresh eyes which bring even the most distant objects into the picture." Moreover, he wishes to see whether he can project the line of development into the future and see what lies ahead. "The coming age," said Shelley, "is shadowed on the Past / As on a glass."[14]

Geoffrey Tillotson has said that the nineteenth century was the first that thought of itself as having a number.[15] Whether or not this be true (one is always cautious about claiming "firsts"), it is certainly true that virtually everybody in the nineteenth century believed that theirs was an "age of transition." According to Walter Houghton, "This is the basic and almost universal conception of the period. And it is peculiarly Victorian. For although all ages are ages of transition, never before had men thought of their own time as an era of change *from* the past *to* the future."[16] Sir Henry Holland said specifically in 1858 that "we are living in *an age of transition*." One of the reasons why Mill wrote his *Autobiography* was that "in an age of transition in opinions, there may be somewhat both of interest and of benefit in noting the successive phases of any mind which was always pressing forward."[17] Arnold wrote of his age as "Wandering between two worlds, one dead, / The other powerless to be born," but his brother Tom anticipated him in 1847, declaring, "We cannot accept the present, and we shall not live to see the future. It is an age of transition; in which the mass are carried hither and thither by chimeras of different kinds, while to the few, who . . . have caught a glimpse of the sublime but distant future, is left nothing but sadness and isolation."[18] Elizabeth Barrett Browning referred, more flippantly, to hers as "An age of mere transition, meaning nought / Except that what succeeds must shame it quite / If God please."[19] Tennyson in 1887 informed his son, "You must not be surprised at anything which comes to pass in the next fifty years. All ages are ages of transition, but this is an awful moment of transition. . . . The wave advances and recedes."[20] Prince Albert, Carlyle, Disraeli, Frederic Harrison, Bulwer-Lytton, W. H. Mallock, Harriet Martineau, John Morley, William Morris, Herbert Spencer, and J. A. Symonds all use the phrase or some variant upon it. All recognize that it is a cliché and that there is nothing original in the idea, but it seems so profoundly true that they cannot refrain from repeating it.

A mirror seems hardly designed to catch so mobile a reflection, and one must admit that the image is not always appropriate. In Pugin's *Contrasts* and Carlyle's *Past and Present,* for example, the Middle Ages are presented not as a reflection of the nineteenth century but as a contrast or paradigm. In other cases it is an underlying spiritual affinity that is felt, neither altogether a likeness nor altogether an ideal. Of course, in the Renaissance the mirror or glass was often the image of an ideal type or pattern, as when Hamlet is called "the glass of fashion and the mould of form"; and when Hamlet tells his mother, "I set you up a glass / Where you may see the inmost part of you," it is actually two pictures, one of her past and one of her present husband, that he exposes. The important point, of course, is not the image of the mirror but the element of self-recognition which the Victorians felt when they looked into history. Because the mirror emphasizes this fact it is perhaps worth retaining as a symbol.

"What pitfalls," said Arnold, "lie in that word Nature!" He might equally well have substituted the word *history*, for any study of this sort is besieged with difficulties. Primary among them is the problem of "truth." It will not do, with some modern critics,[21] to say that the Victorians were simply constructing a "myth" of history, which we could and should criticize exactly as if it were a fiction. The Victorians believed that what they were saying was true, and that belief is an important part of what they were saying. On the other hand, though more, and more accurate, information is available to us today about the past than was available to the Victorians, it is not apparent that we have the "truth" either, or that there is any point in being condescending to the Victorians and showing "how they got it wrong." If their Greeks are figures of serenity and repose because they derive from Winckelmann, whereas ours are irrational and daemonic because they derive from Nietzsche, it may well be that the Nietzschean view will go out in turn and we will come back to Winckelmann. It is clear that we are dealing neither with "myth" nor with "truth" but with that intermediate realm known as "belief"—conceptions of the past which are no doubt inadequate to the truth but have some relation to it. In setting forth these beliefs the great Victorians engaged in a dialogue with each other, which extended over the decades and constituted a running argument about society, religion, culture, science, and art. It is the thesis of this book that that dialogue had a historical dimension, consisting of multiple interpretations of history in conflict with each other. The dialogue is rather like Carlyle's conception of Tradition as a great banyan tree, growing up from one root into a whole overarching labyrinth of trees. "Or rather might we say, it is a Hall of Mirrors, where in pale light each mirror reflects, convexly or concavely, not only some real Object, but the Shadows of this in other mirrors; which again do the like for it: till in such reflection and re-reflection the whole immensity is filled with dimmer and dimmer shapes; and no firm scene lies round us, but a dislocated, distorted chaos, fading away on all hands, in the distance, into utter night."[22]

1

England's Augustan Age

ISTORIANS HAVE COMMONLY MADE a sharp distinction between the Christian linear view of history, extending straight from Creation to the Last Judgment, and the classical cyclical view of writers like Polybius and Machiavelli. Recently, however, G. W. Trompf, in his study of the idea of historical recurrence in Western thought, has urged that so sharp a distinction is unwarranted.[1] Both Christians and pagans had heard of both straight lines and circles, and some element of each conception is to be found in either world. Doubtless the Four Monarchies of the Book of Daniel did not contemplate recurrence, and neither did the Six Ages, corresponding to the six days of creation, into which medieval churchmen divided their subject. But once there was a New Testament to complement the Old, it was perhaps inevitable that some kind of analogy should spring up between them. The analogy that did develop was prophetic or prefigurative: it asserted that events and persons in the Old Testament were types or figures of those in the New. Adam, for example, was the type of Christ, and Moses leading the children of Israel into the promised land is a figure of Christ leading all men from spiritual slavery into the heavenly kingdom. This form of Biblical interpretation, which is known as Typology, has had a continuous history from the time of Origen to our own day, and recent scholars have shown that it had a powerful influence on certain Victorian poets and artists, particularly those in the Evangelical tradition.[2] It was extended in popular usage to include events in either the Old Testament or the New which might be considered types of events in later secular history and particularly in the spiritual life of the individual. It was, then, an example of the Victorian mirror of history operating on Biblical rather than secular materials, and, though it is not a part of the subject of this book, we should note its existence as another powerful force encouraging the practice of analogical thinking.

In the secular world this practice need not be traced back farther than the Renaissance. It began when Petrarch looked back over an intervening period of history to an age with which he felt more spiritually akin and called that age *antiqua* and his own *nova* or modern. Vasari added the essential metaphor of rebirth (*rinascita*) to suggest that the spirit of antiquity had been reborn in the artists of his own day, and thus the one age began to model itself upon the other. The concept of a "middle age" intervening between ancient and modern times is, of course, implicit in the very idea of a renaissance, and we find the terms by which it was known, *media ætas, media antiquitas,* and *media tempora,* as early as the fifteenth century. It was not until the seventeenth century, however, that this tripartite division of history was firmly established by being embodied in the textbooks of the German pedagogue Cellarius.[3] Once it was—once history was conceived as divided into three periods, of which the third was in some sense a *ricorso* or return upon the first— we have the basis for a cyclical or undulatory theory of history.

Sir William Temple gave an early expression to this view in *An Essay upon the Ancient and Modern Learning* (1690). "Science and Arts," he says, "have run their circles, and had their periods in the several Parts of the World. They are generally agreed to have held their courses from *East* to *West,* to have begun in *Chaldæa* and *Ægypt,* to have been Transplanted from thence to *Greece,* from *Greece* to *Rome,* to have sunk there, and after many Ages to have revived from those Ashes, and to have sprung up again, both in *Italy* and other more *Western* Provinces of *Europe.*"[4]

By the mid-eighteenth century this view had undergone some refinement, for Voltaire says in his *Age of Louis XIV* that there are only four ages which count with a person of taste and discrimination: the Age of Periclean Athens, the Augustan Age in Rome, the Age of the Medici in Italy, and the Age of Louis XIV in France. If one groups the first two ages together as "classical antiquity" and the last two as the "Renaissance" and then adds the preceding and intervening "dark ages," one has four large alternating epochs of Superstition and Reason: the river-valley civilizations of the Near East, the classical civilization of Greece and Rome, the Christian millenium, and modern times beginning with the Revival of Letters. In Voltaire's view Christianity represented an advance over the religions of Mesopotamia and Egypt, just as the modern age was an advance over classical antiquity; but it was the tension between the two types of mentality, the credulous and the critical, that constituted for Voltaire (indeed, for the Enlightenment in general) the fundamental pattern of history.[5] In later years the Romantic

movement would reverse this valuation, calling Voltaire's Age of Superstition an "Age of Faith," and his Age of Reason an "Age of Skepticism,"
but it would not disturb the fundamental pattern. And for the moment
it was well established that the Enlightenment, which saw itself as a
continuation of the Renaissance, was resuming a classical tradition
which had unfortunately been broken for a thousand years. "It is not
easy for us," writes Christopher Dawson, "to realize the strength of this
classical tradition [in the eighteenth century]. For three hundred years
men had lived a double life. The classical world was the standard of their
thought and conduct. In a sense, it was more real to them than their
own world, for they had been taught to know the history of Rome better
than that of England or modern Europe; to judge their literature by the
standard of Quintilian, and to model their thought on Cicero and Sen-
eca. Ancient history was history in the absolute sense, and the ages that
followed were a shadowy and unreal world which could only be ratio-
nalized by being related in some way to the classical past."[6]

That way was not always very fundamental. When Queen Elizabeth
was compared to Alexander the Great or King Arthur, the comparison
was a mode of eulogy that was rhetorical rather than historical. William
Prynne had his ears cropped for comparing Charles I to Nero, but that
merely meant that Charles I could recognize an insult when he saw it,
not that Prynne had recognized a parallel. Poems and plays with historical settings were often thought to comment covertly on contemporary politics, but that was a mode of avoiding prosecution and
imprisonment, not of asserting a relation between one century and another. Still, from the Restoration till the late eighteenth century allusions and analogies so cluster about one particular period of history—
the late years of the Roman Republic and the early years of the Empire—
that it appears England really had looked into the mirror of history and
declared itself an Augustan Age.[7] There was a feeling, not systematic or
philosophically based, that the Age of Elizabeth corresponded to the
Roman Republic, that Spain was Carthage, that the Civil Wars corresponded to those between Marius and Sulla, or perhaps between Caesar
and Pompey, and that it was time now for a new Augustus to arise who
would establish authority, bring peace to the country, and patronize the
arts. If so, it was perhaps premature of Edmund Waller in his "Pane-
gyrick to my Lord Protector" (1655) to praise Cromwell by comparing
him to Augustus, but it was entirely reasonable that Dryden in "Astrea
Redux" should so greet Charles II. After the Revolution of 1688, however, it was not possible for writers of any political persuasion to praise
Augustus, and we find that the references to him by Swift, Pope, and

Bolingbroke are primarily hostile and ironic. The best known instance of this is Pope's "Epistle to Augustus" (1737), which, taking advantage of the fact that George II's second name was Augustus, produced an "imitation" of Horace's "Epistle to Augustus" which plays ironically with both the Roman emperor and his modern counterpart. The true focus of the Roman parallel, however, was elsewhere, with Addison's *Cato.*

The presentation of *Cato* at Drury Lane in 1713 produced a political sensation. Addison wrote it hoping that the public would discover an analogy between the followers of Caesar and the Tories, between Sempronius and the apostate Whigs, and between Cato of Utica, the great defender of senatorial liberties, and the band of patriots who still stood firm round Halifax and Wharton. It was not in the interest of the Tories, however, to appropriate to themselves reflections thrown on the great Caesarian leader who, with the support of his legions, had subverted the liberties of the Roman people. Accordingly, though the theater was packed with Whigs, "every shout that was raised by the members of the Kit Cat Club was re-echoed by the High Churchmen of the October; and the curtain fell amidst thunders of unanimous applause." Such is Macaulay's spirited account of the event, and he notes that from this time forth the name Cato was invoked by everyone, of whatever party, who wished to represent himself as a disinterested patriot. The two most famous of these latter-day Catos were John Trenchard and Thomas Gordon, the authors of *Cato's Letters,* a weekly series that assailed the government of Sir Robert Walpole in the early 1720s. There was also, however, a "cult of Cato" among literary men—Swift, Nicholas Rowe, James Thomson, Samuel Boyse, and Colley Cibber—and even the ministry tried to invoke Cato on their own behalf. Ultimately, however, they were forced by the anomalies of their position to select as their sponsor another equally famous Republican, Marcus Tullius Cicero.

The choice of Cicero was dictated in part by the discovery in 1722 of a Jacobite plot (that involving Francis Atterbury, Bishop of Rochester) which presented an obvious parallel with the Catilinarian conspiracy. The parallel was exploited in a government pamphlet, *Clodius and Cicero* (1727), and for the next fifteen years there was a campaign on the part of the Court Whigs to depict Walpole as a reincarnation of "Tully." The point of this campaign, as Reed Browning has noted, was not only to identify Walpole with a popular Republican figure but also to establish tolerance and flexibility as the desirable qualities in political life rather than Cato's inflexible and ultimately quixotic devotion to

principle. Nathaniel Hooke's "Tory" *Roman History* (1738) had represented Cicero as vacillating and sometimes craven, but in 1741 Conyers
Middleton's *History of the Life of Marcus Tullius Cicero* eulogized Cicero
for his great contributions to the state and clearly identified him with
Sir Robert. A medal was struck with Walpole on the obverse and Cicero
on the reverse. Bolingbroke still gloried in his designation "Cato," but
when Walpole stepped down from office in 1742, thus removing the
threat of an aspiring Caesar, the Catonic position seemed more difficult
to maintain. What in the 1720s had seemed like unyielding resistance
now began to appear like inflexibility, and by mid-century Cicero had
become a spokesman for order and liberty to whom almost all writers,
of any political persuasion, could appeal.[8]

In the politics of the early eighteenth century, then, both sides vied
in their devotion to the Roman Republic and both were "anti-Augustan." Indeed, Howard Weinbrot and Reed Browning have shown that
anti-Augustanism was so pervasive in the eighteenth century that one
is left wondering why, in that case, it was called the "Augustan Age."[9]

The answer lies in the cultural meaning of the term. For already in
the seventeenth century the term *Augustan* had come to refer not merely
to a particular period of Roman history and literature but, more generally, to "the period of highest purity and refinement of any national
literature" (*OED*). That period for Italy had been the Age of the Medici
and for France the Age of Louis XIV. It now remained for England, as
it became conscious of its national greatness, to determine which was
its own "Augustan Age." Working on a theory developed by the Roman
historian Florus, that every nation goes through the stages of infancy,
youth, maturity, and decline, writers of the Restoration attempted to
chart the course of English poetry. It was a commonplace that Chaucer
was the "English Ennius," and just as, according to Dryden, there was
"in process of time a Lucilius, and a Lucretius, before Virgil and Horace," so "there was a Spenser, a Harrington, a Fairfax, before Waller and
Denham."[10] Waller and Denham, it was universally agreed, had refined
the language and brought its versification to perfection, so that England
in the late seventeenth century had arrived at a "Silver Age" comparable
to that of Virgil and Horace. Thus, Bishop Atterbury wrote in 1690
that Waller "undoubtedly stands first in the list of refiners, and, for
aught I know, last too; for I question whether in Charles II's reign
English did not come to its full perfection; and whether it has not had
its Augustan age as well as the Latin."[11] Atterbury, as Ian Watt has noted,
was thinking of the perfection of the English language rather than of
its literature, but a generation later John Oldmixon had literature es-

pecially in mind when he wrote that the reign of Charles II "probably may be the *Augustan* Age of *English* Poetry." This view of the Restoration period, though never generally adopted, was implicitly supported by Dr. Johnson in his famous encomium on Dryden: "What was said [by Suetonius] of Rome, adorned by Augustus, may be applied by an easy metaphor to English poetry embellished by Dryden, 'lateritiam invenit, marmoream reliquit,' he found it brick, and he left it marble."[12]

Not everyone agreed with this view. Swift, writing between 1711 and 1745, declared, "The *Epicureans* began to spread at *Rome* in the Empire of *Augustus,* as the *Socinians,* and even the *Epicureans* too, did in *England,* towards the End of King *Charles* the Second's Reign; which is reckoned, although very absurdly, our *Augustan* Age."[13] The comment illustrates very neatly the double use of "Augustan" as a historical period and a normative epithet. In the first part of the sentence Swift acknowledges the historical parallel but then, in the final clause, denies its normative application. Hume also declared (1757), "The reign of Charles the second, which some preposterously represent as our augustan age, retarded the progress of polite literature in this island; and it was then found, that the immeasurable licentiousness, which was indulged or rather applauded at court, was more destructive to the refined arts than even the cant, nonsense, and enthusiasm of the preceding period."[14] Joseph Warton agreed. In his *Essay on the Genius and Writings of Pope* (1756) he declared, "The common opinion that this [the reign of Charles II] was the Augustan age in England, is excessively false. A just taste was by no means yet formed. . . . Our style in prose was but beginning to be polished. . . . If I was to name a time, when the arts and polite literature, were at their height in this nation, I should mention the latter end of King William, and the reign of queen Anne."[15] Goldsmith adopted the view of Warton and Hume in his essay "An Account of the Augustan Age of England" published in *The Bee* in 1759. Defining the term *Augustan Age* as referring to "that period . . . when language and learning arrived at its highest perfection," he notes that "the age of Leo X. in Italy, is confessed to be the Augustan age with them" and that the French "seem agreed to give the same appellation to that of Lewis XIV. but the English are yet undetermined with respect to themselves." "Some have looked upon the writers in the times of Queen Elizabeth as the true standard for future imitation; others have descended to the reign of James I. and others still lower, to that of Charles II. Were I to be permitted to offer an opinion upon the subject, I should readily give my vote for the reign of Queen Anne, or some years before that period."[16] It will be noted of all these writers that they are not asserting a historical parallel between English writers and those of the Roman Augustan Age but are simply taking the term *Augustan* as denoting the period when any national literature attained its highest purity and refinement and are asking what that period was for England. By the end of the century, when the tide was turning against the whole neoclassical period, writers were inclined to deny the term even to the period of Queen Anne. Leonard Welsted in his verse "Epistle to the Duke of Chandos" (1724) had declared, "I see arise a new Augustan Age,"[17] presumably referring to his own; but William Enfield, reviewing Welsted's work in 1789, said, "The author . . . flourished in what is sometimes, though perhaps with no great propriety, called the Augustan Age of English literature." And John Pinkerton declared in 1785 that the "superior good sense and observation of the English" had led them to "fix no Augustan age for their country."[18] After enthusiastically proclaiming its own perfection, the eighteenth century seems to have argued itself out of that view.

How, then, did the idea of an Augustan Age in England come to be established? Curiously enough, as one looks through the manuals, handbooks, and histories of English literature that were written in the nineteenth century, one finds no mention of it. The period is called the Age of Reason, the Neoclassical Age, or simply the Eighteenth Century, but not the Augustan Age. Not until the publication of George Saintsbury's *A Short History of English Literature* (1898) do we encounter the phrase. Andrew Lang then took it up in his *History of English Literature* (1912), and Saintsbury gave it wide currency in his popular *Peace of the Augustans: A Survey of Eighteenth Century Literature as a Place of Rest and Retirement* (1916). In his Preface he notes that "the title of this book has been chosen" in order to bring out the "particular and systematic view" he is taking of the eighteenth century. "That view is of course not new—nothing is. It was taken perhaps for the first time . . . by Thackeray; it has actuated to some extent the novels of Sir Walter Besant and to a much greater the poems and essays of Mr. Austin Dobson."[19] It is, in other words, a part of the late nineteenth-century reaction in favor of the eighteenth century following the Romantic reaction against it. Matthew Arnold had patronized the period as "our excellent and indispensible eighteenth century," but by 1887 Augustine Birrell could write, "We have left off beating the eighteenth century."[20] Thus, in 1916, in the midst of a great World War, Saintsbury could look back to it nostalgically as "a place of rest and retirement" and could assert its relation to an even earlier and greater age. This view was immediately taken up by other scholars who asserted more firmly and seriously the historical relation. Mark Van Doren, for example, declared in the early pages of his *John Dryden* (1920): "For the first twenty years after the Restoration Dryden's London was to reproduce with a certain amount of accuracy the Rome of Ovid. With civil war just past and a common-wealth overthrown, with court and city beginning to realize their power, with peace prevailing and cynicism in fashionable morals rampant, with a foreign culture seeking the favor of patrons and wits, the new city did for a while bear a strange resemblance to the old Empire."[21] Hugh Kenner has pointed out that T. S. Eliot read this passage in May 1921, in the course of reviewing Van Doren's work for the *TLS* for June 9, and that it probably influenced him to make *The Waste Land* an "urban apocalypse" in which the horrors of post-war London are highlighted by being played off against the complex grandeur of Pope's London and the earlier Augustan Age in Rome.[22] It is curious that the modern historical analogy between Augustan England and Rome is not of Augustan but of Victorian origin. For the Augustan parallel, with respect to literature and culture, was purely normative. It was only when the Victorians began to look back to an age that seemed idyllic and pastoral that the scholars, extending the parallel into serious investigations of the relation between the English Augustans and the classics, asserted that parallel to a point where it probably now needs to be revised. Politically, the Augustans were more anti-Augustan than Augustan. Culturally, the analogy meant simply that they, like the Augustans of antiquity, had reached the high point of their culture and thereafter (and this was the less reassuring part) were likely to decline. Indeed, in 1774 Horace Walpole wrote, "The next Augustan Age will dawn on the other side of the Atlantic. There will perhaps be a Thucydides at Boston, a Xenophon at New York, and in time a Virgil at Mexico, and a Newton at Peru."[23]

When the schemes of Mosca and Volpone began to fall apart, Mosca cried, "Let's die like Romans, / Since we have lived like Grecians." From the sixteenth to the eighteenth centuries in England the words *Greek* and *Grecian* in popular usage carried unfavorable connotations as of a nation perfidious, wanton, too "merry," and given to pederasty. If there were noble Greeks, they came from Sparta, not from Athens. This does not mean, of course, that on the higher cultural level neoclassicism was exclusively Roman or that Romanticism was exclusively Hellenic. All the great neoclassicists read their Greek texts just as the Romantics knew their Romans.[24] But Greek was difficult, remote, known by fewer people.

It was, said Samuel Johnson, "like lace; every man gets as much of it as he can." But the corollary is that it was not like homespun or serge, which one would wear for every day. It could not be used as that "second world" to which one would allude as a matter of course, without fear of being misunderstood. The Roman world, on the other hand, which did serve that purpose, was so closely associated with the ideals of neo-classicism that, once those ideals began to fade in the 1760s and 1770s, there was the need for a new world, uncontaminated by such associa-tion, to be the vehicle of what was emerging. What new worlds were available? The Far East with its chinoiserie, the civilizations of the North, the hitherto despised Middle Ages—and all these were in fact used to embody new literary and cultural currents of the day. But there was also the civilization of Greece, which at this time was being redis-covered not through literary texts but through the reports of travelers, dilettantes, artists, and architects, who actually went to Greece and brought back reports which made this old classical civilization seem newly romantic.

This is not the place to tell the story of Romantic Hellenism, which has been well told by others.[25] One may merely say that the movement began with three notable works which appeared in the 1760s. The first was Johann Joachim Winckelmann's *History of Art among the Ancients* (1764), which completely revolutionized the study of art by treating it organically, as a part of the growth of the human spirit, inseparable from racial, climatic, and social conditions. Winckelmann also treated it far more inwardly than had his predecessors, seeking in the evolution of beauty itself the expression of the soul of the artist. Though working exclusively in Rome from Roman copies whose relation to the Greek originals was imperfectly understood, Winckelmann repudiated the ba-roque descendents of Rome in favor of a new imaginative ideal, the "noble simplicity and serene greatness" of Greek art. Meanwhile, over in England, Robert Wood's *Essay on the Original Genius and Writings of Homer* (1767) performed a comparable service for Greek literature, transforming Homer from the elegant neoclassical poet he had been made into by Pope into a rude Romantic poet of primitive genius. He did this, once again, by considering Homer in relation to his age and country, for Wood had traveled extensively in the Near East and was struck by the accuracy of the Homeric topography and by the confor-mity of the manners and customs of the modern inhabitants of the area to those represented in the poem. He did not anticipate Wolf in the theory of multiple authorship, but he did assert that Homer was a wan-dering rhapsodist, unable either to read or to write, who sang his poems in short snatches to the accompaniment of the harp. He also paved the way for Schliemann by searching for the historical Troy, though he reported that "not a stone is left, to certify, where it stood."[26] Finally, James ("Athenian") Stuart and Nicholas Revett, who, between 1748 and 1755, had been sent out by the Society of Dilettanti to draw, describe, and measure the antiquities of Athens, produced in 1762 the first volume of their sumptuously illustrated *The Antiquities of Athens, Measured and Delineated* (1762–94).[27] This work, ultimately in four volumes, was a revelation to the late eighteenth century of the true nature of Greek genius. For hitherto Greek art and architecture had been known largely through the art and architecture of Rome. Now the Apollo Belvedere and the Venus de' Medici were replaced by the frieze and pediments of Phidias, and the "classical" orders derived by Renaissance architects from Vitruvian precepts and Roman practice were replaced by the Doric of the Parthenon and the Ionic of the Erechtheum. The Doric order, in particular, had been virtually unknown to the modern world; in the third volume of Stuart and Revett it was fully and precisely revealed, and with this revelation the way was opened for the Greek Revival. It now became an important part of the training of an architect to visit Athens. Sir Robert Smirke went there in 1802 and on his return designed the first wing of the British Museum and the Royal College of Physicians in Trafalgar Square. William Wilkins also returned from Athens to design the facade of the National Gallery and University College, London. Most important, of course, was the acquisition by the nation in 1816 of the so-called Elgin marbles, for once the question of their authenticity was settled and whether they represented "ideal" or "natural" beauty, they became an integral part of British culture. To Keats they were "mighty things," mingling "Grecian grandeur with the rude / Wasting of old Time," and Benjamin Haydon declared that they "produced an Æra in public feeling."[28]

In addition to the artistic and literary aspect of the Greek Revival there was an important political dimension. Throughout the seventeenth and eighteenth centuries radical thinkers in both England and France had made Sparta rather than Athens the focus of their discussion, but after the 1770s the tide began to turn toward Sparta's more lively and intelligent rival. Tom Paine was apparently the first to declare unequivocally, "We see more to admire, and less to condemn, in that great, extraordinary people, than in anything which history affords." He added, "What Athens was in miniature, America will be in magnitude." Paine was not the first, however, to politicize Grecian history. That had already been done by John Gillies and William Mitford, the authors of the two principal histories of Greece in the last years of the eighteenth century. Gillies, a Tory, declared in the dedication of his work to George III, "Sir, the History of Greece exposes the dangerous turbulence of Democracy, and arraigns the despotism of Tyrants. By describing the incurable evils inherent in every form of Republican policy, it evinces the inestimable benefits . . . of well-regulated Monarchy." Mitford's more considerable work, which was published in ten volumes from 1784 to 1810, was, as Frank Turner has said, "a panegyric, largely derived from Country party ideology, on the virtues of the balanced English constitution and a polemic against those who would undermine that balance in the name of democracy, the people, or antique precedents."[29] It was the standard history of Greece until superseded by Connop Thirlwall's in 1835, but long before that date it had begun to seem reactionary to the rising generation of liberals and philosophic radicals. Macaulay declared that Mitford showed "a marked partiality for Lacedæmon, and a dislike of Athens," and Byron said, "His great pleasure consists in praising tyrants."[30] It was George Grote, the Benthamite banker, who was to redress the balance in his great *History of Greece* (12 vols., 1846–56) by transforming the Athenians into the ancient equivalent of the modern British liberal state. Whether one admired democracy or feared and distrusted it, it was established by Gillies, Mitford, Thirlwall, and Grote that Athens was the place where historically it was to be tried.

Even as Englishmen were debating the Athenian constitution and bringing home remnants of ancient Greek buildings, it became a question whether the most valuable surviving relic of ancient Greece was not the modern Greek people. A series of sentimental French and English travel books from 1770 on drew elaborate parallels between the manners and customs of the ancient Greeks and those of the modern inhabitants of the area and raised the question whether these degenerate people, the oppressed subjects of the Ottoman Empire, could really be the descendants of Plato and Socrates. If they were, could they be regenerated by being given their freedom? With this question the movement for a war of independence began. It was almost exclusively a western idea, the work of young philhellenes from Germany, France, and England, assisted by members of the Greek community who had been educated abroad.[31] Lord Byron was not the first of these young idealists, merely the most famous, and it was he who articulated their views most memorably.

> The mountains look on Marathon—
>> And Marathon looks on the sea;
> And musing there an hour alone,
>> I dream'd that Greece might still be free.

Shelley, asserting in the Preface to *Hellas,* "We are all Greeks"—a statement that no one would have made fifty years earlier—makes clear in the final chorus of his drama the cyclical philosophy on which the regeneration of Greece is to be based.

> The world's great age begins anew,
>> The golden years return,
> The earth doth like a snake renew
>> Her winter weeds outworn.

With Greek independence a "loftier Argo" will cleave the main, "another Orpheus" will sing, and a "new Ulysses" arise. John Stuart Mill declared, "The battle of Marathon, even as an event in English history, is more important than the battle of Hastings."[32] Certainly in the early years of the nineteenth century that was true.

Nonetheless, the main impetus of the Greek Revival hardly lasted beyond 1830. The British Museum and the National Gallery were built in the classical style in the 1820s–40s, but when plans were requested for the new Houses of Parliament in 1835, they were to be in the Gothic or Elizabethan style. Even in Edinburgh, the "Athens of the North," the "Parthenon" proposed for Calton Hill in 1819 was left unfinished, and the "Temple of Theseus" below it (otherwise the Royal High School), built in 1829, was the last gasp of the Athenian conceit.[33] For meanwhile, Sir Walter Scott, the "Wizard of the North," was engaged in a construction, and not only at Abbotsford, that would turn the attention of his countrymen in quite another direction.

2

Scott, Macaulay
and the Progress of Society

SIR WALTER SCOTT never learned Greek properly and by the time he was an adult had forgotten even the alphabet. He knew his Latin classics as a schoolboy does but never followed them up in later years. His attention was turned almost exclusively to the history of his own native land—to Scotland and England in relation to Scotland. As a result, the battle of Hastings was far more important to him than the battle of Marathon (witness *Ivanhoe*), but even more important were the battles of Killiecrankie, Culloden, and Marston Moor. These were the concerns of Macaulay too, for though he was a finished classicist and deeply admired the civilizations of Greece and Rome, even as a youth he had had the Wordsworthian thought that his own country provided subjects as worthy, and perhaps more interesting, than those of antiquity, and by age twenty-five he had already selected as his own the same period that primarily concerned Scott, the seventeenth and eighteenth centuries in Britain. For both men the analogy of history was not with some other civilization at a comparable stage of its development but with their own civilization in an earlier stage. The present could be seen in the past because it had arisen from the past. The circumstances were different but the issues and processes were the same.

In the famous third chapter of his *History of England* Macaulay says that between 1685 and his own day there had occurred a change in his country "to which the history of the old world furnishes no parallel."

> Could the England of 1685 be, by some magical process, set before
> our eyes, we should not know one landscape in a hundred or one
> building in ten thousand. The country gentleman would not recognise
> his own fields. The inhabitant of the town would not recognise his own
> street. Everything has been changed, but the great features of nature,
> and a few massive and durable works of human art. We might find out
> Snowdon and Windermere, the Cheddar Cliffs and Beachy Head. We

might find out here and there a Norman minster, or a castle which witnessed the wars of the Roses. But, with such rare exceptions, everything would be strange to us. Many thousands of square miles which are now rich corn land and meadow, intersected by green hedgerows, and dotted with villages and pleasant country seats, would appear as moors overgrown with furze, or fens abandoned to wild ducks. We should see straggling huts built of wood and covered with thatch, where we now see manufacturing towns and seaports renowned to the farthest ends of the world.[1]

Macaulay is prone to exaggeration, but a modern social historian, Harold Perkin, agrees that one would have to go back to Neolithic times to find a change comparable to that of the Industrial Revolution.[2] In the last years of the eighteenth century, population had increased at a rate never known before. It had also shifted dramatically from the south and east to the northern part of the country. There was a great movement of urbanization. Accompanying and, indeed, producing these changes were profound revolutions in agriculture and industry, and there were vast increases in exports, the national debt, and other measures of trade and commerce.

In Scotland one has to add to these changes the traumatic experience of the Act of Union of 1707, by which Scotland lost her national identity. David Daiches has noted that there were two diametrically opposed reactions to this experience: on the one hand, a nostalgic effort to recover and preserve everything that was distinctly Scottish and, on the other, an effort to create a new civilization that would compete on equal terms with the English.[3] Scott participated in both these efforts. As a child living on his grandfather's farm in the Border country, he had been fascinated by the tales he had heard from country people and servants, tales of bloody clashes between the Scots and English, of wild Border outlaws and wandering minstrels; and when he became older he took advantage of his position as Sheriff of Liddesdale to ride about the country collecting these ballads. The result was the *Minstrelsy of the Scottish Border*, of which he said that his hope was to "contribute somewhat to the history of my native country; the peculiar features of whose manners and character are daily melting and dissolving into those of her sister and ally."[4] Scott began his career, then, as an antiquarian and folklorist, and his work is to be associated with that of the other great antiquarians of the day, Bishop Percy, Thomas Warton, and George Ellis. Still, Scott had a highly ambiguous attitude toward the antiquary, defining him on one occasion as a person who became ill-tempered and dogmatic in direct proportion as the facts with which he was dealing were trivial and uncertain; and the figure of Dr. Dryasdust, to whom

he dedicates several of his novels, embodies his mocking, self-depreca-
tory stance.

Opposed to this antiquarian effort were the men of the Scottish
Enlightenment—David Hume, Adam Smith, Hugh Blair, Dugald Stewart, and others—and Scott was also associated with this group. In particular, in his approach to the past he did not restrict himself to the
poetry and romance of history but was well acquainted with the speculations of the "philosophic historians," a group which included David
Hume (the nephew of the philosopher), William Robertson, Adam Ferguson, and A. F. Tytler. This group was so called because, though lacking in specific facts about many aspects of early societies, they
attempted, through philosophic analysis, to trace the origin and development of social institutions.[5] They took their departure from Montesquieu, but whereas his analysis was largely static, they introduced and
emphasized the idea of progress. Progress for them, however, did not
arise from the perfectibility of human nature, as it did for Hartley and
Godwin, but from each individual's pursuing his own ends and attempting to better himself—a law to which they gave the name the "hetero-
geneity of ends." As a result of this law society moved gradually forward
through a series of "stages," from a hunting to a pastoral, an agricultural, and finally a commercial economy. In cultural terms it passed from
a "savage" to a "rude" or "barbarous" and then a "refined" or "polished"
age. As the terms indicate, this development was generally beneficial,
though there might be temporary setbacks and there certainly would be
losses attendant upon the gains. The progress in material civilization,
for example, might be attended by the selfish narrowness of the "commercial spirit," and a loss of martial ardor would necessarily go with
refinement in manners.

This is the view of history that was accepted by both Scott and
Macaulay as the best and most advanced view of their day. Though
frequently alluded to in their works, it is nowhere fully set forth, simply
because they regarded it as well known, widely accepted, and true. Only
the last phase of it bears directly upon their writings, but that bears
very directly, for they were concerned with the transition from the last
remnants of a feudal to the beginnings of a commercial or industrial
civilization. In Scotland one could actually see this transition occurring,
for in parts of the Highlands there existed pockets of a rude and patriarchal civilization that had changed very little in hundreds of years.
Thus, by traveling from London to the Border country and then up
into the Highlands one could travel back in time almost to the Middle

Ages. As Scott wrote in the "Postscript Which Should Have Been a Preface" to *Waverley*,[6]

> There is no European nation which, within the course of half a century or little more, has undergone so complete a change as this kingdom of Scotland. The effects of the insurrection of 1745,—the destruction of the patriarchal power of the Highland chiefs,—the abolition of the heritable jurisdictions of the Lowland nobility and barons,—the total eradication of the Jacobite party, which, averse to intermingle with the English, or adopt their customs, long continued to pride themselves upon maintaining ancient Scottish manners and customs,—commenced this innovation. The gradual influx of wealth and extension of commerce have since united to render the present people of Scotland a class of beings as different from their grandfathers as the existing English are from those of Queen Elizabeth's time. (I, 447)

Because such a change is gradual, says Scott, one needs to fix one's eyes on a particular point in the past in order to be conscious of it, and that is what *Waverley; or 'Tis Sixty Years Since* proposed to do. It would look back to the Scotland of 1745 and see the Lowlands of that period as in a state analogous to Elizabethan England, the Highlands as analogous to England before the Conquest. And having become conscious of change, it would try to assess the loss along with the gain.

For this purpose Scott needed a method of depicting human life and manners which would steer a middle course between antiquarianism and anachronism. He did not wish to forfeit the interest of his reader by involving him in antiquarian detail; on the other hand, neither would he misrepresent the past by assimilating it to the present. His solution, as stated in the opening chapter of *Waverley*, was to concentrate upon "those passions common to men in all stages of society, and which have alike agitated the human heart, whether it throbbed under the steel corslet of the fifteenth century, the brocaded coat of the eighteenth, or the blue frock and white dimity waistcoat of the present day" (I, 3–4). In other words, Scott accepted the eighteenth-century view of the uniformity of human nature but noted that it manifests itself differently in different ages. The passion of wrath, for example, manifested itself in open and sanguinary violence in the fifteenth century, whereas in the nineteenth it is channeled into legal action. The deep-ruling impulse is the same, and the forms, though different, are equally intelligible. In *Ivanhoe,* where the period is more remote, the problem is more difficult, and Scott indicates he cannot solve it completely unless he were to write the novel in Anglo-Saxon and Norman French. But once again "the passions . . . are generally the same in all ranks and conditions, all countries and ages," and it follows that "sentiments and manners," which spring from the passions, however much they are influenced by the peculiar state of society, must also be largely the same. There is thus an "extensive neutral ground," comparable to the words that are common both to old and modern English, that can be used by the novelist (IX, xxiv–xxv). Scott is not adopting the formula of Bulwer-Lytton in *The Last Days of Pompeii,* who is delighted to discover that the same wheedling, feminine arts that we know today were practiced in ancient Rome; neither is he, like Flaubert in *Salammbô,* reconstructing in detail the paraphernalia of a society.[7] His novels are historical in that they deal with large historical movements, and he is saying that, although there is no such thing as abstract human nature—human nature exists only as modified by particular societies—the reader will find in the struggle of human nature with those large modifying forces a familiar experience.

Because Scott is interested in society and does not wish to embody a "great man" theory of history, his hero has a kind of passivity, or "negative capability," which enables him to register the forces directed upon him but not himself to constitute a force. Hence, for his first hero, Waverley, Scott chose a name that was perfectly neutral, "uncontaminated" with good or evil but suggesting a "wavering and unsettled habit of mind." He then provided his hero with a Hanoverian father and a Jacobite uncle and allowed him during his minority to divide his time equally between their households. Through their negligence he received a desultory education in poetry, romantic fiction, and chivalric romances such as Scott himself had received and which, while cultivating the imagination, taught him little of "what adds dignity to man, and qualifies him to support and adorn an elevated situation in society." Given a commission in the army, he travels north with his regiment, and we become aware that this journey is not merely from England into Scotland, but also from the present into the past, from the Hanoverian succession into Jacobitism, and from prose into poetry. The first stage of the journey, to Tully-Veolan in the Lowlands, is to the home of the Baron of Bradwardine, an old friend of the family, and his daughter Rose. Here Waverley is so entranced with the "enchanted mansion" and "gardens of Alcina," which he sees entirely through the eyes of Spenser and Tasso, that he wholly forgets the depressing poverty of the "Elizabethan" village he came through. Ultimately, the Baron and Rose do not quite meet his ideal. The former has supported the old Pretender in 1715, but since then his Jacobitism has grown mild through disuse, and though he is "the very model of the old Scottish cavalier," this model is so based in the old-fashioned virtues that it does not much appeal to Waverley. Rose too, though reading Tasso, is "too frank, too confiding, too kind" to have "precisely the sort of beauty or merit which captivates a romantic imagination in early youth." Waverley thus decides to press on into the Highlands, and his motive now is not social obligation but mere curiosity. He is also becoming, partly through accidental circumstances, alienated from his regiment, and the more he retreats from duty, the further he penetrates into the spirit of the Highlands. Reaching Glennaquoich, the home of Fergus Mac-Ivor and his sister Flora, he sees their wild, romantic glens through the eyes not of the Elizabethan poets but of the painters Salvator and Poussin. Flora, indeed, singing to him Gaelic songs to the accompaniment of her harp, becomes the very embodiment of the Celtic Muse, and her brother seems like some great romantic chieftain. Both are fanatic Jacobites, but Flora's motives are pure enough that she warns him against her less scrupulous brother and urges that if he is to be involved in the cause, his involvement should "rest upon conviction, and not on a hurried and probably a temporary feeling." Waverley does not take her advice, however, and soon commits himself to the Jacobite cause. Even as he does so, its ill-advised character and the mixture of motives among its leaders become more apparent to him, so that by the time he arrives upon the field of battle at Prestonpans, he has little heart for conflict. Coming upon one of his followers, who is dying, he realizes that he has failed in his responsibilities to these men, and he wishes that he could awake from what now seems like "a dream, strange, horrible, and unnatural." Through the ordeal of battle, in which his role was humanitarian not martial, and through the penance of a wintry meditation by Lake Ullswater, he does awake from his dream: "he felt . . . that the romance of his life was ended, and that its real history had now commenced" (I, 371). Pardoned by the English, he returns, not to his original position, but to the first stage of his journey at Tully-Veolan, and, recognizing the true worth and real heroism of Rose, he marries her and sets about restoring the devastated estate. On his previous visit the Baron had told him he preferred simple prose to poetry but would meet him upon the neutral ground of history. It is upon that ground that they now meet, for British history is not simply the Hanoverian succession but includes some elements of the Celtic Muse.

In *Waverley* Scott found his formula for the historical novel, which he may be said to have invented.[8] Its essence is not simply that its action is set in the past or that its characters are dressed up in fancy costumes, but that it involves a conflict of historical forces and records historic

change. Its real protagonists are not the leading characters but the states
of society out of which they grow, for with great art Scott has contrived
that his characters, though highly individualized and pursuing their
own ends, are nevertheless representative of some aspect of the social
and cultural scene. "Had Fergus Mac-Ivor lived Sixty Years sooner than
he did," we are told, "he would in all probability have wanted the polished manner and knowledge of the world which he now possessed; and
had he lived Sixty Years later, his ambition and love of rule would have
lacked the fuel which his situation now afforded" (I, 118). He had
precisely the barbarism and refinement of a Highland chieftain in the
year 1745, just as the Baron of Bradwardine had precisely the qualities
of a Lowland Jacobite in that year. It is well known that Scott was not
distressed by historical inaccuracies in his novels so long as they involved
mere technicalities of name or date. It is all the more significant, then,
as Duncan Forbes notes, that he was deeply distressed by a "gross defect" in *Marmion,* namely, that Marmion's crime was forgery, "forgery
being the crime of a commercial rather than a proud and warlike age."[9]
In *Ivanhoe* he tolerated anachronisms of two or three hundred years so
long as they did not misrepresent the state of society he was depicting.

David Daiches has noted that Scott's characters are normally spread
out so as to form a spectrum, from extreme to moderate, of the various
factions they represent. In the evolution of his novel the future is always
with the moderates, for Scott believed that history works through compromise, and he also believed that the extreme version of a position is
not its quintessence but its corruption. With both Fergus Mac-Ivor and
Richard Waverley, the father of the hero, the legitimate causes of Jacobitism and the House of Hanover are corrupted by the principle of self,
whereas they are moderate with the Baron of Bradwardine and Colonel
Talbot precisely because they are pure. Having the future of the country
genuinely at heart, Talbot and the Baron can put aside minor differences
and meet on the ground of their common humanity and their common
moral code.

The two virtues which the Waverley hero must have, according to
Francis Hart, are fidelity and prudence.[10] Fidelity, of course, looks toward the past and prudence towards the future, but this does not mean
that one is to be favored over the other. Still, the direction of a Scott
novel is progressive, and it is irreversible. Waverley goes from the dream
of romantic Jacobitism to the reality of the Hanoverian succession, and
he could not possibly go in the opposite direction. This is true not only
because that is not the direction of history but also because it is not the
direction of human maturation. One does not grow more romantic as

one grows older. The triumph of Scott's art is that in a single narrative he can combine the story of a young man who grows up, achieves clarity of vision, and becomes the master of his own soul with the story of a nation which goes through an exactly comparable process. *Waverley* is at once a historical novel and a *bildungsroman,* and this is the answer, surely, to those who ask whether Scott's novels are ultimately about history or about morality. They are about both—about one who, finding himself in the throes of history, attempts to meet the demands of both fidelity and prudence by accommodating himself both to permanence and change.

Nonetheless, as one reads through the prefaces which Scott wrote for the Waverley novels, one is aware that he usually seems to have begun with a historical situation which he then contrived to illustrate by means of character and incident. In *Ivanhoe,* for example, he began with the contrast between the Saxons and the Normans which he found in John Logan's tragedy of *Runnamede.* "It seemed to the Author that the existence of the two races in the same country, the vanquished distinguished by their plain, homely, blunt manners, and the free spirit infused by their ancient institutions and laws; the victors, by the high spirit of military fame, personal adventure, and whatever could distinguish them as the flower of chivalry, might, intermixed with other characters . . . , interest the reader." In *The Monastery* "the general plan . . . was to conjoin two characters in that bustling and contentious age who . . . should, with the same sincerity and purity of intention, dedicate themselves, the one to the support of the sinking fabric of the Catholic Church, the other to the establishment of the Reformed doctrines." In *The Fortunes of Nigel* Scott began with the character of George Heriot, but then, noting that "the most picturesque period of history is that when the ancient rough and wild manners of a barbarous age are just becoming innovated upon . . . by increased or revived learning," he determined to place him in the reign of James I, which "possessed this advantage in a peculiar degree." The same contrast, but at an earlier stage, between the dwindling spirit of chivalry and the rising spirit of egotism is the subject of *Quentin Durward*; and *Redgauntlet,* set in the late 1760s, depicts the final decay of the old Jacobite fervor, opposed by only a few strong fanatic spirits. Scott has quoted Lady Mary Wortley Montagu that "the most romantic region of every country is that where the mountains unite themselves with the plains or lowlands."[11] Scott's Border country is such a region, but it is also the meeting point between two races, two ages, and two societies, whose clashes he chose to depict.

To the Victorians *Ivanhoe* was one of the most wonderful of Scott's

novels, and references to it abound in all the later literature of the age.
Readers were so entranced by what they took to be the vivid picture of
their national past that they did not ask the uncomfortable little questions that are posed by modern critics. David Brown, for example, has
observed that Scott made a clumsy error in the very first chapter.[12] After
emphasizing the hostility that existed between the Normans and the
Saxons after the Conquest, Scott has Wamba the Jester lecture Gurth
the Swineherd upon his oppressed condition by pointing out to him
the familiar distinction between the Saxon terms for barnyard animals
and the Norman names for their flesh as dressed for the table: *swine/
pork, ox/beef, calf/veal*. It is then revealed, however, that Gurth is the
thrall, not of a Norman lord, but of Cedric the Saxon and that it is for
Cedric's table that Gurth's animals are intended. The error is certainly
unfortunate, and yet the central conflict of the novel is not economic
but racial and cultural. For Scott has chosen a period at the very end
of the twelfth century when, as he thought, Saxon and Norman, though
still distinct and hostile races, were on the point of being melded into
the English nation. He illustrated the situation by the state of the language. "French was the language of honour, of chivalry, and even of
justice, while the far more manly and expressive Anglo-Saxon was abandoned to the use of rustics and hinds, who knew no other." To facilitate
communication between the two groups, "a dialect, compounded be-
twixt the French and the Anglo-Saxon" (IX, 3), had been formed, but
"it was not until the reign of Edward the Third," Scott tells us, "that
the mixed language, now termed English, was spoken at the court of
London, and that the hostile distinction of Norman and Saxon seems
entirely to have disappeared" (IX, 447). The striking thing is that both
swine and *pork, ox* and *beef, calf* and *veal* survived in that language.

The French historian Augustin Thierry has described the effect produced upon him and others by finding, in *Ivanhoe*, Saxons and Normans
in the reign of Richard I. Why, he asked himself, should the professional
historians have left such a fact as this to be brought to light by a novelist?[13] The answer may be because it was not true, for E. A. Freeman,
in his *History of the Norman Conquest* (1876), has declared that Scott's
thesis is unsupported by contemporary evidence.[14] Still, it seems to have
been accepted by the nineteenth century as true, for Macaulay says that
this melding of Norman and Saxon, which took place "silently and imperceptibly" in the thirteenth century, was one of the "two greatest and
and most salutary social revolutions which have taken place in England."[15] On the other hand, when Disraeli in 1845 divided England
into "Two Nations," the rich and the poor, he made it perfectly evident

by the choice of names—Marney, De Mowbray, and Egremont on the one hand, Diggs and Wodgate on the other—that these "nations" were the descendants of Norman and Saxon. Arnold too showed himself less a Hellene than a Celt when he protested against the ugliness of the Anglo-Saxon names—"Higginbottom, Stiggins, Bugg!"[16] And it is well known that Tess's expectations were disastrously inflated by her learning that she was a D'Urberville. The racism which Scott thought had been eliminated in the thirteenth century was probably stronger at the end of the nineteenth century than it had been at the beginning, but even in the early Victorian period it was an issue.

In Scott's view both the Saxons and the Normans have good and bad traits. The Saxons are distinguished by their homely manners and the free spirit of their ancient institutions, but also by a rudimentary civilization and a sullen attachment to the past. The Normans, on the other hand, are distinguished by the brilliance of their Gothic architecture and their chivalric accomplishment, but also by a haughty and overweening pride and corrupt morals. It is clear that if the stout homely virtues of the one race could be combined with the high civilization of the other, a noble nation would emerge; and this is just what Ivanhoe, as the mediatorial hero, is prepared to accomplish. He is a Saxon by birth but is alienated from his father because he has gone to court and followed the Norman King Richard to the Crusades. He is in love with the beautiful Rowena, a Saxon princess whom his father hopes to wed to Athelstane, the slow-witted descendant of King Alfred, so as to re-establish the Saxon rule. Richard, however, reconciles Ivanhoe with his father and so accomplishes this fruitful cultural union. Richard too, by wandering incognito among his people, has learned the virtues of the Saxon race and also how unjustly they have been oppressed by the Norman lords, and so he insists on being called not "Richard of Anjou" but "Richard of England." He will be the king of all his people.

In addition to the melding of Saxon and Norman the novel also undertakes an examination of the institution of chivalry. Contrary to popular impression, it is a very mixed report. Of the tournament which concludes the first part of the novel Scott says: "Thus ended the memorable field of Ashby-de-la-Zouche, one of the most gallantly contested tournaments of that age; for although only four knights, including one who was smothered by the heat of his armour, had died upon the field, yet upwards of thirty were desperately wounded, four or five of whom never recovered. Several more were disabled for life; and those who escaped best carried the marks of the conflict to the grave with them. Hence it is always mentioned in the old records as the 'gentle and joyous

passage of arms of Ashby' " (IX, 119–20). Also, during the storming
of the castle of Front de Boeuf, Rebecca, the fair Jewess, attacks the
profession of chivalry by asking Ivanhoe, "What remains to you as the
prize of all the blood you have spilled?" "What remains?" cried Ivanhoe;
"Glory, maiden—glory!" When Rebecca questions whether glory is sufficient reward "for the sacrifice of every kindly affection, for a life spent
miserably that ye may make others miserable," Ivanhoe rather shrilly
declares that it is: Chivalry is "the nurse of pure and high affection, the
stay of the oppressed, the redresser of grievances, the curb of the power
of the tyrant. Nobility were but an empty name without her, and liberty
finds the best protection in her lance and her sword" (IX, 275–76). One
cannot altogether discount Ivanhoe's words, for the philosophic historians did believe that chivalry served this idealizing purpose, but they
also believed there were two phases of chivalry, a purer first phase and
a more sordid second, and we seem here to be well into the second.
Scott grieves to admit that "those valiant barons, to whose stand against
the crown the liberties of England were indebted for their existence,
should themselves have been such dreadful oppressors, and capable of
excesses contrary not only to the laws of England, but to those of nature
and humanity" (IX, 209). He also admits that Richard would have done
more good had he stayed home from the Crusades and taken care of his
kingdom.

The conflict in Scott's novels is essentially one conflict. Whether it
be between the various forms of decaying chivalry and the new nation-
states that are replacing it, between the old aristocracy and the rising
commercial classes, between the Catholic faith and the doctrines of the
Reformed Church, between the wild spirit of individual freedom and
the cautious spirit of civic law, it is essentially a conflict between the
old and the new, between permanence and change. Macaulay, indeed,
says in his *History of England* that there can be but one conflict and that
this was formally recognized in the heart of Scott's period:

> The day [in October 1641] on which the Houses [of the Long
> Parliament] met again is one of the most remarkable epochs in our
> history. From that day dates the corporate existence of the two great
> parties which have ever since alternately governed the country. In one
> sense, indeed, the distinction which then became obvious had always
> existed, and always must exist. For it has its origin in diversities of
> temper, of understanding, and of interest, which are found in all so-
> cieties, and which will be found till the human mind ceases to be drawn
> in opposite directions by the charm of habit and by the charm of nov-
> elty. Not only in politics, but in literature, in art, in science, in surgery
> and mechanics, in navigation and agriculture, nay, even in mathematics,

we find this distinction. Everywhere there is a class of men who cling with fondness to whatever is ancient, and who, even when convinced by overpowering reasons that innovation would be beneficial, consent to it with many misgivings and forebodings. We find also everywhere another class of men, sanguine in hope, bold in speculation, always pressing forward, quick to discern the imperfections of whatever exists, disposed to think lightly of the risks and inconveniences which attend improvements, and disposed to give every change credit for being an improvement. In the sentiments of both classes there is something to approve. But of both the best specimens will be found not far from the common frontier. The extreme section of one class consists of bigoted dotards: the extreme section of the other consists of shallow and reckless empirics.[17]

Except for a slight shading in the tone, Scott the Tory would have agreed with Macaulay the Whig in this declaration, and both would have been found near the common frontier. Coleridge put the matter by saying that "the essential wisdom and happiness [of the Waverley novels] consists in this,—that the contest between the loyalists and their opponents can never be *obsolete,* for it is the contest between the two great moving principles of social humanity; . . . the desire and the admiration of permanence, on the one hand; and . . . the mighty instincts of *progression* and *free agency,* on the other."[18] Scott was more deeply committed than Macaulay to "old, unhappy, far-off things, / And battles long ago," and after the Peterloo Massacre he became more fearful of change. He deeply dreaded the passage of the Reform Bill, which indeed he did not live to see. To Macaulay, on the other hand, this event was the salvation of the state. Still, it is not so much that they were different in temperament as that they were of different generations. The Whig of yesteryear, said Macaulay, is the Tory of today, and the Whig of today is the Tory of tomorrow. Both men espoused what Herbert Butterfield has called "the Whig view of history," that is, the concern with those elements in the past that lead towards the present. To have done otherwise, to have attached oneself to "lost causes and forsaken beliefs," would have seemed to Scott a species of antiquarianism.

The Peterloo Massacre, which drove Scott further into reaction, led the youthful Macaulay temporarily to shed some of his father's Toryism and sympathize with the victims. He assured his parents, however, that he was not being drawn into revolutionary societies but had learned his opinions from Cicero, Tacitus, and Milton. It was inevitable, he said, that any person of reflection, however young, engaged in studying the history and politics of other nations must form notions on such subjects and apply them to his own country.[19] By the time he came to review Mitford's *History of Greece,* however, he had become much more cautious about classical parallels. The work was a good corrective, he wrote, for the "young gentleman who talks much about his country, tyrannicide, and Epaminondas,"[20] but Mitford ought to realize that popular government is not invariably either a blessing or a curse. "The fact is, that a good government, like a good coat, is that which fits the body for which it is designed. A man who, upon abstract principles, pronounces a constitution to be good, without an exact knowledge of the people who are to be governed by it, judges as absurdly as a tailor who should measure the Belvidere [*sic*] Apollo for the clothes of all his customers" (VII, 687–88). In his essay entitled "History" (1828) Macaulay became quite passionate in denouncing this evil. Plutarch and his modern imitators were especially guilty of it, for they took the myths of classical, republican liberty and, ignoring the fact that they had arisen in tiny city-states where, for local causes, the actions might have been justified, applied them to a large, despotic empire and a modern state which afforded no parallel. By the "modern imitators" of Plutarch, Macaulay meant the neo-Harrington True Whigs, the Bolingbrokian "Patriots," and especially the French revolutionaries. For in France the parallel with Rome and Sparta took a virulent form which it had never taken in England. In the National Assembly no issue could be debated without an appeal to classical precedents. Whether Solon or Lycurgus was to be their guide, the educational system of Sparta or the agrarian laws of the Gracchi—these were the burning issues, and the walls of the Assembly hall were lined with statues of Greek and Roman heroes to remind them of their ideal. It was at this time, indeed, that some of the revolutionary leaders began to assume the names of classical heroes, Babeuf initially taking that of Camillus and then of Caius Gracchus. Others exchanged their Christian names for the names of Aristides, Socrates, and Scaevola. In one year, of four hundred male infants named after Republican heroes, three hundred were called Brutus, and Rues de Brutus, de Scaevola, and des Gracques began to spring up in the environs of Paris. During the Thermidorian reaction this fad collapsed, but not before it had done a great deal of harm, in the opinion not only of Macaulay but also of some modern historians.[21]

In England, according to Macaulay, this habit of mind had done less damage, for England had its own tradition of political liberty. "We respect the Great Charter more than the laws of Solon. The Capitol and the Forum impress us with less awe than our own Westminster Hall and

Westminster Abbey. . . . We think with far less pleasure of Cato tearing out his entrails than of Russell saying, as he turned away from his wife, that the bitterness of death was past. . . . Our liberty is neither Greek nor Roman; but essentially English. It has a character of its own,—a character which has taken a tinge from the sentiments of the chivalrous ages, and which accords with the peculiarities of our manners and of our insular situation" (V, 138). Nonetheless, in his *History* Macaulay noted that in 1689, when the proposal was made to create a standing army, the annual debate upon this issue became an occasion for "hopeful young orators, fresh from Christchurch, . . . to deliver maiden speeches, setting forth how the guards of Pisistratus seized the citadel of Athens, and how the Prætorian cohorts sold the empire to Didius." They could not understand, wrote Macaulay, "that what at one stage in the progress of society is pernicious may at another stage be indispensable."[22]

Central to Macaulay's view of history and political science is the idea that "circumstances," by which he means the peculiar social and political institutions, the moral and cultural climate of a nation, determine what is possible and desirable in that country at that time. For this reason he opposed, on the one hand, the "rights of man" and Benthamite schools, which in their different ways attempted to apply abstract principles to particular situations, and, on the other, the Plutarchian or Bolingbroke school, which attempted to apply the examples of individuals to the problems of nations. Neither one was appropriate in what was essentially an empirical situation. The one was too general, the other too specific. Macaulay agreed with Bolingbroke that history was "philosophy teaching by examples," but he noted that the examples depended for their teaching power upon being vividly concrete but upon their generality for being philosophic (V, 122). Most historians fell between these two stools. The ancients wrote vivid narratives but with too little analysis to be philosophically useful; the moderns, like Hallam, wrote analytic histories that were too dry to be moving. Only by turning from the narrative of kings and cabinets to the social history of an entire people could one at once be concrete and yet give a sufficient number of instances to be generally dependable. As history "in small fragments, proves any thing, or nothing, so I believe that it is full of useful and precious instruction when we contemplate it in large portions."[23] It was Macaulay's wish to create a "science of induction" such as would enable the statesman to act with "civil prudence" by combining the method of Sir Francis Bacon with the materials of Sir Walter Scott.

In the essay "History" Macaulay gives a picture of that imaginary "perfect historian" who assuredly would not omit the battles, the sieges, the negotiations, and the ministerial changes but who, along with these,

> would intersperse the details which are the charm of historical ro-
> mances. At Lincoln Cathedral there is a beautiful painted window,
> which was made by an apprentice out of the pieces of glass which had
> been rejected by his master. It is so far superior to every other in the
> church, that, according to the tradition, the vanquished artist killed
> himself from mortification. Sir Walter Scott, in the same manner, has
> used those fragments of truth which historians have scornfully thrown
> behind them in a manner which may well excite their envy. He has
> constructed out of their gleanings works which, even considered as
> histories, are scarcely less valuable than their's. But a truly great his-
> torian would reclaim those materials which the novelist has appro-
> priated. (V, 157–58)

Macaulay is here describing by anticipation his own *History of England*, whose scope and method are presented in almost identical terms in the opening chapter, written a dozen or fifteen years later. To his sister, who inquired how, given the desultory character of his reading, he could be so accurate about details, he explained that as he walked about the city he constructed imaginary romances about the past. "I am no sooner in the streets than I am in Greece, in Rome, in the midst of the French Revolution. . . . I seem to know every inch of Whitehall. I go in at Hans Holbein's gate, and come out through the matted gallery. The conver-sations which I compose between great people of the time are long, and sufficiently animated: in the style, if not with the merits, of Sir Walter Scott's."[24] He drew upon the plays, ballads, lampoons, and broadsheets of the age and says he learned more from the domestic account books of one family than from a whole roll of state papers. He also made it a practice, unlike Hume and Gibbon, but like Scott and the new Romantic historians of his own day, actually to visit the sites he wrote about. He walked twice through the pass of Killiecrankie to be sure how long it would have taken the English army to pass.

It was not merely to make his history vivid, however, that Macaulay turned to sociological detail. It was his view that the truly great revo-lutions in human affairs are those that go on silently and gradually without anybody noticing them until they are either complete or else cannot be completed without a violent revolution in the social and political institutions. These sudden, catastrophic revolutions are merely the adjustment of the earth's surface to the pressure that has long been building up beneath. Far better for the historian to go beneath the surface and concern himself with the pressures in the hearts and minds of the people, so that the statesman may anticipate, and indeed avoid, the violent revolutions which otherwise would follow. What is necesary is that concessions be timely and gracious. If the French aristocracy had accepted Turgot's moderate measures in 1783, they would not have had to endure the violence of 1789.[25] If James II had given graciously in 1686 what he gave ungraciously in 1688, he might have retained his crown. "We know of no great revolution which might not have been prevented by compromise early and graciously made." Small disturbances should be put down unflinchingly. "But no wise ruler will confound the pervading taint with the slight local irritation. No wise ruler will treat the deeply seated discontents of a great party, as he treats the fury of a mob who destroys mills and power-looms. The neglect of this distinction has been fatal even to governments strong in the power of the sword" (V, 238).

Though Macaulay believed there was an analogy between England in 1831 and France in 1783, he did not press this analogy in his speeches, partly because it was all too present to the minds of his hearers and partly because he believed the character and traditions of the two peoples were vastly different. It was rather in seventeenth-century England that he found his analogy, the laboratory where his science of induction might be formed. "Time," he wrote in 1828, "is bringing round another crisis analogous to that which occurred in the seventeenth century. We stand in a situation similar to that in which our ancestors stood under the reign of James the First" (V, 237; cf. *Speeches*, I, 146). The extreme Tories of the 1820s correspond to the intransigent followers of the early Stuarts. Lord Eldon is interchangeable with Laud. The Philosophic Radicals and Benthamites show the same fanatic adherence to political doctrine as did the Puritans to theology infected with politics, and they manifest the same aversion to literature and the fine arts. The issues were basically the same, though on some of them the alignments were strangely confused. On the Catholic question, for example, one would have expected the Tories to have favored emancipation, for in the early eighteenth century they were the ones who were tainted with Jacobitism; and one would have expected the Whigs, the principal architects of the Glorious Revolution and the Act of Settlement which established the Protestant succession, to have opposed it. But in point of fact, Catholic emancipation had now become a "liberal" measure which was opposed by most Tories and supported by most Whigs, and there was no question that, on this issue, the Tories had the majority of the people with them. Thus, to the great chagrin of Macaulay and the Whigs, the Tories were able in 1825 to pose as the inheritors of the Glorious Revolution, and that is why Thomas Arnold said that one must look in the mirror of history to distinguish the true nature of contending parties. It was indeed a "night battle" in which the guidance of history was needed.[26]

Unfortunately, history takes the form of historiography, and the bitter issues of the Civil War had not become less divisive for being written about. Indeed, the party that lost the war had won the battle of interpretation, for initially there had been Clarendon's impressive *History of the Rebellion,* and then in the 1750s David Hume's *History of England* declared that the early Stuarts had governed no worse than the Tudors, that the execution of Charles I was an act of popular madness, that Cromwell was driven by ambition to his career of unjustified violence, and that the whole Puritan phenomenon illustrated the evils of "enthusiasm." The brilliance of Hume's literary style carried his interpretation into general acceptance, and though there were writers in the "radical Whig" tradition, including Catherine Macaulay, a distant relative of the historian, who wrote against Hume, their pens, as Trevor-Roper has put it, "squeaked in vain." It was not until the 1820s, when George Brodie published his anti-Humean *History of the British Empire,* which was favorably reviewed by Jeffrey in the *Edinburgh Review* and by John Stuart Mill in the *Westminster,* that the issue became really warm.[27] It is no wonder that it did. "Where history is regarded merely as a picture of life and manners," wrote Macaulay, "or as a collection of experiments from which general maxims of civil wisdom may be drawn," no very great issue is at stake. "But where history is regarded as a repository of titledeeds, on which the rights of governments and nations depend," then the issue is momentous indeed.[28] So Macaulay saw it in his essay on Milton (1825), which for the first time brought to the debate a literary style, as revolutionary as Hume's was conservative, adequate to rebut Hume. It was not merely that he defended Cromwell and the Puritans; it was also that he regarded the period at which Milton lived as

> one of the most memorable eras in the history of mankind, . . . the very crisis of the great conflict between Oromasdes and Arimanes, liberty and despotism, reason and prejudice. That great battle was fought for no single generation, for no single land. The destinies of the human race were staked on the same cast with the freedom of the English people. Then were first proclaimed those mighty principles which have since worked their way into the depths of the American forests, which have roused Greece from the slavery and degradation of two thousand years, and which, from one end of Europe to the other, have kindled

an unquenchable fire in the hearts of the oppressed, and loosed the knees of the oppressors with an unwonted fear. (V, 23)

For the next fifty years the period of the Civil War continued to have this significance. "We are Cavaliers or Roundheads," wrote W. E. H. Lecky, "before we are Conservatives or Liberals," and even the great Stubbs, admittedly no champion of relevance, declared in 1870 that the period should not be taught to undergraduates, as being too close to contemporary politics.[29]

Macaulay's interpretation of the Civil War in the essay on Milton was a prelude to his use of the Glorious Revolution in the debates on Reform. As early as his undergraduate prize essay, "The Life and Character of King William III," he had developed from this period a theory of history which he now brought into play. He knew and accepted the view of the Scottish philosophic historians that society moved forward through progressive stages—but that was in the long term. In the short term it alternated between oppression and anarchy, and the more severe the repression the more violent the anarchy.[30] This oscillation could be stopped, however, if there were a favorable "conjuncture," a term Macaulay used for a crisis when there was some realignment of parties and a more than usual assemblage of moderates to whom the safety of the whole was more important than the triumph of one part. Joseph Hamburger has argued that Macaulay is to be regarded less as a Whig, who had an ideal of government in mind toward which he consistently worked, than as a classical trimmer, whose highest priority was to preserve the stability and balance of the state by avoiding extremism in politics. George Savile, Marquis of Halifax, wrote in "The Character of a Trimmer" that "This innocent word *Trimmer* signifieth no more than this, That if Men are together in a boat, and one part of the company would weigh it down on one side, another would make it lean as much to the contrary; it happeneth there is a third Opinion of those, who conceive it would do as well, if the Boat went even, without endangering the passengers." Though William III is the hero of Macaulay's *History*, yet Halifax stands by his side as almost equally important. "Our Revolution," wrote Macaulay, "as far as it can be said to bear the character of any single mind, assuredly bears the character of the large yet cautious mind of Halifax."[31]

In Macaulay's view the two parties in the boat, though they were incorporated under the name of Whig and Tory in 1641, had always existed and always would exist, for they represented two essential principles in the state, the one of order, the other of liberty. "One is the moving power, and the other the steadying power of the state" (VII, 205). Macaulay, of course, classed himself with the moving power, and it seemed to him that the history of England was the history of the one group continuously persuading the other to accommodate itself to the great intellectual, economic, and social changes that were continually going on. "The history of England . . . is the history of a government constantly giving way."[32] It is to these concessions that we owe "the Charter of Henry Beauclerk, the Great Charter, the first assembling of the House of Commons, the extinction of personal slavery, the separation from the See of Rome, the Petition of Right, the Habeas Corpus Act, the Revolution, the establishment of the liberty of unlicensed printing, the abolition of religious disabilities." "All these seem to us," wrote Macaulay, "to be the successive stages of one great revolution" (VI, 96), and it was a "preserving revolution." "Reform, that you may preserve."[33]

From the Great Charter to the Glorious Revolution this had been the mode. But now, in 1832, England was confronted by the need for one further reform, in the system of parliamentary representation, and Macaulay drew a graphic picture of the "great and terrible calamities" which would befall the country if it did not respond. In one of his perorations he appealed quite frankly to the argument from fear, but the real basis of his appeal is to history—to change within continuity. "It is now time for us to pay a decent, a rational, a manly reverence to our ancestors—not by superstitiously adhering to what they, under other circumstances, did, but by doing what they, in our circumstances, would have done."[34] Macaulay ever regarded the day of his first speech on the Reform Bill as an epoch in his life and the life of the nation. Hence it was that when, six years later, he first broached the idea of writing a History of England, he proposed extending it from the accession of James II to the passage of the Reform Bill, from "the Revolution which brought the Crown into harmony with the Parliament [to] the Revolution which brought the Parliament into harmony with the nation."[35] He did not live to complete a tenth of the work—the *History* ends with the death of William III—but the character of William and the Glorious Revolution were the essential things. Unlike Carlyle's *French Revolution,* Macaulay's *History* was not written as a warning to the nation but as a hymn of thanksgiving, a celebration of triumphal change. "It is because we had a preserving revolution in the seventeenth century that we have not had a destroying revolution in the nineteenth. . . . For the authority of law, for the security of property, for the peace of our streets, for the happiness of our homes, our gratitude is due, under Him who raises up and pulls down nations at his pleasure, to the Long Parliament, to the Convention, and to William of Orange."[36]

3

Mill, Carlyle
and the Spirit of the Age

*T*HE 'SPIRIT OF THE AGE,' " wrote John Stuart Mill in 1831, "is in
some measure a novel expression. I do not believe that it is to be
met with in any work exceeding fifty years in antiquity. The idea of
comparing one's own age with former ages, or with our notion of those
which are yet to come, had occurred to philosophers; but it never before
was itself the dominant idea of any age."[1] Mill was misinformed on this
point, for, as Friedrich Meinecke has made clear, the phrase *spirit of the
age* and its companion *spirit of a nation* were commonly employed by
continental writers in the seventeenth and eighteenth centuries, particularly by Montesquieu and Voltaire.[2] Nonetheless, Mill was apparently
right that the phrase was not naturalized in English until the early nineteenth century, for the first instance cited by the *OED* is Shelley's
(1820): "It is the spirit of the age, and we are all infected with it."
During the next dozen years it was used by Southey, Henry Crabb Robinson, Landor, Hazlitt, Macaulay, Newman, Carlyle, Mill, Bulwer, and
an anonymous writer in *Blackwood's* (1830), by which time it was established in the language. Indeed, the writer in *Blackwood's* complains,
"That which, in the slang of faction, is called the Spirit of the Age,
absorbs, at present, the attention of the world."[3]

Given this new awareness, it became, said Mill, "a very fit subject
for philosophical inquiry, what the spirit of the age really is; and how
or wherein it differs from the spirit of any other age." Fichte was the
first to analyze it in his lectures, *Characteristics of the Present Age* (1806),
and he was followed in England by Hazlitt's *Spirit of the Age* (1825),
R. H. Horne's *New Spirit of the Age* (1844), and especially by Carlyle's
"Signs of the Times" and "Characteristics" and Mill's "Spirit of the
Age," all published within three years of one another in 1829–31. One
should also mention Edward Lytton Bulwer's "View of the Intellectual
Spirit of the Time," published in *England and the English* in 1833.

The "spirit of the age" differs from the eighteenth-century stages or states of society in being a much more volatile concept. Whereas a state of society might last for many centuries, the spirit of the age might change within a generation—hence the appropriateness of Horne's *New Spirit of the Age* only twenty years after Hazlitt's. The state of society was also an institutional and sociological concept, whereas the spirit of the age carried idealist suggestions of an indwelling spirit which informed all aspects of society and gave it its character. One would, indeed, assume it came to England directly from German Idealism, for its equivalent, *Zeitgeist,* was being used by Herder, Fichte, Goethe, Schiller, and others in the late eighteenth and early nineteenth centuries.[4] Doubtless it was affected by that usage, but the phrase *Zeitgeist,* or "Time-spirit," though used occasionally by Carlyle, did not become current in England until employed, almost ad nauseam, by Arnold in *Literature and Dogma* in 1873. The form of the phrase *spirit of the age* suggests it came to England from French sources (*esprit de l'âge, esprit du temps, esprit du siècle*), and indeed it apparently did carry revolutionary or at least liberal suggestions. To Carlyle it was tinged with rationalism, and the conservative writer in *Blackwood's* complains that he is continually being told he must surrender to revolutionary change simply because it is the spirit of the age. Hence, for his first essay Carlyle selected a phrase whose antecedents are not liberal and continental but Biblical and apocalyptic: "O ye hypocrites, ye can discern the face of the sky; but can ye not discern the signs of the times? A wicked and adulterous generation seeketh after a sign; and there shall no sign be given unto it."[5]

The spirit of the age, according to Mill, "is an idea essentially belonging to an age of change." Men do not think deeply about the character of their own age until they are aware that it differs from the past. Then they divide into those who praise the wisdom of their ancestors and those who extol the march of intellect. "The present times," says Mill, "possess this character. . . . The conviction is already not far from being universal, that the times are pregnant with change; and that the nineteenth century will be known to posterity as the era of one of the greatest revolutions of which history has preserved the remembrance."[6] Carlyle agreed. "The repeal of the Test Acts, and then of the Catholic disabilities, has struck many of their admirers with an indescribable astonishment. Those things seemed fixed and immovable; deep as the foundations of the world; and lo, in a moment they have vanished, and their place knows them no more!"[7] Then followed the July Revolution in France, the burning of ricks all over the south of England, the ominous gathering of the forces of reform, and the Bristol riots when the Reform Bill was not passed. As a result there was a rage of prophecy, and Carlyle recorded in his notebook "a common persuasion among serious ill-informed persons that the *end of the world* is at hand: Henry Drummond, E[dward] Irving, and all that class.—So was it at the beginning of the Christian era; say rather, at the *termination* of the Pagan one."[8] Carlyle did not believe it was the end of the world, but he did believe it was the end of an epoch, and so too did Mill. Indeed, most thoughtful Englishmen during the period of the 1820s and 1830s had a sense, far keener than they had ever had before, that they were living in the stream of history, that they were being swept by some great, irresistible force out of the past and into the future. So powerful, indeed, was this sense of history that the Spirit of the Age became almost a Genius or Daemon, replacing the older conceptions of Providence or Destiny and moving events forward, not in the name of God or Natural Law but of History itself.

It was in this context, in the 1820s and early 1830s, that both Mill and Carlyle developed their philosophy of history. There could hardly have been two young men more diverse in their origin, for Carlyle was raised in the tradition of Scottish Calvinism by devoutly religious parents, whereas Mill, the son of an agnostic, was "one of the very few examples, in this country, of one who has, not thrown off religious belief, but never had it."[9] In the 1820s, however, each experienced a spiritual or mental crisis which brought them together in a common view of society and especially in a view of history. It was not that their paths crossed but rather that they converged for a moment and then moved apart again, though not so widely as before.

Carlyle has given a mythical account of his spiritual crisis in the life story of Diogenes Teufelsdröckh. "Nothing in *Sartor* thereabouts is *fact*," he wrote, "(symbolical myth all) except that of the '*incident* in the Rue St. Thomas de l'Enfer,'—which happened quite literally to myself in Leith Walk, [Edinburgh]. . . . I remember it well and could go yet to about the place."[10] As for the rest, one can trace out in Carlyle's letters and notebooks the entire course of his and Teufelsdröckh's conversion. He had gone up from his native village to Edinburgh at the age of fourteen and there, reading Gibbon and Hume at the University, had lost his faith. He was poor, lonely, in ill health, unable to find meaningful work or spiritual sustenance; and all these rebuffs to his proud and suffering spirit seemed like a cosmic or Everlasting No. "It was God that said Yes:" he wrote in his notebook; "it is the Devil that forever says No."[11] The Everlasting No has two aspects, an objective and a subjective. Objectively, "To me the Universe was all void of Life, of Purpose, of Volition, even of Hostility: it was one huge, dead, immeasurable Steam-engine, rolling on, in its dead indifference, to grind me limb from limb" (I, 133). But subjectively, this produced in Teufelsdröckh a kind of whining Wertherism: "And yet, strangely enough, I lived in a continual, indefinite, pining fear; tremulous, pusillanimous, apprehensive of I knew not what" (I, 134). The distinction between the two aspects of the Everlasting No is important because the experience on Leith Walk freed Carlyle from the one but not the other. In that moment he rose up, in native God-created majesty, and "shook base Fear away from me forever" (I, 135). This act of Protest against the Everlasting No does not lead Teufelsdröckh to the Everlasting Yea but merely to the Center of Indifference, a kind of spiritual No-man's land in which he must wander for a time until he can develop a new faith to replace the old. The culmination of the Everlasting No had come when "Doubt had darkened into Unbelief" (I, 129); but then Teufelsdröckh had exclaimed, "Alas, the fearful Unbelief is unbelief in yourself" (I, 132). In the Protest Teufelsdröckh had freed himself from this second unbelief, had reasserted his own spirituality and separated himself from the material world. He now has to turn outward to that world and study man in society until he can see it too as instinct with spirit—until he sees nature as "the living visible garment of God" and society as a fabric woven by the divine element in man. He then will have achieved the Clothes Philosophy, which is the basis for the Everlasting Yea. He will have seen that the "Man of Sorrows" transcends the "Sorrows of Werther," that blessedness is better than happiness, and that the truly supernatural is a Natural Supernaturalism.

Carlyle worked his way out of his crisis by two routes, philosophy and history. In the German writers and philosophers whom he was reading from 1819 to 1830 he found a mystical or transcendental view of the universe of which he was initially suspicious but which he finally accepted as answering to his deepest needs and to the truth. But he was simultaneously working out, and again partly by their help, a philosophy of history. In the midst of his deepest misery, in January 1824, he wrote, "I have got half a new idea to-day about history: it is more than I can say for any day the last six months." In all likelihood this was the idea about the multidimensionality of history which he confided to his notebook in 1827: "An Historian must write (so to speak) in *lines*; but every event is a *superficies*; nay if we search out its *causes,* a *solid*: hence a primary and almost incurable defect in the art of Narration; which only the very best can so much as approximately remedy.—N.B. I understand this *myself*. I have known it for years; and written it *now*, with the purpose perhaps of writing it at large elsewhere."[12] Carlyle developed this idea more lucidly in his essay "On History" (1830), but he wrote it "at large" in *The French Revolution,* in which his view of "the infinite nature of History,"—of history as "an ever-living, ever-working Chaos of Being, wherein shape after shape bodies itself forth from innumerable elements" (XXVII, 91, 88)—is fully displayed.

There were three species of historian whom Carlyle contemned: first, the sentimental literary historian, or Picturesque Traveller, who constructs elegant narratives of the doings of kings and queens. We come, for example, to the Reformation.

> All Scotland is awakened to a second higher life: the Spirit of the Highest stirs in every bosom, agitates every bosom; Scotland is convulsed, fermenting, struggling to body itself forth anew. . . . We ask, with breathless eagerness; How was it; how went it on? Let us understand it, let us see it, and know it!—In reply, is handed us a really graceful and most dainty little Scandalous Chronicle (as for some Journal of Fashion) of two persons: Mary Stuart, a Beauty, but over-light-headed; and Henry Darnley, a Booby who had fine legs. How these first courted, billed and cooed, according to nature; then pouted, fretted, grew utterly enraged, and blew one another up with gunpowder: this, and not the History of Scotland, is what we good-naturedly read. (XXVIII, 82–83)

The second species was Dryasdust, the antiquarian, a character whom Carlyle borrowed from Sir Walter Scott and whom he represented as a mole burrowing through vast quantities of rubbish without any idea that the past was alive. The third type was the Philosophic Historian, who took the complex reality—nay, the infinitude of history—and reduced it to some finite little formula such as Progress of the Species. To Carlyle, Voltaire did not invent a new mode of history but merely continued the old mode of "philosophy teaching by Experience" according to *his* philosophy rather than that of the monks. But both philosophies were inadequate. Neither saw that history, as Carlyle believed, was "the essence of innumerable biographies"—that is, the inward spiritual life of all the nameless people living in any era. It was the history of the Spirit of the Age, of the Idea realizing itself in the actual.

As a result, the only true historian, according to Carlyle, was the artist or the poet, for only he had the power to lean over the "dark backward and abysm of time" and, by an act of divinization, seize upon its essential character. Only he had the literary art, symbolic or otherwise, to body it forth in its infinite complexity. The *History of Scotland* which elicited the diatribe quoted above was Scott's little potboiler of 1830, but although Carlyle went through a period of considering Scott "the great Restaurateur of Europe" and always lamented that "he had no message" (XXIX, 54), he came to see that his true conception of history was not in his histories but in his novels. "There is something in his deep recognition of the worth of the Past, perhaps better than anything he has *expressed* about it: into which I do not yet fully see." But he soon came to see it. "These Historical Novels have taught all men this truth, which looks like a truism, and yet was as good as un-known to writers of history and others, till so taught: that the bygone ages of the world were actually filled by living men, not by protocols, state-papers, controversies and abstractions of men. . . . History will henceforth have to take thought of it" (XXIX, 77–78). On Scott's death in 1832 he said simply, "He understood what *history* meant; this was his chief intellectual merit."[13]

To Carlyle the best eighteenth-century historian was not Voltaire, Gibbon, Robertson, or Hume, but Boswell in his *Life of Johnson*. "It is not speaking with exaggeration, but with strict measured sobriety, to say that this Book of Boswell's will give us more real insight into the *History of England* during those days than twenty other Books, falsely entitled 'Histories,' which take to themselves that special aim." "The thing I want to see is not Redbook Lists, and Court Calendars, and Parliamentary Registers, but the LIFE OF MAN in England: what men did, thought, suffered, enjoyed; the form, especially the spirit, of their terrestrial existence, its outward environment, its inward principle" (XXVIII, 80–81). For the earlier period Carlyle turned to Shakespeare, for he found "something of *epic* in the cycle of hasty Fragments" which make up the history plays, and he thought that if Shakespeare had done more in that vein, he "could have turned the *History of England* into a kind of *Iliad*, almost perhaps into a kind of *Bible*" (XXX, 26). The *Iliad* and the Bible were for Carlyle the two great histories of antiquity, for if the true historian was a poet, so the true poet was also a historian. More and more literature seemed to Carlyle to be shot through by un-reality, and he cited that strange thesis of his alter ego Sauerteig: "That History, after all, is the true Poetry; that Reality, if rightly interpreted, is grander than Fiction; nay, that even in the right interpretation of Reality and History does genuine Poetry consist" (XXVIII, 79).

What, then, was the right interpretation of reality? What was the poem which God had written upon the fabric of time? In virtually all the new German writers and philosophers whom Carlyle was reading he found a version of history which was much more congenial to his views than the rectilinear Progress of the Species assumed by much French and English thought. It did not conceive, in the first place, that this was the best of all possible ages, and it marked off the past into a series of epochs which vacillated between faith and skepticism, criticism and creation. One of the most elaborate of these schemes was Fichte's in *Characteristics of the Present Age,* a "high priori" work which divided history into five epochs through which mankind must proceed to achieve its goal of Freedom in accordance with Reason. The present age was the third or central one, an age of "completed Sinfulness" which had thrown off the Reason as Instinct of the first age and Reason as external Authority of the second without putting on Reason as Science or Art of the fourth and fifth ages. It is obvious that Fichte's five epochs reduce themselves to the tripartite dialectic—creative/critical/creative—which always occurs when a series of polar opposites succeed upon one another, the second creative epoch transcending and somewhat synthesizing the first two. Herder, Schiller, Novalis, Friedrich Schlegel, and Schelling all had such formulations, but it was in Goethe that Carlyle found the passage that influenced him the most. It occurred in a note, "Israel in der Wüste," which Goethe appended to the *West-östlicher Divan* (1819). Carlyle may have known it as early as March 1826, and it is said that at least a dozen passages in his works show the imprint of it. He translated it twice, once in his Notebook and once in the essay "Diderot," where it is attributed simply to "the Thinker of our time":

> "The special, sole and deepest theme of the World's and Man's History whereto all other themes are subordinated, remains the Conflict of UNBELIEF and BELIEF. All epochs wherein Belief prevails, under what form it may, are splendid, heart-elevating, fruitful for contemporaries and posterity. All epochs, on the contrary, wherein Unbelief, under what form so ever, maintains its sorry victory, should they even for a moment glitter with a sham splendour, vanish from the eyes of posterity; because no one chooses to burden himself with study of the unfruitful." (XXVIII, 248)

Though Goethe here suggests that there are entire epochs which have no history and quite vanish from the annals of the world, the more usual historicist view is that even epochs of unbelief serve their purpose in destroying the old, outworn creeds and making way for the new. In Fichte's scheme it was impossible for mankind to achieve the state of Reason as Science or Art without going through the stage of completed Sinfulness. Thus even the miserable eighteenth century had a purpose. But the reason Carlyle was so deeply affected by this new conception of spiritual periodicity was not merely that it helped him understand

his age but also that it helped him understand himself. "Has the mind
its cycles and seasons like Nature," he asked, "varying from the fermentation of *werden* to the clearness of *seyn*; and this again and again; so
that the history of a man is like the history of the world he lives in? In
my own case, I have traced two or three such vicissitudes: at present if
I mistake not, there is some such thing at hand for me. Feby 1829."[14]
The alternation of creative, critical, and newly creative epochs in world
history exactly corresponds to the three periods in Teufelsdröckh's life:
the period of childhood faith, the Everlasting No and Center of Indifference, and the new faith of the Everlasting Yea. Hence Carlyle applies
this new philosophy of history to his own state at the "Rational University," where "the young vacant mind [was] furnished with much talk
about Progress of the Species, Dark Ages, Prejudice, and the like" till
all were either blown out into windy self-conceit or reduced to impotent
skepticism. "But this too is portion of mankind's lot. If our era is the
Era of Unbelief, why murmur under it; is there not a better coming,
nay come? As in long-drawn systole and long-drawn diastole, must the
period of Faith alternate with the period of Denial; must the vernal
growth, the summer luxuriance of all Opinions, Spiritual Representations and Creations, be followed by, and again follow, the autumnal
decay, the winter dissolution" (I, 90–91). Whether Carlyle adopted the
new philosophy of history because it accorded to the shape of his own
experience or whether he shaped his own experience to accord to the
new philosophy of history, it is clear that they are one and the same.
The history of Teufelsdröckh's conversion is the history of the conversion of his age.

That a better time is coming was first formally announced by Carlyle
in "Signs of the Times" (1829). The title alludes, as we have already
noted, to the doomsday outlook of his contemporaries; neither does
Carlyle initially take a cheerful view. "The grand characteristic of our
age," he writes, is that it is an Age of Machinery. "Nothing is now done
directly, or by hand; all is by rule and calculated contrivance." "Thus we
have machines for Education: Lancastrian machines; Hamiltonian machines; monitors, maps and emblems." "We have Religious machines, of
all imaginable varieties; the Bible-Society. . ." Science no longer depends on a Newton but on a Royal Society, art no longer on a Raphael
but on a Royal Academy, philosophy no longer on a Descartes but on a
Philosophic Institute. As we read on, however, we are aware that the
very process of Carlyle's writing about the age and delineating its essential character begins the process of its spiritualization. Initially, he
had taken machinery in the literal, material sense, but as he proceeded

he made it increasingly metaphoric and symbolic, until at last he exclaimed, "Thus does the Genius of Mechanism stand by to help us in
all difficulties and emergencies." So mechanization itself is spiritualized
by Carlyle, and his essay is itself one of the "signs infinitely cheering to
us . . . that a new and brighter spiritual era is slowly evolving itself for
all men" (XXVII, 62, 81).

John Stuart Mill, eleven years younger than Carlyle, was converging on
the same point from the opposite direction. Educated by his father in
a generally Benthamite atmosphere, he had never read the works of
Bentham himself until the French redaction by Dumont, the *Traité de
Législation,* was put into his hands in the winter of 1821–22. "The
reading of this book," says Mill, "was an epoch in my life; one of the
turning points in my mental history" (45). What primarily impressed
him was "the chapter in which Bentham passed judgment on the common modes of reasoning in morals and legislation, deduced from
phrases like 'law of nature,' 'right reason,' 'the moral sense,' 'natural
rectitude,' and the like, and characterized them as dogmatism in disguise, imposing its sentiments upon others under cover of sounding
expressions which convey no reason for the sentiment, but set up the
sentiment as its own reason. It had not struck me before, that Bentham's
principle put an end to all this. The feeling rushed upon me, that all
previous moralists were superseded, and that here indeed was the commencement of a new era in thought" (45–46). As Mill continues to
describe this experience, the dry prose of his *Autobiography* comes to
life, and one feels that Mill looking into Dumont's Bentham was almost
like Keats looking into Chapman's Homer. "I felt taken up to an eminence from which I could survey a vast mental domain, and see stretching out into the distance intellectual results beyond all computation"
(46). Indeed, it was almost a religious conversion. "When I laid down
the last volume of the Traité, I had become a different being. The 'principle of utility' understood as Bentham understood it, . . . fell exactly
into its place as the keystone which held together the detached and
fragmentary component parts of my knowledge and beliefs. It gave unity
to my conceptions of things. I now had opinions; a creed, a doctrine,
a philosophy; in one among the best senses of the word, a religion"
(47).

This religion lasted for five years. "From the winter of 1821, when
I first read Bentham, . . . I had what might truly be called an object in
life; to be a reformer of the world. My conception of my own happiness

was entirely identified with this object. . . . But the time came when I awakened from this as from a dream. It was in the autumn of 1826. I was in a dull state of nerves, such as everybody is occasionally liable to; unsusceptible to enjoyment or pleasurable excitement. . . . In this frame of mind it occurred to me to put the question directly to myself: 'Suppose that all your objects in life were realized; that all the changes in institutions and opinions which you are looking forward to, could be completely effected at this very instant: would this be a great joy and happiness to you?' And an irrepressible self-consciousness distinctly answered, 'No!' At this my heart sank within me: the whole foundation on which my life was constructed fell down. All my happiness was to have been found in the continual pursuit of this end. The end had ceased to charm, and how could there ever again be any interest in the means? I seemed to have nothing left to live for" (93–94).

As Mill analyzed his crisis in later years, he thought it revealed a psychological defect in Utilitarian theory. According to the theory, the greatest happiness of the greatest number was the end of life, and it was the task of the educator or statesman to create, in the mind of the individual, favorable associations with that end so that his personal happiness would be identified with it. In the case of Mill, however, he was so well acquainted with the theory and so given to intellectual analysis that the indoctrination did not work. He was like the preacher's son who, being "behind the scenes" and seeing his father at work, himself becomes an atheist. His father and Bentham had thoroughly demystified the old absolutes with the result that, for their own disciple, they could not mystify the new. They lacked the psychological and histrionic art to endow the new values with the aura of mystery which centuries of religious tradition had given to the old. Beyond this, Mill felt that there had been a general atrophying of his emotional life, so that his belief in the "greatest happiness of the greatest number" was a mere speculative opinion and was not grounded in genuine benevolence. He knew, and he did not know, that happiness was the end of life.

Mill attempted to find his way back from this dilemma by reading for the first time, in 1828, the poems of Wordsworth, which seemed "the very culture of the feelings, which I was in quest of" (103–04). But he also happened to take up the *Mémoires* of Marmontel, the sentimental French dramatist, and "came to the passage which relates his father's death, the distressed position of the family, and the sudden inspiration by which he, then a mere boy, felt and made them feel that he would be everything to them—would supply the place of all that they had lost. A vivid conception of the scene and its feelings came over me, and I was moved to tears. From this moment my burthen grew lighter. The oppression of the thought that all feeling was dead within me, was gone. I was no longer hopeless; I was not a stock or a stone" (99). This passage is customarily interpreted as a suppressed death-wish on the part of Mill against his harsh and domineering father, but that is surely a shallow interpretation. Mill was clearly aware that he did not love his father and that his father did not love him, but he respected his father as a great and good man and was deeply saddened by his death in 1836. A more plausible interpretation of the episode is that it is a critique of hedonism—it shows the educative power of sorrow. Happiness may be the end of life, but it is tragedy that has the power to elicit the nobleness of men. The actual passage in Marmontel, in which the little boy is elevated to greatness, is so melodramatic that it is a wonder Mill was not moved to laughter rather than tears; but his nerves were ready for tears and it is no wonder that he was cured of his addiction to Bentham-ism by a death-bed scene. Indeed, the moral that Mill drew was spe-cifically formulated by the wise physician whom Marmontel's mother called in to attend the boy in his shock. "The physician . . . told her, that this was an effect of great concentrated grief, and that mine might be attended with the most fatal consequences, if it were not removed by some diversion. 'A journey, absence, and that as soon as possible is,' said he, 'the best remedy that I can indicate to you. But do not propose it to him as a diversion; to that great grief is ever averse: it must be ignorant of the care employed to divert it, and must be deceived in order to be cured.'" "The physician," Marmontel adds, "was right: there are griefs yet more attaching than pleasure itself."[15]

This is the very theory that Mill developed as he recovered from his crisis: namely, that happiness may be the end of life but it should not be proposed as the object of life. Just as Benjamin Franklin discovered that he could not pursue humility directly because, the nearer he came to achieving it, the prouder he became of his humility, so Mill discov-ered that one must make something other than happiness the object of life and one would then achieve happiness by the way. One must both know, and not know, that happiness was the end of life, and to this end one must adopt what Mill calls (though he says that he had never heard of it under that name at that time) the "anti-self-consciousness theory of Carlyle" (100). Mill is presumably referring to Carlyle's essay "Char-acteristics," in which Carlyle makes Self-consciousness, rather than Ma-chinery, the distinguishing characteristic of the age and clearly prefers the unconscious naiveté of the great ages of Belief. But neither Carlyle nor Mill gives any explanation of how one is to go about deliberately cultivating anti-self-consciousness—how one can cease to be conscious of something one previously has known. Nonetheless, "this theory now became the basis of my philosophy of life" (100), and one may see Mill implementing it in the various compromises of these years: the attempt to combine Macaulay's theory of government with his father's, the attempt to meld quantitative with qualitative conceptions of pleasure, and above all the attempt to believe in free will along with necessity. He had long seen that "it would be a blessing if the doctrine of necessity could be believed by all *quoad* the characters of others, and disbelieved in regard to their own," and so now he made a distinction between necessity as applied to human actions and as applied to nonhuman actions which enabled him to achieve that desirable end. As a result, "I no longer suffered under the burthen, so heavy to one who aims at being a reformer in opinions, of thinking one doctrine true, and the contrary doctrine morally beneficial" (119). He could both believe, and not believe, in both free will and necessity.

Under the influence, then, of the Romantic poets and of a whole new stream of ideas and attitudes flowing in upon him from the continent, Mill was carried as far in his reaction against Bentham as he was destined to go. It was at this point that he met Carlyle. They were brought together by the agency of a third party, the Saint-Simonians in France. Claude Henri de Rouvroy, Comte de Saint-Simon, was a nobleman of the ancien régime who had participated in the American and French revolutions and then, in the Napoleonic and post-Napoleonic era, produced a series of brilliant, speculative pamphlets which urged the reorganization of society on the basis of science and technology. His most seminal insight was into the philosophy of history, which he saw as consisting of "organic" and "critical" periods which alternated so as to produce three great epochs of human culture, of which two were past and the third was just beginning. Organic periods were those dominated by a single unified philosophy or religion, which manifested itself in a coherent social system. Critical periods were those in which this overarching authority was lacking, and hence society was a mere agglomeration of individuals motivated by egoism. It was fragmented, atomistic, at war with itself. The transition between the two periods was not abrupt, for the moment one organic period achieved its full development, the process of its dissolution began, and even before that dissolution was complete the elements of the new organic period began to form. The fabric of society was thus never ruptured, but there was a movement back and forth between unity and diversity, criticism and creation.

The first great organic period was that of Polytheism in ancient Greece and Rome, with its attendant social system based on slavery. This period lasted through the age of Pericles in Greece and of Augustus in Rome and was brought to an end by the critical thought of Socrates. The first critical period thus extended from the time of Socrates to the third or fourth century A.D., culminating in the barbarian invasions. The second organic period, the Theological, with its attendant social system of feudalism, began with the promulgation of Christianity, reached its height in the eleventh and twelfth centuries, and lingered on till the time of Leo X in the religious sphere and Louis XIV in the political. The second critical period began with the Reformation and continued through the Enlightenment and the French Revolution right down to the Revolution of 1830. In Saint-Simon's view the world was now in the second phase of the second critical period, that in which the destruction of the old theological world had been completed but nothing new had been introduced in its stead. It was his role to announce the coming of this New Era, which was to be Scientific or Positive in its world-view and Industrial in its social organization. Scientists, engineers, educators, and technologists would organize the industrial resources of the world in behalf of the poor. The motto of the new society would be, "From each according to his capacity, to each capacity according to his work." So organized, society would move forward without the oscillations which had characterized the past, for Saint-Simon was clear that this third stage of society would be the last. "The Golden Age," he said, "which the inspiration of poets has placed in the cradle of humanity, is not behind us but before: it lies in the perfection of society."[16]

It is clear that Saint-Simon has adopted the broad periodization of the eighteenth-century philosophes but has simply reversed their values. Their Ages of Superstition are his Ages of Faith, and their Ages of Criticism are indeed "critical" periods but less favorably conceived. "Looking back at the ages of Pericles, Augustus, Leo X, and Louis XIV, and then at the nineteenth century," said Saint-Simon, "one cannot help but smile; no one would think of drawing a parallel between the periods."[17] Yet these are exactly the ages which Voltaire did parallel with his own age, which he regarded as the acme, not the nadir, of civilization. In Saint-Simon's view both organic and critical periods are necessary to the historical process, and one is technically no "better" than the other. Still, there is a distinct feeling that the organic periods, and the great creative geniuses who bring them about, are superior. The critical periods are dark, violent, and unpleasant, and the duty of everyone is to make them as short and nondestructive as possible. One does this by understanding and facilitating the historical process, and thus the supreme moral imperative is to recognize what one's place is in the stream of history and in which direction it is flowing.

Under the banner of this doctrine Saint-Simon gathered about himself a dedicated group of disciples, including Auguste Comte, who, after their leader's death in 1825, organized his speculations into a creed and attempted to convert not only their fellow countrymen but also their neighbors across the Channel. The leaders of the movement were Saint-Armand Bazard and Barthélemy-Prosper Enfantin, whose brilliant course of lectures, *Doctrine de Saint-Simon; exposition; première année, 1829,* was one of the most important publications of the group. Another of their number was the young scion of a wealthy family, Gustave d'Eichthal, who had met Mill at a meeting of the London Debating Society in May 1828 and, after becoming a Saint-Simonian, sent him a supply of literature, including Comte's *Système de politique positive* (1824). Mill read these materials in the summer of 1829 and was deeply impressed. "I was greatly struck," he says in the *Autobiography,* "with the connected view which they for the first time presented to me, of the natural order of human progress; and especially with their division of all history into organic periods and critical periods. . . . These ideas, I knew, were not peculiar to the St. Simonians; on the contrary, they were the general property of Europe, or at least of Germany and France, but they had never, to my knowledge, been so completely systematized as by these writers, nor the distinguishing characteristics of a critical period so powerfully set forth; for I was not then acquainted with Fichte's Lectures on 'the Characteristics of the Present Age' " (115). In July 1830, during the days of revolution, Mill went over to Paris to observe the state of society and met with Bazard and Enfantin and other leaders of the movement. He was further indoctrinated and from this time on read virtually everything they produced. Indeed, the whole Revolution aroused his "utmost enthusiasm, and gave me, as it were, a new existence" (121).

On coming home, he attempted to embody all his new thoughts and feelings in a series of articles entitled "The Spirit of the Age," which appeared in the *Examiner* from January 6 to May 29, 1831. It was his most Saint-Simonian production. Being less concerned with cultural change than with the transfer of power, he spoke of "natural" and "transitional" periods rather than organic and critical, natural periods being those in which power is exercised by those most fitted to exercise it, and transitional periods being those in which it is not. The present age, he writes, is a transitional period, and the hope is that the people will take their opinions from the cultivated portion of mankind so that Europe can move into a new natural period without violence. "I think you will be pleased with two or three articles of mine in the Examiner," Mill wrote to d'Eichthal. "Although I am not a St Simonist nor at all likely to become one, *je tiens bureau de St Simonisme chez moi*." By November 30, however, he had been brought "much nearer to many of your opinions than I was before; and I regard you as decidedly *á la tête de la civilisation*." Indeed, "if the hour were yet come for England . . . , I know not that I should not renounce every thing, and become, not one of you, but as you." For Mill was now inclined to think that the Saint-Simonian social organization would, under some modification or other, "be the final and permanent condition of the human race." He just did not think it would come as quickly as they did, but would "require many, or at least several, ages."[18]

Meanwhile, in Scotland, Carlyle was also being drawn within the orbit of the Saint-Simonians. His "Signs of the Times," reprinted in the *Revue britannique,* was reviewed sympathetically by the Saint-Simonians, who saw it as the work of one spiritually already with them and only needing to be told about their organization in order to become a convert. In July 1830 d'Eichthal sent Carlyle a copy of their review and also a number of their publications, including the *Nouveau Christianisme,* a proposal for revitalizing Christianity by freeing it of its superstitions and rededicating it to the service of the poor. "Received . . . a strange letter from some *Saint-Simoniens* at Paris," wrote Carlyle, "grounded on my little *Signs of the Times.* These people have strange notions, not without a large spicing of truth, and are themselves among the *Signs.* I shall feel curious to know what becomes of them." After discussing them with Edward Irving while on a visit to London, Carlyle replied to d'Eichthal that he found "little or nothing to dissent from" in their writings—indeed, was in "entire sympathy" with them. Later he mentioned them to Goethe and received from him the warning, "Von der Société St Simonienne bitte Sich fern zu halten"—"From the St. Simonian Society pray hold yourself aloof." But Carlyle did not hold himself aloof. On the contrary, he wrote to his brother in London asking for more Saint-Simonian books, and on December 19 announced that he had translated the *Nouveau Christianisme* and was seeking a publisher. In April 1831 he received another packet of literature from d'Eichthal and told Goethe that the group had "discovered and laid to heart this momentous and now almost forgotten truth, *Man is still a Man,*" though they were "already beginning to make false applications of it."[19]

About this same time, while Carlyle was still in Scotland, he also read Mill's "Spirit of the Age," and saying to himself (as he afterwards told Mill), "Here is a new Mystic," determined on going to London to look up this potential disciple. They met for the first time on September 3, and Carlyle wrote his wife that "we had almost four hours of the best talk I have mingled in for long." The talk was all the better because "the youth . . . seemed to profess almost as plainly as modesty would allow that he had been converted by the Head of the Mystic School" and wished to be his disciple. Two years later Mill would painfully explain to Carlyle that the latter had misinterpreted the degree of their proximity and that he had since been moving further away from him, but for the moment they were united in their admiration of the Saint-Simonians. Mill brought d'Eichthal to meet his new friend, and Carlyle was delighted with this "little, tight, cleanly pure lovable *Geschöpfchen*: a pure martyr and apostle. . . . Mill goes so far as to think there might and should be martyrs: this *is* one."[20]

Mill was right, for the movement was nearing its unfortunate end. The Society was making increasingly bizarre claims to be a new Christianity, with Enfantin as a new Jesus, and it also espoused a freedom between the sexes which Mill could approve but Carlyle could not. Then in December it unwisely sent a mission to London to convert the English, and as the missionaries were handsome bearded youths who were most fantastically dressed in red berets, blue or white drill trousers, and tunics of bluebottle blue revealing white waistcoats embroidered in red, Englishmen naturally feared not only for their religion and their property but also for their wives, and the police had to be called out to prevent a riot. Shortly thereafter the French government began proceedings against the group on charges of unlawful assembly and teaching immorality, and the three main leaders were sentenced to a year in prison. The last Mill and Carlyle heard of them they were setting out to the East in search of a female Messiah whom they expected to find on the banks of the Bosphorus. It seemed to both men a pity that so good and pureminded a group should have ended in such a fiasco, but they felt the whole episode revealed the weakness as well as the strength of the French character.

To both Mill and Carlyle the most valuable and lasting contribution of the Saint-Simonians was their philosophy of history. Mill had read a great deal of history as a child. Not only had he read all the Greek and Latin historians simply as a part of his lessons, but he had also read all the major historians in English of both the modern and the ancient world. The fact that his father was "fond of putting into my hands books which exhibited men of energy and resource in unusual circumstances, struggling against difficulties and overcoming them" (6), indicates that the approach taken to these works was that of "philosophy teaching by examples." When he was a little older it was the typical Enlightenment view of the warfare of Reason against Superstition and Tyranny. When he came to the American war, for example, "I took my part, like a child as I was (until set right by my father) on the wrong side, because it was called the English side" (5–6). And when he came to Mitford's History of Greece, in which he delighted for its vivid narrative, "my father had put me on my guard against the Tory prejudices of this writer . . . with such effect that in reading Mitford my sympathies were always on the contrary side to those of the author" (8–9). In his eleventh and twelfth year he even wrote "a history of the Roman Government, compiled (with the assistance of Hooke) from Livy and Dionysius, [which] . . . was, in fact, an account of the struggles between the patricians and plebeians. . . . Though quite ignorant of Niebuhr's researches, I, by such lights as my father had given me, vindicated the Agrarian Laws on the evidence of Livy, and upheld to the best of my ability the Roman democratic party" (9–10). History for the young Mill and his father was simply a quarry for "ideas respecting civilization, government, morality, mental cultivation" (6), and a narrative of the Progress of the Species, the March of Intellect.

It was only in the years following his mental crisis that Mill came to the historicist view. In his essay on Coleridge he says that Bentham asked of a thing, "Is it true?" whereas Coleridge asked, "What is the meaning of it?" Mill learned from the Saint-Simonians to ask that second question. He learned that an institution may be perfectly rational and yet not be suitable for a particular people at a particular time, or that it may be irrational and yet of great benefit at that stage of their development. It was one of the great merits of the Saint-Simonians, he told d'Eichthal, to have pointed this out with respect to the medieval church, and a second great merit was their insistence that if one wishes to reform society, one needs to know into what stage of civilization society is coming.[21] Otherwise one may propose reforms, good in themselves, which are not adapted to society in that phase of its development.

Mill could hardly fail to see that his father was as much without a developmental child psychology as he was without a developmental conception of history, and that there were certain things in his own education, good in themselves, which were not suitable to the particular age in which they were administered. It was not good for him never to have had a childhood. In an age in which every Victorian lost his religion it was not even good that he never had a religion to lose. He was thereby deprived of one of the great agonizing experiences of his era. Indeed, as Mill examined his own life in the light of the Saint-Simonian philosophy he must have concluded that he was exactly out of phase with his age. For it is clear that his "organic" period—comparable to Teufelsdröckh's idyllic childhood—was the period when Dumont's Bentham united "the detached and fragmentary component parts of my knowledge" and gave "[me] a creed, a doctrine, a philosophy; in one among the best senses of the word, a religion" (47). The trouble is that his organic period was everybody else's critical period, and when he fell into his critical period, under the influence of the Romantic poets, German philosophy, and the Saint-Simonians, that corresponded to the new organic period of the rest of the nation. His Everlasting No, from 1826 to the mid-1830s, was the beginning of Carlyle's Everlasting Yea. And Mill's Everlasting Yea consisted of the compromise or synthesis he attempted to make of these two. For "in this third period (as it may be termed) of my mental progress . . . I had now completely turned back from what there had been of excess in my reaction against Benthamism" (161). Mill insists that although there was a time in which he undervalued Bentham and the eighteenth century, he never joined in the reaction against it, and he was never confused or unsettled in his views. He continually rewove the fabric of his opinions so as to incorporate the new with the old, and he emphasized the necessity of Goethe's "many-sidedness" (114). Thus, though the onset of the Everlasting No was abrupt for Mill, the movement from the No into the Everlasting Yea was not abrupt but was a process. Indeed, it was a continual process, for Mill differs from the Saint-Simonians in not believing that the coming organic phase will be the final one, but that the process of adjusting half-truth with half-truth will go on for at least the foreseeable future.

Thus Mill's assertion in 1831 that the present age is "an age of transition,"[22] remained true for him till the end of his life. In his very last years, when he was writing the final section of his *Autobiography*, he noted that this was a "period of transition, when old notions and feelings have been unsettled, and no new doctrines have yet succeeded to their ascendancy" (178). And it will be remembered that one of his motives for writing the *Autobiography* was that "in an age of transition in opinions, there may be somewhat both of interest and of benefit in noting the successive phases of any mind which was always pressing forward, equally ready to learn and to unlearn either from its own thoughts or from those of others" (1). "The chief benefit which I derived . . . from the trains of thought suggested by the St. Simonians and by Comte, was, that I obtained a clearer conception than ever before of the peculiarities of an era of transition in opinion, and ceased to mistake the moral and intellectual characteristics of such an era, for the normal attributes of humanity. I looked forward, through the present age of loud disputes but generally weak convictions, to a future which shall unite the best qualities of the critical with the best qualities of the organic periods" (116). Mill never reached an organic period in the sense of a period of settled convictions. He moved back from his reaction against Benthamism to a modified Utilitarian position in which he nonetheless took along with him the "many-sidedness" of Goethe. Thus, all his life, like the life of his entire age, was an age of transition. Newman closes his spiritual autobiography by saying, "From the time that I became a Catholic, of course, I have no further history of my religious opinions to narrate . . . no variations to record." Mill, on the other hand, opens the last chapter of his autobiography by saying, "From this time [forth] . . . I have no further mental changes to tell of, but only, as I hope, a continued mental progress" (155).

After his mental crisis Mill continued to read history even more extensively than before and wrote long review-articles on the work of Michelet, Guizot, Grote, Carlyle, and Armand Carrell. The reason for his interest is that in French and German historiography a revolution was occurring of which Englishmen were hardly aware. In Mill's view there were three stages in historical inquiry. The first is that which attempts "to transport present feelings and notions back into the past, and refer all ages and forms of human life to the standard of that in which the writer himself lives." This school has no sense of the "otherness" of the past, but, firmly persuaded that human nature is in all ages the same and that history is "philosophy teaching by examples," attempts to apply present ideas directly to the past. Of course, this kind is better than that which fails to make history live at all (Carlyle's Dryasdust), "and Mitford, so far, is a better historian than Rollin."[23]

The second stage of historical inquiry is that of the Romantic school which "attempts to regard former ages not with the eye of a modern, but, as far as possible, with that of a contemporary; to realize a true and living picture of the past time, clothed in its circumstances and peculiarities."[24] The founder of this school was Sir Walter Scott. Mill writes:

Scott's romances have been read by every educated person in Great

Britain who has grown up to manhood or womanhood in the last twenty years; and, except the memory of much pleasure, . . . they have left no traces that we know of in the national mind. But it was otherwise in France. . . . Scott's romances, and especially 'Ivanhoe,' which in England were only the amusement of an idle hour, [gave] birth (or at least nourishment) to one of the principal intellectual products of our time, the modern French school of history. M. Thierry, whose "Letters on the History of France" gave the first impulse, proclaims the fact. Seeing, in these fictions, past events for the first time brought home to them as realities, not mere abstractions; startled by finding, what they had not dreamed of, Saxons and Normans in the reign of Richard the First; thinking men felt flash upon them for the first time the meaning of that philosophical history, that history of human life, and not of kings and battles, which Voltaire talked of, but, writing history for polemical purposes, could not succeed in realizing. Immediately the annals of France, England, and other countries, began to be systematically searched; the characteristic features of society and life at each period were gathered out, and exhibited in histories, and speculations on history, and historical fictions.[25]

Niebuhr furnished an imperishable model of this school in Germany, and Carlyle (had Mill been writing a little later, he might have added Macaulay) in England.

The third and highest stage of historical investigation is that in which "the aim is not simply to compose histories, but to construct a science of history. In this view, the whole of the events which have befallen the human race, and the states through which it has passed, are regarded as a series of phenomena, produced by causes, and susceptible of explanation." This third stage, which necessarily depends upon the completion of the second, "is rather a possibility to be one day realized, than an enterprise in which any great progress has yet been made. But of the little yet done in this direction, by far the greater part has hitherto been done by French writers."[26] It is clear that Mill has in mind the Saint-Simonians, Comte, and Guizot.

Comte had extended the Saint-Simonian philosophy of history by transforming the three historical epochs, the Polytheistic, the Theological, and the Scientific or Positive, into three stages through which every branch of human knowledge must pass on its way to perfection. These stages were the Theological, in which the causes of phenomena were sought in the direct volition of divine beings; the Metaphysical, in which they were attributed to realized abstractions; and the Positive, in which phenomena themselves and the relations between phenomena were the only object of knowledge. Mill first became acquainted with this scheme from Comte's early Saint-Simonian tract, the *Système de politique positive,* which he read in the summer of 1829. He had good reason to be impressed with its truth because the revolution in his own thinking, when he read Dumont's Bentham in 1821–22, had taken him from the metaphysical to the positive. Having never had a religion, Mill had never known the theological stage, but when Bentham tore the scales from his eyes and showed him that phrases like *Law of Nature, Right Reason,* and *Moral Sense* were not real entities but merely hypostatized fictions, he was catapulted into the positive. When in 1842 he read the fifth and sixth volumes of the *Cours de philosophie positive,* in which Comte's scheme of history is worked out in detail and used as a means of classifying the sciences, Mill was lost in admiration, and it is probable that Comte's law of the three stages exceeded in importance for Mill the three historical epochs of the Saint-Simonians. The only thing he could not tolerate was the monolithic intellectual tyranny which Comte erected in the third stage.

For his general view of a free and pluralistic society he rather turned to Guizot. Guizot observes, according to Mill, "that one of the points of difference by which modern civilization is most distinguished from ancient, is the complication, the multiplicity, which characterizes it. In all previous forms of society, Oriental, Greek, or Roman, there is a remarkable character of unity and simplicity. Some one idea seems to have presided over the construction of the social framework, and to have been carried out into all its consequences." In modern society, on the other hand, there are "a number of distinct forces—of separate and independent sources of power"—the power of knowledge and cultivated intelligence, the power of religion, the power of military skill and discipline, the power of wealth, the power of numbers and physical force, and several others. "We believe with M. Guizot, that modern Europe presents the only example in history, of the maintenance, through many ages, of this co-ordinate action among rival powers naturally tending in different directions. And, with him, we ascribe chiefly to this cause the spirit of improvement, which has never ceased to exist, and still makes progress, in the European nations." If at any time any one power had attained dominance, Europe might have achieved greater perfection in that particular respect, but the whole society "would either have stagnated, like the great stationary despotisms of the East, or have perished for lack of such other elements of civilization as could sufficiently unfold themselves only under some other patronage."[27]

It will be observed that this review of European civilization is really a preview of Mill's essay *On Liberty,* for that essay is also historicist in its assumptions to a degree that Mill's father and Bentham would have

found difficult to understand. In a historical introduction Mill shows
how the problem of liberty has changed over the centuries. At one time
it was thought merely that the people had to be protected against the
tyranny of their rulers, and this was done, first by exacting from the
rulers a recognition of certain immunities (a Magna Carta or Bill of
Rights) and then by establishing constitutional checks. A time came,
however, when it was thought that, rather than tinkering with the ma-
chine, one should set it right once and for all by making the people
their own governors, so that there could be no conflict of interest and
no infringement upon liberty. This was the Benthamite stage. But now
the progress of democracy, particularly in America, has shown that the
people are not their own governors, rather the majority is, and that the
minority, particularly those rare spirits who are in advance of their time,
need to be protected against the majority. Moreover, the real danger
now is not political but intellectual and cultural oppression.

Thus, the problem becomes a cultural issue, and in the remainder
of the essay Mill envisions a Darwinian world (the year is 1859) in
which not merely the survival of truth but also its healthy condition
depend upon struggle and conflict. There have been three great periods
of intellectual ferment in the modern world, Mill says, one in "the condition of Europe immediately following the Reformation; another,
though limited to the Continent and to a more cultivated class, in the
speculative movement of the latter half of the eighteenth century; and
a third, of still briefer duration, in the intellectual fermentation of Germany during the Goethean and Fichtean period. These periods differed
widely in the particular opinions which they developed; but were alike
in this, that during all three the yoke of authority was broken. In each,
an old mental despotism had been thrown off, and no new one had yet
taken its place." Mill does not use the term *critical,* but it is obvious
that he is describing miniature critical periods within the great critical
era of the post-Reformation years. This is particularly apparent in the
chapter "Of Individuality, as one of the Elements of Well-being," where
Mill declares that "the end of man . . . is the highest and most harmonious development of his powers to a complete and consistent whole."
The fact that this quotation comes from Wilhelm von Humboldt (as
does the epigraph to the work as a whole) suggests that it embodies for
Mill the many-sidedness of the Goethean period of German culture. Its
antithesis is then identified with Calvinism. The Calvinistic theory is
that "human nature being radically corrupt, there is no redemption for
any one until human nature is killed within him." In opposition to this
view Mill then quotes Sterling, the Coleridgean under whose influence

he had moved farthest from Bentham: " 'Pagan self-assertion' is one of the elements of human worth, as well as 'Christian self-denial.' There is a Greek ideal of self-development, which the Platonic and Christian ideal of self-government blends with, but does not supersede. It may be better to be a John Knox than an Alcibiades, but it is better to be a Pericles than either; nor would a Pericles, if we had one in these days, be without anything good which belonged to John Knox."[28] The dialectic of history would have produced, in Goethe or von Humboldt, the synthesis of Greek and Christian, of Knox and Alcibiades, which involves self-development *and* self-government. It is clear that Mill's desire is for history no longer to alternate between organic and critical phases but rather to combine the two. It should move steadily forward in a continual process of self-criticism and self-creation.

Prior to encountering the Saint-Simonians, Carlyle's philosophy of history, insofar as he had one, was based on the familiar analogy between the life of the world and the life of the individual. There were three stages: Imagination, Understanding, and Reason. This schema, common in eighteenth-century literary histories, provided the framework for an unfinished "History of German Literature" which Carlyle was commissioned to write by some London booksellers and which he worked on during the winter and spring of 1829–30 until the publishing arrangements collapsed in July of that year.[29] He then quarried his manuscript for three review articles, on the *Niebelungenlied*, "Early German Literature," and on William Taylor's *Historic Survey of German Poetry*, which were published in various periodicals in 1831. From these articles, the manuscript of Carlyle's History, and a letter to Goethe, one can see what Carlyle's plan was. He intended to treat the Swabian Era, the period of the Minnesingers in the twelfth century, as the first great period of German poetry, whose essence was youthful wonder, with chivalry as the appropriate instrument to translate this idealism into action. To this there succeeded a period of Inquiry or Didacticism, which continued through various fourteenth- and fifteenth-century authors until it rose to an almost poetic intensity in Luther and then declined again into theological disputations and superficial refinements. Carlyle saw Lessing as "standing between two Periods, an earnest Sceptic, struggling to work himself into the region of spiritual Truth," but this region was not attained until the era of Goethe and Schiller. "Under you and Schiller," Carlyle wrote to Goethe, "a Third grand Period had evolved itself, as yet fairly developed in no other Literature, but full of

the richest prospects for all: Namely, a period of new Spirituality and
Belief in the midst of old Doubt and Denial: . . . wherein Reverence is
again rendered compatible with Knowledge, and Art and Religion are
one."[30] The three periods, then, are not merely those of Imagination,
Understanding, and Reason but also of Art, Science, and Religion—
periods which Carlyle identifies with the Middle Ages, which is the
youth of the modern world; the Renaissance, Reformation, and Enlightenment, which is its manhood; and the late eighteenth and early nineteenth centuries, which, in a breakdown of the analogy, are not old age
but a new youthfulness on a higher plane.

It is obvious that this scheme, which involves a kind of periodicity
between poetry and didacticism, is easily reconcilable with the Saint-
Simonian philosophy, with its organic-critical-organic periods. As Carlyle first learned about the Saint-Simonians from d'Eichthal in the very
month (July 1830) in which the plan for the History of German Literature collapsed, he must have been delighted to find his tentative views
supported by so systematic and well ordered a scheme. He immediately
plunged into the writing of *Sartor Resartus,* and so it is no wonder that
that work, particularly the biographical portion of it, is full of Saint-
Simonian references. Though Carlyle's philosophy of history first came
to him from English and German sources, it was given its final form by
the Saint-Simonians, as the "organic filaments," the first gossamery
threads of the new society, make clear. The Professor himself, who is
deeply radical, quotes "without censure that strange aphorism of Saint
Simon's," that the Golden Age is not behind us but before, and when,
at the end of the book, he mysteriously disappears, the Editor opines
that he has either been spirited away by the Saint-Simonians or gone to
their headquarters to confront them (I, 188, 236–37).

Carlyle's brilliant contribution to this philosophy of history is the
Clothes metaphor by which it is represented. The metaphor of Machinery, which he had adopted in "Signs of the Times," was not really
successful because, despite his Genius of Mechanization, there was
no smooth way in which Mechanism could modulate into Dynamism.
Neither was the more profound analysis of the age in terms of Self-
consciousness in "Characteristics" satisfactory, since to become unconscious would be simply to return to the original condition and it seemed
psychologically difficult to be "anti-self-conscious." But the metaphor
of clothes was the perfect vehicle to express both the transcendental and
the descendental aspect of Teufelsdröckh's philosophy, for if clothes bod-
ied forth the inner spiritual reality behind appearances, they also, where
that reality was absent or a sham, served as a "clothes-screen" to conceal

the sham. Moreover, they lent themselves to change. New garments could continually be a-weaving, and, on the other hand, the old were easily subject to destruction. By introducing, apparently from German sources, the Phoenix, who expires in a magnificent conflagration and then arises from her own ashes, Carlyle introduced an apocalyptic and catastrophic element which apparently satisfied his Scotch Calvinism but was hardly consistent with the gradualist implications of "organic filaments." He tries to reconcile the two by means of the serpent. " 'In the living subject,' says [Teufelsdröckh], 'change is wont to be gradual: thus, while the serpent sheds its old skin, the new is already formed beneath. Little knowest thou of the burning of a World-Phoenix, who fanciest that she must first burn-out, and lie as a dead cinereous heap; and therefrom the young one start-up by miracle, and fly heavenward. Far otherwise! In that Fire-whirlwind, Creation and Destruction proceed together; ever as the ashes of the Old are blown about, do organic filaments of the New mysteriously spin themselves; and amid the rushing and the waving of the Whirlwind-element come tones of a melodious Deathsong, which end not but in tones of a more melodious Birthsong' " (I, 194–95). The World-Phoenix is apparently of a different species from the ordinary in that it may take two centuries to combust.

The Saint-Simonian philosophy of history seems to have satisfied Carlyle for at least a decade, for it is presupposed in *The French Revolution* and it provides the general structure of the *Lectures on the History of Literature* which Carlyle delivered in 1838. In these lectures, as with the Saint-Simonians, there are two great eras of belief, the Polytheism of the Greeks and Romans, and the Christianity of the Middle Ages, each followed by a period of unbelief. The novel element is that since this is a history of literature and Carlyle has by this time decided that literature *is* self-consciousness—that it is the nation being conscious of its own life rather than living it—he is committed to the theory that great literature does not occur in ages of belief but rather when these ages are beginning to break up. This is the reason for the great efflorescence of literature in the Elizabethan Age, the period when Catholicism and Feudalism were beginning to end. The theory obviously does not account for Dante and Homer, who would seem to be great unconscious geniuses in ages of belief, but Carlyle would say that Dante belongs to religion rather than literature and Homer to history. Shakespeare apparently rises above his age. On the other hand, the theory may explain why Virgil is inferior to Homer. "There is that fatal consciousness, that knowledge that he is writing an epic," which vitiates everything, and "it is remarkable how soon afterwards Roman literature had quite degenerated" into self-consciousness and skepticism. Milton is to Shakespeare as Virgil is to Homer, for "no great man ever felt so great a consciousness as Milton."[31] The theory obviously makes nonsense of literary history and is not consistent with itself, but Carlyle apparently held it as true, at least for purposes of the lecture platform.

A second novel element is his attempt to explain cultural change. In his earlier "History of German Literature" he had avoided doing this, having no faith in "cause-and-effect" philosophers and scornfully rejecting, as reductive, proposed social and material explanations. But in the 1838 lectures he feels the need to explain change, and he hesitates rather lamely between the subjective explanation that systems of belief simply ceased to satisfy after a period and the more objective and progressive view that they were approximations of the truth, good for their time but necessarily superseded when better arrived. Carlyle must have felt less happy with the Saint-Simonian theory when he came to apply it in detail than he did when its novelty first burst upon him. But he never repudiated it, and elements of the system may be found in later works right up to and including *Frederick the Great*. It is supplemented, however, by other schemes which deal more minutely with the period in which Carlyle was chiefly interested, the last two hundred years before his own day.

Indeed, as one reads Carlyle, one feels that his time-scale was considerably shorter than Saint-Simon's and that for him a complete cycle of organic and critical periods had played itself out in the four hundred years of modern history. It is true that he says in several places that Protestantism, Puritanism, and the French Revolution are the three waves of the critical movement that destroyed the Catholic-Feudal system. "Protestantism was a revolt against spiritual sovereignties, Popes and much else. Nay I will grant that English Puritanism, revolt against earthly sovereignties, was the second act of it; and that the enormous French Revolution itself was the third act, whereby all sovereignties earthly and spiritual were, as might seem, abolished or made sure of abolition. Protestantism is the grand root from which our whole subsequent European History branches out" (V, 123, 237). Still, Protestantism and Puritanism, with their heroes, Luther, Knox, and Cromwell, are so much admired by Carlyle that one cannot but think that these periods, though critical with respect to the Catholic-Feudal system, have carried that criticism to a point of intensity that almost constitutes them organic. (One recalls that Carlyle employed the same paradox with respect to Luther in the "History of German Literature": in a Didactic age he carried didacticism to an almost poetic intensity.)

Doubtless Carlyle was projecting his own personal experience upon the backdrop of history, but for him it is the eighteenth century that is critical par excellence.

For that poor, wretched, miserable century he has almost nothing good to say. It was a century of sham, of unreality, of atheism and materialism, of pure formalism and superficial refinement, given to persiflage and mockery, a century of quacks and impostors. By accident several good men were born into it, such as Robert Burns and Dr. Johnson, but its representative figures were Hume and Gibbon in England and Voltaire in France. Voltaire especially was "emphatically . . . the man of his century" (XXVI, 401), the very incarnation of the Spirit of his Age. This being so, Carlyle should have admitted that he had done the work that he came into the world to do, and he does concede, "He gave the death-stab to modern Superstition!" (XXVI, 468). But he cannot quite forgive him for not doing more. " 'Cease, my much-respected Herr von Voltaire,' thus apostrophizes the Professor: 'shut thy sweet voice; for the task appointed thee seems finished. Sufficiently hast thou demonstrated this proposition, considerable or otherwise; That the Mythus of the Christian Religion looks not in the eighteenth century as it did in the eighth. Alas, were thy six-and-thirty quartos . . . all needed to convince us of so little! But what next? Wilt thou help us to embody the divine Spirit of that Religion in a new Mythus, in a new vehicle and vesture, that our Souls, otherwise too like perishing, may live? What! thou hast no faculty in that kind? Only a torch for burning, no hammer for building? Take our thanks, then, and———thyself away' " (I, 154–55). Carlyle could never quite decide whether he wished his Heroes to be Representative Men, embodying all the characteristics of their age, or Great Men, rising above their age. Voltaire was a Representative Man.

The French Revolution to Carlyle was simply the most momentous event since the fall of the Roman Empire—"the crowning Phenomenon of our Modern Time" (II, 212). "Truly, without the French Revolution, one would not know what to make of an age like this at all" (V, 201). Coming at the end of the eighteenth century, it is the negation of a negation—the French people saying No to the Everlasting No. It is comparable to the Protest on the Rue de St. Thomas de l'Enfer (and this may be why Carlyle set that episode in Paris), when Teufelsdröckh stood up in native, God-created majesty and defied the shams with which he was encompassed. In *The French Revolution* Carlyle represents it in terms of titanic natural forces—volcano, earthquake, fire, and raging storm, which destroy the frail wood-and-paper universe of the ancien régime. The trouble was, it issued in nothing. Carlyle's theory, according to Mill in his review, was that "the men . . . who attempted at that period to regenerate France, failed in what it was impossible that any one should succeed in: namely, in attempting to found a government, to create a new order of society, a new set of institutions and habits, among a people having no convictions to base such order of things upon."[32] Thus, the Revolution emerged, not into the New Era which its leaders had promised, but into the Center of Indifference, into a spiritual vacuum. Had there been some great leader with a vision of his own, he might, by inspiring faith in himself, have inspired faith in his vision, but there was not. Mirabeau was truly an Original Man, who moved through the Revolution like a substance and a force, not like the formula of one, but Mirabeau did not live. Thus, at the end there was only Napoleon, a mixture of greatness and quackery, and he was a man of the past, not the future, a Werther or Byron, who wrote his lamentations on the pages of history and with the blood of dying men.

The question is, what lies ahead? In his earlier works, "Signs of the Times," "Characteristics," and *Sartor Resartus,* Carlyle had always ended on a serene and hopeful note. However dark the present age might appear, "the darkest hour is ever nearest the dawn." "Indications we do see . . . , signs infinitely cheering to us . . . , that a new and brighter spiritual era is slowly evolving itself for all men" (XXVII, 81). The ground of this faith was primarily the new literature that was arising in Germany, particularly the writings of Goethe. But Goethe had died in 1832, and although it was not to be expected that his influence be felt immediately—it was rather like a tide which rises in mid-ocean forty-eight hours before it is felt on the shore—still "David Hume is at this hour pontiff of the world, and rules most hearts, and guides most tongues" (XXVII, 378). As a result, the term *New Era* takes on a rather bitter tinge in Carlyle's writings. "Ever the 'new era' was come, was coming, yet still it came not" (XXVII, 379), he wrote in 1832, and in 1839: "One has heard so often of new eras, new and newest eras, that the word has grown rather empty of late" (XXIX, 170). New eras will come, but will they be better than the old and will they come soon? *The French Revolution* was a dire apocalyptic warning that if England did not reform its ways and do justice it would be damned, but if it reformed them in the way that France had it would also be damned. For what issued from the French Revolution was pure democracy, and to Carlyle democracy was not a new order but a transition state. It was the state in which one authority had been destroyed and no new authority had been introduced in its stead. It was a political Center of Indifference.

The universe, said Carlyle, is not a democracy but a hierarchy—a hierarchy of merit. Napoleon had seen this—it was his one new idea: *la carrière ouverte aux talens*—but he himself had lacked talent and had created a false order. Nonetheless, "All human things," said Carlyle, "maddest French Sansculottisms, do and must work towards Order. . . . Disorder is dissolution, death. No chaos but it seeks a *centre* to revolve round. While man is man, some Cromwell or Napoleon is the necessary finish of a Sansculottism" (V, 204). If not Napoleon, then it must be Cromwell.

Cromwell was the very first subject Carlyle seized on for a book. He wrote to his brother in April 1822: "My purpose . . . is to come out with a kind of Essay on the Civil Wars, the Commonwealth of England—not to write a history of them—but to exhibit if I can some features of the national character as it was then displayed."[33] The first thirty pages of his notebook are filled with material relating to this project. Ironically, Cromwell was not then a hero to him, for he had been reading Clarendon's History and had accepted the Royalist estimate. "Cromwell and the rest look much like a pack of fanatical knaves— a compound of religious enthusiasm, and of barbarous selfishness; which made them stick at no means for gratifying both the one and the other. Cromwell is a *very* curious person. Has his character been rightly seized yet?" Apparently he suspected not, for a month later he queried, "*How* was it such noble minds were generated in those times? I know not but think it well worth inquiring into." Still, as late as 1826 he declared, "What a fine thing a *Life of Cromwell,* like the *Vie de Charles XII* [by Voltaire] would be! The wily fanatic himself, in his own most singular features, at once a hero and a blackguard pettifogging scrub; and the wild image of his Times reflected from his accompaniment! I would travel ten miles on foot to see his *soul* represented as I once saw his body in the Castle of Warwick." By the next year he was thinking of a biography of Luther. "Luther's character appears to me the most worth discussing of all modern men's. He is, to say it in a word, a great man in *every* sense; has the soul at once of a Conqueror and a Poet. . . . A picture of the public Thought in those days, and of this strong lofty mind overturning and new-moulding it, would be a fine affair in many senses. It would require immense research.—Alas! alas!—When are we to have another Luther? Such men are needed from century to century: there seldom has been more need of one than now." And a few days later: "Begin to think more seriously of discussing *Martin Luther.* The only Inspiration I know of is that of Genius: it was, is, and will always be of a divine character."[34]

Throughout 1833–34 Carlyle hesitated between a history of John Knox and the Scottish Reformation and a history of the French Revolution—quite a hesitation! He ultimately settled on the latter, but when he finished it in 1837 he determined to return to Cromwell, whom he now saw as a much maligned man. Luther, Knox, and Cromwell all figure as heroes in *Heroes and Hero-worship* (1841), but Carlyle thought Cromwell deserved a book to himself. He had trouble getting on with it, however, because his mind was distracted by the desperate plight of the poor. Then, in September 1842, as he was pursuing his researches in the East Anglian region associated with the Lord Protector, he came upon two places, quite unrelated to Cromwell, which deeply impressed his imagination—the ruined abbey of Bury St. Edmunds and the modern workhouse at St. Ives. These two institutions, the one symbolizing a harmonious society suffused with religion, the other a bankrupt modern world united only by the cash-nexus, represented for Carlyle the Past and the Present. On returning to London he began reading about the monastery and found in the Latin *Chronicle* of Jocelin of Brakelond an account of the ministry of Abbot Samson so inspiring that he was momentarily diverted from Cromwell and seventeenth-century Puritanism into an account of medieval Catholicism.

Carlyle's influence on Ruskin and Morris was so great that he has always been accounted a major figure in the Victorian revival of Medievalism, but in truth he knew little about the Middle Ages and was not deeply committed to it. He wholeheartedly accepted the nineteenth-century reversal of the values of the Enlightenment, accounting the Roman Augustan Age a period of sensualism and skepticism and the Middle Ages a period of faith and youthful wonder. In his unfinished "History of German Literature" he had described the Swabian Era as an era of great poetry, and in his *Lectures on the History of Literature* he had said bluntly: "The Middle Ages used to be called Ages of Darkness, Rudeness, and Barbarity. . . . But it is universally apparent now that these ages are not to be so called." Even the barbarian invasions were "a great and fertile period,"[35] accomplishing for the Roman Empire the same favorable destructive purpose as was accomplished for the ancien régime by the French Revolution. William the Conqueror was not a bloody tyrant but one who performed needful surgery upon the English nation. Feudalism, which even the Saint-Simonians had seen as only less oppressive than the slave-owners of antiquity, Carlyle saw as a system of mutual responsibility and interdependence. Summoning the dubious argument of etymology, he declared that in those days a Lord really was a *Law-ward* or guardian of the law, a Lady really was a *Hlaf-dig* or giver of the loaf, a Duke really was a *Dux* or leader, and a King really was the most knowing or able (*Can-ning*) (I, 198; X, 193, 211, 245). It so happened that Jocelin was the exact contemporary of Ivanhoe, and so Carlyle could make frequent use of that book, which, like most of his contemporaries, he read as far more favorable to the Middle Ages than it was. None of Scott's criticism of chivalry, for example, seems to have come through to him, and Gurth, the thrall of Cedric the Saxon whom Scott describes with mild acerbity as having a brass collar round his neck, Carlyle sees as perfectly happy. "Gurth's brass collar did not gall him," says Carlyle. "Cedric *deserved* to be his master. The pigs were Cedric's, but Gurth too would get his parings of them. Gurth had the inexpressible satisfaction of feeling himself related indissolubly, though in a rude brass-collar way, to his fellow-mortals in this Earth. He had superiors, inferiors, equals." He did not have liberty, but then " 'Liberty to die by starvation' is not so divine!" (X, 212).

There is no question but that Carlyle was favorable to the Middle Ages, but there is really very little in *Past and Present* that is specifically medieval.[36] The life in the monastery is not noticeably interdependent, and the Catholic religion is almost embarrassingly absent. Abbot Samson, who is a rude, practical, overbearing peasant with amazing spiritual and physical force, seems more like a pre-incarnation of Cromwell, or of Carlyle's father, than a medieval Abbot. Indeed, the thing that seems most powerfully to have drawn Carlyle to this material was not the contrast between Bury St. Edmunds and the workhouse but the contrast between the treatment of Cromwell's corpse and the enshrined and embalmed body of St. Edmund. For far and away the most dramatic scene in *Past and Present* is that in which Samson and eleven of his fellows, in the dead of night, open the coffin of their patron saint and reverently look in upon the relic (two of them touching it) before they transfer it to its newly enriched shrine. Saints are the Heroes of the Middle Ages, and those ages knew how to worship them aright. Cromwell's body, on the other hand, after having been buried in Westminster Abbey, was, at the Restoration, torn from its coffin and hanged on the gallows at Tyburn from 10 A.M. until sunset. The head was then cut off with an axe by the common hangman and mounted on a pole on top of Westminster Hall—the rest of the body being buried in a pit beneath the gallows. This, said Carlyle, is the way the modern world treats its Heroes, and in a chapter entitled "Two Centuries" he traces the spiritual desiccation of England not from the twelfth century but from the seventeenth.

The second episode in Jocelin's narrative in which Carlyle is most deeply interested is the election of Samson as Abbot. An election, says

Carlyle, "is a most important social act; nay, at bottom, the one important social act. Given the men a People choose, the People itself, in its exact worth and worthlessness, is given. . . . Nor are electoral methods, Reform Bills and such like, unimportant. A People's electoral methods are, in the long-run, the express image of its electoral *talent*" (X, 75–76). The electoral methods of the monastery were superficially very complicated but at bottom very simple: good men simply got together and chose the one they thought best in the sight and fear of the Lord. It happened that the one they chose was of low birth, and in this too he was like Cromwell, who rose from a country squire to be the most powerful and "the Ablest Man in England, the King of England" (X, 222). Burns, on the other hand, was allowed to weigh out malt in eighteenth-century England.

When Carlyle treated Cromwell in *Heroes and Hero-worship,* he put him in the very last chapter along with Napoleon under the title "The Hero as King." This is surprising because all the other heroes are in chronological order. Indeed, the work has a historical thesis that the divine spirit, incarnating itself in Heroes, accommodates itself to the degree of civilization of the age, so that one goes through the series: Hero as Divinity (Odin), as Prophet (Mahomet), as Poet (Dante and Shakespeare), as Priest (Luther and Knox), as Man of Letters (Johnson, Rousseau, and Burns), and as King (Napoleon and Cromwell). Carlyle insists, despite the apparent secularization, that there is no falling off in the central heroic stuff, merely an accommodation of the divine to the spirit of the age. But it is obvious that the King is not the old-fashioned King by divine right of which Charles I and Louis XVI were a faint relic, but the new post-revolutionary King who comes to impose an order upon Sansculottism. He is, then, a King of the future, not of the past, and the fact that England had its revolution in the seventeenth century does not matter in this essentially philosophical development.

The association of Cromwell with Napoleon was not original with Carlyle: it was, indeed, a commonplace in his century. For, as we have already seen, Cromwell had been so maligned by all parties immediately following the Restoration that he was, in Pope's words, "damn'd to everlasting fame." Throughout most of the eighteenth century he was regarded as a monster both in private and in public life. Two Nonconformist biographies early in the century somewhat modified this view, but then there was nothing for three-quarters of a century until Napoleon's career suddenly "explained" Cromwell to both the British and the Continental public. The antiquarians meanwhile had been printing a great many documents, and there was a sudden flurry of new biographies, none of which really changed the traditional view. Carlyle, who had been suffering through these documents for nearly twenty years and who had arrived at the conclusion that Cromwell was England's greatest national leader, wished to publish a new biography of his own, but reluctantly decided that the only way was to let the facts speak for themselves. He thus edited in two (later three) volumes the letters and speeches of Cromwell (1845) with a voluble commentary so that not even the dullest could miss the point. The result was a great triumph. The Lord Protector's character and personality stood clear for the first time both of the distorting lies of his detractors and also of the accumulated rubbish of the historians, and, as Hilaire Belloc says, a new myth was born. For such was the growing affluence and power of the Nonconformists, such the hatred of the Tractarians, and such too the feeling that England was being called to imperial greatness, that Cromwell was raised to the position of a national hero. "He stood somehow, consciously or unconsciously, for the English people." "He was a practical mystic," said Lord Rosebery, "the most formidable and terrible of all combinations, uniting an inspiration derived from the celestial and supernatural with the energy of a mighty man of action. . . . no hypocrite but a defender of the faith, the raiser and maintainer of the Empire of England."[37]

With Cromwell, the Once and Future King, Carlyle came to the end of his historical myth, and the six volumes on Frederick the Great were really unnecessary. Frederick was the last real King *before* the Revolution, a Reality in an age of shams, and that is doubtless the reason for Carlyle's interest in him. Feeling more and more out of phase with his age himself, he wanted to see how one had managed who was completely out of phase. But Frederick, as Carlyle admitted, was "a questionable hero" (I, 14). The two elements of a Hero were vision and will. Cromwell mediated the vision of John Knox to the English people, but Frederick did not mediate that of Luther, merely of Voltaire and his own realpolitik. More and more Carlyle emphasizes will in his heroes at the expense of vision, doubtless because he is impatient that the New Era does not come. How long will it take? "Will *one* century of constant fluctuation serve us," he asks in 1831, "or shall we need two?"[38] By *Sartor Resartus* he has concluded that two would be a bargain (I, 189). "Two centuries; hardly less;" he exclaims in *The French Revolution*, "before Democracy go through its due, most baleful, stages of *Quack*ocracy; and a pestilential World be burnt up, and have begun to grow green and young again" (II, 133). But by the end of *Frederick the Great* he declares, "Centuries of it yet lying ahead of us . . . ! Say Two Centuries yet,—say even Ten of such a process: before the Old is completely burnt out, and the New in any state of sightliness. Millennium of Anarchies!" (XIX, 2).

Obviously, the new Industrial Age in which the Captains of Industry are directed by the Scientists did not have to wait a thousand years. It is here already. But that is only the lesser side of the world that Carlyle envisoned. He envisioned a world based on social justice in which religion would be a living reality again. But it would be religion with a difference—a religion in which "Man is still Man" and Nature is not fallen but erect. "The Universe, I say, is made by Law; the great Soul of the World is just and not unjust. Look thou, if thou have eyes or soul left, into this great shoreless Incomprehensible: in the heart of its tumultuous Appearances, Embroilments, and mad Time-vortexes, is there not, silent, eternal, an All-just, and All-beautiful; sole Reality and ultimate controlling Power of the whole? This is not a figure of speech; this is a fact. The fact of Gravitation known to all animals, is not surer than this inner Fact, which may be known to all men" (X, 229). Carlyle's use of *fact* where we would say *value,* and *Reality* where we would say *God,* is a part of his Natural Supernaturalism. Heaven and Hell, he declares, "are not a similitude, nor a fable nor semi-fable: . . . they are an everlasting highest fact!" (X, 145). One may say that they *were* a fact until Carlyle and his generation demystified them and made them into a fable, and the effort now to take the psychological or moral truth which that fable represents and transform it back into a fact is not easy. It is Mill's problem all over again. Having been catapulted from the Metaphysical into the Positive stage, it is difficult to climb back up into the Metaphysical. We can see Carlyle trying to do it by his capital letters, which attempt to make Real Entities out of subjective feelings, by his Biblical language and assumption of the garb and mien of Jehovah, and by his creation of a band of Heroes, who are his version of the Visible Church. But it will not do: he cannot be both inside history and outside it. He cannot believe both that every age has its own validity in the historic process and also that there are some ages, such as the eighteenth century, that have "no history at all." He cannot have his Heroes both Representative Men and Unrepresentative Men. He cannot say that Belief is of transcendent importance, with the strong implication that it does not matter what one believes, and still urge his countrymen to believe this or that particular thing. He cannot see religion both as relative to the state of society it is in and as of absolute significance to those within that state. He cannot say that Might makes Right, even in the long-range sense that the real forces in the world do tend to legitimize themselves in history, and at the same time thunder against the Might that has made Wrong. He has effected a quasi-divinization of history and a quasi-secularization of God, and it is difficult to assimilate the one to the other. "Man lives at the conflux of two eternities," Carlyle was fond of saying. He obviously had a deep-seated need to live at the conflux, but also to feel that there were eternities before and after.

In some of his later works Carlyle tended to see history not as a matter of alternating periods but of radiating lineal descent. He found in Norse mythology the metaphor of the tree of Igdrasil, which expressed his deeply felt sense that nothing in the past is lost.

> I like, too, that representation they have of the Tree Igdrasil. All Life is figured by them as a Tree. Igdrasil, the Ash-Tree of Existence, has its roots deep-down in the kingdoms of Hela or Death; its trunk reaches up heaven-high, spreads its boughs over the whole Universe: it is the Tree of Existence. At the foot of it, in the Death-Kingdom, sit Three *Nornas,* Fates,—the Past, Present, Future; watering its roots from the Sacred Well. Its 'boughs,' with their buddings and disleafings,—events, things suffered, things done, catastrophes,—stretch through all lands and times. Is not every leaf of it a biography, every fibre there an act or word? Its boughs are Histories of Nations. The rustle of it is the noise of Human Existence, onwards from of old. It grows there, the breath of Human Passion rustling through it;—or stormtost, the stormwind howling through it like the voice of all the gods. It is Igdrasil, the Tree of Existence. (V, 20)

The metaphor expresses Carlyle's strong sense of the organic unity of the present with the past, of the fact that nothing true in the past is ever lost. Therefore, the past, whether analogous to the present or not, is at least relevant to the present. "Let us search more and more into the Past; let all men explore it, as the true fountain of knowledge; by whose light alone, consciously or unconsciously employed, can the Present and the Future be interpreted or guessed at. For though the whole meaning lies far beyond our ken; yet in that complex Manuscript, covered over with formless inextricably-entangled unknown characters,— nay, which is a *Palimpsest,* and had once prophetic writing, still dimly legible there,—some letters, some words, may be deciphered" (XXVII, 89).

4

Thomas Arnold
and the Idea of Modernity

THE WORD *modern* in its currently favorable sense seems to have entered the language in the first third of the nineteenth century, probably about the same time that *spirit of the age* became popular. In the older literature, apart from its purely chronological meaning, *modern* was generally used in the unfavorable sense of "commonplace" or "trivial," as in Shakespeare's "Wise saws and modern instances." Johnson in his *Dictionary* gives only two definitions, the purely chronological one, "late; recent; not ancient; not antique," and the Shakespearean, "vulgar; mean; common." In the nineteenth century, however, there developed a use of the term to designate, favorably, a style and sensibility, a complex of attitudes, which certainly were characteristic of the modern world but which were not limited to that era, as when Lowell speaks of Montaigne as "the first really modern writer" or Emerson praises the "modernness" of Plato.[1] The Quarrel between the Ancients and the Moderns in the late seventeenth century was a step in this direction, but only in the sense that it raised the value of those who were chronologically modern. No seventeenth-century defender of Aristotle would have defended him on the ground that he was "modern," nor did the Moderns assert that intrinsic desirability of modernness. It was only when the idea arose that anyone who looked forward to or anticipated the modern world was peculiarly interesting that the favorable conception of modernity developed. It is the "Whig interpretation of history" manifesting itself in language, and it is no accident that it arose as that interpretation of history arose. Thomas Arnold and the group known as the Liberal Anglican historians are partly responsible for that usage.

The figures whom Duncan Forbes treats in *The Liberal Anglican Idea of History* are Thomas Arnold, Julius Hare, Henry Hart Milman, Arthur P. Stanley, Connop Thirlwall, and Richard Whately.[2] They were a part of the Broad Church group within the Anglican communion, though one should be conscious that the term *Broad Church* was not employed during the period from 1825 to 1840 when Arnold and his colleagues were most active. Jowett says that it was first proposed, in his hearing, by Arthur Hugh Clough as a kind of joke. If there were a High Church and a Low, presumably there ought also to be a Broad, if only on the model of the Latitudinarians of the seventeenth century. By 1850 the term was colloquially familiar in Oxford circles, and in 1853 it was used by W. J. Conybeare in an article entitled "Church Parties" in the *Edinburgh Review*. Conybeare says that the Broad Church party was marked by a spirit of tolerance and comprehensiveness which attempted to mediate between the High Church party and the Low. It is true that there were these three parties in the Church, but it is probably better to think of the Broad Church theologians as mediating among three extreme positions rather than two. Mill says that the two seminal minds in the early nineteenth century were Coleridge and Bentham, but in addition to the Romantic and the Utilitarian positions there was also the traditional Christian humanist position, which took the form of orthodoxy within the Established Church. The peculiar feature of the religious situation in the early nineteenth century was that each of these three wings within the Anglican Church had a more extreme version which had broken out of the Church and thus constituted a danger to its existence. Beyond the Low or Evangelical wing were the various forms of Dissent, which constituted the religious manifestation of Romanticism. Beyond the Liberal wing were Unitarianism, Socinianism, and skepticism, which constituted the religious manifestation of Benthamite rationalism. And beyond the High Church or Tractarian party, especially after 1833, was Roman Catholicism, the extreme manifestation of the orthodox or dogmatic ideal. The Broad Church party mediated among all three groups, having affiliations with them all. It has been said that it is the direct descendant of Coleridge, and this is true, but it must be remembered that Coleridge himself had moved, between the days when he was truly a seminal mind and the days at Highgate when he was in contact with the Liberal Anglicans, from a Romantic to a quasi-Victorian position. Moreover, the Broad Church group itself represented quite a spectrum. C. R. Sanders has distinguished between an Oxford contingent, which was more Aristotelian and rationalist, and a Cambridge contingent, which was more Platonic and intuitive.[3] The former included the Oriel "Noetics," a group comprising Edward Copleston, Edward Hawkins, Blanco White, Richard Whately, and Thomas Arnold. So far were they from Coleridge that it has been said the Oriel Common Room "stunk of logic," a charge that could not have been made of the Cambridge "Apostles" and their great leader, Frederick Denison Maurice. In its breadth and comprehensiveness the Broad Church position has been called the "Victorian compromise," though if it were not for some looseness and inexactitude in its thinking it might be called the "Victorian synthesis."

Thomas Arnold was preeminently the historian of this group. At the age of eight he read Joseph Priestley's *Lectures on History*, and at Winchester, according to his pupil Stanley, "he was a diligent student of Russell's *Modern Europe*; Gibbon and Mitford he had read twice over before he left school." At Oxford, deciding it would be beneficial to master some one period, he chose the fifteenth century with Philip de Comines as his text. He of course went through all the classic historians thoroughly and wrote out an analysis, under the title "Thoughts on History," of the characteristics of the chief ancient historians. Livy he despised for his slovenliness and inaccuracy; the Greek historians he much preferred, placing Thucydides highest but Herodotus not far below. Indeed, he had so imbued himself with the style of these two writers, according to his friend J. T. Coleridge, that "he could write narratives in the style of either at pleasure with wonderful readiness, and as we thought with the greatest accuracy." Though he is known as the historian of Rome, Greek history was actually the more sympathetic to his mind. His edition of Thucydides he began with the intention of illustrating the work historically rather than philologically, and in the early 1820s he wrote a short sketch of the rise of the Greek nation which he carried down to the Persian wars. Greek or Roman, ancient or modern, the events of the past had for him a vivid reality, so that it seemed to his students as though he had actually witnessed the siege of Syracuse or been present at the battle of Marathon. "The images of the past were habitually in his mind," wrote Stanley, "and haunted him even in sleep with a vividness which would bring before him some of the most striking passages in ancient history—the death of Caesar, the wars of Sylla, the siege of Syracuse, the destruction of Jerusalem—as scenes in which he was himself taking part." Aristotle too was a passion with him. So imbued was he with Aristotle's ideas, says Coleridge, that in conversation "his language was quaintly and racily pointed" with phrases from the *Ethics* and the *Rhetoric*. "I never knew a man who made such familiar, even fond use of an author: it is scarcely too much to say, that he spoke of him as of one intimately and affectionately known and valued."[4]

It is doubtless because of this power to realize vividly the Greek and Roman classics that Edward Hawkins said of Arnold in recommending him for the position of Headmaster of Rugby School that, if elected, he would "change the face of education all through the public schools of England."[5] Lytton Strachey, in his delightfully outrageous caricature of Arnold, has said that he did no such thing but continued essentially the same classical curriculum which had obtained since the Renaissance. It is true that Arnold went only a little way toward the introduction of modern subjects, but what he did was to revolutionize the teaching of the classics by substituting for the elegant verbal scholarship of the eighteenth century the use of the classics as a key to Greek and Roman culture. "He was the first Englishman," says Stanley, "who drew attention in our public schools to the historical, political, and philosophical value of philology [i.e., the study of literature] and of the ancient writers, as distinguished from the mere verbal criticism and elegant scholarship of the last century."[6] Whereas a previous generation of schoolboys had written Latin verses and construed their texts with a keen eye for an ablative absolute and a dative of reference, Arnold deprecated verse-writing and insisted that his students translate extempore, turning a whole sentence of Greek or Latin into a whole sentence of English, so that they could get the meaning of what they read. He never lectured but used the Socratic method, endeavoring by his questions to direct the boys to the real point of the subject and to teach them what they knew and what they did not know. "You come here," he said, "not to read, but to learn how to read." He gave the death blow (as he said) to themes on "Virtus est bona res," and gave instead "historical or geographical descriptions, imaginary speeches or letters, etymological accounts of words, or criticisms of books, or put religious and moral subjects in such a form as awakened a new and real interest in them."[7] Style he prized less than originality of thought, for his real purpose was not to teach the Greek and Roman classics but to train the mind by means of the classics.

Each half year at Rugby was divided into two equal parts, called "language time" and "history time." The poets and orators were read principally during "language time," history and geography during "history time." Under the latter were included Eutropius, parts of Justin, Xenophon's *Anabasis* and *Hellenics,* Florus, Arrian, Paterculus, Herodotus, Livy, Thucydides, and Tacitus; also Markham's *History of England* and *History of France,* the *History of Greece* issued by the Useful Knowledge Society, Russell's *Modern Europe,* Sir James MacIntosh's *England,* Hallam's *Middle Ages,* and (in the French division) Guizot's *Histoire de la révolution de l'Angleterre* and Mignet's *Histoire de la révolution française.* With a strong sense of what was appropriate at different ages

Arnold started off the little boys with volumes of prints of the famous men of all periods and then moved on to the poetical and heroic part of history, to the stories that would enlist their interest. This done, he gradually filled in the narrative substance and then, in the Sixth Form, brought them to some philosophical historian who would enable them to rise to "the causes of things." For the main purpose of this study was not to give the student a knowledge of any particular period of history but to "enable him to read all history beneficially; . . . [to] teach him what to look for in it, how to judge of it, and how to apply it."[8] It will be apparent that for the little boys Arnold's system was essentially that of "philosophy teaching by examples," but that for the Sixth Formers he has moved on to the view of the Scottish philosophical historians that history enables one to make generalizations about society which can then be applied to the modern world. If the Battle of Waterloo was won on the playing fields of Eton, Arnold would have said that England's future statesmen were being formed in the classrooms of Rugby.

The school, indeed, was but an image of the mighty world, and the evil which dismayed Arnold among the boys dismayed him even more in contemporary society. The period 1815 to 1840 was a dark one in English history, with the economic collapse following the Napoleonic wars, the oppressiveness of the Tory reaction, the agitations surrounding the Catholic emancipation and the first Reform Bill, the hopes and fears of the Revolution of 1830, the Bristol riots and rick-burning, the fearful suffering of the poor. "I cannot tell you," he wrote in 1826, "how the present state of the country occupies my mind, and what a restless desire I feel that it were in my power to do any good." And in January 1840: "The state of the times is so grievous, that it really pierces through all private happiness, and haunts me daily like a personal calamity." Readers of Strachey assume that Arnold was a puzzle-headed reactionary, but in point of fact he was regarded at this time as an almost dangerous radical. The Revolution of 1830 he hailed as "a most blessed revolution, spotless beyond all example in history." Indeed, so open was he in his admiration of it that he was constrained to deny a report that he was setting revolutionary themes for the boys and distributing tricolor cockades. "If any man seriously considers me to wish for a revolution here, with my seven children and a good house to lose, to put it on no other ground, why he must even continue to think so. But I do admire the Revolution in France—admire it as heartily and entirely, as any event recorded in history." In an effort to disseminate his views he established in 1831 a weekly newspaper, *The Englishman's Register,* which he carried on as long as he was financially able; he then transferred

his views to the *Sheffield Courant*. Arnold was no leveller—indeed, he
believed that the oligarchical spirit was essential to the welfare of the
nation—but he was deeply concerned with the antagonism which had
arisen between the working classes and their employers, and he urged
the aristocracy to come forward and make the necessary concessions
before it was too late. If the Reform Bill were delayed even five years he
thought there would be a bloody tumult, and all would go "if the convulsion which I dread really comes to pass." "There is nothing so revolutionary," he wrote in November 1830, "because there is nothing so
unnatural and so convulsive to society as the strain to keep things fixed,
when all the world is by the very law of its creation in eternal progress."[9]

When, in the midst of these troubles, the cholera appeared in England, men of a religious turn of mind could not but think of it as
having a preternatural significance. Writing to Whately in August 1831,
Arnold says, "The old Persian and Egyptian philosophers held that there
were certain periodical revolutions of time, fraught with evil to the
human race, and others, during which they were exempt from the worst
sort of visitations. This is mysticism; yet, from Thucydides downwards,
men have remarked that these visitations do not come single." Many
people at this time thought that the end of the world was approaching,
and one of the strangest phenomena was the speaking in tongues which
had arisen among female parishioners in the church of Edward Irving,
Carlyle's friend. Writing of this in October 1831, Arnold declared, "If
the thing be real, I should take it merely as a sign of the coming of the
day of the Lord. . . . However, whether this be a real sign or no, I believe
that 'the day of the Lord' is coming, i.e. the termination of one of the
great αἰῶνες [eons] of the human race; whether the final one of all or
not, that I believe no created being knows or can know. The termination
of the Jewish αἰών in the first century, and of the Roman αἰών in the
fifth and sixth, were each marked by the same concurrence of calamities,
wars, tumults, pestilences, earthquakes, &c., all marking the time of one
of God's peculiar seasons of visitations." Then, after the usual Scriptural
references, Arnold adds, "But I have not the slightest expectation of
what is commonly meant by the Millennium, and I wonder more and
more that any one can so understand Scripture as to look for it. As for
signs of the times in England, I look nowhere with confidence: politically speaking, I respect and admire the present government."[10]

Under the influence of this crisis, the same which provoked Carlyle's
"Signs of the Times" and Mill's "Spirit of the Age," Arnold began to
think deeply about the meaning of history and about the place of his
generation in the historical process. He was much given to historical

parallels. In 1819 at the time of the Peterloo massacre he declared, "I think daily of Thucydides, and the Corcyrean sedition, and of the story of the French Revolution, and of the Cassandra-like fate of history, whose lessons are read in vain even to the very next generation."[11] But then in 1827 he entered in his Book of Themes the warning: "of the Use of Examples in Argument and the Cautions to be used in taking them from the history of other Times and Countries."[12] What had happened between 1819 and 1827 to make Arnold thus cautious about the pragmatic use of history? Undoubtedly it was that during these years he became acquainted with the work of Barthold Niebuhr and Giambattista Vico, his two masters in historical method, who revolutionized his thinking about history. They carried him from the eighteenth-century philosophers who generalized about society to the nineteenth-century emphasis upon development.

Vico's *Scienza Nuova,* published in 1725, was largely unknown outside of Italy until, adopted by the Risorgimento, it was carried by Italian expatriates to Germany, France, and England in the early nineteenth century. There was a German translation in 1822 and an abridged French translation by Michelet in 1827. Coleridge was the means of its introduction into England. He was lent a copy of the 1816 edition of Vico's works by Gioacchino de' Prati, an Italian patriot, in the spring of 1825 and was so taken with it that he immediately introduced an epigraph from it on the verso of the titlepage of *Aids to Reflection.* By his discussing the work and lending it to friends and disciples it became widely known, and it was doubtless from this group that Arnold learned about it. Probably he read it in Michelet's translation. On the other hand, he knew Italian, and since he had traveled in Italy in 1825 and 1827 and consulted with Chevalier Bunsen and Savigny about his Roman history, he may well have known it in the original. In any case, he is the first Englishman to acknowledge publicly indebtedness to Vico.[13]

Vico held that one can know perfectly only that which one has made. Man is assuredly the author of his own society and hence his knowledge of it is potentially as perfect as God's knowledge of nature. Only, however, if he does not project back upon early ages concepts which are entirely foreign to them but rather enters sympathetically into the mind of a primitive people. He will then see that mythologies are really poetic histories that will yield genuine historical information if rightly interpreted. He will see that the Egyptian hieroglyphs are not, as the philosophes would suppose, the stratagems of crafty priests to impose upon a vulgar people but are a rude, symbolic language which adumbrates poetic truth. Homer he will learn to think of not as an individual but as the embodiment of the entire Greek people, being claimed by seven cities because he did, in fact, live everywhere and being thought of as both early and late because the wandering rhapsodists did their work over several centuries. By this "New Science" of interpretation Vico looked back through the mists of history and discerned three distinct periods through which man had developed—an Age of Gods, an Age of Heroes, and an Age of Men, each with its own characteristic language, literature, religion, and jurisprudence. Vico traces these ages through the two exemplar states of Greece and Rome and then shows how, after their disintegration into a second barbarism, the cycle repeats itself in the Christian era. The early Christian monarchy corresponds to the Age of Gods, the feudal aristocracy to the Age of Heroes, and the modern world to the Age of Men. In no case should the similarities between civilizations be interpreted as a case of transmittal: there is "an ideal eternal history traversed in time by the history of every nation in its rise, development, maturity, decline and fall."[14]

Arnold regarded much of Vico's work as disfigured by "strange extravagancies," but he also believed it was "in its substance so profound and so striking" that in his "Essay on the Social Progress of States" (1830) he imitated its broad outlines.[15] He declared that every state passes through a cycle of three phases, which he called Childhood, Manhood, and Old Age. This is true for the great exemplar states of Greece and Rome and also for Christian civilization, which is regarded as a single cycle with the Middle Ages as its childhood, the Renaissance as its young Manhood, and the period from 1688 to 1830 as a transition into the period of Old Age. These periods are not presented in broadly cultural terms, as in Vico, but rather in terms of the successive dominance of social classes. Thus, the first period is dominated by the aristocracy, whose attribute is noble birth (based originally on military prowess and superior wisdom); the second by the middle classes, whose attribute is wealth; and the third by the common people, whose only attribute is numbers. Arnold's periods do not correspond chronologically with Vico's, for Vico's first two periods are largely prehistoric, the Age of Men beginning as early as the Peloponnesian War in Greece and the Second Punic War in Rome. Arnold's first period roughly comprehends the first two periods of Vico, and he divides Vico's Age of Men into two in order to provide for both the middle classes and the common people. Indeed, the details of Arnold's three ages bear very little resemblance to Vico's, and one feels that he may have learned more from Plato's evolution of the state from Timocracy (the rule of the "spirited" element in man) to Oligarchy (i.e., plutocracy), to Democracy.

Though Arnold's metaphor of Childhood, Manhood, and Old Age suggests that the social progress of states is a purely natural process which requires no explanation, in fact the explanation of it is class conflict. In the first phase the conflict is between the aristocracy and the middle class, in the second between the middle class and the common people. Hence, Arnold's important law that the popular party in the first phase becomes the anti-popular party in the second phase. This is the reason why an understanding of the inevitable development of states is so important. Otherwise one might "appeal to examples which are nothing to the purpose, because they are taken from a different stage of a nation's existence from that to which they are applied." As Arnold saw it, his own society was in that critical transition period between the second stage and the third, between wealth and numbers. The transition between birth and wealth was not normally dangerous because by the time it came to pass the original superiority in strength or wisdom on which the distinction of birth had been based had become largely unreal. The commons were as well qualified as the nobles to conduct the affairs of state. But in the contest between wealth and numbers the distinction was real, and it tended to become more, rather than less, acute. Thus, "wherever [this contest] has come to a crisis," says Arnold, "I know not that it has in any instance terminated favourably." The corresponding crisis in Greek history was that of "the bloody factions of Corcyra and Megara" in the Peloponnesian War, that in Roman history "the civil wars of Marius and Sylla, of Caesar and Pompey, of Brutus and Cassius against the triumvirs." The effort of all men of good will should be to enable the nation to make this transition without violence, primarily by recognizing its inevitability. If one recognizes that the natural "tendency of society is to become more and more liberal,"[16] then one will not oppose all change until the discontent breaks out in violence.

Applying this concept of analogous periods in history, Arnold saw that the bitter conflict in Roman history over the Licinian or Agrarian Laws had a direct bearing upon the social problems of his own day. For this insight he was indebted to his second great master, Barthold Niebuhr. Niebuhr's *Römische Geschichte* had been published in 1811–12, but it was almost unknown in England when Julius Hare, then engaged with his colleague Connop Thirlwall in translating it, introduced Arnold to it in 1824. Arnold learned German for the purpose of reading it and immediately found himself in a new intellectual world. He had been writing articles on Roman history for the *Encyclopædia Metropolitana,*[17] and he now realized how elementary was his knowledge and that of his English colleagues compared with the researches of the learned Germans—how provincial, indeed, England was altogether to have cut itself off from Continental learning. There were two things, in particular, which he regarded as Niebuhr's greatest achievements and for which he was especially grateful. The first concerned the nature of early Roman history. Arnold himself had written an article in the *Quarterly Review* for 1822 demonstrating the worthlessness as history of the standard sources, Livy and Dionysius, but Arnold did not know (though he chides his countrymen for their ignorance) that Niebuhr had the answer.[18] It was that the stories in Livy were the relic of early popular lays which had been transmitted orally from generation to generation and had ultimately been embedded in this historical narrative. It is, of course, the Viconian solution, though Vico was apparently unknown to Niebuhr. The suggestion had, indeed, been made even earlier by the seventeenth-century Dutch scholar Perizonius, but at that time no one had ever seen a living popular ballad. It was only when the ballads were recovered in England, Scotland, Germany, and Spain in the late eighteenth century that F. A. Wolf thought of applying the thesis to Homer, and Niebuhr, who had long been interested in popular poetry, saw the application to Livy. Returning to his text, he discovered under its surface the form and structure, even the very words and titles, of these lays, and he urged that anyone who had the "boldness" to restore them to poetical form should do so in the style of the native popular poetry.[19] Macaulay, living at that time in India, responded to this call by translating the very legends that Niebuhr had distinguished into the ballad measure of Sir Walter Scott. He called his work *Lays of Ancient Rome* (1842).

Arnold was a little slow to accept Niebuhr's hypothesis, but by the time he came to write his *History of Rome* (1838) he had accepted it, and his solution was to retain the stories, which were too beautiful to be sacrificed, but to tell them in a slightly antiquated style that would clearly distinguish them from the surrounding text. Unfortunately, as his friend Coleridge pointed out, they sounded rather like the King James version of the Bible, but Arnold stoutly defended his principle. "I regard them as poetry, in which the form is quite as essential as the substance of the story. It is a similar question, and fraught with similar difficulties, to that which regards the translation of Homer and Herodotus. If I were to translate Herodotus, it were absurd to do it in my common English, because he and I do not belong to analogous periods of Greek and English literature; I should try to translate him in the style of the old translation of Comines rather than that of Froissart; in

the English of that period of our national cultivation which corresponds
to the period of Greek cultivation at which he wrote. . . . If I could do
it well, I would give all the Legends at once in verse, in the style and
measure of Chapman's Homer."[20]

The second great achievement of Niebuhr for which Arnold was
especially grateful was his explanation of the true nature of the Agrarian
Laws. In the early days of the Republic a popular tribune, C. Licinius,
had proposed and carried a law limiting the amount of land which any
citizen might possess to five hundred jugera (about 330 acres).[21] The
law fell into disuse but remained a rallying point in the struggle between
patricians and commons, and in 133 B.C. it was revived in a modified
form by the tribunes Tiberius and Caius Gracchus. The interpretation
of the actions of the Gracchi was a central issue between the Whig and
Tory interpretations of Roman history throughout the eighteenth century, from Swift's *Contests and Dissentions in Athens and Rome* (1701),
which characterized the entire history of the Roman Republic as a gradual and pernicious encroachment of the commons on the rights of the
nobles, to Nathaniel Hooke's *Roman History* (1738–71), which defended Gracchus as a patriot. It will be remembered that John Stuart
Mill, at the age of eleven, compiled a Roman history "with the assistance
of Hooke" and, "though quite ignorant of Niebuhr's researches, . . .
vindicated the Agrarian Laws on the evidence of Livy, and upheld to
the best of my ability the Roman democratic party."[22] Arnold was of
course strongly drawn to the democratic side, but he could not countenance the invasion of private property which the Laws seemed to imply. Therefore in his articles on Tiberius and Caius Gracchus for the
Encyclopædia Metropolitana, written in 1821–23, and in his 1822 article
for the *Quarterly Review* he characterized the Laws as "wildly imprac-
ticable," "mischievous," and "pernicious." To propose such laws today,
he said, would imply a high degree of "profligacy or folly."[23] But three
years later, after reading Niebuhr, Arnold had a totally different view.
It now appeared that the land which Rome had acquired by conquest,
the "Ager publicus," was *"the joint property of all the citizens"* (Arnold's
italics). Some of these lands were from time to time divided among the
citizens and became their private property. But there were other public
lands, which had not been divided, that certain favored individuals,
chiefly the nobility, were allowed to occupy, presumably on the payment
of a tithe; and, although they had no legal title to the land and could
theoretically be dispossessed, practically it was difficult to do so. "To
check this evil was the object of the famous Licinian law, which had
nothing to do with private property as has been commonly supposed,

but only limited the amount of undivided national land which might be occupied by any one individual." Arnold obviously saw in the Roman situation an analogy to the monopolization of land in England through the enclosure system, primogeniture, and the entailing of estates. And in the Agrarian Laws he saw the remedy. They were, he declared, "among the fairest means ever devised for obviating the necessity of poor laws, and providing for the wants of a redundant population."[24] If England could learn from the Corcyrean revolution in Greece and the Agrarian Laws in Rome, it might avoid the savagery of the French Revolution in England.

The Vician idea that all states go through analogous periods of development was widely accepted among the other Liberal Anglican historians. Arthur Stanley declared in his Oxford prize essay (1840) that "it has been one of the chief boasts of modern historical science to establish and elucidate" these natural periods. "We must judge whether a nation is in an early or an advanced stage, by these epochs; by them we learn what periods of civilization are alone truly analogous; by them we discover a modern history in the ages of Greece and Rome, and an ancient history in the nations of modern Europe; an affinity between the heroic ages of Paganism and the feudal ages of Christendom; between the era of Thucydides and the era of the Reformation; between the times of Alexander and Augustus and the times of Louis XIV."[25] Stanley was only twenty-five when he wrote this, and so it is natural that he should have echoed the words of his master. But in his mature *Lectures on the History of the Eastern Church* (1861) he declared that "the history of the Russian Empire and Church presents a parallel to the history of the whole European Church, from first to last, not merely fanciful and arbitrary, but resulting from its passage through similar phases." And in his *Lectures on the History of the Jewish Church* (1863–76), so much admired by Matthew Arnold, he said, "I know not where we shall find a better guide to conduct us, with a judgment at once just and tender, through the medieval portion of Christian ecclesiastical history than the sacred record of the corresponding period of the history of the Judges."[26] Julius Hare summed up the matter epigrammatically in his meditation on history in *Guesses at Truth* (2d ed., 1848): "The natural life of nations as well as of individuals, has its fixed course and term. It springs forth, grows up, reaches its maturity, decays, perishes."[27]

Hare's way of putting it raised a question which deeply troubled the Liberal Anglicans, namely, whether their cyclical scheme of history, based on an analogy with the life of the individual, did not involve a fatalism, a pessimism, even a paganism that was sharply at variance with their liberal Christian philosophy. The scheme certainly was pagan in origin, for it is found in Polybius and Tacitus and was recovered for the modern world by Machiavelli. Even Vico asserted that his laws applied only to the gentile, not to the Jewish, nations. Moreover, the fullest development of the scheme was by Florus, an author widely used as a textbook in the seventeenth and eighteenth centuries, whose dark picture of the degeneracy of the second half of the third period in ancient Rome cast a pall over England's claim to be an Augustan Age.[28] For, after all, if one had reached the height of perfection, there was nothing to look forward to but decline, and this prospect made the metaphor unattractive to all who believed in progress. The Saint-Simonians rejected it for that reason: "Some refer to the childhood, youth, and manhood of societies," wrote Bazard, "telling us that we are in a period of old age and persuading old and weary Europe to look to young America." Hegel and Comte accepted the metaphor but avoided its implications by replacing Old Age with Maturity.[29] Indeed, Arnold in "The Social Progress of States" rather finessed the matter by saying a great deal about Childhood and Manhood but leaving Old Age virtually unmentioned.

Young Stanley, however, was asked to face the problem, for the title of his prize essay is "Whether States, like individuals, after a certain period of maturity, inevitably tend to decay." His answer was No. The analogy is twofold, moral and physical, but only the former half is valid. There is nothing in the nation corresponding to the physical body of the individual which will inevitably decay; indeed, the nation is renewed by the successive generations of its citizens. But it does have a moral and spiritual life comparable to that of the individual, and just as no individual loses his moral life except through his own agency, so the same is presumably true of the nation. The fall of Rome and the destruction of Jerusalem were owing to internal dissolution and inevitable only for that reason. A Christian nation, operating under God's providence, may save itself from decay and move on to higher things.[30]

Julius Hare found a similar solution. Using Coleridge's distinction between culture and civilization, he rejected the radicals' belief in the perfectibility of man in favor of a belief in man's moral progressiveness. This pertained only to mankind as a whole, however, guided by its Christian faith; the individual nation states were still tied to the wheel of their development. Thus the whole course of civilization was a wayward one, moving generally forward but with many eddies and returns upon itself. "It is like the motion of the earth, which, beside its yearly course round the sun, has a daily revolution through successive periods of light and darkness."[31] Arnold, in his *Introductory Lectures* as Professor of Modern History at Oxford, gave a more somber determination. For it seemed to him that a nation—that is, a racial stock—really was exhausted by its civilizing effort. Hence, in his Inaugural Lecture, which preceded by only a few months his own death, he declared that "modern history appears to be not only *a* step in advance of ancient history, but *the* last step; it appears to bear marks of the fulness of time, as if there would be no future history beyond it." For we have had the gift of Greek intellect and the gift of Roman law and government, and now to the northern Teutonic nations has been entrusted the supreme gift of Christianity. But where do we turn from here? "Looking anxiously round the world for any new races which may receive the seed (so to speak) of our present history into a kindly yet a vigorous soil . . . , we know not where such are to be found." There are no unexplored portions of the world in which new races lurk, standing to us as the barbarians did to the Roman Empire. Therefore, if "we are living in the latest period of the world's history,"[32] it behooves us to work, for the night cometh wherein no man can work.

If Arnold's life had been spared and he had lectured for the next generation to the Oxford from which Newman was just then retiring, one has an idea how he would have gone about his "work." In the first place, he would not have been troubled by the paradox that he had been appointed Professor of *Modern* History despite the fact that his reputation was based entirely on his *History of Rome* and his edition of Thucydides. For he had long ago proposed "a more sensible division of history than that which is commonly adopted of ancient and modern. . . . There is in fact an ancient and a modern period in the history of every people. . . . Thus the largest portion of that history which we commonly call ancient is practically modern, as it describes society in a stage analogous to that in which it now is; while, on the other hand, much of what is called modern history is practically ancient, as it relates to a state of things which has passed away."[33] In Oxford the Professor of Modern History was responsible for everything since the fall of Rome, and there is no question but that the medieval period is part of what Arnold considered "practically ancient." Indeed, he proposed to start his first series of lectures with the fifteenth century, since that was the period he had worked up as a young man, and "it gives you the middle ages still undecayed, yet with the prospect of daybreak near. I could not bear," he wrote to Stanley, "to plunge myself into the very depths of that noisome cavern, and to have to toil through centuries of dirt and darkness." Upon its being represented to him, however, that this hardly gave a fair view of the Middle Ages, he agreed to go back to the fourteenth century, though he warned his listeners he intended to use "the habitual language of our age; which calls itself civilized, and the middle ages as in comparison half civilized."[34]

On the basis of this new conception of modernity, then, he doubtless would have advised his students that political and religious parties are of no importance as compared with the underlying social forces that affect the progress of states. Indeed, if he had had time he might have gone on to write that "noble work" which he once outlined to Chevalier Bunsen "on the Philosophy of Parties and Revolutions, showing what are the essential points of division in all civil contests, and what are but accidents." "It seems to me," he had declared, "that the real parties in human nature are the Conservatives and the Advancers; those who look to the past or present, and those who look to the future. . . . The Conservatism may sometimes be ultra democracy, (see Cleon's speech in Thucydides, III.), sometimes aristocracy, as in the civil wars of Rome, or in the English constitution now; and the Advance may be sometimes despotism, sometimes aristocracy, but always keeping its essential character of advance, of taking off bonds, removing prejudices, altering what is existing."[35] The term *Liberal* would not come in for another decade as the accepted name of a political party, which is perhaps why Arnold used the rather awkward term *advance*. Still, it has the advantage of making it clear what he means, that that party should move forward in the direction in which history is going. In order to know what that direction is, however, one must look back to the analogous period in Greece. That period was the age of Thucydides, which "belongs properly to modern and not to ancient history." "Where Thucydides, in his reflections on the bloody dissensions at Corcyra, notices the decay and extinction of the simplicity of old times, he marks the great transition from ancient history to modern, the transition from an age of feeling to one of reflection, from a period of ignorance and credulity to one of inquiry and scepticism." No other period did that with equal clarity. There was a similar transition in the sixteenth century, but it was less radical than that in Greece, and though the comparable period in Roman civilization, from the times of the Gracchi to the Antonines, was "far more completely modern," it was less adequately represented in history and literature. In any case, "in freedom of inquiry no greater range was or could be taken than that which the mind of Greece had reached already. . . . Not the wildest extravagance of atheistic wickedness in modern times can go further than the sophists of Greece went before them; whatever audacity can dare and subtilty contrive to make the words 'good' and 'evil' change their meaning, has been already tried in the days of Plato, and by his eloquence, and wisdom, and faith unshaken, has been put to shame."[36] In such a manner would Arnold have preached to the undergraduates at Oxford.

Indeed, the real motive of Arnold's conception of modernity probably lies less in a philosophy of history than in the belief of a great teacher in the relevance of the classics to the lives of his students. He extended that belief, however, to the life of the nation. He took a broad view, from the perspective of history, of the political, social, religious, and cultural problems of his age, and he strove mightily to resolve them. He was not in sensibility and outlook a thoroughly modern man, and he was not always clear in his thinking. But he was, without irony, an "eminent Victorian." When Mill was distinguishing among the three stages through which historical studies might develop (the third, scientific history, being as yet largely unrealized), he singled out Arnold's *Introductory Lectures* as having at least foreshadowed the third and completely realized the second.[37] And his son Matthew, reading J. T. Coleridge's *Memoir* of Keble many years after his father's death, wrote to his mother, "There is much to interest me, and there must be more to interest you; but my one feeling when I close the book is of papa's immense superiority to all the set, mainly because, owing to his historic sense, he was so wonderfully, for his nation, time, and profession, European, and thus so got himself out of the narrow medium in which, after all, his English friends lived. I said this to Stanley last night, and he quite agreed."[38] There is some filial piety in this remark, and if Arnold had been speaking of Newman instead of Keble, he would have had to change his tone. For Newman, though fighting all his life against the Liberalism that Thomas Arnold represented, was ultimately, perhaps, far more "modern" than he.

5

Newman and the Oxford Counter-Reformation

*I*T WAS THOMAS ARNOLD who first called the Tractarian Movement a "new counter-reformation," declaring that the true historical antecedents of Newman and his associates were the Non-Jurors of King William's, Queen Anne's, and George I's reign— those who, after the Revolution of 1688, refused to swear allegiance to the new monarch. Even the term "Oxford Malignants," which he applied to the Tractarians in his *Edinburgh Review* article, was not mere name-calling, for that was what Cromwell called the small group of Oxford clergymen who stubbornly held out against the Commonwealth. Though with respect to the social crisis of 1830 Arnold looked back to Greek and Roman history, with respect to the religious crisis of a few years later he looked back to the Reformation. "The '*Idea*' of my life," he wrote to J. T. Coleridge in 1835, "to which I think every thought of my mind more or less tends, is the perfecting the 'idea' of the Edward the Sixth Reformers,—the constructing a truly national and Christian Church, and a truly national and Christian system of education."[1] By his enemies Arnold has been called an Erastian, a follower of the sixteenth-century Swiss reformer who advocated the subservience of the church to the civil power, but Arnold's true desire was for a complete infusion of the national life by Christian principles. He wanted a non-dogmatic Christian nation, and in his pamphlet on Church Reform (1833) he proposed that the parish church be made available to all religious bodies, from Catholic to Unitarian, who would use it in rotation on different days of the week.

Actually, Arnold's interest in the Reformation was linked to his interest in the history of Rome, for he believed that the evils which the Reformation came to correct had their origin in the latter days of the Roman Empire. Like most Victorians, he both admired and detested Gibbon, and it was his ambition, had he lived, to rewrite Gibbon in a way more satisfactory to his own age. "My highest ambition," he said, "and what I hope to do as far as I can, is to make my history the very reverse of Gibbon in this respect,—that whereas the whole spirit of his work, from its low morality, is hostile to religion, without speaking directly against it; so my greatest desire would be, in my History, by its high morals and its general tone, to be of use to the cause, without actually bringing it forward." To this end, according to Stanley, he would have unfolded "the rise of the Christian Church, not in a distinct ecclesiastical history, but as he thought it ought to be written in conjunction with the history of the world." He would have brought his story right down to the coronation of Charlemagne in 800 A.D., for at that point "we shall have passed through the chaos which followed the destruction of the old western empire, and shall have seen its several elements . . . organized again into their new form. That new form exhibited a marked and recognized division between the so called secular and spiritual powers, and thereby has maintained in Christian Europe the unhappy distinction which necessarily prevailed in the heathen empire between the church and the state." Arnold's detestation of the medieval period was based largely on this separation of church and state, whereby the national life was not infused with Christian principles but rather with the spirit of chivalry, which emphasized honor and allegiance to a superior rather than justice and the brotherhood of man. Indeed, he believed that except among the Anglo-Saxons there had been only a nominal or pretended conversion of the peoples to Christianity in the fourth and fifth centuries, and that the real conversion came in the Reformation. But now a second Reformation was needed, for Arnold adhered to Niebuhr's doctrine that "1517 must precede 1688, and so . . . for a better than 1688, there needs a better than even 1517."[2] The work of the eighteenth century must be incorporated into the Establishment, and the new Judaizers, the new Non-Jurors, the new bloody fanatics who would once again separate church and state must be combatted.

There were times when John Henry Newman would have conceded that he was indeed a "bloody fanatic," for he had very early entered into a dogmatic conception of Christianity. As a boy of fifteen he had undergone a religious conversion which was so definite an experience that he could date its first and last days as August 1 and December 21, 1816.[3] Though the faith into which he was brought had an Evangelical cast, Newman always emphasized its dogmatic character. "I fell under the influences of a definite Creed, and received into my intellect impressions of dogma." Of the reality of this experience, he wrote some fifty years later, "I am still more certain than that I have hands and feet." Indeed, the experience tended to confirm him in his mistrust of the reality of material phenomena and made him rest in "the thought of two and two only absolute and luminously self-evident beings, myself and my Creator."[4] One may say that Newman spent the rest of his life working out the relationship between these two beings. In a notebook of 1820–21 he wrote, "The reality of conversion: —as cutting at the root of doubt, providing a chain between God and the soul (i.e. with every link complete). I know I am right. How do you know it? I know I know. How? I know I know I know."[5]

Newman never tired of pointing out what different theologies are implied by different conceptions of God. If one means by God a sentiment in the human breast, then theology is certainly not a body of knowledge but a matter of feeling which will vary from one individual to another. One is in the realm of Private Judgment, which leads to the multiplication of sects, to Protestantism, Evangelicalism, and extreme dissent. If, on the other hand, one believes that God is the collective public morality, then theology again is not a body of knowledge but a social construct, which leads to the Broad Church movement, to Erastianism, and to various forms of secularism. Only if one believes, as did Roman Catholics and the first race of Protestants, that God has objective existence as "an Individual, Self-dependent, All-perfect, Unchangeable Being,"[6] is theology a branch of knowledge. In that case, certain things can be said about God and not others. The very existence of God implies the dogmatic principle. "From the age of fifteen," wrote Newman in the *Apologia,* "dogma has been the fundamental principle of my religion: I know no other religion; I cannot enter into the idea of any other sort of religion; religion, as a mere sentiment, is to me a dream and a mockery. As well can there be filial love without the fact of a father, as devotion without the fact of a Supreme Being. What I held in 1816, I held in 1833, and I hold in 1864. Please God, I shall hold it to the end" (54).

As long as Newman held just to the dogmatic principle, his religion was incomplete, for although he could answer the question, "How do you know?" by the words, "I know I know," so too could others, and the principle of Private Judgment would reign supreme. Thus, there was a need for some institution on earth to be the authoritative interpreter of religious truth, and the antecedent probability that God should have provided such an institution, joined with the historical fact that he apparently had, led Newman to his second principle, that of the Visible Church. This principle he did not have, and could not have had, during his Evangelical phase, but in 1822 he was elected a Fellow of Oriel and so came "under very different influences from those to which I had hitherto been subjected" (20). These influences were those of the Liberal wing of the church, particularly the Oriel Noetics—Edward Copleston, Richard Whately, Edward Hawkins, Blanco White, and Thomas Arnold. Paradoxically, this group of people, in whom, of course, the elements of the orthodox tradition had survived, taught him the very doctrines which, when fully realized and acted upon, would carry him beyond Liberalism into the High Church party. Of these doctrines the most important was that of Apostolical Succession, the doctrine that there has been an uninterrupted succession, from the Apostles to the present day, of bishops and priests consecrated by the laying on of hands and that this succession is essential to the validity of sacramental ministrations. It was at this point that history took up a central place in Newman's thought, for if a revelation had been made at a certain point in time and if there was a Visible Church which was the interpreter of that revelation and whose sacraments and rites were the channel of invisible grace, then continuity with that church was essential for salvation.

The third question, then, was, which was the church that was continuous with the Primitive Church? and to this question Newman replied in 1833 that it was the Anglican, not the Roman. In Newman's view the Roman Catholic Church had gradually during the Middle Ages made unwarranted additions to the original depositum of faith such that, when these were confirmed by the Council of Trent, it was no longer a pure but a corrupted channel of grace. The Reformed Churches of Luther and Calvin, on the other hand, had so overreacted against these corruptions that they had stripped away not merely the human additions but also some part of divine revelation, and so stood shorn and impoverished. Only the Anglican Church had followed a via media between Romanism and Protestantism and preserved the full round of original doctrine pure and uncorrupted. At least it had up until the Revolution of 1688, but within the past hundred and fifty years, under the impact of rationalistic thought, it too had been shorn of its full Catholic heritage and had been reduced to a pale Erastian image of its former self. The solution, according to Newman and the Tractarians, was to raise up the church from its fallen state and restore it to its former grandeur. Thus Newman agreed with Arnold that "there was need of a second reformation" (40), but it would be a reformation not to continue the work of the eighteenth century but to undo it. And it would be, said Newman, "a better reformation, for it would be a return not to the sixteenth century, but to the seventeenth"—to the church of Andrewes, Laud, Hammond, Butler, and Wilson (50, 71).

Newman assumed at this date that a return to the Anglican divines
of the seventeenth century was a return to the Primitive Church, but it
was the Primitive Church that was his first love. Indeed, at the time of
his boyhood conversion he had "read Joseph Milner's Church History,
and was nothing short of enamoured of the long extracts from
St. Augustine, St. Ambrose, and the other Fathers which I found there.
I read them as being the religion of the primitive Christians" (20). A
decade later, when, under the influence of the Oriel Noetics, he was
"drifting in the direction of the Liberalism of the day" (26), he con-
tracted "a certain disdain for Antiquity" which manifested itself in
"some flippant language against the Fathers" (25) in some articles he
was writing for the *Encyclopædia Metropolitana*. He was rudely awakened
from this dream at the very end of 1827 by two great blows—a severe
illness which came upon him while an Examining Master in the Schools,
and the sudden death of his sister Mary. Newman saw in these two blows
the chastising hand of God rebuking him for intellectual pride, and the
new mood of religious fervor into which he was plunged was for him
the real beginning of the Tractarian movement. Once again he was saved
by the Fathers. He had asked Pusey, who was then in Germany, to purchase for him as many volumes of the Fathers as he could, and the books
had arrived in the autumn of 1827. He began to read them chronologically, beginning with St. Ignatius and St. Justin, in the Long Vacation
of 1828, and from this time forth they were the dominant influence on
his thought. They represented for him the *"beau idéal* of Christianity."
So well known was his devotion to them that when he retired from the
tutorship at Oriel in 1831 his pupils and friends presented him with a
valuable set of thirty-six volumes of the Fathers. "They are so fine in
their outsides," wrote Newman, "as to put my former ones to shame—
and the editions are the best."[7] Out of these volumes Newman wrote
his *Arians of the Fourth Century* (1833), his equivalent of the Ph.D.
dissertation, which made him a scholar and gave him a "field." "What
principally attracted me," he says, "in the ante-Nicene period was the
great Church of Alexandria, the historical centre of teaching in those
times. Of Rome for some centuries comparatively little is known. The
battle of Arianism was first fought in Alexandria; Athanasius, the champion of the truth, was Bishop of Alexandria; and in his writings he
refers to the great religious names of an earlier date, to Origen, Dionysius, and others, who were the glory of its see, or of its school. The
broad philosophy of Clement and Origen, carried me away. . . . Some
portions of their teaching, magnificent in themselves, came like music

to my inward ear, as if the response to ideas, which, with little external to encourage them, I had cherished so long" (36).

It is sometimes said that Newman was "a modern medievalist," and we hear of the "medievalism" of the Tractarian movement. This is a misconception. Hurrell Froude, as Newman noted, was "powerfully drawn to the Medieval Church" (34), but Newman himself knew little about the Middle Ages and did not consider it a significant period. He preferred the Palladian to the Gothic architecture and was generally classical in his tastes. For him the great period to which he looked back, with an almost romantic devotion, was the period of the third to the fifth century A.D., when the Christian Church was taking form and beginning to establish its dogma. Thomas Arnold thought that he should have looked back earlier, to the Age of the Apostles,[8] but Newman's religion was not founded upon scripture but upon scripture as interpreted by the church. There was an oral tradition, along with the written, that was well known to the early Fathers, and as this tradition drew itself up into creeds and formularies and was sanctioned by general councils, it gave rise to the authoritative teaching church, of which the Anglican Church was the uncontaminated descendant.

Antiquity, then, was the note or criterion of the true church. "I do not know," wrote Newman in the *Apologia,* "when I first learnt to consider that Antiquity was the true exponent of the doctrines of Christianity and the basis of the Church of England; but I take it for granted that the works of Bishop Bull, which at this time [1831] I read, were my chief introduction to this principle" (36). In order to implement the principle historical research was required, for both the early Fathers and the seventeenth-century divines were almost unknown in England at this time. As a result, Newman and his young colleagues plunged into the work of reading, writing, editing, and translating, in order to make known to the English people their goodly heritage. Newman had already published a short life of Apollonius of Tyana and *The Arians of the Fourth Century.* For three years, beginning in 1833, he ran a series of sketches in the *British Magazine,* under the title "The Church of the Fathers," whose purpose was to illustrate "the tone and modes of thought, the habits and manners of the early times of the Church."[9] Its object was to show that, whatever the early Church was, nothing comparable to Protestantism was there to be found. In 1836, the Library of the Fathers was started, which ultimately extended, though long after Newman had ceased to be associated with it, to forty-eight volumes. He himself contributed two volumes of the *Select Treatises of*

St. Athanasius. In 1839 the translation of Claude Fleury's *Ecclesiastical History* was begun and in 1842 the series of the "Lives of the English Saints." Thus, when Newman delivered his *Lectures on the Prophetical Office of the Church* in 1836, he could say, "Primitive doctrine has been explored for us in every direction, and the original principles of the gospel and the Church patiently and successfully brought to light. But one thing is still wanting. . . . We have a vast inheritance, but no inventory of our treasures. All is given us in profusion; it remains for us to catalogue, sort, distribute, select, harmonize, and complete."[10]

The church needed a positive theory of the via media to discriminate it from Protestantism on the one hand and Romanism on the other. This theory Newman found in the Canon of St. Vincent of Lerins (434 A.D.), that what has been taught "always, everywhere, and by all"—*Quod semper, quod ubique, quod ab omnibus*—is to be believed. Thus Newman's personal canon, that if asked, "How do you know?" he would answer, "I know I know," is converted into a matter of history. How do we know that Ambrose, Leo, and Gregory were right in receiving St. Paul's Epistles? "The answer would be, that it is a matter of history that the Apostle wrote those letters which are ascribed to him. And what is meant by its being a matter of history? why, that it has ever been so believed, so declared, so recorded, so acted on, from the first down to this day; that there is no assignable point of time when it was not believed, no assignable point at which the belief was introduced; that the records of past ages fade away and vanish *in* the belief; that in proportion as past ages speak at all, they speak in one way, and only fail to bear witness, when they fail to have a voice. What stronger testimony can we have of a past fact?"[11] *Quod semper, quod ubique, quod ab omnibus.*

In the *Prophetical Office of the Church* Newman elaborates the Vincentian Canon into the three notes of Catholicity, Antiquity, and the Consent of the Fathers. It is apparent, however, that the Consent of the Fathers (*ab omnibus*) is really contained in the other two, for the consent of those distributed through time (*semper*) is the note of Antiquity, and the consent of those distributed though space (*ubique*) is the note of Catholicity. In the *Apologia* Newman does in fact reduce the notes to these two, saying that in the controversy between the Anglican and the Roman Catholic Church, the Anglican takes his stand upon Antiquity, the Roman upon Catholicity. The Anglican says to the Roman: "There is but One Faith, the Ancient, and you have not kept to it." The Roman retorts, "There is but One Church, the Catholic, and you are out of it" (101). Without admitting in 1836 that the Roman claim was just, Newman did admit that the strong point of the one church was in the one area and of the other in the other. "It is a fact, however it is to be accounted for, that Rome has added to the Creed; and it is a fact, however we justify ourselves, that we are estranged from the great body of Christians over the world" (106–07). Our strong point is the argument from Primitiveness, theirs from Universality. We have the Note of Schism lodged against us, they the Note of Idolatry. "There was a contrariety of claims between the Roman and Anglican religions," wrote Newman, "and the history of my conversion is simply the process of working it out to a solution" (106).

The process began, as we have already noted, in the Long Vacation of 1839, when Newman, thinking to put aside controversy for a while and indulge himself in his favorite subject of the early Fathers, took up the history of the Monophysites. "Of all passages of history," he wrote, "since history has been, who would have thought of going to the sayings and doings of old Eutyches, that *delirus senex,* as (I think) Petavius calls him, and to the enormities of the unprincipled Dioscorus, in order to be converted to Rome!" (108). But so it was, for the perspective of fourteen hundred years enabled Newman to see his own church in its true light. Eutyches, Archimandrite of a monastery in the suburbs of Constantinople, a man of unexceptionable character and seventy years of age, was condemned in 448 by a Council of Constantinople for holding and teaching the doctrine of one, instead of two, natures in Christ. He was supported by the imperial court and by Dioscorus, the Patriarch of Alexandria, and at a general council summoned for the ensuing summer at Ephesus, a council known as the Latrocinium or "Gang of Robbers" because of its violence, he was honorably acquitted and his doctrine received. It should be noted that there was much to be said in support of his view, including evidence from scripture, the creed, and the Fathers. It should also be noted that very early in the controversy Dioscorus and the majority of the bishops withdrew from the extreme view originally enunciated by Eutyches and formed a moderate party known as the Monophysites. Yet it was this party that, by the power of Pope Leo acting through his Legates, was condemned by the Council of Chalcedon in 451.[12] Newman, reading this controversy through the lens of history and being concerned, of course, not with the doctrinal question but simply with the relation of the parties one to another, saw, "as it seemed to me, Christendom of the sixteenth and the nineteenth centuries reflected. . . . The Church of the *Via Media* was in the position of the Oriental communion, Rome was where she now is; and the Protestants were the Eutychians" (108).

Two years later, while engaged on his translation of St. Athanasius,

Newman encountered the same phenomenon in the history of the Arian controversy. He had not observed it while writing on this subject in 1832, but now "I saw clearly, that in the history of Arianism, the pure Arians were the Protestants, the semi-Arians were the Anglicans, and that Rome now was what it was then" (130). The Nestorian controversy presented many of the same features, and thus, said Newman, "I saw that the general theory and position of Anglicanism was no novelty in ancient history, but had a distinct place in it, and a series of prototypes, and that these prototypes had ever been heretics or the patrons of heresy. The very badge of Anglicanism, as a system, is that it is a *Via Media*; this is its life; it is this, or it is nothing. . . . The *Via Media* appeals to the good sense of mankind; it says that the human mind is naturally prone to excess, and that theological combatants in particular are certain to run into extremes. Truth, as virtue, lies in a mean; whatever, then, is true or not true, extremes certainly are false. And, whereas truth is in a mean, for that very reason it is ever moderate. . . . Dispassionateness, forbearance, indulgence, toleration, and comprehension are thus all of them attributes of the *Via Media*."[13] For that reason it is especially acceptable to the civil magistrate, who works by compromise and moderation. But is it acceptable to the dogmatic church, whose truth may very well lie in an extreme? Newman saw clearly that the Anglican Church tended in its essential idea toward latitudinarianism and Erastianism.

In the autumn of 1839, while Newman was still reeling from the Monophysite controversy, he received a second blow, this time from an article in the *Dublin Review* by Nicholas Wiseman, Rector of the English College in Rome. The article charged that the Anglican Church had put itself in a state of schism at the Reformation, and to support this charge it adduced the parallel of the Donatist controversy in the fourth century. That controversy was already well known to Newman and considered by him to be not parallel. It was a jurisdictional dispute within the African church, not between that church and Rome. But the anxious friend who had brought the article to Newman's attention pointed out to him the "palmary words" of St. Augustine which were quoted in the review: "Securus judicat orbis terrarum." "He repeated these words again and again," says Newman, "and, when he was gone, they kept ringing in my ears. . . . By those great words of the ancient Father, interpreting and summing up the long and varied course of ecclesiastical history, the theory of the *Via Media* was absolutely pulverized" (110–11).

Newman emphasizes the incantatory power of the words, and one suspects that he was partly influenced by the internal rhyme of Augustine's sentence: "Quapropter SECURUS judicat *orbis terrarum,* bonos non esse qui se dividunt ab *orbe terrarum,* in quacumque parte *orbis terrarum.*" (My italics—"Wherefore, it is the untroubled judgment of the entire world, that those cannot be good who, in any part of the world, cut themselves off from the rest of the world.") It is the impressive power of the "entire world" judging a part of the world that is emphasized. Wiseman had pointed out in his article that this "golden sentence" of St. Augustine ought to be "an axiom in theology," because it constituted "a general rule applicable not merely to the Donatist case, but to all future possible divisions in the Church."[14] This too was Newman's point: "they were words which went beyond the occasion of the Donatists: they applied to that of the Monophysites. . . . They decided ecclesiastical questions on a simpler rule than that of Antiquity; nay, St. Augustine was one of the prime oracles of Antiquity; here then Antiquity was deciding against itself" (110). The Canon of St. Vincent of Lerins was already ambiguous in having three criteria: what if one were at variance with another? Newman did not think this possible since he had reduced them to two, Antiquity and Catholicity, and thought of them as operating in different planes, the one in time, the other in space. But Catholicity was also a factor in antiquity, and here was Antiquity testifying in behalf of Catholicity. If the Anglican claim to Antiquity had already been weakened by the example of the Monophysite controversy, it was now further weakened by this voice from the past pronouncing against it.

The coup de grace, however, was given by the modern Anglican Church, which in the summer of 1841 simply repudiated Newman's conception of the via media. It did this by two acts: by the bishops' in their charges condemning Tract 90, in which Newman had attempted to show that the Thirty-Nine Articles were patient of a Catholic interpretation, and by the government's establishing, in cooperation with the Prussian Court, a joint Anglican–Evangelical Bishopric in Jerusalem, which would minister to all Protestants in the area and offset the prestige of France and Russia as the protectors of the Catholic and Greek Orthodox communions. There could hardly be any act more distinctly Erastian and anti-Apostolic, and doing it in Jerusalem was a particularly egregious symbol.

So from the end of 1841 Newman was on his "death-bed," as he phrases it, with regard to his membership in the Anglican Church, and though a process of time was required before he could think of changing his religion, there was also an intellectual process to be gone through.

There was the "difficulty" of the apparent elaborations and additions to the creed of the Primitive Church that had been made by the Roman Church over the centuries and that were thought by the Tractarians to constitute "corruptions." The presence of these corruptions weakened the Roman Church's claim to the note of Antiquity. The Anglican Church had neither the note of Antiquity nor that of Catholicity. Was there some means by which the Roman Church could be found to have both? It was essentially a historical problem: the discovery of continuity within change or change within continuity.

As became his anti-Erastianism, Newman distinguished sharply between secular and religious history. Thomas Arnold had wanted to describe the rise of the Christian Church, "not in a distinct ecclesiastical history, but . . . in conjunction with the history of the world"; and Pusey, who did not always see very deeply into these matters, had advised Newman, in writing his *Arians,* that the church councils, which are generally "the driest portion of Ecclesiastical History, . . . might be made both interesting and improving, by exhibiting them in reference to, and as characteristic of the age in which they occurred."[15] It is difficult to imagine Newman, however, presenting the *Homoousia,* or Consubstantiality of our Lord, as being defined essentially by the Spirit of the Age. For Newman the unchanging Christian revelation and the changing course of empire were quite distinct, though doubtless there were areas in which they interacted.

Newman's secular philosophy of history is presented most fully in a series of lectures which he gave at the time of the Crimean War—"The History of the Turks in their Relation to Europe." Toward the end of the lectures he speaks of the transitoriness of all states and empires.

All human power has its termination sooner or later; states rise to fall; and, secure as they may be now, so one day they will be in peril and in course of overthrow. Nineveh, Tyre, Babylon, Persia, Egypt, and Greece, each has had its day; and this was so clear to mankind 2,000 years ago, that the conqueror of Carthage wept, as he gazed upon its flames, for he saw in them the conflagration of her rival, his own Rome. 'Fuit Ilium.' The Saracens, the Moguls, have had their day; those European states so great three centuries ago, Spain and Poland, Venice and Genoa, are now either extinct or in decrepitude. What is the lot of all states, is still more strikingly fulfilled in the case of empires; kingdoms indeed are of slow growth, but empires commonly are but sudden manifestations of power, which are as short-lived as they are sudden. Even the Roman empire, which is an exception, did not last beyond five hundred years; the Saracenic three hundred; the Spanish three hundred; the Russian has lasted about a hundred and fifty, that is, since the Czar Peter; the British not a hundred; the Ottoman has reached four or five.[16]

These states and empires may be divided into "barbarous" and "civilized." The former have their life in "objects of *imagination*," by which Newman meant "such as religion, true or false . . . , divine mission of a sovereign or of a dynasty, and historical fame." The latter have their life in "objects of *sense*, such as secular interests, country, home, protection of person and property." The former are stagnant and destroyed by external causes, such as foreign wars, insurrection of slaves, and natural disasters. The latter are progressive but not infinitely so, for ultimately the very cultivation of reason and spread of knowledge which produced their greatness leads to their fall. They, therefore, are destroyed by internal causes, or what may be called "succumbing to a natural death."[17] In other words, secular history goes by cycles, and therefore it would be possible for the British by studying Roman history to learn something about the probable cause of their own decline. But since both these civilizations have their life in objects of sense, what they would learn would be relatively trivial compared with what they might learn by studying the history of religion. For that would bear upon the salvation of their immortal soul.

Christian doctrine Newman had ever regarded as simply immutable. Revelation was a body of Truth which had been vouchsafed by God at the beginning of time and would last until the fullness of time. True, Protestantism had denuded the Creed and Rome had corrupted it, but "our [Creed] is fixed once for all."[18] Bossuet had declared it an axiom that variation in religion is always a sign of error. "The Church's doctrine is always the same," he wrote; "false doctrine . . . is recognized at once, whenever it appears, merely because it is new."[19] There was a tendency in the eighteenth century to admit the possibility of progress in theology, but the Tractarians brought the discussion back to Bossuet, merely claiming his canon for Anglican rather than Catholic theology. But now Newman was faced with the necessity of seeing whether there was not some mode of human variation that was compatible with unchanging divine truth. One possible solution to the problem, which had become popular in his own day, was the so-called doctrine of accommodation.

This doctrine had become notorious with the publication of Henry Hart Milman's *History of the Jews* in 1829. Milman has been called "a kind of Christian Gibbon, without the indecency and without the fun,"[20] but he was really a Liberal Anglican clergyman who was trying to apply to the Chosen People the same historical methods he would have applied to the Greeks and the Romans. Since this had never been done before, it was immensely shocking to people to hear Abraham called a "Sheik or Emir," and they did not like his minimizing of the Old Testament miracles. Lot's wife, for example, was turned into a pillar of salt by the volcanic action and sulphurous vapors still visible in the neighborhood, and in telling how the bitter waters of Marah were made sweet by the branch of a tree, Milman added, "whether from the natural virtue of the plant seems uncertain." Milman's underlying principle was that the ancestors of the Jews, except for being "the depositaries of certain great religious truths," did not differ from the other semibarbaric peoples of the area. They went through the normal stages of a hunting, pastoral, and agricultural society, and God, in his dealings with them, necessarily accommodated himself to the state of civilization in which he found them. He manifested himself as rude and primitive when they were primitive, as ignorant when they were ignorant, and had to wait upon their refinement to become the civilized deity of later times.[21]

The outcry against Milman's work was immediate and sensational. Dr. Faussett, Margaret Professor of Divinity at Oxford, preached a sermon against it in St. Mary's, and Bishop Mant addressed two letters to the author imploring him to withdraw the work from publication, a step which was eventually taken.[22] Newman himself wrote to Pusey that he thought it "a very dangerous work," but on the whole his judgment was less severe and based upon rather different grounds than that of many of his contemporaries. To a young friend who was still writing *his* protest more than a year later, Newman advised that it was unnecessary and, moreover, that he himself did not always agree. "Sometimes I am on M[ilman]'s side against you," he declared. "It seems to me that the great evil of M's work lies not in the *matter* of the history, but in the profane *spirit* in which it is written. In *most* of his positions I agree with him but abhor the irreverent scoffing Gibbon-like tone of the composition."[23]

A decade later, when Milman's *History of Christianity* appeared ("worse, and just in the same line"), Newman wrote a lengthy review in the *British Critic,* in which he set forth fully and precisely his objections to treating sacred history in the same manner as profane.[24] It was not that the two subjects did not have an element in common or that this element could not be isolated and treated in a strictly historical manner, but simply that in sacred history this element was completely trivial. If Christ really was the son of God, then that was the most momentous fact about him, and to leave it out of account in a history of his work was to ignore the very reason for our being interested in that work at all. As for the doctrine of accommodation, Newman did not disagree with the substance of what Milman said, but he did violently disagree with his manner of saying it.[25] As Milman himself noted, the *word* was partly at fault, for it suggested a subservience of God to civilization, as if he were limited in what he could do. It seemed to apply to the Supreme Deity the adage "When in Rome do as the Romans do," ignoring the fact that he had created Rome and all its inhabitants and could destroy them in an instant. It ignored the fact that if civilization evolved and revelation were gradual, it was because God had established those laws as ministering to his purpose, and it emphasized the relativity of human understanding at the expense of the absolute character of Divine Law. Nevertheless, the solution which Newman proposed to the question of change was not unrelated to the doctrine of accommodation. It really was that doctrine viewed from the other end, but by that shift in emphasis its character was changed completely.

Newman arrived at his theory of the development of Christian doctrine so gradually that in later years he said, "I cannot trace the steps of my conviction."[26] One of the earliest steps, however, must have been his discussion, in *The Arians of the Fourth Century,* of two practices of the early church, the *Disciplina Arcani* and the Economy. The former is the practice of concealing from heathen and catechumens the more sacred and mysterious doctrines and rites of the church, either by not mentioning them at all or by mentioning them only in enigmatical language. The motive for this was partly to prepare the candidate gradually for the reception of sacred truths and partly to preserve the mysteries from violation and sacrilege. The Economy is a more general term which refers to a mode of communicating a truth, with caution and reserve, so as to make it more acceptable to the mind of the hearer. It was commonly used with children and people of limited understanding, but it might also be used with persons to whom a doctrine would be startling or offensive if the entire truth were flashed upon them all at once. Like any form of rhetoric, it is capable of both abuse and misunderstanding, and it is one of the concepts that got Newman into trouble with Charles Kingsley. Newman makes it clear, however, that "substantial truth" must always be preserved.[27]

It is obvious that the Disciplina Arcani and the Economy are related to accommodation in that they involve a gradual revelation of doctrine to the individual as he becomes capable of receiving it, but they are not an explanation of the development of doctrine within the church as a whole. Still, in the view of the Fathers, the Economy was also a method employed by God in his dealings with his people. It is, in fact, the method of accommodation, and Newman actually employs that word as a synonym for the Economy, at the same time indicating that Milman has made a wrong application of it.[28] For in Newman's view the Economy is part of the mystical or sacramental principle whereby God has made all visible and material things types and symbols of the divine (36–37). It is only in this high mystical sense, then, of a Christian Platonism, that Newman speaks of accommodation. God has accommodated himself to man in the sense of embodying spiritual truths in a material form available to man's senses, but it is evident that man will grow in his ability to penetrate those truths, not by becoming more civilized but by becoming more Christian.

Newman had, then, from very early years the conception of Christian doctrine as an unfathomable mystery that can only gradually be elucidated by the church operating under divine guidance. In 1841 he began considering the actual mechanism by which this elucidation occurred, and on February 2, 1843, he gave his first, preliminary statement of the theory of development in a sermon at St. Mary's, the last he ever delivered there as University Preacher. The next year, perceiving that his position in the church absolutely depended upon the validity or non-validity of this theory, he began to write *An Essay on the Development of Christian Doctrine,* resolving that if, at the end of it, his conviction in favor of the Roman Church were not weaker, he would take the necessary steps for admission into her fold. Never was any book written which so completely fulfilled itself in the process of writing, for as Newman advanced in his argument his difficulties so cleared away that on October 8, 1845, he was received into the Catholic Church—"and the book remains in the state in which it was then, unfinished" (211).

The *Essay* is far less mystical than the *Arians* or even the sermon; it is, indeed, a treatise conducted in psychological and historical terms. It takes the view that revelation, which for Newman is not a verbal statement in Scripture but a body of facts and experiences, was given fully and completely by God at the beginning of the Christian dispensation but that it has required a process of time for the human mind to enter into and master its various aspects. This, indeed, is the way we apprehend any large, complex fact or seminal idea. We see it initially more or less as a whole; then we walk around it and view it first in this aspect and then in that. Gradually we perceive its bearing upon other related facts and experiences; we draw out inferences and pursue analogies, develop corollaries and observe consequences, until at last, out of a meager original datum, we have built up a complex philosophical system. Thus, out of the simple idea of private property might emerge a complex legal code, and, similarly, out of the original Depositum of Faith has come the rich and elaborate system of Catholic theology. And yet there is nothing in the latter that was not implicitly in the former. It is just that it has been drawn out and made explicit. Newman does not for a moment hold that the Apostles were "rude and primitive" Christians to whom God had to accommodate himself more than to a nineteenth-century Englishman: they held the full round of Christian doctrine but some of it implicitly rather than explicitly. Such, indeed, is the case with children and uneducated Christians today. There are many doctrines of which they have never heard, and yet they do believe them implicitly in that they believe the great central doctrines in which they are included. The first two centuries of Christianity had something childlike about them in that the Church found it unnecessary, and was also reluctant, to impose religious tests and formularies. It was only as false developments of doctrine grew up that these became necessary. "No doctrine is defined," wrote Newman, "till it is violated." Heresies had this advantage that they were the means by which the Church was forced to become conscious of the true meaning of its own doctrines and draw these out into definitions. "It is well known," wrote Newman in his *Lectures on Certain Difficulties Felt by Anglicans,* "that, though the creed of the Church has been one and the same from the beginning, yet it has been so deeply lodged in her bosom as to be held by individuals more or less implicitly, instead of being delivered from the first in those special statements, or what are called definitions, under which it is now presented to us, and which preclude mistake or ignorance. These definitions . . . are the work of time; they have grown to their present shape and number in the course of eighteen centuries . . . , and they may of course receive still further additions as time goes on."[29]

The problem is to know true developments from false, and to this end Newman set forth seven Notes, or distinguishing marks, which he thought characterized a true development. They are: (1) Preservation of Type, (2) Continuity of Principle, (3) Power of Assimilation, (4) Logical Sequence, (5) Anticipation of its Future, (6) Conservative Action upon its Past, and (7) Chronic Vigour. Newman would hardly contend that these Notes are a blueprint for determining the true Church. He had come to believe that the Vincentian Canon was virtually useless because it was so difficult to apply, but he could not pretend that these were much easier. What they do is introduce the element of change into a previously static system. They replace the note of Antiquity with that of Continuity or substantial Identity. It will be observed that the seven Notes are evenly divided between the ideas of permanence and change, 1, 2, and 6 being oriented toward the past, 3, 5, and 7 being oriented towards the future, and 4 (Logical Sequence) participating in both. The idea of a progressive transition or continuous development in Christian doctrine is one of Newman's most profound and seminal ideas. Others had hinted at it before, but he first brought it into the mainstream of Christian thought.[30] He introduced change and history into an unchanging science, and in so doing he forged a link between those two luminously self-evident beings, himself in the nineteenth century and God at the beginning of time.

It seems likely that Newman was influenced in the *Essay on Development* by contemporary discussions on the subject of evolution. It is true that he says, at the very beginning of the *Essay,* that *"physical* developments, as the growth of animal or vegetable nature,*"* do not come into consideration in his argument, except as "they may be taken as illustrations" of theological developments.[31] But it is evident that three of his seven Notes, Preservation of Type, Power of Assimilation, and Chronic Vigour, are metaphors from the life sciences, and far and away the largest source of illustration and analogy is the world of living and growing things. His metaphor for a false development is "corruption," and of course the Theory of Development is itself the nineteenth-century term for evolution. This is not to say that Newman anticipated Darwin, for his theory obviously has nothing to do with natural selection. The equivalent of natural selection, applied to the development of Christian doctrine, would be the cynical and soul-destroying view that doctrines are engaged in a kind of struggle for existence and that those which win out and get themselves accepted are called "orthodox" and those which do not are called "heterodox." Such would be the view logically resulting from Utilitarianism or pragmatism, but it is not Newman's view. Newman's view, however, does have much in common with that put forward in Robert Chambers's *Vestiges of the Natural History of Creation,* which was published in October 1844, just as Newman was beginning to work on the *Essay on Development* but before he had begun to write. *Vestiges* went through four editions by April 1845, five months before Newman's work was published in September 1845. There is no evidence that Newman read it, but as it was the most notorious book of the decade he could hardly have failed to know about it. Chambers's view is an attack on "successive creationism," which is the equivalent in the biological field of Milman's successive revelations to an evolving mankind. In Chambers's view this was an uneconomical hypothesis, for just as the inorganic world "has one final comprehensive law, GRAVI-

TATION," so "the organic, the other great department of mundane things, rests in like manner on one law, and that is,—DEVELOPMENT."[32] In the chapter entitled "Hypothesis of the Development of the Vegetable and Animal Kingdoms" Chambers puts forth the view that God initially created life in the simplest and most primitive forms but that these then developed, by a kind of internal self-perfecting tendency, into higher and more complex forms. Newman also sees doctrines as having a kind of life of their own, as developing from simpler to more complex forms, and as proliferating in the mind of the Church so as to occupy evey niche in the ecology of belief. The one point on which he differs from Chambers—and it is a momentous one—is that he does not admit the development of new species. His illustrations are always from the life of the individual, and his Note of Preservation of Type (to which he devotes nearly a quarter of the book) indicates that the transmutation of species is not contemplated. Protestantism is, indeed, the church which has developed into a new type, that of the anti-dogmatic, Erastian church, whereas Cathoicism through all its changes has remained faithful to the type of the Primitive Church.

It should not be thought, however, that Newman feared the evolutionary hypothesis. In his review of Milman's *History of Christianity* he mentions speculations about "man's being originally of some brute nature, some vast mis-shapen lizard of the primeval period, which at length by the force of nature, from whatever secret causes, was exalted into a rational being." "Such a theory," he adds, "is of course irreconcilable with the letter of the sacred text, to say no more," but it is so much in accord with the way revelation works, which is by "addition, substitution," that it is in no wise unacceptable so long as one understands that at some point man received an immortal soul.[33] A generation later, when the Darwinian version of this hypothesis was being canvassed, Newman, commenting on the uneconomical character of "special creationism," declared, "I will either go whole hog with Darwin, or, dispensing with time and history altogether, hold not only the theory of distinct species but that also of the creation of fossil-bearing rocks." And on Easter Eve, 1874, he wrote to a friend, "I see nothing in the theory of evolution inconsistent with an Almighty God and Protector."[34] Four years later, Mark Pattison, thanking Newman for the gift of a new edition of the *Essay on Development,* wrote, "Is it not a remarkable thing that you should have first started the idea—and the word—Development, as the key to the history of church doctrine, and since then it has gradually become the dominant idea of all history, biology, physics, and in short has metamorphosed our view of every science, and of all knowledge."[35]

Newman was not quite so original as Pattison suggests, but it can be said that the Tractarian movement began simultaneously with the publication of Lyell's *Principles of Geology* and culminated simultaneously with the publication of Chambers's *Vestiges of Creation,* and that its crowning work, the *Essay on Development,* applied to the subject of church doctrine the language, concepts, and illustrations of biological evolution, only stopping short of the transmutation of species.

Having said this, one should then admit that Newman's primary model in the *Development of Christian Doctrine* was the development of his own life. Just as in Mill's and Carlyle's spiritual autobiographies we discerned a tendency to pattern their philosophies of history on the experiences they themselves had undergone, so was it with Newman. For it should be remembered that Newman's conversion to the Catholic Church, though humanly a rupture with his past, was not religiously a rupture at all but simply a development and working out of those principles which he had held from the beginning. The great conversion of Newman's life was that which he suffered at the age of fifteen, "with experiences before and after, awful, and known only to God." So dramatic was it that he could "look back at the end of seventy years as if on another person," for before that time he was essentially a pagan, but after that a Christian. The conversion introduced into his intellect "impressions of dogma," and so occupies in his life the place occupied in the history of the world by revelation. From that time forward there was no material change, for Newman's whole point in the *Apologia* is that in his conversion to Rome there was no rupture, no break with the past, no inexplicable development, no Jesuit in disguise, but merely the working out of the ultimate implications of his boyhood conversion. Given a belief in God, there follows the Dogmatic Principle. Given that, there follows the principle of the Visible Church; and once that is given, there merely follows the historical problem of determining which modern church is the successor to that of antiquity. It was not Newman that had changed but rather the Church of England, and on the principle that ontogeny recapitulates phylogeny, Newman could even be said, during his brief Noetic period, to have undergone the Reformation. But then he underwent the Counter-Reformation and ended up in Rome.

The *Apologia pro vita sua* was prompted by Charles Kingsley's attack on Newman in *Macmillan's Magazine* for January 1864. A decade before this, however, Newman and Kingsley, who were antithetical personalities in virtually every aspect of their lives and thought, had a preliminary skirmish in the form of two historical novels, *Hypatia* and *Callista*. Hypatia was a beautiful Neo-Platonic philosopher, head of the Alexandrian School in the fifth century A.D., whose story was first introduced into English by John Toland, the deist, and then was recounted by Gibbon in his forty-seventh chapter. Caught in a political struggle between the Roman magistrate and Cyril, Archbishop of Alexandria, Hypatia was dragged from her chariot, stripped naked, and torn to pieces by a blood-maddened Christian mob. "The murder of Hypatia," says Gibbon, "has imprinted an indelible stain on the character and religion of Cyril of Alexandria." Since the School of Alexandria was Newman's beau idéal of Christianity and since Athanasius, Cyril's predecessor, was the source to which Newman appealed above all others for doctrinal purity, Kingsley saw in this anti-clerical story the perfect vehicle for an attack on the Tractarians. Moreover, since Cyril with his dirty and fanatic monks had established a theocracy which challenged the power of the civil magistrate, Kingsley also had a comment on the so-called "Papal Aggression" by the reestablishment of the Catholic Hierarchy in England in 1850, and it is very likely that his Cyril was intended to suggest Dr. Wiseman. It was in 1851, the year after the Papal Aggression and in the midst of a vehement "No-Popery" agitation in England that Kingsley began to think seriously about writing a romance on the subject of Hypatia.

Kingsley's target, however, was not confined to the Tractarians. In Hypatia he saw the ancient counterpart, as he wrote to his friend Maurice, of "modern Neo-Platonism—Anythingarianism," by which he meant "Emerson, Fichte, and the whole of the German, American, English Spiritualists" (though not Carlyle). Mulling over the contrast between these "spiritualists" and Christian Socialists like himself and Maurice, he had come to the conclusion that "there are two great views of men. One as a spirit embodied in flesh and blood, with certain relations, namely, those of father, child, husband, wife, brothers, . . . [which] are the symbols of relations to God." The second view, found principally among the upper classes, is that "man is not a spirit necessarily embodied in, and expressed by an animal; but a spirit accidentally connected with, and burdened by an animal." The ideal of this second group is to deny the animal part of man and to strive after a nonhuman or angelic state.

> Now this [second] anthropology was held and carried out by the Neo-Platonists, by Plotinus, Libanius, Hypatia, Isidore, Proclus, and others. And we know whither it led them. To aristocratic exclusiveness; to absolute hatred of anything which looked like a gospel for the merely

human masses; to the worship of the pure and absolute intellect, and the confusion of it with the understanding. . . . I appeal to history whether my account is not correct. And I appeal also to history whether the same phases, in exactly the same order, but with far more fearful power, did not develop themselves in the medieval Church, between the eleventh and sixteenth century, ending in the lie of lies—the formulised and organised scepticism of Jesuitry. And I do assert, that the cause of that development was the same in both—the peculiar anthropologic theory which made an angel the ideal of a man, and therefore celibacy his highest state.[36]

This grandiose anthropology Kingsley intended to apply to *Hypatia.* "My idea in the romance," he wrote to Maurice, "is to set forth Christianity as the only really democratic creed, and philosophy, above all, spiritualism [i.e., Neo-Platonism], as the most exclusively aristocratic creed."[37] Thus, the conflict in the novel between Christianity and paganism is ultimately secondary to that between aristocracy and the populace, between otherworldliness and a healthy materialism. Though Kingsley is doubtless revolted by the murder of Hypatia, he has to balance that in his mind with the fact that she had no room in her lecture hall for publicans and sinners, and that Cyril and his monks were at least "democratic."

The novel is resolved by a world-weary Jew, Raphael Aben-Ezra, who wanders over the Mediterranean world enlarging his sympathies with the poor and is ultimately converted to a form of Broad Church Christianity by a "philosophic" bishop much like Kingsley. Raphael communicates this message, that God is Love and that he is the Father of all his people, to Hypatia just before her death, but it is uncertain whether she dies in that new faith or in her old aristocratic creed.[38]

The subtitle of *Hypatia* was *New Foes with an Old Face,* which Kingsley explicates in the final paragraph of the novel. "And now, readers, farewell. I have shown you New Foes under an old face—your own likenesses in toga and tunic, instead of coat and bonnet. One word before we part. The same devil who tempted these old Egyptians tempts you. The same God who would have saved these old Egyptians if they had willed, will save you, if you will. Their sins are yours, their errors yours, their doom yours, their deliverance yours. There is nothing new under the sun." Kingsley is expressing the standard view that human nature is uniform in all ages and that the great laws of truth and righteousness, of sin and folly, are everywhere the same. But in his letter to Maurice he also expressed the historicist view that "the same phases, in exactly the same order" had carried ancient philosophy, medieval theology, and modern Transcendentalism and Tractarianism to the same pitch of aristocratic exclusiveness which boded their destruction. Certainly he intends his picture of Alexandria—swarming, sensual, degraded, tempestuous; a cockpit of contending creeds, races, and philosophies—to be seen as a city not unlike London, more violent perhaps in its sharp contrasts of good and evil but not more certainly doomed to destruction. For by an unlikely gesture Kingsley has also introduced into this early fifth-century scene a tribe of playful Goths, who have just come from the invasion of Greece and the sacking of Rome, and the implication is that this debased and effeminate city must likewise be destroyed if it is to regain wholeness. It has lost "the very ideas of family and national life — those two divine roots of the Church," and so there is need of "some infusion of new and healthier blood," such as Carlyle also recommended, if the city is to regain "comparative purity of morals; sacred respect for woman, for family life, law, equal justice, individual freedom, and, above all, for honesty in word and deed."[39]

Who were to be the Gothic invaders of modern London, Kingsley did not say, but he was clearly a catastrophist in his philosophy of history. "I am the prophet of the coming convulsion," he wrote to his publisher. "I cannot cry peace, peace where there is none. I see all things in Christendom drifting toward the hurrican-circle of God's wrath and purifying storms."[40] In the lectures *Alexandria and Her Schools* which, on the strength of *Hypatia,* he was called upon to deliver before the Edinburgh Philosophical Institute he said, "I cannot but subscribe to the opinion of the many wise men who believe that Europe, and England as an integral part thereof, is on the eve of a revolution, spiritual and political, as vast and awful as that which took place at the Reformation; and that, beneficial as that revolution doubtless will be to the destinies of mankind in general, it depends upon the wisdom and courage of each nation individually, whether that great deluge shall issue, as the Reformation did, in a fresh outgrowth of European nobleness and strength, or usher in, after pitiable confusion and sorrows, a second Byzantine age of stereotyped effeminacy and imbecility."[41]

Though it is not known for certain that Newman read *Hypatia,* it is usually assumed that he did and that *Callista* is in some sense a reply to it. There is, first of all, the coincidence of the dates. Newman began *Callista* in the early spring of 1848 and wrote the greater part of chapters 1, 4, and 5. He seems to have been led to his subject by his interest in St. Cyprian, the third-century Bishop of Carthage, whose

Treatises and *Epistles* he and Pusey had edited in the Library of the Fathers in 1839 and 1844. The sort of thing he had in mind is suggested by his reply to J. M. Capes, editor of the *Rambler*, who proposed that he write, from a Catholic point of view, something similar to what he had done as an Anglican under the title "The Church of the Fathers." "I heartily wish I could promise you a series like the Church of the Fathers," wrote Newman in February 1849, "but *when* is it to be? If you can use my name honestly, without pledging me, I should be glad. As to the middle ages, I could not go on to *them*. What I should like, would be to bring out the ἦθος [ethos] of the heathen from St Paul's day down to St Gregory, when under the process, or in sight of the phenomenon, of conversion; what conversion *was* in those times, what the position of a Christian in that world of sin, what the sophistries of Philosophy viewed as realities influencing men. But besides the great difficulty of finding time, I don't think I could do it from history. I despair of finding facts enough—as if an imaginary tale could alone embody the conclusions to which existing facts *lead*." The project of "an imaginary tale," however, seems to have been abandoned, for on August 31, 1851, Newman offered to send J. D. Dalgairns, a young Oratorian whom he was urging to do a life of St. Cyprian, the notes he made on the historical and topographical background.[42] He himself was entirely preoccupied with the Catholic University of Ireland.

Then in January 1852 Kingsley's novel began to appear in *Fraser's Magazine* and continued until April 1853, when it was also published in book form. The notoriety of the work may have had an effect not only on Newman but also on other quarters, for towards the end of 1853 Burns and Lambert, the Catholic publishers, began to organize a Popular Catholic Library, perhaps to counter the effect of works like Kingsley's. The plan for the Library was approved by Cardinal Wiseman, who suggested that it include "a series of tales illustrative of the condition of the Church in different periods of her past existence. One, for instance, might be called 'The Church of the Catacombs'; a second, 'The Church of the Basilicas'; each comprising three hundred years; a third would be on 'The Church of the Cloister'; and then, perhaps, a fourth might be added, called 'The Church of the Schools.' " Wiseman himself offered to do the first in the series, and his *Fabiola; or, the Church of the Catacombs* appeared late in 1854. Newman thought Wiseman's plan a "beautiful" one but declared he had no time for writing while he had the University on his hands.[43] Nevertheless, when he returned from Dublin to Birmingham in July 1855, he took up his unfinished tale and completed it within two or three months. It is evident that the original conception goes back to 1848 and that the stimulus for finishing it came from Cardinal Wiseman. But it is likely that Kingsley played some role too, for in form and substance *Callista* is an answer to *Hypatia*, whether intentionally so or not.

This does not mean that Newman learned his fictional art from Kingsley, for one has only to read the opening sentences of *Callista* to see that he learned it from Sir Walter Scott, whose novels he used to read as a boy in bed, in the early summer mornings. With the second volume of *Ivanhoe* he was so delighted that he apostrophized, "Author of Waverley, thou art a second Shakespeare!" In 1821 J. G. Lockhart, Scott's son-in-law, applied his father-in-law's methods to the early Christian period in *Valerius, A Roman Story*, which Newman read as an undergraduate at Oxford. He found it "well worth reading . . . [and] very improving," though he thought the author "*could* have made much more of his subject."[44] It was the story of a young Briton who, coming to Trajan's Rome, fell in love with a noble Roman girl who was secretly a Christian, rescued her from martyrdom, and took her home to his native isle. Since Newman mentions *Valerius* in the Postscript to *Callista* as a precedent for his treatment of history, it is probable that this was his fictional model, though he borrowed character types from Scott himself and from his favorite Romantic poet, Southey.

The relation between *Callista* and *Hypatia* lies primarily in their characters. Both novels have as their heroine a beautiful representative of Greek culture, the one in its philosophic, the other in its aesthetic aspect. In both the hero is a young Christian of uncertain faith who has his faith tested by his encounter with Greek culture. Both make use, though in different ways, of the contrast between a brother and sister of Greek origin, and both have an ancient crone (Miriam and Gurtha) who dabbles in black magic. Both have, in Orestes and Cornelius, representatives of the Roman civil power, and both give prominent roles to a Christian bishop, Cyril of Alexandria and Cyprian (called Caesilius) of Carthage. Within these parallels and the general fact that both are early Christian novels set in North Africa, the relationship is primarily one of contrast.

Kingsley set his novel in the fifth century, by which time Christianity had become an overweening power which provided an analogy, in his view, with the Papal Aggression of 1850. Newman naturally chose an earlier period when it was still a persecuted rather than a persecuting sect. Specifically, he chose the middle of the third century, when the "long peace of the Church," a period of relative toleration in which the faith and discipline of Christians had become lax, was broken by the edict of Decius requiring all Christians to sacrifice to the Emperor. In a sense, a similar period of peace in the English church had been broken in the years 1829–1832, when the impending struggle between church and state sharply tested the faith of Christians who had grown lax and easy under the Georgian era, but more specifically Newman had in mind the No-Popery agitation of 1850 and following. He had vividly described and analyzed this prejudice in his *Lectures on the Present Position of Catholics in England* in 1851, and *Callista* was in part a projection of the contemporary scene back upon the annals of the early church. But it was more especially the message which the faith of that early age could have for distraught and bewildered Catholics of the nineteenth century.

In order to dramatize that message Newman has ranged his characters not in national blocks, as did Kingsley, but in subtle gradations from Christian holiness to pagan sin. At the top of the spectrum is the Christian saint or martyr, Cyprian himself and Callista after her conversion. Considerably below them comes Agellius, the young hero of the novel, a Christian whose faith is sound but who, lacking the support of an active church and Christian community, has not been kept up to his duty and can actually contemplate marriage with Callista, a heathen, without facing what that means—particularly without facing the fact that his first duty is to win her for his Master, not for himself. He can do this because Callista, whose name suggests the Greek word for beauty, represents the most enlightened form of Greek culture and has such delicate moral scruples, such a shrinking from any kind of grossness or immorality, that she might very easily be mistaken, so far as externals are concerned, for a true Christian. Callista herself, however, is very much aware of the difference, for she is not happy in her humanism and has vivid memories of a Christian slave girl, Chione, who had a joyous strength unlike anything she has seen before or since. Hence, with this deep need for an Object to love, she is disappointed that Agellius offers her only gallantry. Below Callista is Aristo, Callista's brother, whose name also indicates his nobility but who, lacking her delicate moral instincts, sees nothing wrong with the proposed marriage to Agellius and ultimately abandons her when she insists on martyrdom. He, indeed, becomes indistinguishable in principle from Jucundus (*agreeable, pleasant*), Agellius's uncle, the original promoter of this marriage, who, though a good, kindly man who wishes well to both parties, is ultimately seen as a kind of spiritual pander. Newman devotes a great deal of attention to Jucundus, for he is the respectable hedonist, the "gentleman," who believes in law and order and also pleasure, and who cannot see in Christianity anything other than a sullen obstinacy, a morose refusal to conform and do the decent thing. He becomes a darker and less agreeable figure when we see his connection with Juba, Agellius's younger brother, who was a Christian but who, through a spirit of pride and independence (his name means *mane* or *crest*), has lapsed into mere self-assertion. He too is a hedonist, but whereas Aristo and Jucundus are refined and cultured hedonists, Juba is gross and animal and shows the connection of that philosophy with pagan nature. Indeed, the source of his "religion," the lowest of the low, is Gurtha, his mother, who has lapsed into a witch, the practitioner of the most obscene pagan rites, the very representative of Satan on earth. For the heathen religion that is really operative in North Africa, the religion of the people, is not the relatively respectable Roman pantheon but the dark obscenities of the Punic religion, Astarte and Cybele, the powers of sex and blood. Gurtha is the product of the dank, steaming heat of Africa, as Callista is of the bright, pure light of Greece; but it requires the darkness of the prison or the Christian caves to nourish the Christian martyr.

All these character types existed in nineteenth-century England as well as in third-century Africa, but what the African scene makes clear is the stark antithesis between Christianity and even the most specious forms of polite culture. Newman was never concerned in his practical writings with the gross forms of evil or rampant atheism, which he thought would expose themselves, but only with the subtler forms of philosophism, humanism, or liberal culture which could masquerade as Christianity and yet were worlds away from it. The "gentleman" was not a Christian. However valuable he might be as the product of civilization, he was not the equal in spirituality to the ignorant peasant who believed. The value of the historical setting was that through the insensible gradations from Callista to Gurtha one could see the unbroken connection between the loveliest forms of Greek humanism and the most obscene forms of ancient paganism, and one had the edict of the Emperor which forced the individual to choose between them and Christianity. In third-century Africa there had occurred the same life-and-death struggle between Christianity and paganism which Newman believed was still taking place in his own day, but through the perspective of sixteen hundred years and through the clear air and vivid colors of the Mediterranean world one could see its shape and meaning more clearly.

James Anthony Froude, by fifteen years the younger brother of Hurrell, tells how the family was dazzled by the new views of history which Hurrell brought home from Oxford. It seems that the old view of the Reformation was all wrong. Antichrist was not the Pope but liberalism and revolution. "Charles I was to be our holy and blessed martyr St. Charles. The Pretender was to be called James III. The Revolution of 1688 was a crime. The nonjurors were the true confessors of the English Church."[45] Anthony, whose mind had already been opened by his boyhood reading of Sharon Turner and Gibbon, did not really believe this and never would believe it, but when he went up to Oxford in 1836, he fell insensibly under the influence of Newman, who was kind to him for his brother's sake. Newman was at that time organizing a series of Lives of the English Saints, which would serve at once to occupy the restless young men of the movement and also explore the question of the continuity of the supernatural in the English Church. Froude was invited to join and chose the Life of St. Neot, a Cornish contemporary of King Alfred. The usual account given of this episode is that Froude, under Newman's guidance, dutifully set to work narrating one miracle after another, each more incredible than the last, until, unable to stomach any more, he ironically concluded his work with the words, "This is all, and perhaps rather more than all, that is known of the life of the blessed St. Neot." Waldo H. Dunn, however, has noted that these words do not in fact occur in Froude's Life, though something like them—but with quite a different meaning—does occur in the immediately preceding "Legend of St. Bettelin" by Newman and J. D. Dalgairns. Indeed, as one reads Froude's "Legend of St. Neot"—for such it is called, not "Life"—one discovers that he has not at all strained his historical integrity in recounting it, for it is not presented as historically true but merely as morally edifying. This, indeed, is the theory on which Newman intended these early saints' lives to be written, for he himself has provided an introduction to the "Legend of St. Gundleus" which was evidently intended to apply to the entire volume of Hermit Lives. In it he asserts that these legends are profitable to read as containing spiritual truth even if they are not factually accurate. "It is not that we may lawfully despise or refuse a great gift and benefit, historical testimony, and the intellectual exercises which attend on it, study, research, and criticism," but in the case of these early saints we do not have the facts. Therefore the popular mind "develops its small portion of true knowledge into something which is like the very truth though it be not it, and which stands for the truth when it is but like it. Its evidence is a legend; its facts are a symbol; its history a representation; its drift a moral."[46] Newman's approach is roughly analogous to the Niebuhrean view of early Roman history.

It was not in writing "A Legend of St. Neot," then, that Froude lost his faith but in a long process of critical and historical investigation made over the next few years. Turning to the lives of the Irish saints, he found himself in a veritable morass of pseudo-history. Whereas the Protestants distinguished sharply between the Biblical miracles and those of later date, grounding their faith in the former on the inspiration of Scripture, and whereas the Tractarians extended their faith in the Gospel miracles to those of the early Church, Froude found that the incredibility of the later miracles infected his belief in the earlier. As he read English and German criticism and learned that the four Gospels could not be proved to have existed in the form in which the Church has received them until the latter half of the second century and that their authorship was quite uncertain, he realized that it was not on historical grounds that the truth of Christianity could be established. "The religion with which we were to direct our lives in this world, and on which we build our hopes for the future must be a present fact, a reality independent of time, a part of the constitution of the universe, to be verified, like all other knowledge which we possess, by living experience, not dependent on whether certain incidents alleged to have happened 1,800 years ago in Palestine could be established by critical enquiries."[47] Unfortunately, Froude did not reach this conclusion until after he had taken the step, irreversible in those days, of taking Deacon's orders. He could not go back, and yet other professions, by the law of the land, were closed to him. Newman was going over to Rome, whither Froude, despite his continuing admiration of the man, could not follow him. Indeed, Carlyle, rather than Newman, was becoming his intellectual mentor, and as the temper of the times moved towards 1848 and his friends Clough and Tom Arnold were making their revolutionary gestures, Froude also made his by writing an autobiographical novel, *The Nemesis of Faith*. "Faith with a Vengeance" his friends called it, for it was the scandal of the year on its publication in 1849. It told the story of a youthful clergyman who, unable to believe all the tenets of the official religion, drifted into immorality and ultimately into monasticism and despair. Morality—such is the thesis of the book—requires for its support "a strongly believed religious faith," and therefore to insist that the Christian religion assume a form which the modern mind cannot believe opens the way to immorality, which is "the nemesis of faith." William Sewell, rector of Froude's college, was so incensed by this thesis that he publicly denounced the book and burned it in Hall before the undergraduates. Froude was forced to resign his fellowship, was abandoned by his family, and found himself in real difficulties as to earning a living. It was while he was in these straits that Charles Kingsley and his wife kindly took him in, and within a few months Froude had married the sister of Mrs. Kingsley, who had been on the point of entering a Roman Catholic nunnery. They settled in Wales, and within a few years Froude repudiated all the fume and fret of his Wertheresque novel and conformed to the Church of England, not because it was or was not the successor of the Apostles but because it was the form in which religion was by law established. He was thus more Erastian than Thomas Arnold. "To me religion is presented under the form of the law of the land. I acknowledge it as I do the common law or the civil law, and so I left and so I leave a question into which I am not required to examine further."[48]

It was inevitable, then, that Froude should turn to the period in English history when this establishment was effected. Initially, after his marriage, he thought of writing a book on " 'The Era of Tacitus,' a sort of philosophical-historical survey of the state of things, internal and external, from Nero to Trajan."[49] But he was soon led, both by his earlier reading and by his personal interest, to the history of the English Reformation. In Oxford the Reformation had been used by both sides as an instrument of party politics. On the one hand, Hurrell Froude's *Remains* (pt. I, 1838), which had been published after his death by Newman and Keble as a party manifesto, had presented the Reformation as an unfortunate incident which destroyed the unity of the Church. On the other hand, in reply to this the anti-Tractarians proposed to erect in Oxford a monument to the "Martyrs of the Reformation," Cranmer, Latimer, and Ridley, which Newman correctly perceived as a scheme to embarrass the Tractarians, for if they subscribed they would appear to be making amends for previous harsh words and if they refused they would appear to be disloyal to their Church. Nonetheless, Newman, Keble, and Pusey did refuse, and the subscription so far languished that the monument, originally conceived on a more elaborate plan, was reduced to the form of a Gothic cross, which may still be seen in front of Balliol College. Then, in the autumn of 1841, the contest for the Poetry Professorship, which had been held by Keble, was lost to the anti-Tractarians, and the new incumbent, the Reverend James Garbett, immediately set Cromwell as the subject for the Newdigate Prize for 1843, a prize which was won by the young Matthew Arnold, but with an interpretation more Byronic than Carlylean.[50] Thus, everything about the

Reformation during these years was freighted with modern import, and Froude could not take up the subject without writing against his brother's and Newman's views.

He began with individual essays on Mary Queen of Scots, John Knox, Elizabeth, Cardinal Wolsey, and Mary Tudor, but he soon felt himself able to undertake some larger work of serious consequence. "More and more I had become interested in the political aspect of the Reformation as distinct from the doctrinal. If it was a revolt against idolatry and superstition, it seemed to me still more of the laity against the clergy, and of the English nation against the Papal supremacy." Originally, Froude's interest was chiefly in the reign of Elizabeth, but it happened that just at this time a large collection of valuable manuscripts relating to the reign of Henry VIII was placed in the hands of John Parker, the publisher, who was asked to find a historian capable of utilizing them. He chose Froude. Thus, Froude's history began with Henry VIII, who had been presented as violent and despotic by Lingard, Hallam, and others and of whom Froude had hitherto taken the conventional view. He was gradually forced by his documents to enter a qualified defense, and so he presented a portrait of Henry which was considered revolutionary. Elizabeth he found less talented than he had supposed: her wisdom was the wisdom of her ministers, especially Burghley. But both she and her father were Carlylean Heroes. If the country had been left to itself, it would have destroyed itself in theological wars as did its contemporaries on the continent. The interregnum of Edward and Mary had sacrificed the national interest, in the one case to Protestant, in the other to Catholic interests. But Henry had controlled the conflict by law, and when Elizabeth came to the throne she took up the policy of her father. The result was that "the English character and the English intellect unfolded with a splendour which has never been exceeded; never, if the test of a nation's greatness be the men whom it produces, attained again." In 1891, when he was adding a supplementary volume to his history, he declared that he found nothing of substance to change. "I believe the Reformation to have been the greatest incident in English history; the root and source of the expansive force which has spread the Anglo-Saxon race over the globe, and imprinted the English genius and character on the constitution of mankind."[51]

Froude embodied this belief in two great scenes which form the climax of his *History*, the execution of Mary Queen of Scots and the defeat of the Spanish Armada. Mary is presented as England's own private Whore of Babylon. Dressed entirely in scarlet, she hopes to make of her execution a scene that will convert thousands, but when the executioner holds up her head, the false hair falls off and there is exposed "the withered features of a grizzled, wrinkled old woman." It is Duessa unmasked by Prince Arthur once again. With her power broken there followed the defeat of the Armada, for Froude considered 1588, not 1688, the great date in English history, and he summed up its meaning in a sentence: "The names [of the ships] on both sides, either by accident or purpose, corresponded to the character of the struggle; the St. Matthew, the St. Philip, the St. James, the St. John, the St. Martin, and the Lady of the Rosary, were coming to encounter the Victory, the Revenge, the Dreadnought, the Bear, the Lion, and the Bull: dreams were ranged against realities, fiction against fact, and imaginary supernatural patronage against mere human courage, strength, and determination."[52] It is obvious that in the defeat of the Armada Froude saw a reenactment of his own personal drama, when Newman's Saints were routed by Carlyle's Heroes.

Froude never cared for Kingsley's historical fiction, for he felt it was the task of fiction to deal in universals rather than in the peculiarities of past ages. Kingsley may himself have felt that in *Hypatia* he had not chosen the most advantageous ground for doing battle with Newman, for in his next novel he shifted the scene from the early Christian period to the Reformation. *Westward Ho!* (1855) was, indeed, suggested by Froude's essay "England's Forgotten Worthies" (1852), which dealt with the sea-dogs of the Elizabethan era. Kingsley took these bully-boy mariners out to the West Indies, where they trounced the Spaniards, whose cruelty is seen as closely related to their Catholicism. The work is infused with the bellicosity of the Crimean War, and Caroline Fox is doubtless right in saying, "For Spaniards read Russians." But Henry Crabb Robinson, who also read the book, declared, "I fear it has been produced by the wish to induce a vulgar hatred of Popery."[53]

Kingsley's hatred of all things Popish was doubtless increased by a snub he received in 1863 at the University of Oxford. His name had been put forward for an honorary degree and he fully expected to receive it, but at the last moment Pusey, who had disliked *Hypatia*, announced his intention of calling out *Non Placet* when the voting took place, and so Kingsley, to avoid a public scandal, had to withdraw. It is understandable, then, that in January 1864, in the course of reviewing the seventh and eighth volumes of Froude's *History*, Kingsley cast the slur on Newman which resulted in the *Apologia*. "Truth for its own sake," he wrote, "had never been a virtue with the Roman clergy. Father Newman informs us that it need not, and on the whole ought not to be; that cunning is the weapon which Heaven has given to the saints wherewith to withstand the brute male force of the wicked world which marries and is given in marriage. Whether his notion be doctrinally correct or not, it is at least historically so."[54] It is appropriate that a historical analogy (false, in Newman's view) between Newman and the pre-Reformation clergy should have provoked the Newman–Kingsley quarrel.

Froude, though sharing Kingsley's view of history and Roman Catholicism, never shared his loathing of Newman. Indeed, in 1881 he published, in *Good Words,* his "Reminiscences of the High Church Revival," in which he gave one of the most beautiful and moving tributes to Newman that has ever been written. The tribute came to Newman's attention at the Oratory, and Newman, now eighty years of age, wrote to thank Froude for this "evidence of your affectionate feelings towards me, for which I was not prepared and which has touched me very much."[55] Froude later republished the essay in *Short Studies on Great Subjects* under the title, "The Oxford Counter-Reformation," and although he does not make any comparison between the Oxford movement and the European movement of the late sixteenth century, he implies that if the Reform movement of the 1830s was a second Reformation of the English Church, as it was, then the Tractarian movement was a second Counter-Reformation. That was its place in history.

6

Matthew Arnold
and the Zeitgeist

*I*N 1871 MATTHEW ARNOLD WROTE TO NEWMAN at the Oratory expressing the strong "interest with which I used to hear you at Oxford, and the pleasure with which I continue to read your writings now." Then, with a quaint apology for not having become a Catholic, he added, "We are all of us carried in ways not of our own making or choosing, but nothing can ever do away the effect you have produced upon me, for it consists in a general disposition of mind rather than in a particular set of ideas." A few months later he added, "There are four people, in especial, from whom I am conscious of having learnt—a very different thing from merely receiving a strong impression—learnt habits, methods, ruling ideas, which are constantly with me; and the four are—Goethe, Wordsworth, Sainte-Beuve, and yourself. You will smile and say I have made an odd mixture and that the result must be a jumble."[1] Arnold would not, of course, have said directly to Newman what he said in his lecture on Emerson a few years later, that "Cardinal Newman . . . in the Oratory . . . has adopted, for the doubts and difficulties which beset men's minds to-day, a solution which, to speak frankly, is impossible."[2] But though Arnold believed that Roman Catholicism was an anachronism in the modern world, he also deeply admired the ethos and temper of that religion and of the Tractarian movement which led up to it. He saw that Newman and the Tractarians had been doing in the realm of religion what he was trying to do in the realm of culture. The Private Judgment which they regarded as the central error of Protestantism was but a version of the provinciality, the eccentricity, which he regarded as the besetting sin of the English. Both he and they believed that this sin and this error could be rectified only by creating a center of authority whereby the individual could correct and discipline his own nature. But whereas Newman believed that authority was divine, Arnold believed it was human. In a certain sense

Arnold believed in the Dogmatic Principle—there was such a thing as Truth, but it was set on a mountain top where human beings could never reach it, though it was appropriate they should spend their lifetime trying. Hence, Arnold could not go along with Newman on the idea of the Visible Church. He saw the logical necessity for it if subjectivity and individualism were to be avoided, and in his essay "The Literary Influence of Academies" he so enlarged upon the value to France of the French Academy that one expected him to recommend a comparable institution for the English. But at the end of the essay he shied away from it and, like Adam, who is to find a "Paradise within thee, happier far," recommended that each individual construct his own personal "academy" through a process of self-discipline and culture.

Arnold was a generation younger than Newman and Carlyle, and hence his youth fell upon the crisis of 1848 rather than that of 1830–33. But in those years he underwent a conversion very similar to Carlyle's and not totally unlike Newman's. His was from the subjectivity and *Sturm und Drang* of his early poetry to the calm and objectivity of his critical prose, and as with those other writers it provided a paradigm for his conception of history. This conception was initially embodied in a myth which constitutes the central organizing symbol of all his poetry and which continues to undergird his thought even when he moves from poetry into prose.[3] The myth is played out upon a symbolic landscape which is divided into three regions, representing the period of childhood and early youth, the period of young manhood and maturity, and the period of old age or death. In accordance with Arnold's usage, we may call them the Forest Glade, the Burning or Darkling Plain, and the Wide-Glimmering Sea. Through these regions runs the River of Life or Time, carrying both the individual and the whole of humanity from a period of unity of being, when one lived in harmony with nature and oneself, to a period of fragmentation, when one is alienated from God, divorced from nature, and at odds even with one's own soul, to a final period of restored unity, which is a synthesis of the innocence of the first period with the bitter knowledge of the second. Arnold's poetry necessarily regards this myth from the point of view of the second period (the present), looking back nostalgically to the freshness of the early world and forward hopefully to the future. The third period, when it comes, will recover the Joy of the first period but without its elements of romantic illusion and aristocratic exclusiveness; it will be a "Joy whose grounds are true" and a "Joy in widest commonalty spread." It is a period which Arnold does not reach in his poetry and which is barely adumbrated in his prose.

It is clear that Arnold's myth of history is simply the universal tripartite myth of all who take a tragic view of life. It is related to the cycle of birth, death, and rebirth which was the basis of Greek tragedy, and to the cycle of Paradise, the expulsion from Paradise, and the "Paradise within" which is the substance of Christian myth. Since the third period of the myth is a synthesis of the first two, it may also be considered as forming the first period of a new cycle, and the threefold pattern as accommodating itself to the alternating organic-critical-organic periods of Carlyle and the Saint-Simonians. When Arnold first read Carlyle, he must have felt that his own sense of history was being reinforced, and that the pattern of Teufelsdröckh's idyllic childhood, his Everlasting No with its transitional Center of Indifference, and his Everlasting Yea corresponded to his own three periods. Like Carlyle, Arnold acted out his myth in his own life, and in the volume *Empedocles on Etna, and Other Poems* (1852) he has left us a spiritual autobiography not unlike *Sartor Resartus*.

The central spiritual crisis in Arnold's life, corresponding to the episode in the Rue St. Thomas de l'Enfer in *Sartor,* occurred in September 24 to 27, 1849, when Arnold went on a soul-searching expedition up into the Bernese Alps.[4] He was involved with a girl whom we have hitherto known only as "Marguerite" but whom Park Honan has recently identified as Mary Claude.[5] Mary, born in Berlin of French ancestry, was brought by her father to Liverpool while she was still a child. After his death in 1828 her mother bought a summer home at Rothay Bank, Ambleside, less than a mile from the Arnold's home at Fox How, and it was in that way that she and Arnold got acquainted. She was a tall, pale, beautiful girl, very intense, somewhat given to melancholy but concealing her melancholy under a light, mocking laughter. She was devoted to modern French and German literature, and among the authors whom she and Arnold must have read was Étienne Pivert de Senancour, author of the Wertheresque novel *Obermann*. Senancour was one of those second- or even third-generation Romantic writers for whom protest has faded into fretfulness, the "unstrung will" of modern life. Arnold had first encountered his work in 1847 and, feeling that it expressed exactly the mood of his generation, had taken Senancour as the "master of my wandering youth." So much so, indeed, that when he went to Oxford in November 1848 and found himself repelled by the superficiality of the place, he wrote to Clough, "I . . . took up Obermann, and refuged myself with him in his forest against your Zeit Geist." "Better that," he added, "than be sucked for an hour even into the Time Stream in which they and [you] plunge and bellow."[6]

Ultimately, however, it was not the modern Obermann but his ancient counterpart, Empedocles, with whom Arnold refuged himself, for
in the summer of 1849 J. C. Shairp wrote to Clough: "I saw the said
Hero—Matt—the day I left London. He goes in Autumn to the Tyrol
with Slade. He was working at an 'Empedocles'—which seemed to be
not much about the man who leapt in the crater—but his name & outward circumstances are used for the drapery of his own thoughts."[7] How
much they were so used Shairp would have realized if he could have
followed Arnold to Switzerland (his actual destination rather than the
Tyrol) and seen him act out his own drama in the Bernese Alps.

This drama involved making some decision about "Marguerite,"
who had come to represent for Arnold the disturbing element of sexual
passion and also a soul which knew not itself in any depth. He also had
to decide what kind of person he was and what he was to do. "I am
here," he wrote to Clough from Thun, "in a curious and not altogether
comfortable state: however tomorrow I carry my aching head to the
mountains and to my cousin the Blümlis Alp." The flight to the mountains was evidently for the purpose of self-mastery and self-discovery,
for earlier in the letter Arnold had confided to Clough: "What I must
tell you is that I have never yet succeeded in any one great occasion in
consciously mastering myself: I can go through the imaginary process
of mastering myself and see the whole affair as it would then stand, but
at the critical point I am too apt to hoist up the mainsail to the wind
and let her drive. However as I get more awake to this it will I hope
mend . . . [My] one natural craving is not for profound thoughts,
mighty spiritual workings etc. etc. but a distinct seeing of my way as
far as my own nature is concerned."[8]

The process of self-mastery for Arnold involved putting behind him
not only Marguerite but also all other morbid things that troubled without advancing him, and that included Obermann. And so as Arnold
walked up into the Obermann country (for Senancour's novel is set
partly in the mountains around the Baths of Leuk), he exorcised the
spirit of that unproductive thinker. Specifically, he composed the "Stanzas in Memory of the Author of 'Obermann,' " which records, he tells
us, "my separation of myself, finally, from him and his influence."[9] This
act—the act by which Arnold separated himself from Obermann—was
certainly the most important spiritual act of his entire life, for it put
behind him all the turbulence and unrest, the *Sturm und Drang*, that
had troubled him in previous years.

Unfortunately, when Arnold exorcised the spirit of Obermann in
September 1849, he was already engaged upon his drama *Empedocles on*

Etna, which was the very essence of all that he had put behind him. He had chosen Empedocles because, as he said in his Preface, into the feelings of this last of the Greek religious philosophers "there entered much that we are accustomed to consider as exclusively modern; . . . the dialogue of the mind with itself has commenced; modern problems have presented themselves; we hear already the doubts, we witness the discouragement, of Hamlet and of Faust" (I, 1). He was determined to analyze, as lucidly and pitilessly as did Obermann, the modern situation. "Woe was upon me," he wrote to Clough, "if I analysed not my situation: and Werther, Réné, and such like, none of them analyse the modern situation in its true *blankness* and *barrenness,* and *unpoetrylessness.*" Shairp had declared that Arnold was merely using the philosopher as a cloak for his own thoughts and feelings, and this is true. But when Arnold reached the top of the mountain, he did not, like Empedocles, throw himself into a volcano. Rather, in rejecting Obermann, he threw his own personal Empedocles into a volcano and came back down, a whole man, to lead a useful life in the cities of the plain. In one sense *Empedocles on Etna* dramatizes what Arnold did, but in another it dramatizes what he did not do. It dramatizes what he was saved from doing by the fact that he did it vicariously in the realm of art.

Of course, he had to do it again and again, for such affirmations are not accomplished once and for all. And although the writing of *Empedocles on Etna* acted as a catharsis for Arnold, he must have been aware, as Goethe was in the case of *Werther,* that upon others it might have a deleterious effect. Therefore in the autumn of 1853 he decided to exorcise Empedocles as he had previously exorcised Obermann. He was led to this decision partly by the example of Froude. Froude, who was four years older than Arnold, had been through his Empedoclean phase three years earlier when he had published his *Nemesis of Faith,* but now he had gotten married, settled down, and was turning himself into a historian. Arnold visited him at his Welsh home of Plas Gwynant in August 1852 and wrote to Clough: "I should like you to see Froude— quantum mutatus! He goes to church, has family prayers—says the Nemesis ought never to have been published etc. etc.—his friends say that he is altogether changed and re-entered within the giron de l'Eglise— at any rate within the giron de la religion chrétienne: but I do not see the matter in this light and think that he conforms in the same sense in which Spinoza advised his mother to conform—and having purified his moral being, all that was mere fume and vanity and love of notoriety and opposition in his proceedings he has abandoned and regrets. This is my view. He is getting more and more literary, and vise au solide instead of beating the air. May we all follow his example!"[10] Arnold did follow Froude's example, for he went straight from Plas Gwynant to Fox How, where, in the month of September, he wrote the preface to *Poems* (1853) in which he repudiated *Empedocles on Etna* and formulated his new poetical creed.

That creed involved the rejection of romantic subjectivism in favor of a more classical art in which feelings find a "vent in action" and so are resolved. The whole tenor of Arnold's Preface is toward a greater degree of objectivity: through the selection of an action rather than one's own feelings as a subject, through a concern with the architectonics of a work of art rather than its subordinate parts, and through a subordination of language and expression to plot and theme. Unfortunately, the critics saw the issue as Arnold's choice of an ancient rather than a modern subject. For thirty years this had been a burning controversy with the Spasmodic poets and their supporters, the "march-of-mind" men, and Arnold's poem had been reviewed unfavorably by several critics for this reason. Arnold felt he could not allow it to be supposed that he was omitting the drama from his new collection in deference to this opinion, and therefore he declared that his real reason was that, being unresolved, it did not "inspirit and rejoice" the reader, as Schiller said art should. It is odd, given the fact that Arnold says explicitly in the Preface that into the feelings of Empedocles there had entered "much that we are accustomed to consider as exclusively modern," that he did not take his father's line of defense and boldly declare that the chronologically ancient is, in this case, philosophically and culturally modern. In the end, he admits that date is of no importance. What is important is that one should have a great action which "powerfully appeal[s] to the great primary human affections: to those elementary feelings which subsist permanently in the race, and which are independent of time" (I, 4). But it ultimately appears that mere antiquity *is* important to Arnold, partly because the modern age is "wanting in moral grandeur" (I, 14) and so does not provide many great actions, partly because the artist treating a modern subject tends to focus on the trivial details of the social scene rather than the essentials of the inward man, and partly because the mere antiquity, the otherness of the past, has a strengthening and steadying effect upon the artist. It takes him out of himself into another world. In other words, the trouble with *Empedocles on Etna,* in Arnold's view, was that it was *too* modern— morbidly so—and although Arnold had doubtless gone to the legend of the Sicilian philosopher because he thought he could deal with his problem more easily under that alien guise than if he had written a drama about Obermann or some fictitious hero of his own, still, it was not alien enough. The Sophists were too patently the Utilitarians, Callicles too patently the Keatsian poet, Pausanias too patently the bewildered Anglican clergyman, and Empedocles too patently himself. His father was right that the ancient was modern, but if there were disease then as now, one did not wish to import it.

Arnold dealt more directly with the question of modernity in his lecture "On the Modern Element in Literature," delivered in November 1857 to inaugurate his appointment as Professor of Poetry at Oxford. He had been present fifteen years before when his father delivered his Inaugural Lecture as Professor of Modern History, and he undoubtedly felt that he was in some sense continuing his father's work. Indeed, several years later when he wrote "Rugby Chapel," the elegy to his father, he added to it the date "November 1857" as if to indicate that it was at this point that he had grown into such sympathy with his father as to make that tribute possible. In some ways the Inaugural Lecture is an even greater tribute because it consists almost entirely of his father's ideas. Its central thesis is that modernity is a quality of mind or spirit that may be found in men of any age and that there are periods of antiquity, such as fifth-century Greece and the Augustan Age in Rome, that are more "modern" than relatively recent periods. Arnold exemplifies this by contrasting Thucydides' critical spirit in handling the Peloponnesian War with the fantastic credulousness of Sir Walter Raleigh in his *History of the World*. Children, however, who follow in their father's footsteps like to differentiate themselves from their father, and Arnold did this, as indeed his professorship required, by concentrating upon literature rather than history. Whereas his father had said that by studying the history of these analogous periods we would come to understand our own and then, by purifying and reinvigorating our religious faith, would find the strength to deal with them, the son turned to the literature of those periods for his stay and remedy. He introduced the term "adequacy" ("a term I am always using," he confided to his brother) and asserted that whereas the literature of fifth-century Greece was supremely adequate in the sense that it reflected fully "the highly developed human nature of that age" (I, 28), the literature of the Augustan Age was not adequate. The Augustan Age was in some ways a fuller and more significant period than the Age of Pericles, but of its greatest writers Lucretius is characterized by depression and ennui, Virgil is tinged with an "ineffable melancholy," and Horace, though enchanting to men of taste and cultivation, is without faith, without enthusiasm, and without energy.

It is a little uncertain exactly what Arnold means by "adequacy," for if Horace and Lucretius accurately depict the spiritual malaise of their time, as Arnold seems to suggest they do, then they are adequate interpreters of their age and it is presumably the age itself that is at fault. If, on the other hand, what he means by "adequacy" is the power not merely to reflect the age but in some way to rise above it, to offer an interpretation and criticism of life that is permanently valid, then Arnold needs some other term than "adequacy"—perhaps "high seriousness." It is apparent that this is what Arnold is moving toward, for he declares that the need of any age that calls itself modern is for "intellectual deliverance" (I, 19–20), and by this deliverance he means an emotionally satisfying synthesis of the vast and confusing array of facts with which such an age is confronted. Sophocles, who "saw life steadily, and saw it whole," presented such a synthesis, but Empedocles, another fifth-century Greek, did not. Both Empedocles and Lucretius were "modern," but neither was "adequate." They represented the complexity of modern life but not a synthesis of that complexity, and by 1857 that is what Arnold wants.

Arnold developed his conception of "adequacy" in a letter to his brother Tom written just six weeks after the delivery of the Inaugural Lecture.

> A great transformation in the intellectual nature of the English, and, consequently, in their estimate of their own writers, is, I have long felt, inevitable. When this transformation comes the popularity of Wordsworth, Shelley, Coleridge, and others, remarkable men as they were, will not be the better for it. I am very much interested in what you say about Pope. I will read the Essay on Criticism again—certainly poetry was a power in England in his time, which it is not now. . . . You ask why is this. I think it is because Pope's poetry was *adequate*, (to use a term I am always using), to Pope's age—that is, it reflected completely the best general culture and intelligence of that age: therefore the cultivated and intelligent men of that time all found something of themselves in it. But it was a poor time, after all—so the poetry is not and cannot be a first-class one. On the other hand our *time* is a first class one—an infinitely fuller richer age than Pope's, but our poetry is not *adequate* to it; it interests therefore only a small body of sectaries. . . . But it is a hard thing to make poetry adequate to a first-class epoch. The eternal greatness of the literature of the Greece of Pericles is that it is the *adequate* expression of a first-class epoch. Shakespeare again, is the infinitely *more than adequate* expression of a *second class* epoch. It is the immense distinction of Voltaire and Goethe, with all their shortcomings, that they approach *near* to being adequate exponents of first-class epochs. And so on— . . . It is singular—but all this

is the very matter debated in my inaugural lecture, & the debating of
which will be continued in the two next.[11]

The most striking thing in this letter is the different estimate Arnold
now gives of his own age. A decade before these were "damned times,"
but now it is a "first-class epoch." The reason for this is partly that the
times really had changed, as England moved from the "hungry forties"
into the economic prosperity and serenity of the mid-fifties, and partly
that Arnold's personal situation has changed. It is not that he has moved
off the burning plain but that he at least sees the wide-glimmering sea
in the distance. The age is still characterized by complexity, but this
complexity is less a loss of unity of being than it is a challenge to discover
a new unity. Thus, the very morbidity which made Empedocles and
Lucretius seem so modern now begins to seem a little old-fashioned.
At least, Arnold would like to *make* it old-fashioned by putting it further
behind him, and the Inaugural Lecture is a repudiation of Lucretius,
as the Preface of 1853 was of Empedocles, and the "Stanzas in Memory
of the Author of 'Obermann' " was of Obermann. The truly modern, it
now appears, will be that literature which, with a full awareness of the
complexity of the modern world upon it, will offer "deliverance" from
that world into the next phase of being.

Arnold continued to pursue the theme of the "modern element in
literature" through the entire first series of his Oxford lectures, tracing
it from antiquity up through the Middle Ages. Unfortunately, his knowledge was not equal to the subject and so he never published these lectures. Among the topics treated were the troubadours, Dante, the
scholastic philosophy, and feudalism (I, 225), and it would be interesting to know how he handled them because neither he nor his father
considered the Middle Ages to be a "modern" epoch. Doubtless he
found the effort strained and unsatisfactory, for in the next year he
turned to an author who had been mentioned in the Inaugural Lecture
as supremely adequate but less interesting to us because his age is less
interesting—Homer. That Homer could offer "intellectual deliverance"
to the modern age seemed likely from a story which Arnold found in
Robert Wood's *Essay on the Original Genius and Writings of Homer*
(1775). Wood says that at the end of the Seven Years' War he waited
upon Lord Granville, then President of the Council, with the preliminary articles of the Treaty of Paris and found him so languid "that I
proposed postponing my business for another time; but he insisted that
I should stay, saying, it could not prolong his life to neglect his duty;
and repeating the following passage out of Sarpedon's speech":

> Ah, friend, if once escaped from this battle, we were for ever to be ageless and immortal, neither would I fight myself in the foremost ranks, nor would I send thee into the war that giveth men renown, but now—for assuredly ten thousand fates of death do every way beset us, and these no mortal may escape nor avoid—now let us go forward, whether we shall give glory to other men, or others to us (XII, 322–28)

"His Lordship repeated the last word several times with a calm and determinate resignation; and, after a serious pause of some minutes, he desired to hear the Treaty read, to which he listened with great attention, and recovered spirits enough to declare the approbation of a dying statesman (I use his own words) 'on the most glorious war, and most honourable peace, this nation ever saw' " (I, 107–08).

Lord Granville, of course, quoted Sarpedon's speech in the original Greek, and so too does Arnold in retelling the story.[12] But the middle classes of Arnold's day did not know Greek, and therefore the possibility of Homer's sustaining them, as he did Lord Granville, depends on the adequacy of translation. Arnold's lectures *On Translating Homer,* then, are concerned with exactly the same problem as Newman's *Development of Christian Doctrine*. For if Homer is the supreme source of value standing at the head of the classical tradition, as revelation is at the head of the Christian tradition, then there is the problem for Arnold, as there was for Newman, of transmitting that value substantially unchanged and yet adapted to the modern mind. *Translatio* is the technical term for the transmission of culture from one civilization to another, and translation, both in the literal and the extended sense, is exactly what is here involved. Arnold discovered, as he surveyed the tradition of English translations of Homer, that it had hitherto been conducted in accordance with the doctrine of accommodation, each translator adapting his author to the Spirit of the Age—Chapman translating him into Elizabethan, Pope into neoclassical, Cowper into eighteenth-century Miltonic, and Maginn and others into romantic ballads in accordance with the theories of Wolf and the taste of Sir Walter Scott. Worst of all was the most recent translation, that which was the principal occasion of Arnold's lectures, by F. W. Newman, brother to the great Oratorian—but no more a brother than Esau was to Jacob—who had translated Homer into the very image of a nineteenth-century crochety Englishman. F. W. Newman was a very learned Professor of Latin at University College, London, but he had married a member of a small dissenting sect, the Plymouth Brethren, had gone on an ill-advised missionary expedition to Syria, and then had returned to translate *Hiawatha* into

Latin and *Robinson Crusoe* into Latin and Arabic. Not only in religion
but also in lifestyle he was the very "Dissidence of Dissent and the
Protestantism of the Protestant Religion," and he was now translating
this greatest of all world classics into a mirror image of himself. How,
Arnold wondered, can the ordinary provincial Englishman lose his provinciality by reading such a work as this?

Arnold's solution was to do as John Henry Newman had done, set
up certain Notes or criteria which would distinguish a true development, or translation, from a false. In his view there were four: Homer
was rapid, plain and direct in style, plain and direct in ideas, and noble.
(In F. W. Newman's view he was "quaint, garrulous, prosaic, and low.")
One may concede that Arnold is translating Homer into his own image
as much as F. W. Newman is into his, and that the conflict between them
is a part of the contest between the two older universities and the new
University of London. One may also concede that Arnold's Apollonian
conception of Homer, derived from Winckelmann and Goethe, would
soon be replaced by a more Dionysian conception, and that his attempt
at a "Visible Church"—"the modern Greek scholar of poetical taste"—
was unsatisfactory (Newman preferred more scholarship and less taste).
Still, Arnold differed from Newman in at least trying to distance Homer
from himself rather than engorge him. In writing his tragedy *Merope* he
had learned how different the world created by the Greek imagination
is from our own,[13] and he thought that difference, that sense of otherness, ought to be preserved.

In the end the conflict came down to the question of how archaic
was Homer's diction. Did he sound to Sophocles as antiquated as Chaucer sounds to a Victorian? It is fascinating that the question should have
taken this form, for one might think that Homer could be translated
into modern English on the grounds that there was some time in the
past when his Greek sounded modern. But Thomas Arnold had said
that ancient authors ought to be translated into the English of the period analogous to their period of civilization. Thus, he would have translated Herodotus into Elizabethan English but Thucydides into modern.
Matthew, imitating his father, thinks of himself as standing in fifth-
century Athens and wants Homer to sound to him the way it sounded
to Sophocles. He cannot accept the idea that Homer is "medieval." He
is rather of the age of the King James version of the Bible, and it is in
that diction that Arnold would have him clothed (I, 155–56, 165–66).
There is, of course, the additional reason that he sees him as a secular
version of Scripture.

But if Homer was supremely adequate, he was not really modern.

His age did not have the complexity of a modern age, and therefore he could not offer "intellectual deliverance" from it. For this reason, in his next book, the *Essays in Criticism* (1865), Arnold represents himself as a "seeker still," still wandering in the wilderness of modern Philistia and saluting the promised land from afar. "That promised land," he said, alluding to the great creative epochs of Aeschylus and Shakespeare, "it will not be ours to enter, and we shall die in the wilderness: but to have desired to enter it, to have saluted it from afar, is already, perhaps, the best distinction among contemporaries" (III, 285).

The opening essay, "The Function of Criticism at the Present Time," presents a poignant picture of one who lives in "an epoch of dissolution and transformation" (III, 288). The poet Wordsworth has said that the critical faculty is always lower than the creative, and Arnold is acutely aware of the fact that he has not published a volume of poetry for the past ten years. His excuse is that the production of great works of literature "is not at all epochs and under all conditions possible." Literature works with ideas, the best ideas current at the time. "And I say *current* at the time, not merely accessible at the time; for creative literary genius does not principally show itself in discovering new ideas, that is rather the business of the philosopher. The grand work of literary genius is a work of synthesis and exposition, not of analysis and discovery." It is the business of the critical power "in all branches of knowledge . . . to see the object as in itself it really is" and so to establish "an order of ideas, if not absolutely true, yet true by comparison with that which it displaces. . . . Presently these new ideas reach society, the touch of truth is the touch of life, and there is a stir and growth everywhere; out of this stir and growth come the creative epochs of literature" (III, 260–61).

One might have thought that such an epoch would come out of the stir of the French Revolution, but, on the one hand, the Revolution rushed too directly into practical projects for the improvement of mankind and, on the other, in England it created in opposition to itself an "epoch of concentration," of which Burke was the great voice. On the continent for the past many years the main effort has been a critical effort, but not so in England. England was so frightened by the Revolution and the external danger of Napoleon that it withdrew into itself and fortified itself in the old order. That work of retrenchment and self-protection was the work of the aristocracy, and well have they done it. They had just the firmness and heroic temper of mind to do it well, and it needed to be done. But now the danger is past, and Arnold senses that a new epoch, an "epoch of expansion," is about to open upon his country. For the work of that epoch a new class more receptive to ideas than the aristocracy will be needed, for the qualities now required are not heroic firmness of mind but openness and flexibility of intelligence. England is wandering between two worlds, one dead, the other no longer "powerless to be born" but requiring a great critical effort to be born, and that is "The Function of Criticism at the Present Time." It is obvious that the words *at the Present Time*—the phrase omitted by T. S. Eliot from the title of his comparable essay—are for Arnold the operative words, for at an earlier time, that of Gibbon and Voltaire, for instance, its function might have been quite different—to destroy the old order rather than create the new—and in a later, more poetic time it might have no function at all. But if that later time is ever to be reached, if we are to achieve "deliverance" from modern Philistia, then we need critics who, "by a disinterested endeavour to learn and propagate the best that is known and thought in the world" (I, 283), can establish a current of fresh and true ideas that will make great poetry possible once more. Just as Newman turned at this point from Antiquity to Catholicity, so Arnold turned from Homer to the literature of continental Europe to examine its adequacy for the modern world.

The individual essays of which *Essays in Criticism* is composed had originally been lectures delivered by Arnold as Professor of Poetry at Oxford, and all had then been published in periodicals. But when Arnold suggested to Macmillan that they be collected into a volume, he added, "I am not at all clear that the papers should be printed in the order in which I have put them down."[14] He had put them down simply in the chronological order of their delivery and publication, but when the volume appeared they had been rearranged in what one can only call the order of Arnold's historical myth. That is to say, they are in the order in which their subjects ought to have lived had they followed the intellectual development of the modern world. Thus, after the two opening theoretical essays Arnold had placed first Maurice de Guérin, a French Keatsian poet who had a happy faculty of interpreting nature but not of the moral interpretation of man. He was obviously an inhabitant of the forest glade and, while very charming, was no guide to the modern world. Even less suitable was his sister Eugénie, who lived in the glade of the Roman Catholic religion but, fretting against herself, had not even achieved happiness in that outmoded religion. Heine, the subject of the third essay, was a true inhabitant of the modern world. From his "mattress-grave" in Paris he had shot against the ramparts of Philistinism arrowy shafts of irony and satire. He had been an effective dissolvent of the old European system, but, says Arnold, he was an acrid dissolvent, deficient not only in love but also in dignity and self-respect. Hence, though a brilliant soldier in the war of the liberation of humanity, he was not "an adequate interpreter of the modern world." He offers us "a half-result, for want of moral balance, and of nobleness of soul and character" (III, 132).

At this point—after three subjects on whom he has passed a primarily negative judgment and before the three on whom he will pass a primarily positive judgment—Arnold inserts the pivotal historical essay of the book, "Pagan and Mediæval Religious Sentiment." As the title indicates, it is a contrast between the religious sentiment of the pagan world, as exemplified in Theocritus's fifteenth idyll and that of the medieval world, as exemplified in St. Francis's "Canticle of the Sun." The former is the religion of pleasure, gay, natural, cheerful, and it is a very good religion, says Arnold, so long as things are going well. It served Heine beautifully during the early years of his life, but in old age, when he was sick and sorry, he took refuge in irony and satire. This, however, is a refuge for the few, not the many, and it is now asserted that the test of the satisfactoriness of a religion is its ability to minister to the many. In this, Christianity, the religion of sorrow, is vastly superior, but it too, in its extreme of otherworldliness, overruns the normal limits of humanity. Monte Alverno is as far from us as Pompei, the Reformation as the Renaissance. "The poetry of later paganism lived by the senses and understanding; the poetry of mediæval Christianity lived by the heart and imagination. But the main element of the modern spirit's life is neither the senses and understanding, nor the heart and imagination; it is the imaginative reason" (III, 230). With this key statement Arnold has moved beyond his initial historical analysis of alternating critical and creative periods into a perception of what the new creative period must be like.

The last three subjects in the book, though all inhabitants of the burning plain, are at least looking forward to the new age. Joubert is for Arnold the very type of the Buried Life, the obscure author whose fame has been suppressed during his own lifetime because he lived in an uncongenial epoch, but who can be recognized by the "outskirmishers" of the next generation, its quick-witted, light-armed troops, as being one of the sacred family, and so rescued and set aside. It is obvious that Arnold regards himself as one of these quick-witted, light-armed troops who is now in the process of rescuing Joubert—bringing the river of his Buried Life to the surface so that it can contribute to the broadening stream flowing on into the future. Spinoza, the subject of the next essay, also looks to the future because he put religion on a basis suitable to the modern mind. Without the mockery of Voltaire or the passion for demolition of Strauss, he made the purely intellectual love of God the summum bonum of life. Thus his works, aridly metaphysical as they are, will soon be recognized as the central point in modern philosophy.

Finally, Marcus Aurelius, chronologically the most remote of all the subjects, is spiritually the most modern—"a truly modern striver and thinker" (III, 136). He was, says Arnold, "perhaps the most beautiful figure in history" (III, 140). Moreover, he was so not in an age of medieval Catholicism, which made it easy for a St. Louis or a King Alfred to be beautiful, but in an age essentially like our own, an age of imperial paganism. In such an age Epictetus could attain to morality but nothing more. Marcus Aurelius, however, could suffuse morality with something like the emotion of Christianity. Still, though he could suffuse morality with emotion, he could not light it up with emotion, as does the New Testament. In this respect he was imperfect, and Arnold ends the essay by noting that it is through this very imperfection that Marcus Aurelius appeals to men today. "It is because he too yearns as they do for something unattained by him." What if he had been able to enter into Christianity? "Vain question!" says Arnold, "yet the greatest charm of Marcus Aurelius is that he makes us ask it. We see him wise, just, self-governed, tender, thankful, blameless; yet, with all this, agitated, stretching out his arms for something beyond—*tendentemque manus ripæ ulterioris amore*" (III, 156–57).

This is the last sentence in the essay, and it is also the last sentence in the book. We are struck by its resemblance to the last sentence in "The Function of Criticism at the Present Time," where Arnold says, "There is the promised land, towards which criticism can only beckon. That promised land it will not be ours to enter, and we shall die in the wilderness." It is obvious that Arnold has arrived in his quest at the point at which Marcus Aurelius had arrived in his. Each stood on his respective Mt. Pisgah, the one looking into the promised land of Christianity, the other into that new birth of Christianity to be effected by *Literature and Dogma*.

Arnold seems to have begun thinking seriously about history in the mid-1840s, when he subjected himself to an intensive course of reading in the Romantic German philosophers and historians. He was particularly impressed by the idea of the Zeitgeist. The concept of the Spirit of the Age had been introduced into England from French sources about the time of the Revolution of 1830, but now, in the time of the Revolution of 1848, Arnold reintroduced it from German sources. He probably first encountered it in Carlyle, who uses it in "Characteristics" and *Sartor Resartus*,[15] but he seems always to have associated it with Goethe. His first use of it was in a letter to Clough on July 20, 1848: "Goethe says somewhere that the Zeitgeist when he was young caused everyone to adopt the Wolfian theories about Homer, himself included: and that when he was in middle age the same Zeitgeist caused them to leave these theories for the hypothesis of one poem and one author: inferring that in these matters there is no certainty, but alternating dispositions."[16] Fifteen years later he alluded to the same passage in Goethe's *Schriften zur Literatur* (the section entitled "Homer noch einmal (1827)") and went on to say, "Intellectual ideas, which the majority of men take from the age in which they live, are the dominion of this Time-Spirit; not moral and spiritual life, which is original in each individual" (III, 77). Style is also original with the individual. "In a *man*," Arnold wrote to Clough, "style is the saying in the best way *what you have to say*. The *what you have to say* depends on your age."[17] Style he evidently thought of as subjective; the moral and spiritual life, though also unique to the individual, is surely in some degree objective. It is the area in between the subjective and objective—the vast area of human culture—that depends upon the age. The phrase "alternating dispositions" indicates that Arnold was thinking in terms of critical and creative or organic and mechanical periods.

The phrase "Zeitgeist" differs from the "Spirit of the Age" in its greater emphasis on Time and therefore change. It notes that the Spirit of the Age changes continuously with the passage of time, although it may be only at moments of revolutionary change, as in 1830 and 1848, that people become conscious of the fact and comment upon it. As to why change occurs, Arnold does not say. There is a large fatalistic element in his thought, and the image of the River of Life or Time, which is as pervasive in his prose as in his poetry, suggests that change is simply a cosmic process. It is an aspect of Time. Without change, external or internal, there would be no Time. In the area of knowledge, though not in that of the arts, Arnold believes in progress, though perhaps only *en ligne spirale,* as Goethe did. But in other areas he suggests a law of action and reaction, possibly because life, as he sees it, is a harmonious balance of opposing qualities. Hence, whenever one element, such as Hebraism, becomes dominant there is a natural reaction in favor of its opposite, Hellenism. This law is thus a self-protective device on the part of life itself to preserve the good health of the organism. It is a kind of spiritual sensor which detects in advance changes which need to be made by the body politic if it is to be in harmony with its own inward life. For Arnold agrees with Carlyle that changes are initially spiritual and that the forms of society (Carlyle's "clothes") are continually lagging behind. He does not frequently use his father's analogy between the life of the individual and the history of the world, but he certainly thinks of society as alive and as changing because it is alive.

The changes society undergoes are both positive and negative, for the Time-Spirit is both a Creator and a Destroyer. Fraser Neiman, who has studied this matter in detail, says that Arnold had two widely differing conceptions of the Zeitgeist, in the forties thinking of it as "the temper of the times, with the additional idea that time is a local, changeable phenomenon opposing eternal values;" in the seventies, when he was writing on the Church and the Bible, thinking of it as "an aspect of the eternal, promoting change as a manifestation of its own being."[18] It may be, however, that it was not Arnold's conception of the Zeitgeist that changed but rather the position from which he viewed it. When Arnold felt himself on the burning plain, he necessarily found the Zeitgeist inimical and attempted to refuge himself from it; but when he felt he was approaching the wide-glimmering sea, then the Zeitgeist was working in his favor and he naturally elevated it to a cosmic process. It was the same power in both cases, but in the one operating as the destroyer of the old world, in the other as the creator of the new.

Throughout his life Arnold varied in his view of the Time-Spirit, sometimes regarding it as a mere metaphor for collective shifts in human opinion and sometimes hypostatizing it as a real entity that produced those shifts. He tells his sister, for example, "It is only in the best poetical epochs (such as the Elizabethan) that you can descend into yourself and produce the best of your thought and feeling naturally . . . ; for then all the people around you are more or less doing the same thing. It is natural, it is the bent of the time to do it; its being the bent of the time, indeed, is what makes the time a *poetical* one."[19] The Elizabethan age is poetical *because* many people were then writing and reading poetry. On the other hand, in *St. Paul and Protestantism* Arnold makes the Zeitgeist independent of individual human actions, identifying it with the logic or life in ideas themselves. He associates it with the power which Newman made responsible for the development of Christian doctrine and with St. Paul's "divine power *revealing* additions to what we possess already" (VI, 92). The ambiguity of Arnold's feeling is apparent in the fact that he sometimes uses the phrase Zeitgeist along with another phrase—"the 'Zeit-Geist' and the general movement of men's religious ideas" or "the 'Zeit-Geist' and the mere spread of what is called *enlightenment*"—where one cannot tell whether the second phrase is in addition to or in explanation of the first (VI, 121, 236). Generally speaking, in view of Arnold's (along with Goethe's) "imperturbable naturalism" one is inclined to think that the reification of the Time-Spirit is less a matter of real belief on Arnold's part than of rhetorical strategy. Just as he will personify Culture or Criticism in order to give authority to his own ideas and will chastise the provinciality of the English by telling them what "Europe" thinks of them, so here he undertakes to speak for "History." The Time-Spirit is a device whereby Arnold can project his own sense of change onto a persona that is simply irresistible. The change is coming whether people like it or not. On the other hand, when Arnold defines God as "the stream of tendency by which all things seek to fulfill the law of their being" (VI, 10), one does not feel that this is a mere rhetorical strategy. There is a distinct element in Arnold that reaches forward to a Bergsonian Life Force, and the only Absolute he really believes in is placed within the evolving forms of life itself. He may mythologize the Time-Spirit for rhetorical purposes, but when he divinizes it, he is probably being serious.

The Time-Spirit embodies itself in external institutions and then, moving on, creates a sense of discordancy between these institutions and its own inner life. This discordancy grows until at last the institutions break up, either rapidly by revolution or more slowly by gradual change, and at such times we feel we are at the end of an era. Thus, the periodization of history is created by the breakup of systems rather than by the more or less constant movement of the Zeitgeist itself.

It is sufficiently obvious that this view of history derives from the Philosophy of Clothes in Carlyle's *Sartor Resartus* and from his German and French sources. Some scholars have perceived in Arnold's work the influence of Vico,[20] but Arnold never quotes Vico, and although the *Scienza Nuova* appears in his reading lists for 1876, there is no evidence he read it. He of course knew his father's "Essay on the Social Progress of States," but his father had so far modified Vico, reducing his Ages of Gods, Heroes, and Men to periods dominated by the aristocracy, the middle class, and the populace, that there was little left peculiar to the Italian. Both father and son did, of course, hold that every society, at least ideally, goes through a threefold evolution and therefore that modern societies tend to repeat the development of those in antiquity. To that extent they are Viconian. But Arnold could have gotten this scheme more easily from Goethe and Carlyle.

Like his predecessors, he does not apply the scheme rigorously or

systematically. The alternating epochs tend to fall into a threefold dialectical pattern, but this is not always the case. Moreover, the pattern
may be on a very extended time-scale, as with the great divisions of the
Middle Ages, the Renaissance, and modern times, or it may be so reduced that epochs of concentration and expansion come and go with
bewildering rapidity. In all likelihood Arnold believed that there are
cycles within the great cycles of human history, even down to the cycles
of individual human life. Thus, though the Middle Ages is a kind of
childhood of the world, followed by a harsh maturity from the Elizabethan age on, Romanticism is certainly a miniature childhood within
that larger cycle. Moreover, it should be understood that individual
nations do not necessarily move in phase. England in 1848 was *"far
behind* the Continent,"[21] according to Arnold, and the French Revolution, which produced an epoch of expansion in the country in which it
occurred, provoked in England an epoch of concentration. Even within
a country the various aspects of national life were not always in phase,
and it goes without saying that Arnold held different views of different
periods at different times. He had a particularly hard time making up
his mind about the Elizabethan period, whether it was, as he said in his
letter to Tom, a "second-class epoch" with an occasional genius like
Shakespeare or one of the great synthetic periods of world history like
its counterpart in Italy. Arnold read much history and thought deeply
about it, but he was neither an accurate historian of the past nor a
systematic philosopher of history. His aim was to draw from the past a
paradigm of the stages through which nations and individuals ideally
would pass in realizing their full potential.

Arnold applied his philosophy of history in three main areas, the
evolution of political society, the course of literary culture, and the
history of religion. As might be expected, his terminology and concepts
vary from one field to another. In the area of politics Arnold believed,
along with his father, that society was moving inevitably towards a
greater degree of democracy. Thus, it would evolve through periods
dominated by the aristocracy, the middle class, and the populace. But
whereas his father believed that in 1830 England was at the crisis point
between the second phase and the third, Arnold regarded the process
as much less advanced and likely to be less catastrophic. He acknowledged that 1688 was an important date but held that the aristocracy
was still well in charge through 1815 and that even after the first Reform
Bill the actual reins of government were in their hands. The problem
now was to persuade them to relinquish their power, for as Arnold
looked back through history he thought he saw that the Roman aris-

tocracy had fallen because it was unable to deal with the ideas of the mature period of Roman history after the Punic Wars,[22] and that the Venetian and French aristocracies had fallen because they were unable to deal with the ideas of modern Europe (I, 83–84; II, 6). An aristocracy is naturally unsympathetic to ideas, which it regards as visionary and even dangerous, and thus, as the old order ceases to satisfy, there is a need for a new class to come into power that will be sympathetic to ideas. This will be the middle class, and despite Arnold's recognition of the narrowness and lack of intelligence of this group, he believes that it does have the capacity for that role. The "master-thought" of his political writings is the need to educate the middle class so that it can properly perform its role in history. As for the ultimate transfer of power to the people, that is a more distant event which Arnold regards with some unease but as in itself desirable.

In his literary essays Arnold initially used the Goethean-Carlylean terminology of critical and creative periods, saying, in *On Translating Homer* and "The Function of Criticism at the Present Time," that the main effort of the intellect of Europe, for now many years, has been a critical effort, and that the exercise of the creative power in the production of great works of literature is, in the present epoch, simply impossible. But then, a little way into the essay, Arnold shifts to "epochs of concentration" and "epochs of expansion," doubtless because these have a broader cultural application. The two sets of terms are not identical. An epoch of concentration is that great centripetal movement in society whereby a culture draws in upon itself, orders and consolidates its world-view, and defends that view against external enemies long after it has ceased to be alive. It is the epoch of aristocracies, and although it presupposes an earlier act of creation, it really comprehends only the last phase of that act and the first, destructive phase of criticism. An epoch of expansion, on the other hand, is the great centrifugal movement whereby a culture creates, initially through criticism, a new worldview which it then enhances and brings into relation with the lives of men through artistic creation. Arnold differs from Carlyle primarily in his insistence that criticism is creative too and, living as he did a generation later than Carlyle, in his emphasis on its creative rather than its destructive aspect. His terms focus on the systole and diastole of human society rather than on the moment of stasis when either criticism or creation is at its height.

It is not difficult to relate these terms to Arnold's political thought. The epoch of concentration is that of the fading of the aristocracy and the epoch of expansion that of the rise of the middle class, but presum-

ably at some time in the future there will be a new epoch of concentration as the middle class attempts to hold on to its power against the
new expansive movement of the populace. There is a certain sense in
which the three social classes correspond to the three regions of Arnold's imaginative world, for the aristocracy is the childhood of the
world, the middle class is transitional, and democracy is the period in
which joy will be "in widest commonalty spread." But Arnold's experience of history is limited to the first two classes, and so he tends to
see the new expansive movement of the middle class (it is not irrelevant
that it is his own class) as the "wide-glimmering sea." He records its
coming very precisely in his essays. In the *Essays in Criticism* (1864–65)
he is living in "an epoch of dissolution and transformation"—the last
phase of an epoch of concentration—and the promised land is far in
the distance. "But epochs of concentration cannot well endure for ever;
epochs of expansion, in the due course of things, follow them. Such an
epoch of expansion seems to be opening in this country" (III, 269).
Five years later it apparently had opened, for in *Culture and Anarchy*
(1869) Arnold asks, "Is not the close and bounded intellectual horizon
within which we have long lived and moved now lifting up, and are not
new lights finding free passage to shine in upon us? For a long time
there was no passage for them. . . . But now the iron force of adhesion
to the old routine . . . has wonderfully yielded" (V, 92). And a few pages
later he speaks of "epochs of expansion . . . , such as that in which we
now live" (V, 124). In 1880 he reiterated his entire doctrine in a letter
to M. Fontanes,[23] the French critic, and in 1886 declared, "The epoch
of concentration has ended for us, the ice has broken up." "We are living
in an epoch of expansion" (XI, 130, 139).

Arnold seems never to have applied the terms *epoch of concentration*
and *epoch of expansion* to any except the modern period, but in *Culture
and Anarchy* he devised another set of terms which he could use of the
entire course of civilization. Hebraism and Hellenism originally denote
two constituent elements in human nature: on the one hand, the impulse
to right conduct, obedience to God, and strictness of conscience; on
the other, the impulse toward intelligence, seeing the object as it really
is, and spontaneity of consciousness. But because these two elements
are embodied, the one in the Judaeo-Christian, the other in the Graeco-
Roman tradition, they may also be observed in human history. They
have but one aim, human perfection, but they pursue this aim by different means and each is disposed to regard itself not as a contribution
to the whole but as the *unum necessarium,* the one thing needful. Therefore history has proceeded by alternating epochs, in which an exclusive

pursuit of one quality has led to a practical neglect of the other and so produced a reaction into the opposite error, which had to be corrected in turn. The bright promise of Hellenic culture, for example, was ultimately found to be unsound simply because it had not provided the indispensable basis of conduct and self-control. It led into the moral enervation and self-disgust of late paganism. In that context Christianity, a more inward and spiritual form of Hebraism, came as a rebirth of the human spirit, but it led, through the austerities of St. Paul, into medieval asceticism and so provoked the Renaissance, a second phase of Hellenism. Arnold pondered deeply about the Renaissance and its relation to the Reformation. He sharply disagreed with Froude that "the Reformation caused the Elizabethan literature." It was rather that "both sprang out of the active animated condition of the human spirit in Europe at that time. After the fall of the Roman Empire the barbarians powerfully turned up the soil of Europe—and after a little time when the violent ploughing was over and things had settled a little, a vigorous crop of new ideas was the result."[24] The Reformation was the "subordinate and secondary side" of the Renaissance, and though it was a Hebraising revival within the church, it was so infused with the subtle Hellenic spirit that "the exact respective parts, in the Reformation, of Hebraism and of Hellenism, are not easy to separate" (V, 171–72). This great hybrid movement, in other words, which initiated the modern world, was in some degree a synthesis of antiquity and the Middle Ages. Nonetheless, even with the Reformation, the Renaissance had its side of moral weakness, just as later paganism had, and in England Puritanism came as the reaction of Hebraism against this weakness precisely as primitive Christianity had at the time of St. Paul.

> Yet there is a very important difference between the defeat inflicted on Hellenism by Christianity eighteen hundred years ago, and the check given to the Renascence by Puritanism. . . . Eighteen hundred years ago it was altogether the hour of Hebraism. Primitive Christianity was legitimately and truly the ascendant force in the world at that time, and the way of mankind's progress lay through its full development. Another hour in man's development began in the fifteenth century, and the main road of his progress then lay for a time through Hellenism. Puritanism was no longer the central current of the world's progress, it was a side stream crossing the central current and checking it. (V, 174–75)

If one asks how Arnold knows that it is a side stream, his reply is that it is only in England that this happened. On the continent Hellenism remained the dominant movement from the Renaissance to the present time, but in England, in the seventeenth century, the middle class "entered the prison of Puritanism, and had the key turned upon its spirit there for two hundred years" (VIII, 294). If Arnold were speaking to the French, he would doubtless recommend some additional Hebraism, but speaking to the English, he recommends their peculiar deficiency, Hellenism.

Though both Hebraism and Hellenism have both critical and creative phases, Hebraism, as Arnold views it, is often simply the moral and religious aspect of an epoch of concentration and Hellenism the cultural aspect of an epoch of expansion. The new terms have the virtue, however, of denoting the powers which produce this systole and diastole of human history and so are more useful for tracing the development of civilization. But Arnold also needs to analyze a development within the Hebraic tradition, and for this he turns, in *Literature and Dogma,* to another set of terms, verifiable religious experience *vs. Aberglaube.*

The Bible, in Arnold's view, is not a theological work which sets forth in precise, scientific terms the dogmas of the Christian religion, but is simply the literature of the Hebrew people. Like any literature it is couched in the language of metaphor and symbol, for these alone could shadow forth the profound spiritual experiences of the Old Testament prophets. At least in the early golden years the people had no difficulty interpreting it. Gradually, however, as they suffered misfortunes and weakened in faith, they began to interpret these insights literally, to look for a miraculous change that would restore their fallen fortunes—to expect a Messiah. These new beliefs were not such as could be verified by experience. They were "extra-beliefs"—*Aberglaube*—not exactly superstitions but beliefs *in addition* to what they knew by their own experience of the moral law to be true. When the Messiah did come, then, his function was not to fulfill this mechanical religion but to renew and deepen the experience on which true religion was based—to renew it by the method of inwardness, the secret of renunciation, and the mildness of his own temper. Unfortunately, his followers were once again prone to take literally what he meant only spiritually, and so once again a new Aberglaube, that of Christian theology, grew up. By Arnold's day it had become so entangled in metaphysics and the supernatural that the masses of men were ready to reject the Bible altogether rather than believe what they were told it meant. And so Arnold, who believed the Bible was the greatest repository of spiritual wisdom the world possessed, broke through this web of musty theology to re-present the Bible, as Coleridge and his father had before him, as the religious experience of the Hebrew people. So viewed, the joy announced by Christ would become a "joy whose grounds are true" and so would once again be accepted by the masses, as a "joy in widest commonalty spread." Far more truly than by the advent of democracy or of a new Hellenism, this would bring about the New Heavens and the New Earth that Arnold desired.

The period that Arnold found most analogous to his own was the period of late paganism immediately before the birth of Christ. For twenty years Arnold tried to write a tragedy on Lucretius, for he found the passage at the end of the third book where Lucretius depicts the tedium and ennui of the Roman noble, driving furiously abroad in order to escape from himself and then driving furiously home again, one of the most powerful and solemn in all literature. He quoted it in his lecture "On the Modern Element in Literature" (I, 32–33) and used it again in "Obermann Once More." To Clough he wrote in 1835, "We deteriorate in spite of our struggle—like a gifted Roman falling on the uninvigorating atmosphere of the decline of the Empire."[25] The later period covered by Gibbon he was not so interested in, but when he was passing through Arles in the south of France, he wrote to his sister, "I cannot express to you the effect which this Roman south of France has upon me—the astonishing greatness of the ancient world, of which the provincial corners were so noble—its immense superiority to the Teutonic middle age—its gradual return, as civilization advances, to the command of the world—all this, which its literature made me believe in beforehand, impresses itself upon my senses when I see these Gallo Roman towns. I like to trace a certain affinity in the spirit of these buildings between the Romans and the English; 'you and the Romans,' Guizot said to me the other day, 'are the only two governing nations of the world.'"[26] This was in 1859; a dozen years earlier he had written in his notebook:

> The Roman world perished for having disobeyed reason and nature.
> The infancy of the world was renewed with all its sweet illusions.
> but infancy and its illusions must for ever be transitory, and we are again in the place of the Roman world, our illusions past, debtors to the service of reason & nature.
> O let us beware how we again are false to them: we shall perish, and the world will be renewed: but we shall leave the same questions to be solved by a future age.[27]

In "Obermann Once More," alluding to the birth-time of Christianity, he said,

> 'Oh, had I lived in that great day,
> How had its glory new
> Fill'd earth and heaven, and caught away
> My ravish'd spirit too!'

But he added that in the modern rebirth of Christianity one must remain "unduped of fancy," lest one be doomed to repeat the Middle Ages all over again.

Of the Middle Ages Arnold wrote to his sister, "I have a strong sense of the irrationality of that period, and of the utter folly of those who take it seriously, and play at restoring it; still, it has poetically the greatest charm and refreshment possible for me. The fault I find with Tennyson in his *Idylls of the King* is that the peculiar charm and aroma of the Middle Age he does not give in them. There is something magical about it, and I will do something with it before I have done."[28] Oxford, "steeped in sentiment as she lies, spreading her gardens to the moonlight, and whispering from her towers the last enchantments of the Middle Age," was for Arnold the very symbol of that magic, but it was also the "home of lost causes, and forsaken beliefs, and unpopular names, and impossible loyalties" (III, 290)—in particular, of Newman, who had vainly attempted to revive there the dream of the Catholic Church. Of the Celtic people, whom Arnold treated in his lectures *On the Study of Celtic Literature,* the bard had said, "They went forth to the war, *but they always fell*" (III, 346). They were characterized by sentiment, the willful rebellion against the despotism of fact, and though they contributed to English poetry its element of "natural magic," they contributed nothing more. The Middle Ages was the childhood of the modern world, and though one might yearn for the beauty and charm of one's childhood, it was impossible to return. It was impossible to return to the monastery of the Grande Chartreuse, whose religion offered a refuge, but the refuge of the tomb. One of Arnold's sharpest criticisms of the Romantic poets was that they did seek to return. When he wished to say that Wordsworth "voluntarily cut himself off from the modern spirit," he said that he "retired (in Middle-Age phrase) into a monastery" (III, 121). At the same time "Scott became the historiographer-royal of feudalism," and Coleridge took to opium. The same was true of the German Romantics. Carlyle had declared that Tieck, Novalis, Richter, and others were the chief inheritors and continuators of Goethe's work, but Arnold declared that they were a minor current; the main current flowed from Goethe to Heine. "The mystic and romantic school of Germany lost itself in the Middle Ages, was overpowered by their influence, came to ruin by its vain dreams of renewing them. Heine, with a far profounder sense of the mystic and romantic charm of the Middle Age than Görres, or Brentano, or Arnim, Heine the chief romantic poet of Germany, is yet also much more than a romantic poet: he is a great modern poet, he is not conquered by the Middle Age, he has a talisman by which he can feel,—along with but above the power of the fascinating Middle Age itself,—the power of modern ideas" (III, 119).

To Arnold the Renaissance put European civilization back upon the right road after the long detour of the Middle Ages. He quotes again and again in his notebooks the remark of Renan, "*La Renaissance—ce grand éveil, qui replaçait l'humanité dans la voie des grandes choses*"; and again, "*The Renaissance. le retour à la vrai tradition de l'humanité civilisée.*"[29] Uniting as it did Hebraism and Hellenism, the senses and understanding of late antiquity with the heart and imagination of the Middle Ages, it was one of the great epochs of the "imaginative reason," the beginning of the modern world. Moreover, Arnold had somehow persuaded himself that the high culture of the Renaissance pervaded a large body of the community, creating a current of fresh ideas, and that it is this broad basis of culture that is "the secret of rich and beautiful epochs in national life; the epoch of Pericles in Greece, the epoch of Michael Angelo in Italy, the epoch of Shakespeare in England" (II, 316; cf. III, 121, 262–63). It created a "national glow of life and thought" that made for a great creative and expansive epoch. Raphael, Arnold thought, was probably the ideal representative of this age, but unfortunately Arnold knew little about Raphael or Michelangelo, and so he had to confine himself to his own country. There he was less enthusiastic. Though he never said publicly what he said in a private letter to Tom, that the Elizabethan Age was a "second-class epoch" (indeed, he always acknowledged that it was England's greatest), he did not consider it really modern. It retained too much of the Middle Ages upon it, had not really entered into the classical decorum. Or rather, having been so long repressed by the Middle Ages, it burgeoned forth into a fantasticality and playfulness that was simply extravagant. It did so partly because it did not have a complex body of thought and feeling to wrestle with and so could devote itself to curious and exquisite expression. For this reason Arnold did not think it provided a good model for the modern poet. "More and more I feel that the difference between a mature and a youthful age of the world compels the poetry of the former to use great plainness of speech as compared with that of the latter: and that Keats and Shelley were on a false track when they set themselves to

reproduce the exuberance of expression, the charm, the richness of images, and the felicity of the Elizabethan poets."[30] Indeed, the literature
of the eighteenth century was simply "a long reaction against this eccentricity" (I, 140), and ultimately it perished through its own provinciality. On the continent, however, Goethe and Voltaire had created a
great critical effort which, in the completeness of its culture, was almost
the equivalent of a true creative age. It only lacked the "national glow
of life and thought" which one finds when ideas are widely diffused
among the people and not derived from books. Moreover, it was in the
eighteenth century that Hellenism, checked by the Puritan reaction,
achieved its full development, and Arnold was strangely drawn to the
period. "I am glad you like Gray," he wrote to his wife; "that century
is very interesting, though I should not like to have lived in it; but the
people were just like ourselves, whilst the Elizabethans are not."[31]

The truly great synthetic epoch in the past is the Periclean Age in
Athens. "There is a century in Greek life," wrote Arnold, "the century
preceding the Peloponnesian war, from about the year 530 to the year
430 B.C.,—in which poetry made, it seems to me, the noblest, the most
successful effort she has ever made as the priestess of the imaginative
reason, of the element by which the modern spirit, if it would live right,
has chiefly to live. Of this effort . . . the four great names are Simonides,
Pindar, Æschylus, Sophocles" (III, 230–31). Arnold does not claim that
these poets are perfect, but no other poets have so well balanced the
thinking power by the religious sense. As he contemplates their work,
he is impressed by their objective excellence and solidity: they are like
a group of statuary seen at the end of a long dark vista. "I know not
how it is," he says in the Preface to *Poems* (1853), "but their commerce
with the ancients appears to me to produce, in those who constantly
practise it, a steadying and composing effect upon their judgment, not
of literary works only, but of men and events in general. They are like
persons who have had a very weighty and impressive experience: they
are more truly than others under the empire of facts, and more independent of the language current among those with whom they live" (I,
13). The Periclean Age is modern in the sense that it has a deep, inward
affinity with contemporary life, but it rises so far above the level of that
life that it is an ideal rather than an analogy.

In his later years Arnold turned more and more from the Greeks to the
Hebrew scriptures. Indeed, he had no sooner recommended an increase
of Hellenism to the English people than he began to think that an

increase of Hebraism was what they needed. "If I was to think only of the Dissenters," he wrote to Kingsley in 1870, "or if I were in your position, I should press incessantly for more Hellenism; but, as it is, seeing the tendency of our *young* poetical litterateur (Swinburne), and on the other hand, seeing much of Huxley. . . , I lean towards Hebraism, and try to prevent the balance from on this side flying up out of sight."[32] It was, of course, balance that Arnold was trying to maintain. He was in no sense a relativist, saying that whatever the Zeitgeist brought was to be accounted a blessing. It was rather that the whole course of history presented an ideal of totality or comprehensiveness, the harmonious development of one's powers that was lacking in any particular age. It was also lacking in any particular nation. Just as Newman sought the note of Catholicity by looking to Rome and the note of Apostolicity by looking to Jerusalem, so Arnold also sought these values by looking, on the one hand, to the modern civilizations of France and Germany and, on the other, to the Graeco-Roman tradition. But after the Franco-Prussian War of 1870 he became increasingly disgusted with the modern French. *Madame Bovary* was not to be recommended, and Balzac, unlike Arnold's beloved George Sand, was to be deplored. Whereas previously the French had been characterized by their widespread intelligence, they were now a nation of *hommes sensuels moyens* who worshipped the goddess Lubricity, and their downfall was only a matter of time. "[It] is mainly due" wrote Arnold to his mother, "to that want of a serious conception of righteousness and the need of it, the consequences of which so often show themselves in the world's history, and in regard to the Graeco-Latin nations more particularly. The fall of Greece, the fall of Rome, the fall of the brilliant Italy of the fifteenth century, and now the fall of France, are all examples."[33] Earlier it was the inability to cope with modern ideas that had produced these downfalls.

As Arnold swung back from the Latin to the Saxon races and from Hellene to Hebrew, he turned increasingly to the Old Testament. In 1872 he published an edition of the Second Isaiah for school use and declared in the Introduction that the work provided a key to "universal history." "Many of us have a kind of centre-point in the far past to which we make things converge, from which our thoughts of history instinctively start and to which they return; it may be the Persian War, or the Peloponnesian War, or Alexander, or the Licinian Laws, or Caesar. Our education is such that we are strongly led to take this centre-point in the history of Greece or Rome; but it may be doubted whether one who took the conquest of Babylon [538 B.C.] and the restoration of the Jewish exiles would not have a better. Whoever began with laying hold on this series of chapters [40–66] as a whole, would have a starting-point and lights of unsurpassed value for getting a conception of the course of man's history and development as a whole" (VII, 71). Here, then, is an alternative to the Age of Pericles, the slightly earlier age of the Second Isaiah. One reason that Arnold so prized it was that the majority of people require joy in their literature, "and if ever that 'good time coming,' for which we all of us long, was presented with energy and magnificence, it is in these chapters" of the Second Isaiah. Hence, in the lecture "Numbers," which Arnold delivered on his tour of America, he contrasted Plato's conception of the "remnant," the small band of honest followers who, in the madness of the multitude, seek shelter under a wall till the storm is over and then depart in mild and gracious mood, with Isaiah's "remnant" (in this case the first Isaiah's), who will actually restore the state. Isaiah's hope is foolish, says Arnold, for the numbers, either in Athens or in Israel, are far too small. But Arnold's father had told him that numbers were the characteristic of democracy, and so in America's fifty millions there will perhaps be found a remnant of sufficient magnitude to accomplish the task.

Arnold's conception of the remnant seems overstrained and dubious, but it is not unrelated to a conception much more fundamental to his thought, that of the lonely individual who carries on, in a climate uncongenial to his genius, to transmit to the future the values of civilization. Such a man was Marcus Aurelius, a "truly modern striver and thinker" who nonetheless had "a sense of constraint and melancholy" upon him because he longed for something more than his age could provide. Such a man was Falkland, a martyr of moderation and tolerance amid the violence of the English civil war. "Shall we blame him for his lucidity of mind and largeness of temper?" By no means. "They are what make him ours; what link him with the nineteenth century. He and his friends, by their heroic and hopeless stand against the inadequate ideals dominant in their time, kept open their communications with the future, lived with the future" (VIII, 204). Such a person was Gray, a born poet who fell upon an age of prose and so "never spoke out." "Coming when he did, and endowed as he was, he was a man . . . whose spiritual flowering was impossible. The same thing is to be said of his great contemporary, Butler" (IX, 200–01). It may be said too of Joubert, who, though passing with scant notice through his own generation, was singled out by the light-armed troops of the next as a person to be preserved and, like the lamp of life itself, handed on to the next generation. It is as one of these that Arnold saw himself, not as a great poet but as one who, living in the days of the Philistines, yet kept his gift pure and so was a forerunner, a preparer, an initiator of the age to come.

"I think," Arnold wrote to his sister in 1863, "in this concluding half of the century the English spirit is destined to undergo a great transformation; or rather, perhaps I should say, to perform a great evolution."[34] He never ceased to think so or to aid in that evolution. Unlike some of his contemporaries he did not settle down into a fixed position as old age came upon him. By looking to the past he kept himself oriented towards the future. He had in his mind's eye the image of a society in which the whole body of men should come to live with a life worthy to be called *human*. "This, the humanisation of man in society, is civilisation" (IX, 141–42). He knew, however, that this ideal was simply to be sought; it would never be reached once and for all. "Undoubtedly we are drawing on towards great changes; and for every nation the thing most needful is to discern clearly its own condition, in order to know in what particular way it may best meet them. Openness and flexibility of mind are at such a time the first of virtues. *Be ye perfect,* said the Founder of Christianity. . . . Perfection will never be reached; but to recognise a period of transformation when it comes, and to adapt themselves honestly and rationally to its laws, is perhaps the nearest approach to perfection of which men and nations are capable" (II, 29).

7

Ruskin and
Victorian Medievalism

I T IS GONE!" cried Burke in his famous lament over Marie Antoinette.
"The age of chivalry is gone. That of sophisters, economists, and
calculators has succeeded; and the glory of Europe is extinguished forever." Burke was echoing the final speech of Götz von Berlichingen, the
hero of Goethe's drama set at the very end of the fifteenth century: "The
age of frankness and freedom is past—that of treachery begins. The
worthless will gain the upperhand by cunning, and the noble will fall
into their net."[1] Whether or not the age of chivalry ever existed in the
form in which Burke and Goethe envisioned it, it is certainly true that
it was not "gone" but was at that very moment being brought into
existence in the form of the nineteenth-century myth of medievalism. It
was through nostalgia such as theirs for an older, simpler form of society
which was being replaced by the competitive commercialism of the industrial age that this myth arose. Indeed, it was by a simple expansion
of their *topos* that a new literary genre arose in the third decade of the
nineteenth century—the comparison of the medieval and the modern
world to the detriment of the latter.[2] Southey, Cobbett, Pugin, Carlyle,
Ruskin, and Morris all practiced this mode, and we must realize, as we
read their works, that although to them it was a genuinely historical
analysis, they were, in a sense, doing in the historical mode what the
eighteenth century had done by means of a visitor from Persia or China
or a voyage to Lilliput or Brobdingnag. They were criticizing their own
society in the light of an ideal, but because that ideal was not rational-
istically arrived at, it was important to them that it be set not in a distant
land but in the historic past. Whether or not it was strictly "medieval"
did not seem to matter to the writers in question. It could be placed
well into the sixteenth and seventeenth centuries, and Cobbett even
found it in the rural England of his own boyhood. What was important
was that this "old order" which "yieldeth place to new" should be chi-

valric in manners and sentiment, feudal in social structure, agrarian in economy, and unspoiled in the natural scene. Its religious character was an open question.

Throughout the period of the Enlightenment the Middle Ages had been "down." Hume felt a contempt for it. In his view the human mind had reached very nearly its state of perfection about the age of Augustus Caesar and thereafter had declined into "ignorance and barbarism." Society remained in this state for nearly a thousand years, and there was no utility in studying the medieval period, for "the adventures of barbarous nations, even if they were recorded, could afford little or no entertainment to men born in a more cultivated age." Robertson was less contemptuous but regarded the early ages of Scottish history as merely preliminary to the modern period. "Nations, as well as men," he wrote, "arrive at maturity by degrees, and the events, which happened during their infancy or early youth, cannot be recollected, and deserve not to be remembered." Even Hallam, writing as late as 1818 and on the specific subject of the Middle Ages, prefaced his work by saying, "Many considerable portions of time, especially before the twelfth century, may justly be deemed so barren of events worthy of remembrance, that a single sentence or paragraph is often sufficient to give the character of entire generations, and of long dynasties of obscure kings."[3]

It was the new historicist approach which led to the recovery of the Middle Ages. Bishop Hurd, whose *Letters on Chivalry and Romance* (1762) was important in this process, urged that the institution of chivalry should not be condemned as absurd without our enquiring "when, and where, and how it came to pass that the western world became familiarized to this *Prodigy.*" It arose naturally out of feudal society, and Hurd tells us that if we would understand the *Faerie Queene,* we must read it under the idea of a Gothic, not a classical poem. Over the past two hundred years reason has driven out romance, and though England has gained by this revolution "a great deal of good sense," what it has lost is "a world of fine fabling."[4] "Fine fabling" was now coming into its own, and the Middle Ages were its natural habitat. Hence Chatterton's pseudo-medieval Rowley poems, Macpherson's Ossianic bard, the old ballads of Percy's *Reliques,* the Gothic novel and the Gothic revival in architecture, even some aspects of the "graveyard school" of poetry. More dramatic, perhaps, was the recovery of King Arthur. Malory's *Morte d'Arthur* had gone through seven black-letter editions between 1485 and 1634, but then it was not reprinted for nearly two hundred years until, at the height of the Romantic movement, there were three different editions within two years, 1816–17. In the eighteenth century

Arthur had been a semi-comic character. Tennyson, reading as a boy in the tiny duodecimo edition of 1816, drew therefrom the ideal figure he developed in the *Idylls of the King.*

In its earliest phase the medieval revival was primarily literary and picturesque, appealing to the supernatural and the fabulous, but by the second decade of the nineteenth century attention had turned to its social and religious character. Sharon Turner's *History of the Anglo-Saxons* (1799–1805) provided a wealth of new information about the early period; the *History of England* (1819–30) by John Lingard, a Catholic priest, presented the age from a new religious point of view; and Henry Hallam's *View of the State of Europe during the Middle Ages* (1818), though continuing the Enlightenment tradition, emphasized the legal and constitutional aspect of feudalism. Thus, the Middle Ages came to be less and less a world of fable and romance, more a real society that had existed at some time in the past and had virtues and qualities of its own.

Moreover, by the third decade of the nineteenth century the average Englishman was becoming increasingly disenchanted with his own age. As the effects of the Industrial Revolution spread across the land, blackening the once-green fields and crowding people together in factories and tenements, there was a yearning for an older, simpler, agrarian society that seemed idyllic in comparison. The French Revolution had shown how fearfully fragile was the modern social order, and as a corresponding unrest swept across English society in the Peterloo Massacre and the disturbances of the 1830s, there was a longing for some form of community in which people were bound together not just by the "cash nexus." The Catholic Church too was seen as an institution which may once have functioned in a way that the various Protestant sects no longer did. When the new Poor Law was passed in 1834, it seemed as though there ought to be a better solution for poverty than locking able-bodied people up in "workhouses" while the industrious part of the population paid for their upkeep. Thus, there arose what Alice Chandler, the historian of Victorian medievalism, has called "a dream of order," a partly historical, partly mythical vision of the Middle Ages as a society whose indwelling religious faith had manifested itself in a social order, a hierarchy in which every individual had a place, bound together by a system of mutual responsibilities.

Rosemary Jann has noted that this was not the only vision of the Middle Ages in the nineteenth century.[5] There was also the Whig view— put forth by Hallam and Macaulay, by John Kemble in *The Saxons in England* (1849), and later by the Oxford School of William Stubbs,

E. A. Freeman, and J. R. Green—that the free institutions of the Anglo-Saxons, particularly the folkmoot and witenagemot, were the cradle of English liberties, that this tradition had been only briefly interrupted by the absolutism of the Norman Conquest, and that England's future lay in regaining continuity with its native Teutonic heritage and developing it in accordance with the needs of the day. Finally, in the later years of the century, there was a third, socialist view, intuited by Cobbett but developed by Marx, Thorold Rogers, H. M. Hyndman, and William Morris, that as a result of the peasant uprisings in the fourteenth century there had been a brief period of freedom and well-being for the English laborer but that this had been lost in the sixteenth century when the tenants were driven from the land and made the victims of the rising commercial system. There were thus three views of the English medieval past depending on which part of the Middle Ages one invoked: the Whig view, which returned to the Anglo-Saxons; the conservative view, which returned to the feudal system of the Normans; and the radical socialist view, which returned to the brief interval between the decline of the feudal and the rise of the commercial system. In the first third of the centrury, however, it was the conservative view which attracted most attention, partly because of the distinguished literary talents enlisted in that cause and partly because it really did seem, both to conservatives and to radicals, that something had been lost from English society that was very valuable.

The religious question was particularly vexed, for since England during the Middle Ages was Catholic, the question arose how much the peculiar virtues of its social system were to be attributed to the specific form of its religion. Moreover, it happened that the most violently agitated political question of the 1820s was that of Catholic Emancipation, and while this was a purely modern issue, as to whether Irish Catholics should be eligible to take a seat in Parliament, it somehow got involved with the medieval question. It was, for example, the occasion for William Cobbett's writing his *History of the Protestant "Reformation"* (1824–26). Cobbett was a self-educated Englishman of yeoman stock who was a member of the Church of England more because it was English than because it was a church—indeed, he cared not at all for the doctrinal question. But he saw Roman Catholics being vilified and abused by Anglicans and Dissenters who, on the whole, were less sympathetic to reform than they, and on reading Lingard's *History of England* a whole new conception of the national past opened upon him. He saw, or thought he saw, that the Roman Catholic Church prior to the Reformation had not been corrupt, that the Reformation was not a reformation at all but a spoliation or devastation (indeed, he always placed the word within inverted commas in his book), that it was "engendered in beastly lust, brought forth in hypocrisy and perfidy, cherished and fed by plunder."[6] The tithes, originally designed for the support not only of the clergy but also of the poor, had been appropriated by the parsons for themselves. The monasteries and other great religious houses were not merely centers of worship and learning; they also served a useful communal purpose by providing hospitality to the wayfarer, employment to the community, a place of refuge to younger sons and unmarried daughters, and, above all, alms to the poor. The Reformation had destroyed a beneficient institution and put nothing in its place. As a result, in the reign of "Bloody Bess" (Cobbett's name for Queen Elizabeth) Poor Laws were instituted for the first time, and the newly enriched class began its work of funding, stockjobbing, banking, borough-mongering, and tithe-hunting: in fact, the whole system of social and political exploitation and corruption which Cobbett brilliantly called "The Thing." Cobbett's work is far too one-sided to be called history. In fact, it is a political pamphlet masquerading as history, but it was superbly effective. Issued in numbers, it achieved a sale of forty thousand copies in that form and then went on to authorized and pirated editions, to translations into French, Spanish, and other European languages. It swept Ireland and America and in England created the base of popular support which made Catholic Emancipation possible. It also contributed to the thought of Carlyle, Pugin, and Ruskin.[7]

Robert Southey was far too dour a Protestant to be swayed by either Cobbett's short-term or long-term views, and that is perhaps why he goes back only to the Reformation, though to a Catholic representative of that period, Sir Thomas More. By a foolish device which prepares us for the foolishness of some of his conclusions he has the ghost of the great martyr visit him in his study at Keswick, where they prose dreadfully through two volumes over a wide range of subjects. These *Colloquies on the Progress and Prospects of Society* (1829) apparently arose out of Southey's belief that he and More were similarly circumstanced and shared a considerable body of opinion. Both men lived during "one of the grand climacterics of the world," and both had speculated in their youth upon the possible improvement of society. Thus, if they were to compare "the great operating causes in the age of the Reformation, and in this age of revolutions," they might gain insight into the prospects of society. Neither is very hopeful. They agree that Englishmen are less well off in the nineteenth century than their forefathers were when Caesar first invaded the island, but they think there was a point in between—

indeed, precisely during the lifetime of More—when their condition was better than it has been either before or since. "The feudal system had well nigh lost all its inhuman parts, and the worse inhumanity of the commercial system had not yet shown itself." More explains how this could be. "No man in those days could prey upon society. . . . Every person had his place. There was a system of superintendence every where, civil as well as religious. They who were born in villenage, were born to an inheritance of labour, but not of inevitable depravity and wretchedness. If one class were regarded in some respects as cattle, they were at least taken care of: they were trained, fed, sheltered and protected; and there was an eye upon them when they strayed." These comforting reflections are balanced by More's view of the modern world: "The fact is undeniable that the worst principles in religion, in morals, and in politics, are at this time more prevalent than they ever were known to be in any former age."[8]

The flaw in the *Colloquies* is that there is not enough difference of opinion between More and Montesinos (as Southey calls himself for purposes of the dialogue) to produce a clash of opinion. This defect was remedied when Macaulay reviewed the book, as he did in one of his wittiest and most savage essays. He ridicules Southey's idealization of the past and informs him, out of his greater knowledge of the period, exactly what he would have had to eat, how he would have been housed, and what would have been his life expectancy, had he lived at that period. He then casts his eye forward to the year 1930 and prophesies the marvels of wealth, technology, and social organization that will have been ushered in by that date. He did not hit it right in every particular, but even those who prefer Sir Thomas More to Macaulay will hardly say that on this point Southey won the argument.

Though Southey saw an analogy between his age and the Reformation, the Victorian medievalists generally saw only a contrast. As we have already noted, they used history as a mirror only in the sense in which Hamlet shows his mother her own soul by holding up before her contrasting pictures of her former and her present husband. "Look here upon this picture, and on this." Such is literally the method of A. Welby Pugin in *Contrasts* (1836), a biting, satiric work which presents a series of plates contrasting "the Noble Edifices of the Middle Ages, and Corresponding Buildings of the Present Day."[9] These plates, of which there are twelve in the first edition and fifteen in the second, present dual images of parochial churches, royal chapels, altar screens, sepulchral monuments, college gateways, episcopal residences, town halls, public inns, market crosses, and even public conduits as they were handled by the great architects of the Middle Ages and the "leading men of the day." All is then summarized in a print depicting a "Catholic town in 1440" and "the same town in 1840." In the former all of the sixteen numbered buildings except the guildhall bear the name of a saint, suggesting the religious unity out of which the pointed architecture arises, whereas in the latter these buildings are replaced by Mr. Evan's Chapel, the Unitarian Chapel, New Church, the Wesleyan Centenary Chapel, the New Christian Society, the Quakers' Meeting, and the Socialist Hall of Science. What was once pleasant open ground is now encumbered by the gas works, the iron works, and, looming up in the front of the picture, the New Jail and the Lunatic Asylum. Pugin was a recent convert to Catholicism, and his main point is that it was the spirit of the Catholic religion that gave rise to Gothic architecture and that only a renewed faith will revive it again.

One of the plates which Pugin introduced into his second edition (1841) is entitled "Contrasted Residences for the Poor." One feels that Carlyle may well have consulted it before writing *Past and Present* (1843), for it embodies essentially the same contrast which he encountered in the Workhouse at St. Ives and the Abbey of St. Edmundsbury. The "Modern Poor House" consists of a Benthamite Panopticon, laid out like the spokes of a wheel so that a single warden can keep his eye on a variety of inmates. The "Antient Poor House," on the other hand, is a spacious monastic establishment set amid pleasant fields with gardens and orchards and a great Gothic church towering up at one side. Carlyle would have agreed with the contrast, but he would have agreed with Pugin on little else. For he did not want to take England back to the Middle Ages but rather forward to the new faith which would animate a very different future. The portion of Carlyle's work which deals with the past presents the image not of an organic society but of a man, Abbot Samson, whipping together a totally disorganized society by means of his indomitable will. Indeed, one of the reasons why Carlyle's work fits in so poorly with Victorian medievalism is that it was not based on an idealized vision of the Middle Ages but on a real twelfth-century chronicle, that of Jocelin of Brakelond, who shows the monks and their contemporaries quarreling as vigorously about money and privilege as any members of a commercial society. *Past and Present* was certainly read by the Victorians as a "medieval" work, but it presents a good example of how the pervasive metaphor of the Middle Ages caught up some nineteenth-century thinkers whose real intellectual affinities lay elsewhere.

In the very year in which Carlyle was writing *Past and Present,* Disraeli was forming his Young England group which, in reaction to the "Toryism without principle" of Peel, attempted to rally the younger aristocrats to a sense of their social responsibilities so that they would bridge the gap between the "Two Nations" of the rich and the poor. "There is no community in England," laments one of the characters in *Sybil*; "there is aggregation, but aggregation under circumstances which make it rather a dissociating than a uniting principle."[10] The Young Englanders were partly influenced by a strange young Irish antiquary, Kenelm Henry Digby, who as an undergraduate at Cambridge studied medieval romances until (one is tempted to say) his brains were addled and he produced a book entitled *The Broad Stone of Honour, or Rules for the Gentlemen of England* (1822). He is a kind of nineteenth-century Don Quixote, for his aim was to provide the youth of England with a code of chivalric conduct which would teach them the lessons "of piety and heroism, of loyalty, generosity, and honour." He must have succeeded to some degree, for Julius Hare declared that, had he a son, he would place the book in his hands, charging him to love it next to his Bible. Even in its longer four-volume edition it was read and prized by many Victorians, including Ruskin, Morris, and Burne-Jones, well into the third quarter of the century. It may also have been responsible, however, for some absurdities, including the medieval tournament which the Earl of Eglinton staged at his castle in the north of England in August 1839. This famous affair, which was attended by tens of thousands of spectators and featured jousts between knights on horseback in full armor, a Queen of Beauty, jesters, heralds, pavilions, and a banquet replete with roast boar, was turned into a fiasco by two days of torrential rain which reduced the lists to a sea of mud. Mark Girouard suggests that the image of knights on horseback holding green umbrellas over their dripping steeds put an end to the more absurd manifestations of Victorian medievalism—but only to those.[11]

The most intense period of Victorian medievalism ran from the late 1820s to 1850s, and, given the fact that its practitioners had so little in common—they included Tories and radicals, Roman Catholics and Dissenters, aristocrats and commoners—it can only be explained as a reaction against the forces dominating English life at this time: the Whigs, Utilitarians, and liberal reformers. Disliking intensely what they saw taking place in England, they took refuge in another age, and that age was large enough, various enough, sufficiently unknown and even mythical, that each person could find there what he wanted—a hierarchy, a community, a code of conduct, a form of hero-worship, a system of ritual, a charitable establishment, a style of architecture, a resplendent wardrobe. Victorian medievalism meant many different things to different people, and there is no question but that the metaphor attracted some adherents whose real affinities lay elsewhere. It is also true that Victorian medievalism is rather different from some of the other uses of history that we are concerned with in this book. For one thing, it was peculiarly static. The Middle Ages seem not to have been related by their admirers to the present by any process of historic change but are simply set over against the present as an ideal or paradigm. That is perhaps why there is so much emphasis on costume, armor, castles, feudal relations, hierarchy, and ritual—and so little on events. It is a fully formed "state of society," a "dream of order." For this reason the image of the mirror, as we have noted, is strictly inappropriate. Yet Carlyle continues to use it in *Past and Present,*[12] apparently feeling that he saw something in Jocelin's Chronicle that pertained to his own age, even if it was a reverse image, an image of what was not. "The nineteenth century dislike of Realism," said Wilde, "is the rage of Caliban seeing his own face in a glass. The nineteenth century dislike of Romanticism is the rage of Caliban not seeing his own face in a glass."[13]

Ruskin began writing in the early 1840s just as this movement culminated, and he inherited the whole of it. He did not begin, however, as a medievalist but as an interpreter of modern art. It is, indeed, a paradox that his first volume should be called *Modern Painters,* for, as Cook and Wedderburn point out in the Index to the Library Edition of his works, "To collect in one article all references to Ruskin's indictments of modernism would involve much repetition."[14] Originally, it had been Ruskin's intention to call his work *Turner and the Ancients,* as if it were a part of the Quarrel of the Ancients and the Moderns, and he did not intend to refer to any modern painter other than Turner. But then, "in deference to the advice of friends" (VII, 441n) (presumably his father), he altered his title to *Modern Painters: Their Superiority in the Art of Landscape Painting to all the Ancient Masters proved by examples of the True, the Beautiful, and the Intellectual, from the Works of Modern Artists, especially from those of J. M. W. Turner, Esq., R. A.* (1843). It should be understood that by "Ancient Masters" he did not mean Leonardo, Michelangelo, and Raphael but those seventeenth- and eighteenth-century Dutch and French masters whose conventional representations of nature had been praised above Turner's. By "Modern Artists" he meant a group of English landscape painters whom he took to form a school along with Turner.[15] But then in 1845 he traveled to Italy and began for the first time to learn something about the history of art and indeed about history in general. "Formerly," he wrote to his father, "I hated history, now I am always at Sismondi [*Histoire des républiques Italiennes du moyen âge* (1807–18)]. I had not the slightest interest in polit[ica]l science, now I am studying the constitutions of Ital[y with] great interest." If he were to go back to college now, he declared, "the histories & mysteries, and myths, which were a mere task, would now be a subject of real pleasurable investigation—my mind is strangely developed within these two years."[16] In preparation for the journey he had read Alexis François Rio's *De la poésie chrétienne dans son principe, dans sa matière et dans ses formes* (1836), a work of the Catholic reaction, which states in its opening paragraph that it is written from a rather different point of view than the ordinary formalist histories of art. For "if it were only a question of imitating nature more or less faithfully by lines and colors, what would it matter to the happiness or dignity of the human species if this imitation were crude in one age and admirable in another?"[17] The *history* of art is significant only when one regards it as the vehicle of man's moral and religious aspirations. Despite Ruskin's view that nature was the revelation of God, he could not but feel that his exclusive preoccupation with Turner's "truth" relative to that of his predecessors was rather narrow, and so he saw the early Italian painters with a new eye. Indeed, he saw the world around him with a new eye. Whereas previously he had treated the whining of the beggars as a nuisance or at best had seen their distress "more as picturesque than as real,"[18] now he saw it as real. They were the hideous present in contrast to the glorious past, and architecture, which at once was tumbling down and being restored out of existence, was the connection between the two. By 1848, when the combined efforts of revolutionaries and restorers seemed to threaten all the heritage of the great cathedrals, Ruskin's evolution was complete. He had shifted his attention from nature to man in society, from beauty and truth in the abstract to beauty and truth in history. It was the crisis of 1848 and the years following that focused his attention upon the past, just as it had been the crisis of 1832–33 that did the same for Mill, Carlyle, Newman, and Thomas Arnold.

Hence, *The Stones of Venice* (1851–53), the product of this new outlook, begins with these prophetic words:

> Since first the dominion of men was asserted over the ocean, three thrones, of mark beyond all others, have been set upon its sands: the thrones of Tyre, Venice, and England. Of the First of these great powers only the memory remains; of the Second, the ruin; the Third, which

inherits their greatness, if it forget their example, may be led through
prouder eminence to less pitied destruction. (IX, 17)

Ruskin feels like Milton, who, as he sees Satan approach the Garden of
Eden, cries, "O for that warning voice, which he who saw / Th' *Apocalypse,* heard cry in Heav'n aloud." Of what does he wish to warn England? Doubtless of many things, for Ruskin has described himself as
"a Tory of the old school" (XXXV, 13), that is, of the school of Sir
Walter Scott and Homer, who believed in the traditional virtues and in
the religious and political sanctions which enforce them. He sees a generally liberal England moving in a direction which he, a "violent Il-
liberal" (XXVII, 14–15), cannot countenance. In particular, he is
concerned about the English reaction to the so-called "Papal Aggression."[19] The Pope had decided in October 1850 to re-establish the Catholic hierarchy in England, and a letter from Cardinal Wiseman
announcing this fact, imprudently dated "from without the Flaminian
Gate," had provoked a violent anti-Catholic reaction. Lord Russell
brought in an Ecclesiastical Titles Bill designed to prevent the Catholic
bishops from taking up the titles assigned to them, but it ran into
trouble with the Irish and Catholic members of Parliament and the
Peelite Tories. A muted reference in the first chapter of the *Stones of
Venice* to "the temper of our present English legislature" (IX, 27) indicates the fury Ruskin felt that Parliament could hesitate over so obvious a measure. Letting Irish Catholics into Parliament in the first place
by the Act of 1829 had been bad enough; now its consequences were
apparent. It was clear that religious toleration was religious indifference,
for whereas a purely Anglican legislature could extend the national faith
to national policy, a polyglot legislature could only act on secular principles. Ruskin thought he saw an ominous parallel between what was
about to happen in England and what had happened in Venice over four
hundred years before.

The day on which the fall of Venice commenced, according to Ruskin, was May 8, 1418, the date of the death of Carlo Zeno, soldier-hero
of the Republic. Since Zeno's passing is not otherwise celebrated by
historians of Venice, one may wonder why Ruskin gave it this importance.[20] Doubtless part of his reason was his predilection for precise
dates, and perhaps also a desire to do honor to this octogenarian hero
who had died just after a pilgrimage to the Holy Land. But the reason
for his choice of that decade is made apparent in Appendix 5; it was
then that Venice, in a spirit of secularism and religious neutrality, began
systematically to exclude the representatives of the Papacy from the

grand Council (IX, 420–22). "Now, let it be observed," says Ruskin, "that the enforcement of absolute exclusion of the clergy from the councils of the State, dates exactly from the period which I have marked for the commencement of the decline of the Venetian power" (IX, 423). It might be thought, in view of Ruskin's attitude toward the Papal Aggression that he would have welcomed this gesture of independence on the part of the Venetians, but in Venice the Roman Catholic religion was the national religion and therefore to exclude representatives of the Papacy was to exclude religion altogether. Individual Venetians of course remained staunch in their faith, but "the stopping short of this religious faith when it appears likely to influence national action" seems to Ruskin "correspondent . . . and that most strikingly" (IX, 27) to the situation in England. "If they were to blame, in yielding to their fear of the ambitious spirit of Rome so far as to deprive their councils of all religious element, what excuse are we to offer for the state, which, with Lords Spiritual of her own faith already in her senate, permits the polity of Rome to be represented by lay members?" (IX, 423). The source of the evil is the Emancipation Act of 1829.

Venice fell, then, because as a nation it had turned away from its religious faith to the pride and infidelity, the worldliness and corruption, that constitute the Renaissance. Ruskin had learned from Rio to see this change reflected in Italian painting; now he saw it even more graphically in Venetian architecture. England was squarely in the Renaissance tradition, and Venice was a particularly good object-lesson because she had become a byword in song and story for a debased and depraved beauty. In Shakespeare and Otway, in the dramas of Byron and the poetry of Rogers, her glory and her corruption are celebrated, and the process by which the Queen of the Adriatic became the Whore of Venice is Ruskin's theme. "Now Venice," he wrote, "as she was once the most religious, was in her fall the most corrupt, of European states; and as she was in her strength the centre of the pure currents of Christian architecture, so she is in her decline the source of the Renaissance. . . . It is in Venice, therefore, and in Venice only, that effectual blows can be struck at this pestilent art of the Renaissace" (IX, 46–47).

Ruskin notes that "the history of Venice divides itself, with more sharpness than any other I have read, into periods of distinct tendency and character" (XXIV, 240). For example, the first period, after its independence from the cities of old Venetia, lasted six hundred years, from 697 to 1297—to be exact, February 28, 1297. The second period lasted five hundred years (or rather 501), from 1297 to 1798, when a French general declared an end to the Republic. In a later sketch of Venetian history in *St. Mark's Rest* Ruskin divided the narrative into four periods, of which the first ran from the fifth to the eleventh century—"Accurately, from the Annunciation day, March 25th, 421, to the day of St. Nicholas, December 6th, 1100" (XXIV, 254). The second period, which is characterized by the religious passion of the Crusades, "lasts, in accurate terms, from December 6th, 1100, to February 28th, 1297; but as the event of that day [the closing of the Council] was not confirmed till three years afterwards, we get the fortunately precise terminal date of 1301" (XXIV, 254–55). Ruskin rejoices in these round numbers, partly for pedagogical reasons but also because he sees in them the hand of Providence. It is, for example, "to my mind a most touching and impressive Divine appointment" that "there is a kind of central year about which we may consider the energy of the Middle Ages to be gathered; a kind of focus of time, which . . . has been marked for us by the greatest writer of the Middle Ages, in the first words he utters; namely, the year 1300, the 'mezzo del cammin' of the life of Dante. Now, therefore, to Giotto, the contemporary of Dante, who drew Dante's still existing portrait in this very year, 1300, we may always look for the central mediæval idea in any subject" (X, 400–01). The central idea in this case is that Giotto represents Cupid as one of the companions of Satan and Death, whereas the Renaissance artists represent him as the plaything of the Graces. Finally, if the Middle Ages may be fixed around the year 1300, the Renaissance may also be dated, for it began in Venice on March 27, 1424, when the first hammer was lifted up against the old palace of Ziani. "That hammer stroke was the first act of the period properly called the 'Renaissance.' It was the knell of the architecture of Venice,—and of Venice herself" (X, 352).

Ruskin draws our attention to a whole series of these crucial moments. The tomb of the Doge Tomaso Mocenigo, who died in 1423, only five years after the commencement of the Fall, is dignified and true; but when Ruskin put a ladder up to the tomb of the Doge Andrea Vendramin, who died in 1478 after a short reign of two disastrous years, he found that the sculptor had not bothered to finish the hand or the side of the face turned towards the wall. The effigy was, in short, a "base and senseless lie," and he thought it not insignificant that the author of this culminating pride of Renaissance art *"was banished from Venice for forgery in 1487"* (IX, 52, Ruskin's italics). Or take the case of the capitals of the Ducal Palace. Those on the seaward side and some of those on the Piazzetta side are fourteenth-century work; the rest are of the fifteenth century. The fifteenth-century architect, however, who built under Foscari in 1424 (six years after the commencement of the Fall), had not wit enough to invent new capitals and so copied the old. Several of these represent the eight Virtues, of which one, in the original, shows Hope praying, while above her hand is seen emerging from the sunbeams the hand of God. In the fifteenth-century copy, however, Hope is praying to the sun only: *"The hand of God is gone."* "Is not this a curious and striking type," says Ruskin, "of the spirit which had then become dominant in the world, forgetting to see God's hand in the light He gave; so that in the issue, when that light opened into the Reformation on the one side, and into full knowledge of ancient literature on the other, the one was arrested and the other perverted?" (IX, 55). Finally, of the three sculptures at the three principal angles of the Ducal Palace, the first two, which belong to "the old, or true Gothic, Palace," have as their subject the Fall of Man and the Drunkenness of Noah, whereas the third, which belongs to the Renaissance imitation, has as its subject the Judgment of Solomon. "It is impossible to overstate . . . ," says Ruskin, "the significance of this single fact. It is as if the palace had been built at various epochs, and preserved uninjured to this day, for the sole purpose of teaching us the difference in the temper of the two schools" (X, 359).

Ruskin declared that he devoted so much time to Venice, not because her architecture is the best in existence, but because "it exemplifies, in the smallest compass, the most interesting facts of architectural history" (VIII, 13). The Ducal Palace in particular was "the central building of the world" (IX, 38). Moreover, the history of its religion and policy were "intense abstracts of the same course of thought and events in every nation of Europe. Throughout the whole of Christendom, the two stories in like manner proceed together. The acceptance of Christianity—the practice of it—the abandonment of it—and moral ruin. The development of kingly authority—the obedience to it—the corruption of it—and social ruin" (XXIV, 258). Thus, when he turned to the northern Gothic, both before and after writing *The Stones of Venice,* he found the same evolution, from medieval purity to Renaissance pride. It is illustrated in the evolution of tracery. Tracery arose from the gradual enlargement of the penetrations of the stone in the head of early windows. "Now, it will be noticed that, during the whole of this process, the attention is kept fixed on the forms of the penetrations, that is to say, of the lights as seen from the interior, not of the intermediate stone. All the grace of the window is in the outline of its light . . . , at first in far off and separate stars, and then gradually enlarging, approaching, until they come and stand over us, as it were, filling the whole space with their effulgence." It is no accident that

Ruskin speaks here almost as if it were the eve of Christ's nativity, for "it is in this pause of the star, that we have the great, pure, and perfect form of French Gothic" (VIII, 88–89). Unfortunately, that pause did not last fifty years. The perfect form of it is to be found in a panel decoration in the north door at Rouen. Up to the time of that panel the architect's eye had been on the openings only, on the stars of light. But then the stone "flashed out in an instant, as an independent form," and the line was substituted for the mass as the new principle in decoration. It was the most important change ever made, says Ruskin, in the spirit of Gothic architecture, and it was not gradual but sudden. It was "as marked, as clear, as conspicuous to the distant view of after times, as to the distant glance of a traveller is the culminating ridge of the mountain chain over which he has passed. It was the great watershed of Gothic art" (VIII, 89–91).

The same development occurred in the treatment of moldings, which were originally considered (as they actually are) stiff and unyielding, but were then regarded as ductile, even penetrable, and allowed to pass through one another when their paths coincided. This form of falsity destroyed Gothic architecture. When it "lost its essence as a structure of stone," then "fell the great dynasty of mediæval architecture. . . . It was not because its time was come; it was not because it was scorned by the classical Romanist, or dreaded by the faithful Protestant. That scorn and that fear it might have survived and lived; . . . but its own truth was gone, and it sank for ever" (VIII, 92, 98).

Why it is that a great art no sooner achieves perfection than it passes beyond it is a mystery, but Ruskin had no doubt that it was so. In a lecture on "The Deteriorative Power of Conventional Art over Nations" (1858) he declares that we find everywhere this "apparent connection of great success in art with subsequent national degradation." It is not merely that nations which possess a refined art are always subdued by those who possess none, as the Lydian by the Mede, the Athenian by the Spartan, the Greek by the Roman, and the Roman by the Goth. It is also that "even where no attack by any external power has accelerated the catastrophe of the state, the period in which any given people reach their highest power in art is precisely that in which they appear to sign the warrant of their own ruin; and that from the moment in which a perfect statue appears in Florence, a perfect picture in Venice, or a perfect fresco in Rome, from that hour forward, probity, industry, and courage seem to be exiled from their walls, and they perish in a sculpturesque paralysis, or a many-coloured corruption" (XVI, 263–64). The ultimate reason for this is the self-regarding or solipsistic tendency of art. The artist's duty is to exhibit and interpret the great objective facts of God, nature, and human life, and so long as he keeps his gaze steadily upon them he has before him an element of the infinite which he can never fully compass, and so he continues to live and grow. "But a time has always hitherto come," says Ruskin—hoping, perhaps, that one day it will not come—"in which, having thus reached a singular perfection, [art] begins to contemplate that perfection, and to imitate it, and deduce rules and forms from it; and thus to forget her duty and ministry as the interpreter and discoverer of Truth. And in the very instant when this diversion of her purpose and forgetfulness of her function take place— . . . in that instant, I say, begins her actual catastrophe; and by her own fall—so far as she has influence—she accelerates the ruin of the nation by which she is practised" (XVI, 269). Ruskin calls it a "fall," and indeed this turning away from God to self is the very act by which Satan, and Adam and Eve in the Garden, fell. In history it is a part of the dynamic of human life.

It is in the chapter "The Nature of Gothic" that Ruskin lays out his distinction between the "glory of the imperfect" and the deadliness of perfection and associates the former with the art of the Middle Ages, the latter with the Renaissance. The terminology is deliberately paradoxical (X, 202), and doubtless the chapter would lose much of its power if Ruskin had said simply that he preferred asymmetrical art to symmetrical, an element of the infinite to the finite, Romantic art to neoclassical. Purely as aesthetic analysis, however, it would have been better if he had adopted a more neutral and simply descriptive terminology, for we are inclined to wonder, if the rude technique of the Gothic workman succeeds in shadowing forth his conception of infinitude, whether that technique, far from being "imperfect," is not indeed perfect for its peculiar purpose. How could one know what the Gothic workman was trying to express unless he had in fact expressed it? and in that case his technique must not be rude and imperfect but rather highly sophisticated. In an earlier treatment of the subject in volume I Ruskin conceded that it was difficult to tell when this apparent imperfection was due to incapacity and when it was due to a deliberate simplification—to an abstraction and stylization by the architect of the object to be represented. But in "The Nature of Gothic" he returns to the idea of imperfection, attributing it on the one hand to the Christian humility of the workman, who offers, with trembling hands, his unworthy gift to the greater glory of God, and, on the other, to the understanding of the master, who accepts his humble gift as of greater worth than dead perfection. Ruskin is now more interested in the internal elements of Gothic than in its external forms, and he asserts that the nobleness of Gothic depends on the "happiness" of the workman. It is apparent that a powerful social purpose has disturbed this part of the book, and indeed this is the part in which the present bears most powerfully upon the past. The modern factory worker insensibly displaces the medieval artisan in the discussion, despite the fact that they are not really parallel. Cathedrals have never been mass-produced in any age, nor is it to be expected that the manufacture of pins should parallel that of gargoyles. Nevertheless, this is the contrast that Ruskin makes, between the medieval artist who, in Ruskin's view, is responsible for the entire process of his art and so remains a fully integrated human being, and the modern factory worker who, fragmented by the new technique of the division of labor, performs one minute, mechanical task over and over and so is alienated both from himself and society. In Ruskin's view it is this, rather than the worker's economic condition, that has turned him into a revolutionary (X, 194), and it is revolution that Ruskin fears. That probably explains why he has adopted a political metaphor to describe the three great systems of architectural ornament: the Servile, the Constitutional, and the Revolutionary.

The metaphor applies to the degree of subordination or insubordination both of the ornament to the overall design and of the workman to the master architect. Through the latter application it becomes a history of labor relations through the ages. In the Servile system of ornament found in Assyrian, Egyptian, and, to a lesser extent, Greek architecture, the executive power of the workman is absolutely subordinated to the inventive power of the builder. The workman is, in fact, a slave. The task of the builder, therefore, is to simplify his designs to the capacity of the worker, train him to a rigid standard of excellence, and so secure a product that is perfect within its kind. We may admire it, but it is impossible to go back to it, because it is based upon a ruthless political absolutism.

The medieval or Constitutional system of ornament is based upon the Christian philosophy which, recognizing the value of the individual human soul but also its fallen condition, gives full rein to the creative energies of the workman but within the limits of an overall conception. In other words, it was a voluntary rather than an enforced subjection of the executive to the conceptive power. Exactly how a harmonious whole is to arise out of inharmonious parts is a problem which Ruskin solves differently in the different places in which he treats it. In the *Seven Lamps of Architecture* he seems to accept Sir Charles Eastlake's "noble principle" that the fullest realization in sculpture shall be of the noblest object, that is, of human figures above animals, of animals above plants, and that this "graduated scale of abstraction" (VIII, 173–75) will unite the parts with the whole. But then again he will say that in the medieval system "everything is realised as far as possible, leaves, birds, and lizards, quite as carefully as men and quadrupeds," and that "the subordination is chiefly effected by symmetries of arrangement, and quaintnesses of treatment" (IX, 286–88). Nonetheless, he warns against the "dangers" of full realization and suggests several "safe-guards," as if he thought revolution were in the offing, though whether on the part of the workmen or the ornaments is uncertain. In "The Nature of Gothic," however, he puts all these problems behind him and depends simply on the spirit of religion, which animates both workman and builder to bring their work to a glorious issue.

It is odd that Ruskin should use the term *Constitutional,* which is an eighteenth- and nineteenth-century term of Whig political theory, to describe the ornament of the Middle Ages. *Feudal* would have been more exact and would have revealed how far he was idealizing the Gothic workman. But he has transplanted the whole question into the modern world, describing the Middle Ages with a term that properly applies to British politics following the Revolution of 1688 and describing the Renaissance with a term freighted with the fears of 1789 and 1848. Like *Constitutional,* the term *Revolutionary* does not quite fit. For one would expect that Revolutionary ornament would be that in which both the ornament and the inferior workman would rise up and revolt against the overall design and the designing mind. Presumably something like the Reign of Terror ought to result. It is true that this does result in the sense that the workman is now equalized with the master and the inferior ornament becomes principal (X, 189). If Servile ornament is enforced submission and Constitutional ornament is voluntary submission, then Renaissance ornament is willful self-assertion. But it is self-assertion in the name of perfection. The new perfectionism is on a higher level than that of the Servile system, for the slave is now educated: he produces "educated imbecilities"—the scrolls and flowers, the shields and grapes which adorn Renaissance buildings from St. Peter's to Regent Street. This "relentless requirement of perfection," which arises in Renaissance architecture, is "the first cause of the fall of the arts of Europe" (X, 204); but it is odd to call it revolutionary. One would have thought that the "Savageness" of Gothic more nearly merited that title. Ruskin is, of course, drawing upon Catholic reactionary thought which found the seeds of the French Revolution in the Renaissance, but more to the point is the fact that he hated the Renaissance and feared revolution.

The problem is in relating Ruskin's metaphorical revolution in ornament to his fear of real revolution in the land. For although he was clear that nineteenth-century architecture was still in the Renaissance tradition (XI, 4, 45)—the line goes direct from Palladio to Gower Street—the modern factory worker was not already a revolutionary; rather he was so much a slave that Ruskin feared his becoming a revolutionary. The parallel to the factory worker making pins or glass beads is the Greek helot cutting beads and dentils by rule and line, and this *is* the parallel that Ruskin draws (X, 190, 193, 202). Though England in its art might be in the egregious moral state of Renaissance ornament, its factory workers were in the oppressed condition of Greek or Assyrian slaves. Economically, England was a throwback to pagan antiquity, and what was needed was to bring it up into the modern world. Something comparable in the arts and the economy to the constitutional government England had achieved in the eighteenth century was what England wanted, and that was to be found in the Middle Ages. It is a mixed bag of metaphors, but then it is a complicated social and historical situation, about which Ruskin felt deeply.

Ruskin was confronted with one profound dilemma in his treatment of medieval and Renaissance architecture, namely, that medieval architecture was the outgrowth of the Catholic faith and Renaissance architecture was contemporaneous with the Reformation. This dilemma had been posed by Pugin and was implied by the association of the Gothic Revival with the Tractarian movement, but it was the purpose of Ruskin in the *Seven Lamps of Architecture* to resolve it and to reclaim medieval architecture for Protestantism. He did this by asserting that prior to the Reformation the Church was simply the Church Universal and that not until it was corrupted by Romish superstition did any stigma attach to it. At that point it was confronted by two great and opposite powers, the Reformation in the north and the Revival of Letters in the south. The former was an unlettered movement which, attempting to purify the church, rejected the arts associated with it, much to its own injury; whereas the latter was a pagan and rationalistic movement which, attempting to refine and sophisticate the external form of the church, continued its internal corruption (IX, 44–45, 58; XIX, 247–48). Between Paganism on the one side and Rationalism on the other the arts of the sixteenth to eighteenth centuries were divided, and no good had been done. Ruskin's desire was to recover for the impoverished Evangelical chapels of his own day the uncorrupted heritage of the medieval church.

R. G. Collingwood, attempting to answer the question whether Ruskin had a nucleus of ideas which might be called a philosophy, declared that he did and that it belonged not to the traditional, empirical philosophy of Britain but to the newer continental school of historicism. "Of this historical movement Ruskin was a whole-hearted adherent, and every detail of his work is coloured and influenced by the fact. In a quite real sense he was a Hegelian." Collingwood hastens to add that Ruskin had not read Hegel, a fact which was confirmed by his father, W. G. Collingwood, who was Ruskin's secretary and who, also believing in the Hegelian influence, had asserted that it must have been "gathered orally from some enthusiastic friend."[21] The single reference to Hegel in the Index to the *Works* suggests it was not very explicit. The most important parallel between Ruskin and Hegel is in the law of contradiction. Like Plato and Aristotle, Ruskin believed that truth is arrived at dialectically through a series of contrary propositions, but, unlike Hegel, he did not apply this process to history. Servile and Revolutionary ornament are the thesis and antithesis of a system of which Constitutional ornament is the synthesis—but historically the synthesis came *before* the antithesis. Of course, one could posit a Revolutionary phase (perhaps the Barbarian invasions or Alexandrianism) between the Servile and the Constitutional, or a Servile phase (neoclassicism) between the Renaissance and the new synthesis of Romanticism. That would accord reasonably well with the facts and perhaps is what Ruskin ought to have said. But he did not say it and his thinking does not take that form. He does not share Hegel's optimism that the Idea works itself out in history. Rather, believing in a myth of the Fall, he thinks of going back in history for his synthesis. The synthesis—or perhaps one should call it a mean between two extremes—is something to be recovered from the past rather than worked out in the future.

This fact may be illustrated by two other triadic groups presented in "The Nature of Gothic." The first divides all men, with respect to their artistic qualifications, into three great classes: men of facts, men of design, and men of both. Ruskin admits that these classes "pass into each other by imperceptible gradations" (X, 217); still there is a difference between the person who primarily wishes to convey accurate information about the tendrils of a vine and the person who dimly suggests these tendrils in the course of creating a design. The great Gothic builders of the Ducal Palace did both, and that is the highest form of art. The two extremes are both healthy unless the men of fact or design either despise or envy their opposite, and then one gets such dangerous errors as Chinese ornament on the one hand or Dutch painting on the other. The great pre-Raphaelite painters of earlier ages are healthy examples of men of design.

The second triad considers these same three classes with respect to their pursuit of facts and, assuming that nature presents them with a mixed spectacle of good and evil, divides them according to their tendency to filter out the evil and present only the good (the Purists), to dwell eagerly upon the evil (the Sensualists), or to render all that they see in nature unhesitatingly, sympathizing with the good and yet confessing and permitting the evil (the Naturalists). As with the earlier triad there is a quasi-historical distribution of painters among these groups. To the Purists belong the early Italian and Flemish painters, Angelico, Memling, Perugino, Francia, Gozzoli, Raphael "in his best time," Giovanni Bellini, and the modern English artist Stothard. To the Naturalists belong Giotto, Orcagna, Michelangelo, Leonardo, Tintoretto, Hogarth, and Turner. Raphael "in his second time," Titian, and Rubens are transitional. To the Sensualists belong Salvator Rosa, Caravaggio, Murillo, Zurbaran, Procaccini, Rembrandt, and Teniers (X, 222–23, 231, 231n; cf. V, 103–08). There is obviously an analogy between the Purists and the men of design, the Sensualists and the men of fact, and the Naturalists and the men of both fact and design. The Purists depend upon symbol to depict the spiritual good with which they are primarily concerned, the Sensualists are inevitably drawn to material fact by their preoccupation with evil, and the Naturalists are concerned with both fact and design. There is a less complete analogy, however, between these two triads and the systems of architectural ornament, for although the Revolutionary corresponds to the Sensualist and some men of fact, the Servile corresponds only to the debased form of Purist and the men of design. Furthermore, it requires two categories in painting, the Purists and the Naturalists, to cover the medieval period covered by the one category, Constitutional, in architecture. This means that for Ruskin the Fall in painting could not occur at the same date that it did in architecture.

In *The Stones of Venice* Ruskin had attempted to correlate the two events. "It will be remembered," he declared, "that I put the commencement of the Fall of Venice as far back as 1418." He then notes that Giovanni Bellini was born in 1423 and that he and his brother Gentile "close the line of the sacred painters of Venice." "The most solemn spirit of religious faith animates their works to the last." But Titian was born in 1480, and "there is no religion in any work of Titian's." This was not because Giovanni Bellini was a religious man and Titian was not; it was because both were thoroughly representative of the ages in which they were brought up and "Bellini was brought up in faith; Titian in formalism. Between the years of their births the vital religion of Venice had expired" (IX, 31). The same is true of Tintoretto, born a generation later than Titian. "The mind of Tintoret, incomparably more deep and serious than that of Titian, casts the solemnity of its own tone over the sacred subjects which it approaches, and sometimes forgets itself into devotion; but the principle of treatment is altogether the same as Titian's: absolute subordination of the religious subject to purposes of decoration or portraiture." So too with Veronese and every succeeding painter: "the fifteenth century had taken away the religious heart of Venice" (IX, 32).

Ruskin must have written these words with anguish and uncertainty, for when he had first come to Venice in 1845 he had been "overwhelmed" by Tintoretto. He had begun his education in Italian art in Florence at the feet of Fra Angelico. Being still in his narrow Evangelical phase, he found his *Annunciation and Adoration of the Magi* "as near heaven as human hand or mind will ever, or can ever go." Beside him "Perugino is prosaic—and Raphael sensual." Raphael and Michelangelo were "great fellows, but from all I can see they have been the ruin of art."[22] It was, indeed, in the very midst of Raphael's painting of the Stanza del Segnatura that the Fall of Italian art occurred. With his penchant for round numbers Ruskin observes that it was "in *the very centre of [Raphael's] available life,*" that is, halfway between the age of twelve (the age at which Christ went up to the temple at Jerusalem) and Raphael's death at thirty-seven, that he was summoned to Rome to decorate the Vatican for Pope Julius II, and "having until that time worked exclusively in the ancient and stern mediæval manner, he, in the first chamber which he decorated in that palace, wrote upon its walls the *Mene, Tekel, Upharsin* of the Arts of Christianity." He wrote it in this manner, says Ruskin. "On one wall of that chamber he placed a picture of the World or Kingdom of *Theology,* presided over by *Christ.* And on the side wall of that same chamber he placed the World or Kingdom of *Poetry,* presided over by *Apollo.* And from that spot, and from that hour, the intellect and the art of Italy date their degradation" (XII, 148). The significance of this act is not in the mere use of the figure of a heathen god to indicate the domain of poetry—for such use had been made in the best times of Christian art—but in the fact that Raphael, in the very palace of the "so-called" head of the Church, *"elevated the creations of fancy on the one wall, to the same rank as the objects of faith upon the other."*

"The doom of the arts of Europe went forth from that chamber" (XII, 149–50).

As a result Ruskin split Raphael in two and placed half of him in the highest and half of him in the lowest of his categories of painters. For during his study at Florence in the summer of 1845 he had arrived, he told his father, at "my scale of painters. I may shift about here & there a little—I am not sure of the places of all—but I regard them pretty nearly in this order, and I shall not alter very much." He then gives four classes of painters, with the individuals within each class ranked by number. The first class is "Pure Religious art. The School of Love"—obviously the group that will later become the Purists. First among them is Fra Angelico—"Forms a class by himself—he is not an *artist,* properly so called, but an inspired saint." The second class is a groping attempt to define the Naturalists: "General Perception of Nature human & divine, accompanied by more or less religious feeling. The School of the *Great* Men. The School of Intellect." Included are 1. Michelangelo, 2. Giotto, 3. Orcagna, 4. Benozzo, 5. Leonardo, 6. Ghirlandajo, and 7. Masaccio. The third class is "The School of *Painting* as such," which includes the great Venetians and Rubens, Rembrandt, and Velasquez; and the fourth class is the "School of Errors and vices," the forerunner of the Sensualists. Raphael "in his early works" is number 5 in class 1, but "in his last manner" he is number 1 in class 4,[23] a far wider bifurcation than Ruskin will make in "The Nature of Gothic," where he has Raphael transitional between Naturalism and Sensualism but inclining to the former. But the interesting thing is that Ruskin at this point does not know what to do with the great Venetians on a moral and religious scale. He cannot say they delight in evil, but neither can he say that they seek the good, and so he puts them simply in "The School of *Painting* as such." He does not yet perceive that he ought to throw class 3 together with class 2 and call them simply the Naturalists.

He would begin to make this discovery later in the summer when he proceeded from Florence to Venice after a brief stay in the mountains. He wrote his father that he did not intend to stay long at Venice because "John & Gentile Bellini are the only people I care about studying here, my opinions about Titian & Veronese are formed, and I have only to glance at their pictures that I may know what there are."[24] But then, three days later, he was "overwhelmed . . . by a man whom I never dreamed of—Tintoret." "I never was so utterly crushed to the earth before by any human intellect as I was today, before Tintoret. Just be so good as to take my list of painters, & put him in the school of Art at the top, top, top of everything [previously he was seventh], with a

great big black line underneath him to stop him off from everybody—
and put him in the school of Intellect, next after Michael Angelo. . . .
As for *painting,* I think I didn't know what it meant till today—the
fellow outlines you your figure with ten strokes, and colours it with as
many more."[25] Though Ruskin says he was crushed to the earth by Tintoretto, he wrote many years later in the Epilogue to volume II of *Modern Painters,* "I had seen that day the Art of Man in its full majesty for
the first time; and [felt] that there was also a strange and precious gift
in myself enabling me to recognize it, and therein ennobling, not crush-
ing me" (IV, 354).

Titian's *Assumption,* which he saw for the first time in the Academy,
was also a "staggerer"—"a complete Turner, only forty feet high."[26] Ruskin had already decided that Titian was wholly without religion, and
Tintoretto, though a more deeply solemn man, painted on the same
principle. "Conceive the weight of this problem . . . ," wrote Ruskin,
"on my inner mind—how the most perfect work I knew . . . could be
done 'wholly without religion' " (XXIX, 88). It was understandable that
the higher arts of painting and sculpture could be continued by individual geniuses even after the society as a whole was corrupt, whereas
architecture, which was much more the product of society and was ex-
ecuted by inferior workmen, could not. But these men had in their very
sensuality and worldliness something that seemed to serve them like
religion and that gave to their work an opulence and power not to be
found in purely religious art. He did not come to this conclusion easily.
Though he was "overwhelmed," "crushed," and "staggered" by the experience of 1845, he still presented Fra Angelico as the supreme painter
in *Modern Painters* II (1846). Indeed, all his books "to the end of the
Stones of Venice, were written in the simple [Evangelical] belief I had
been taught as a child" (XXIX, 87). Not until 1858 did the pressures
against this belief accumulate to the point of accomplishing a complete
reversal.

Ruskin has told the story of his "unconversion" in several different
places and with different emphases, but it seems that in July 1858, after
a spell of geologizing, he had come down out of the Alps somewhat
disillusioned with mountains and receptive to the values of civilization.
He went to the Gallery at Turin and was impressed with the unvarying
nobility of Titian and Veronese in contrast with the baseness of some
of the religious painters. "Certainly," he wrote to his father, "it seems
intended that strong and frank animality, rejecting all tendency to asceticism, monachism, pietism, and so on, should be connected with
the strongest intellects. Dante, indeed, is severe; at least, of all nameable

great men, he is the severest I know. But Homer, Shakespeare, Tintoret, Veronese, Titian, Michael Angelo, Sir Joshua, Rubens, Velasquez, Correggio, Turner, are all of them boldly Animal. Francia and Angelico, and all the purists, however beautiful, are poor weak creatures in comparison. I don't understand it; one would have throught purity gave strength, but it doesn't. A good, stout, self-commanding, magnificent Animality is the make for poets and artists, it seems to me" (VII, xl). He then recounted the incident which had prompted these reflections. He had been copying Veronese's *Solomon and the Queen of Sheba,* and one day while working from the beautiful maid of honor in the picture, he was "struck by the Gorgeousness of life which the world seems to be constituted to develop" (VII, xli). Then, one Sunday, with the glory of this picture still upon his senses, he went into "a Waldensian chapel, where a little squeaking idiot was preaching to an audience of seventeen old women and three louts, that they were the only children of God in Turin; and that all the people in Turin outside the chapel . . . would be damned. I came out of the chapel, in sum of twenty years of thought, a conclusively *un*-converted man" (XXIX, 89).

So Ruskin wrote in *Fors Clavigera* in 1877, but, as several critics have pointed out,[27] when the incident is retold in *Praeterita* in 1888, the crucial moment is placed not in the Waldensian chapel but afterwards, before Veronese's picture.

> I walked back into the condemned city, and up into the gallery where Paul Veronese's Solomon and the Queen of Sheba glowed in full afternoon light. The gallery windows being open, there came in with the warm air, floating swells and falls of military music, from the courtyard before the palace, which seemed to me more devotional, in their perfect art, tune, and discipline, than anything I remembered of evangelical hymns. And as the perfect colour and sound gradually asserted their power on me, they seemed finally to fasten me in the old article of Jewish faith, that things done delightfully and rightly were always done by the help and in the Spirit of God. (XXXV, 495–96)

This later version emphasizes the positive value of the experience rather than the loss of religious faith, and it is true that from this point on Ruskin moved into a religious humanism which allowed him to admire, without conflict, the great worldly panoply of Venetian art. He came to the conclusion, which altered "from that time forward, the tone and method of my teaching,—that human work must be done honourably and thoroughly, because we are now Men;—whether we ever expect to be angels, or ever were slugs, being practically no matter. We *are* now Human creatures, and must, at our peril, do Human—that is to say, affectionate, honest, and earnest work" (XXIX, 88). This was Ruskin's creed for the next sixteen years, and it affected not only his personal development but also his view of history. For it allowed him to move forward out of the religious atmosphere of the Middle Ages into the humanism of the Renaissance.

This development is seen most clearly in a series of lectures which Ruskin gave in the early 1870s as the Slade Professor of Fine Art at Oxford. All these lectures are historical in their approach to Italian painting, all divide the subject up into three or four distinct periods, and all select as the culminating period a time which is a little later than Ruskin would have chosen in the 1850s. It is a time, moreover, in which Christianity has lost some of its vitality without as yet being corrupted. In "Verona, and Its Rivers," for example, the culminating period is not the Gothic (1200–1400), though that was the period of "vital Christianity," but the first period of the revival of the arts of Greece, a period for which Ruskin has no name, for it was neither antique nor Christian but simply the "Age of the Masters." In that period of fifty years, centering around the year 1480, there is produced, for the first time in the world's history, "perfect" work. "Perfect. It is a strong word. It is also a *true* one. The doing of these fifty years is unaccusably Right, as art" (XIX, 435, 442–43). Right it may be, but one remembers a time when "perfect" was the most damaging epithet Ruskin could assign to a work of art—when he much preferred the rude artisan aspiring to a perfection he never achieved to the Master whose achievement was "dainty, delightful, and perfect" (XIX, 444).

In the lecture on "The Relation between Michael Angelo and Tintoret," the third culminating period is a period of compromise between the fully formed conscience of the race and its sense of the inconvenience of obeying its own precepts, so that for a brief period there is a magnificent display, an iridescence of collapsing powers, that constitutes the great period of art. It lasts this time for forty years, from 1480 to 1520, the period of Michelangelo, Titian, and Raphael. That period is at once the culmination of Italian art and also the period of its "deadly change." Then came Tintoretto, who "stands up for a last fight; for Venice, and the old time. He all but wins it at first; but the three together are too strong for him. Michael Angelo strikes him down; and the arts are ended" (XXII, 82–83). It was Michelangelo's science of anatomy and Tintoretto's effort to emulate him in that science that brought about the end of Italian art. In the compositions of those two men "the art of Italy consummated itself and expired" (X, 161).

"Thus then it went with me," says Ruskin, "till 1874, when I had lived sixteen full years with 'the religion of Humanity.' " He then found himself at Assisi and, making a copy of Giotto's *The Marriage of Poverty and St. Francis,* he experienced what one may call a "reconversion." For sixteen years he had believed that not only the three great Venetians but also Velasquez, Reynolds, Gainsborough, and Turner—those seven men, "quite indisputably giants in the domain of Art . . . stood, as heads of a great Worldly Army, worshippers of Worldly visible Truth, *against* (as it seemed then to me), and assuredly distinct from, another sacred army . . . , headed by Cimabue, Giotto, and Angelico; worshippers not of a worldly and visible Truth, but of a visionary one, which they asserted to be higher; yet under the (as they asserted—supernatural) teaching of the Spirit of this Truth, doing less perfect work than their unassisted opposites!" Now, while making this drawing of Giotto, Ruskin discovered "the fallacy under which I had been tormented for sixteen years,—the fallacy that Religious artists were weaker than Irreligious. I found that all Giotto's 'weaknesses' (so called) were merely absences of material science. He did not know, and could not, in his day, so much of perspective as Titian,—so much of the laws of light and shade, or so much of technical composition. But I found that he was in the make of him, and contents, a very much stronger and greater man than Titian; . . . and that his work, in all the innocence of it, was yet a human achievement and possession, quite above everything that Titian had ever done!" (XXIX, 89–91).

In his 1845 "scale of painters" Ruskin had grouped Giotto among the Naturalists, but he doubtless now thought of himself as going back to the Purists and to an earlier medieval world-view. Still, there is some element of synthesis in his new position, for he now saw Giotto's work as a "human achievement" and saw in the naiveté of the early painters not imperfection but perfection in another mode. In any case, he went back over his early works, which he had been refusing to republish, and annotated them affirming their essential soundness and indicating, in some instances, how little he knew about the subject when he first treated it. Of a passage in the *Seven Lamps* he wrote in 1880: "I did not know the history of Venice when I wrote it. . . . The real strength of Venice was in the twelfth, not the fourteenth century: and the abandonment of her Byzantine architecture *meant* her ruin" (VIII, 130). Thus, though in 1851 Ruskin knew the precise day on which Venice fell, he later decided he had been wrong about the century.

It is clear that Ruskin tended to see his own life, at least when he looked back upon it from the perspective of later years, in terms of the Evangelical religious conversion. He was Saul on the road to an aesthetic

Damascus. Beginning with an admiration for the physical power of Rubens (VII, 9), he experienced apocalyptic moments before Fra Angelico's *Annunciation and Adoration of the Magi* in 1845, before Veronese's *Solomon and the Queen of Sheba* in 1858, and before Giotto's *Marriage of Poverty and St. Francis* in 1874. Actually, when one examines the contemporary evidence it appears that these revelations were not always as dramatic as they were represented as being. One of the most momentous episodes in *Praeterita*, for example, is that in 1842 in the Forest of Fontainebleau when Ruskin, drawing an aspen tree, found that it "composed itself" and that he did not have to impose a composition upon it (XXXV, 314–15). This surely was an important moment, marking Ruskin's breakthrough from the picturesque to a naturalist form of art, but in the diaries of the period there is little indication that anything important occurred. Indeed, there is a suspicion that Ruskin has transferred to himself a revelation that actually occurred to his drawing instructor.[28] Similarly, though the "unconversion" at Turin is described in *Fors Clavigera* as precisely that—the abrupt end of twenty years of Evangelical thinking—in the contemporary "Notes on the Turin Gallery" Ruskin seems uncertain how to resolve the dilemma of Veronese and the Waldensian preacher. "I don't understand it," he says to his father. "It is a great mystery" (VII, xl–xli). And in a contemporary letter to Charles Eliot Norton he says of his new view, "I had been inclining to this opinion for some years; but I clinched it at Turin."[29] One assumes that many of the changes were of this sort, a building up of pressure for many years and then a sudden slippage, as in a geological fault.

One of the most important developments in Ruskin's life was not apocalyptic but gradual—his loss of the landscape-feeling. From earliest childhood he had had a pleasure in all mountain ground and scenery "infinitely greater than any which has been since possible to me in anything" (V, 365). This "joy in nature," he declared, was "the pure landscape-instinct," and it remained with him in its full intensity "till I was eighteen or twenty, and then, as the reflective and practical power increased . . . , faded gradually away, in the manner described by Wordsworth in his *Intimations of Immortality*" (V, 368). As Ruskin learned more about the art of the past he realized that the landscape-feeling was peculiar to the modern world. The Greeks and Romans did not paint mountains and lakes, and neither did the artist in the Middle Ages. They were concerned with the gods and human life and would have thought that modern art lacked seriousness and purpose. "The simple fact, that we are, in some strange way, different from all the great races that have existed before us, cannot at once be received as the proof of our own greatness" (V, 196). Indeed, it may indicate the precise opposite. Ruskin felt a need to enlarge his context and see how modern art stood not only to the Middle Ages and the Renaissance but also to the classical world.

The key to the modern landscape-feeling is the "pathetic fallacy," an unfortunate phrase, since we now assume that all fallacies are bad, particularly those that are pathetic. What Ruskin meant, of course, is that the modern sensibility projects its own *pathos* or feeling upon the natural world and that this is so far a fallacy in that the feeling is really an attribute of the observer, not the observed. The fallacy is to be deplored, however, only when it is done in cold blood, as in the neoclassical artists and poets, not when it is an expression of sincere feeling. It is always, by implication at least, a metaphorical mode of speaking. This is the first point to be made about the classical writers' handling of nature, that they do not use the pathetic fallacy. They believe there is a god *in* the wind or *in* the sea, and so describe it in terms at once strongly naturalistic and spiritual, but they do not mix the two. Furthermore, they do not like wild nature but "only such portions of the lower world as were at once conducive to the rest and health of the human frame." "Thus, as far as I recollect, without a single exception, every Homeric landscape, intended to be beautiful, is composed of a fountain, a meadow, and a shady grove." In the description of the garden of Alcinous, for example, the notable things are, "first, the evident subservience of the whole landscape to human comfort . . . ; and, secondly, that throughout the passage there is not a single figurative word expressive of the things being in any wise other than plain grass, fruit, or flower" (V, 234–35).

In Dante, who is the representative mind of the Middle Ages as Homer is of the ancient world, Ruskin finds a passage (*Purg.,* xxviii, 40–63), which "embodies in a few syllables the *sealing* difference between the Greek and the mediæval, in that the former sought the flower and herb for his own uses, the latter for God's honour; the former, primarily and on principle, contemplated his own beauty and the workings of his own mind, and the latter, primarily and on principle, contemplated Christ's beauty and the workings of the mind of Christ" (V, 280). This is a declaration of the central purpose of medieval landscape and of the spirit in which it is to be understood. For in medieval painting landscape is distinctly subordinate to the religious subject, being normally reduced to a bit of background in the distance. As Ruskin follows out the development of this element, he traces it from the highly stylized and conventional representation of sky in early art to the more naturalistic mode of the Renaissance painters. The crucial point is at the close of the fourteenth century when the pure gold or chequered color background gives way to a blue sky gradated to the horizon, thus dividing early Christian art into two distinct phases, Symbolic and Imitative. It is curious, says Ruskin, how quickly the change is completed once it is begun. The moment the sky is introduced, "the spirit of art becomes for evermore changed, and thenceforward it gradually proposes imitation more and more as an end, until it reaches the Turnerian landscape" (V, 263).

Scott and Turner are the representative minds of the modern age, and the landscape they prefer is not the neat, ordered, sunny realm of the classical and medieval ages but a realm of cloud and mist, of nature in its wilder and more irregular aspects, dark, broken, and turbulent. It is an aspect of the picturesque, which represents nature in association with ruins, with crumbling cottages and broken windmills, as if to emphasize decay. It shows man as a part of time and history, his works arising out of the natural world and sinking back into it again. To Ruskin the very epitome of the picturesque is the old church tower in Calais which "completely expresses that agedness in the midst of active life which binds the old and the new into harmony. We, in England, have our new street, our new inn, our green shaven lawn, and our piece of ruin emergent from it,—a mere *specimen* of the Middle Ages put on a bit of velvet carpet. . . . But, on the Continent, the links are unbroken between the past and present. . . . A building of the eighth or tenth century stands ruinous in the open street; the children play round it, the peasants heap their corn in it. . . . No one wonders at it, or thinks of it as separate, and of another time; we feel the ancient world to be a real thing, and one with the new: antiquity is no dream; it is rather the children playing about the old stones that are the dream." There is, of course, a low picturesque, which is merely sentimental, but there is also a noble picturesque, which is the expression of unconscious suffering "nobly endured by unpretending strength of heart" (VI, 11–14). It is the human world seen under the aspect of time and death, and so is peculiarly modern. The classical world accepted time and death as natural facts and did not overly preoccupy itself with them. The medieval world denied them as illusory, and this was the source of its weakness. But with the Renaissance came the Resurrection of Death, which some men, like Holbein, Dürer, and Salvator, fought stoutly against, but which most tried to escape by fleeing into sensuality. As a result, the art of this period is cold, heartless, and dead. "There is *no* entirely sincere or great art in the seventeenth century" (V, 400).

But then Ruskin perceives that a new "contemplative reaction is taking place in modern times, out of which it may be hoped a new spiritual art may be developed" (VII, 264). This art is based on what must be acknowledged to be a new religion, the religion of nature. It will embody the tender feelings towards nature first engendered by Christianity but will also perceive it as subject to sin and death. Indeed, it will principally record it in association with the history of man. Whether the religion on which it was based is "a permanent and healthy feeling, or only a healthy crisis in a generally diseased state of mind" (V, 353), Ruskin was uncertain. It had been the "ruling passion" (V, 365) of his own life, and he desperately wanted to believe that it had a beneficent impact upon those who lived under its sway. But he had seen the avalanche and he had seen the Swiss peasant, and he had to acknowledge that nature was a manifestation of God's anger and power as well as of his wisdom and glory. There is a Mountain Gloom as well as a Mountain Glory, and the Contemplative School recorded both.

In order to record the Gloom and the Glory art must employ the pathetic fallacy, but Ruskin insisted that in the work of Turner the result was not merely "subjective," in the sense of being infused into nature by the observing mind. It is rather related to the "power" in an object to produce certain emotions in the observer. It does derive, however, from what Locke would call the secondary rather than the primary qualities of an object. It is concerned with how something appears to an observer rather than how, in its inner nature, it is. For, as Ruskin says at the end of his long treatment of landscape in *Modern Painters* III, "There is a science of the aspects of things, as well as of their nature; and it is as much a fact to be noted in their constitution, that they produce such and such an effect upon the eye or heart . . . as that they are made up of certain atoms or vibrations of matter.

"It is as the master of this science of *Aspects,* that I said, some time ago, Turner must eventually be named always with Bacon, the master of the science of *Essence.* As the first poet who has, in all their range, understood the grounds of noble emotion which exist in landscape, his future influence will be of a still more subtle and important character" (V, 387, 353). The classical poet saw a god *in* nature. The medieval poet saw God apart from nature. The modern artist found in nature "noble grounds for the noble emotions," primarily because he saw nature in conjunction with the tragic history of man.

In 1864 Froude sent Ruskin a copy of his Royal Institution lecture, "The Science of History," to which Ruskin replied, "There is no law of history any more than of a kaleidoscope. With certain bits of glass— shaken so, and so—you will get pretty figures, but what figures, heaven only knows. . . . The wards of a Chubb's lock are infinite in their chances. Is the Key of Destiny made on a less complex principle?" (XXXVI, 465). Ruskin was a little unjust to Froude, who was engaged in that very lecture in rebutting Henry Thomas Buckle's view that there was such a thing as the Science of History, and even declared, "It often seems to me as if History was like a child's box of letters, with which we can spell any word we please."[30] Ultimately, he took the position that history teaches us precisely because, like Shakespeare's plays, it is not didactic but simply represents the world as it is. In some great periods of history, like that of Elizabeth and Mary Queen of Scots, it will be quite as dramatic as Shakespeare. With this Ruskin would have agreed. In the Fall of Venice he had found a great and instructive drama, but as he turned the kaleidoscope in later years the bits of glass slipped and fell into a new pattern, which was also very instructive. The result, however, was not cynicism but rather enlargement of mind. Ruskin gradually perceived that his original views about art and history had been too narrow and that there were many different kinds of art, the product of different societies and different religions, which yet were very good. Though he never came to like Renaissance architecture or the French or Dutch painting of the seventeenth century, he did perceive an unbroken artistic tradition from antiquity to his own day—or at least until the day when, like many of us, he stopped being receptive to new things. His return to Giotto in 1874 was perhaps less a return to the Middle Ages than simply to an individual who "in the make of him" was a greater man than Titian. Indeed, Ruskin did not at any time think that anyone ought to "return" to any period in the past. If the northern Gothic was the best form of architecture to use in modern buildings, it was because it was beautiful and strong, not because it was medieval. At Bradford in 1859 he contrasted the hideousness of modern Rochdale with the beauty of Pisa in the Middle Ages, but he did not suggest, *à la* Pugin, that his audience should build a new Pisa in Bradford. Indeed, he was at that moment so impressed with the selfish violence and pride of life of all great periods of art that he would not have had them go back to any of them. "The great lesson of history is, that all the fine arts hitherto . . . have only accelerated the ruin of the States they adorned; and at the moment when, in any kigdom, you point to the triumphs of its greatest artists, you point also to the determined hour of the kingdom's decline. The names of great painters are like passing bells: in the name of Velasquez you hear sounded the fall of Spain; in the name of Titian, that of Venice; in the name of Leonardo, that of Milan; in the name of Raphael, that of Rome. And there is profound justice in this; for in proportion to the nobleness of the power is the guilt of its use for purposes vain or vile." And therefore Ruskin suggested that England abandon the hope of emulating the luxuriousness of Italy for "the loftier and lovelier privilege of bringing the power and charm of art within the reach of the humble and the poor. . . . Between the picture of too laborious England, which we imagined as future, and the picture of too luxurious Italy, which we remember in the past, there may exist—there will exist, if we do our duty—an intermediate condition, neither oppressed by labour nor wasted in vanity—the condition of a peaceful and thoughtful temperance in aims, and acts, and arts." When Ruskin wrote these words in 1859 he thought mankind was "about to enter on a period of our world's history in which domestic life, aided by the arts of peace, will slowly, but at last entirely, supersede public life and the arts of war" (XVI, 341–42). Ten years later, after the passage of the Second Reform Bill, he was declaring that "we are on the eve of a great political crisis," that of "a struggle . . . between the newly-risen power of democracy and the apparently departing power of feudalism; and another struggle, no less imminent, and far more dangerous, between wealth and pauperism" (XVIII, 494). The kaleidoscope of history had turned a little further.

8

Browning and the
Victorian Renaissance

O F THE THREE MAJOR VICTORIAN POETS Browning was undoubtedly the most learned, and he was also the only one who did not
have a university education. Coming from a strong Dissenting background, he could not have subscribed the Thirty-Nine Articles of the
Anglican Church, which was required of all students on matriculation
at Oxford and on receiving the degree at Cambridge. He did, however,
have the freedom of his father's remarkable library, and, being possessed
by an ungovernable thirst for knowledge and having no tutor to hold
him back and tell him it was not "customary" for youths to read books
of which their betters had never heard, he acquired an odd, eccentric,
and irregular knowledge of the past which was no doubt partly responsible for his poetic originality. For whereas we feel that Tennyson and
Arnold were both traditional poets, the one looking back to the pre-
Romantics, Milton, Spenser, and the Roman poets of the Silver Age,
the other to Byron, Wordsworth, Goethe, and the Greeks, we feel that
Browning looks forward to something as yet unexampled and undefined.
Or rather he looks back to an age which was temporarily out of fashion,
which indeed had suggestions of something evil and sinister, but which
in his view had the energy and vitality to promise a new birth in the
Victorian age as it had in the Renaissance. Being a Dissenter in England
in the nineteenth century was analogous to being a Protestant in the
sixteenth, but Browning was both a Protestant and a Renaissance man.

This was already apparent in his first three published poems, *Pauline, Paracelsus,* and *Sordello. Pauline* (1833) is a confessional poem in
which a youthful poet traces for his beloved the violent and disastrous
course of his own soul. Gifted with "a most clear idea of consciousness /
Of self" and with "a principle of restlessness / Which would be all, have,
see, know, taste, feel, all," he was inspired by Shelley to dreams of human
perfectibility, from which, by a failure of imagination, he awoke and fell

into the "dim orb of self"—into pride and solipsism. He has now
learned that the true end of life is not to be God but to love God, and
he hopes, with Pauline's help, to find his way back to health. It is evident, however, that he is near to death, a broken and a blasted man. To
this poem Browning prefixed two quotations, the first from the French
poet Clément Marot: "Plus ne suis ce que j'ai été, / Et ne le sçaurois
jamais être;"[1] the second from the German doctor and occult philosopher Heinrich Cornelius Agrippa. The second is a long quotation in
Latin from the *De Occulta Philosophia* and says in essence, "This is a
poisonous work—do not read it," offering in excuse, "I wrote this work
when I was less than a youth." The bearing of these quotations on the
poem is sufficiently clear, but the question is, why, in this poem of a
modern setting, Browning wished to direct the attention of the reader
to two nearly contemporaneous figures of the early Renaissance.
Agrippa lived from 1486 to 1535, Marot from about 1496 to 1544.
Both had stormy careers in which they were driven from one country
to another by their enemies, chiefly monks and ecclesiastical authorities,
and both spent much time in prison, dying in poverty and exile. Though
they remained Catholics, they were thought to be tainted by the new
heretical opinions of Melanchthon and Luther. They were thus advanced
thinkers who, in a transitional age, represented the new spirit of the
Renaissance and Reformation before it had fully emerged from the Middle Ages. That Browning was specifically interested in them and not
merely in the quotations he culled from their works is evident from the
fact that both men are connected with his later poems. Marot reappears
as a character in "The Glove," where he now represents an older poetic
style against the more advanced work of Ronsard, and Agrippa leads
into *Paracelsus,* whose protagonist, also an occult philosopher, had as
his preceptor the very Abbot Trithemius who advised and assisted
Agrippa in the composition of *De Occulta Philosophia.* Browning evidently saw in these two Renaissance overreachers a symbol of the Romantic overreacher whose glorious failure he had depicted in his own
poem.

　　Indeed, Browning apparently thought of himself in these terms. He
tells us in a note which he wrote in the famous copy of *Pauline* sent to
John Stuart Mill for review, "The following Poem was written in pur-
suance of a foolish plan which occupied me mightily for a time, and
which had for its object the enabling me to assume & realize I know
not how many different characters;—meanwhile the world was never to
guess that 'Brown, Smith, Jones, & Robinson' (as the spelling-books
have it), the respective authors of this poem, the other novel, such an

opera, such a speech, etc. etc. were no other than one and the same individual."[2] In other words, he was apparently planning to write a series of poems, plays, novels, operas, dramatic speeches, etc., each under a different assumed name and then to startle the world by revealing that all were the work of one "Renaissance man," Robert Browning. But after the abysmal failure of *Pauline* he added, "Only this crab remains of the shapely Tree of Life in the Fool's Paradise of mine—R.B."[3] Nevertheless, Browning did not give up his conviction that gloriously to fail was better than lowly to succeed.

This, indeed, is the theme of *Paracelsus*. But this time Browning chose as his actual protagonist an occult philosopher and physician, the exact contemporary of Marot and Agrippa, who wandered about the world in search of esoteric knowledge and died so execrated by his countrymen that one remains uncertain whether he was a great genius or a charlatan. We are told by Mrs. Orr that the subject was suggested to Browning by his friend the Count Amédée de Ripert-Montclar.[4] Browning, however, must already have been acquainted with the philosopher, not only through his reading in Agrippa but also because Paracelsus's works, in the edition of Bitiskius, were in his father's library. Beyond that, in view of Shelley's *Prometheus* and Goethe's *Faust,* the world was obviously ready for a Faustian or Promethean work on Paracelsus. And so Browning, suppressing in his notes at the end of the volume the more disreputable details of Paracelsus's career, makes him into one who seeks infinite knowledge—nothing less than "the secret of the world, / Of man, and man's true purpose" (I, 276–77). The trouble is that Paracelsus proposes to seek knowledge to the exclusion of love, to seek it in total disregard of the accomplishments of his predecessors, and not even to refresh himself with the normal rewards and pleasures of life along the way. His friends Michal and Festus, who in their deeply religious and prudential outlook, seem to represent the medieval worldview, urge him to be "lowly wise" and even suggest he may be more interested in glory and power than in true knowledge. He laughs at their fears and proceeds on his way, but after many years of aspiration and failure he returns home with nothing accomplished except the realization that true attainment consists simply in aspiration. Rising from his death-bed and putting on his priestly robes, he delivers a magnificent final speech, which is nothing less than his vision of the entire hierarchy of creation. This hierarchy, however, is not a static Great Chain of Being, as in the eighteenth century; rather it is an evolutionary ladder ascending and descending in time, as the lower forms aspire to the higher and the higher condescend to them in turn. It is this latter aspect that Par-

acelsus has neglected, contemning not only his predecessors but also
his own students and countrymen, and so, like the protagonist in *Pauline,* he has learned not to be God but to love God, and to love man
too.

His deficiency is emphasized as early as the third part, when the
name of Martin Luther is introduced. In one sense Paracelsus is regarded as "another Luther" ("Luther alter"[5]), the physician of the body
as Luther was of the soul. His greatest achievement, and the one that
gave him most satisfaction at his death, was that he had cured the great
Erasmus. But more profoundly he and Luther are opposed, for when
Festus describes Luther as "a wondrous soul," Paracelsus replies:

> True: the so-heavy chain which galled mankind
> Is shattered, and the noblest of us all
> Must bow to the deliverer—nay, the worker
> Of our own project—we who long before
> Had burst our trammels, but forgot the crowd,
> We should have taught, still groaned beneath their load:
> This he has done and nobly.   (III, 982–88)

He even acknowledges that the peasants' rebellion suggests "men seem
made, though not as I believed, / For something better than the times
produce;" (III, 991–92) but then declares, "Well, well; 'tis not my
world!" (III, 996). It is, however, the world of Festus and Michal. The
drama runs from 1512 (originally Browning had made it 1507) to 1541.
In the beginning Festus and Michal, who live in a "sequestered nest"
(I, 36) by St. Saviour's, seem part of a self-enclosed medieval world,
but by part 3, set in 1526, nine years after Luther had nailed his Theses
to the door of the Castle church in Wittenberg, Festus has come out of
his nest and is carrying messages between Zuinglius and Luther (III,
951–62). Luther is really a more perfect and complete hero than Paracelsus, and just as Carlyle would soon include him in his *Heroes and
Hero-Worship* (1841), so one feels that Browning, whose roots were deep
in the Protestant tradition, perhaps should have written a drama about
Luther rather than Paracelsus. Indeed, in "Bishop Blougram's Apology"
he introduced Luther as the very type of untroubled religious faith—a
life "incomparably better than my own," acknowledges Blougram. "He
flared out in the flaring of mankind" (568–74). But the truth is that
Browning wanted a hero who would fail rather than succeed, and so,
while declaring in the notes that "there is no doubt of the Protestantism
of Paracelsus, Erasmus, Agrippa, etc.," and even that "the noncomfor-

mity of Paracelsus was always scandalous,"[6] in the drama he makes Paracelsus more a Renaissance figure, one who placed himself "alongside" or even "beyond" Celsus, the great Roman physician, and who repudiated the dead dogma of the Middle Ages. "Come," says Paracelsus at one point,

> I will show you where my merit lies.
> 'Tis in the advance of individual minds
> That the slow crowd should ground their expectation
> Eventually to follow.   (III, 870–73)

Like a great wave that sweeps over a strip of sand and thus enables the little waves to follow, he precedes his age (III, 887).

> For men begin to pass their nature's bound,
> And find new hopes and cares which fast supplant
> Their proper joys and griefs; they grow too great
> For narrow creeds of right and wrong . . . :
> Such men are even now upon the earth,
> Serene amid the half-formed creatures round
> Who should be saved by them and joined with them.
> Such was my task, and I was born to it—   (V, 778–87)

Paracelsus performed his task in a flawed and imperfect manner. Still, he has been a portent in world history, so that even lowly men like Festus exclaim, "And this was Paracelsus!" (V, 908).

Paracelsus is contrasted not only with Luther but also with Aprile, a Shelleyan poet whose spirit appears in a strange episode in part 2. As Paracelsus aspired to KNOW infinitely, so Aprile aspired to "LOVE infinitely, and be loved!" (II, 384–85). They are alike in that each pursued an exclusive goal without limitation, but they are opposed in their goals. Moreover, Paracelsus is evidently the successor to Aprile as the poet-king commissioned to save the world. For in a lyric speech apparently uttered by Paracelsus we learn of a central doctrine of Browning, one that appears explicitly in many of his poems and is presupposed by all the others, that all the poets of the world constitute a band or company commissioned by God to utter the spiritual truth that is in them. For in accordance with Browning's doctrine of the "subjective" poet later expressed in the "Essay on Shelley," truth is within the poet (I, 725–37), and it is there he will find the nearest approximation of God's truth, which he is required to utter. In this transcendent task he will necessarily fail, and Browning imagines that all the poets of the past are looking over his shoulder as he writes to see how he will perform. Will he dauntlessly raise the slug-horn to his lips as Childe Roland did, or will he betray the cause as did Wordsworth in "The Lost Leader"? Aprile, the Shelleyan poet, necessarily "failed," and in a long speech of Aprile's Browning seems to say it was through a want of constructive or architectonic power and through ignoring the resources of the literary tradition (II, 490–609)—essentially what Arnold would later say of both Keats and Shelley. But if Aprile is a Shelleyan poet, then Paracelsus, who is his successor, figures forth the new Victorian poet whose task is to master the vast amount of new knowledge pouring in upon the age, and whose defect will be to allow his poetic faculty to be atrophied by intellectual analysis. From Coleridge, who feared that by "abstruse research" he had damaged his imagination, to Mill, whose "mental crisis" was caused by such a regimen, to the Spasmodic poets and Arnold, whose Empedocles was such a hero, there was a recognition of the new "intellectual hero" who was superseding the older "affective hero" of the Romantic age.[7] Knowledge was replacing Love, and since Love was often in the Romantic view the characteristic of the Middle Ages, that process can be symbolized by the advent of a new Renaissance figure like Paracelsus. Of course, he is not the end of the process, either for his own time or for the Victorian Age, for the drama ends with Paracelsus urging that men should "Regard me, and the poet dead long ago / Who loved too rashly; and shape forth a third / And better-tempered spirit, warned by both" (V, 886–88). Robert Browning, however, will never be the poet of that "better-tempered spirit."

Sordello, which was begun before *Paracelsus* but not completed until 1840, is focused around the siege of Ferrara in 1224 and so may be considered to be medieval in its setting. Various scholars have pointed out, however, that Sordello is presented as the precursor of a new age rather than the culmination of an old.[8] Alluding to the fact that he was known in the nineteenth century chiefly through his appearance in Dante's *Purgatorio,* Browning introduced him as "thy forerunner, Florentine! / A herald-star" (I, 348–49) who has been absorbed into the greater fame of Dante. His very faults—a refusal to compromise, to stoop, or be confined within the limits of the possible—are explained in terms of the ebullient temper of the age. "Born just now, / With the new century, beside the glow / And efflorescence out of barbarism" (I, 569–71), he is the contemporary of Nicolo and Giovanni Pisano, the latter the architect of the Campo Santo, innovators of a new classical style, and of Guido da Sienna, pregnant with the new birth of Saint Eufemia's sacristy. The concept of a "Renaissance of the Twelfth Century" had not yet been formally so labelled by Charles H. Haskins, but the idea of such a renaissance in both the twelfth and the thirteenth century had been expressed by Gibbon, Hallam, and William Roscoe.[9] A few years later in his notable volume on the Renaissance in his *Histoire de France* (1855) Michelet would declare, "That era [the Renaissance] would certainly have been the twelfth century, if things had followed their natural course."[10] It was Browning's desire to disengage Sordello from Dante's fame and also from the false legend which made him a warrior-poet, and to show how, if he had performed as he ought to have performed, the course of history might have been different.

Sordello, however, is not merely a precursor but also a successor-poet, for just as Paracelsus was defined in relation to Aprile, so is Sordello in relation to Eglamor, whom he triumphs over in the Court of Love. Eglamor, as Herbert Tucker says, is the formalist poet whose work consists in the patient rearrangement of other men's materials, in the turning out of finished verses.[11] At the Court of Love he retells the myth of Apollo, but since Sordello is trying to "be" Apollo, he is able, in a magnificent improvisation, to draw from his own experience of the myth a spiritual truth which far transcends the limited art of Eglamor. If Eglamor suggests the neoclassical poetry of the eighteenth century, Sordello suggests the new Romantic poetry of Shelley, the more so in that, crowned the laureate of the new age, he then retires into the romantic castle of Goito, ignoring the needs of his own people. Events finally bring him forth, and the last three books of the poem are occupied with Sordello's struggle to decide how he can or should contribute to the perfection of man in society. He very quickly realizes that progress must be gradual, and he perceives in the struggle between Emperor and Pope a struggle between Strength and Knowledge, of which both are necessary for true progress. Charlemagne represented "Strength by stress of Strength," Pope Gregory VII, three centuries later, "Knowledge by stress of Strength" (V, 134, 176–77). The ideal is "Knowledge by stress of merely Knowledge," but for this the world is not yet ready. "For the next age / Or two . . . Knowledge, part by Strength and part / By Knowledge" is needed. "Then, indeed, perchance may start / Sordello on his race" (V, 211, 226–29). Sordello, the Guelf poet, and Salinguerra, the grizzled warrior of the Ghibelline interest, are the representatives of Knowledge and Strength within the poem, and the question is, how, in this transitional age, to combine the two. Sordello is subjected to two opposite temptations: to accept the badge, symbol of the headship of the Romano family, which Salinguerra cynically flings about his neck, and so abandon the realm of poetry for that of practical action, or, on the other hand, to conclude that nothing can be done and not attempt to use his poetic power effectively. He resists the former but succumbs to the latter, though only after uttering a magnificent final speech, comparable to Paracelsus's final vision, which declares that poets are the "unacknowledged legislators of the world" (V, 505–51). Of this speech Browning declares,

> I tell you, what was stored
> Bit by bit through Sordello's life, outpoured
> That eve, was, for that age, a novel thing:
> And round those three [Sordello, Palma, and Salinguerra]
>   the People formed a ring,
> Of visionary judges whose award
> He recognised in full.   (V, 453–58)

The Guelf is the popular party as against the aristocratic Ghibellines, and so Sordello's visionary judges are not merely his own peers (V, 547) but also the people. Still, he has not served them well by wholly renouncing authority, for as a result of his death, Ecelin the Cruel came to power and established one of the most oppressive tyrannies the world has ever known.[12] The light of Italian liberty was put out, the Renaissance was pushed back two hundred years, and Dante was unable to accomplish what he might have, had Sordello truly prepared the way. Browning tells us that "we suffer at this day" because of what Sordello "should have been, / Could be, and was not—the one step too mean / For him to take." "Had Sordello dared that step alone, / Apollo had been compassed" (VI, 829–37). By this Browning means that with the advent of Dante a poet would have ruled the world.

Unfortunately, Bacchus, not Apollo, was "compassed." Alan Johnson has noted that throughout the poem there is a network of allusion which associates Sordello with Apollo, and Salinguerra with Bacchus.[13] Salinguerra, though a man of action, is singularly dependent on some guiding figure, and once he loses the support of Sordello and Palma he turns into a sensualist who ends his life "fat and florid" (VI, 730–31). He thus represents a side of the Renaissance which won out over a chaster, purer ideal—not specifically the "early Christian" art espoused by A. F. Rio (for Sordello is not notably Christian), but the art of the early Renaissance as opposed to the later florid art detested by Ruskin. It is no wonder, then, that Rossetti and his fellows were so enthusiastic about *Sordello*, which is in a way the first pre-Raphaelite poem. While the rest of the world was making inane witticisms on the unintelligibility of

Sordello, Rossetti and Hunt did not find it unintelligible at all. They carried it with them on their trip through northern France and Flanders and only found it unintelligible that men should press round the Old Masters, while "no man asks of Browning."[14] For them Browning was not "the Author of *Paracelsus,*" as he was for the rest of the world, but "the Author of *Sordello.*"

At the end of *Sordello* Browning says that all that has survived of Sordello's works is a snatch of song that may be heard sung by a barefoot boy as, early in the morning, he crosses a "hill-side of dew by sparkling Asolo" (VI, 853–70). The boy seems to have evolved in Browning's mind into the little silk-weaver of Asolo, Pippa, who, in her drama published the next year, also sings of a "hill-side dew-pearled" and touches with her song the lives of four sets of people. It is as if Browning, through her, had taken up the work Sordello let fall six centuries before and was attempting to be "earth's essential king." In order to see how he does this we need to turn for a moment from history to myth in the three great areas of Browning's interest, love, art, and religion.

It is generally agreed that the central myth in Browning's love poems is that of Perseus and Andromeda or, in its Christianized version, St. George and the Dragon.[15] Even before he enacted this myth in his own life by rescuing Elizabeth Barrett from the Dragon of Wimpole Street, Browning had a copy of an eighteenth-century engraving of Caravaggio's *Perseus and Andromeda* hanging over his desk,[16] and he says in *Pauline* that in moments of despair this gave him faith "some god / To save will come in thunder from the stars" (666–67). The myth takes various forms in Browning's poetry, some incomplete or truncated, some with unhappy endings. The fullest development is that in *The Ring and the Book,* but there are also versions in "My Last Duchess," "Count Gismond," "In a Gondola," "The Flight of the Duchess," "The Glove," and "The Statue and the Bust." The essential elements in the myth are three: the maiden lashed to the rock, the monster about to devour her, and her rescuer. The maiden changes little from one poem to another, for she is independent of time and circumstance, the very embodiment of life and love. The "spot of joy" called up in the cheeks of "my last Duchess" is a symbol of the inner radiance and vitality of these maidens, who are all creatures of absolute purity and innocence, a portion of the ideal. The rescuer varies widely from poem to poem, for although he is God's emissary, enacting divine justice upon earth, he necessarily takes a form appropriate to his own time and place. The dragon in some poems carries suggestions of the "old dragon" Satan, but more often he is part of a society whose fossilized institutions would destroy life and love if this were not prevented by some higher power. The conflict, then, in these poems is between Nature, God, and Society, though Nature, in the person of the maiden, is sometimes so divinized that she is almost more saintly than her rescuer, who, conversely, is sometimes closer to outraged nature than an avenging god.

The inciting moment of the myth is always the "glance of recognition" exchanged between the maiden and her rescuer. By this revelation of their inmost souls they make the "leap of faith" and dedicate themselves to one another for life. When Count Gismond steps forth into the arena, the lady looks at him and instantly knows that she is saved. So from balconies or open windows or boxes in the theater the other maidens look down upon their knights, their eyes meet, they communicate silently with one another and either are saved or are not saved. In "The Statue and the Bust" they unfortunately temporize and so are damned. "Cristina" is entirely about the glance with which the lady in that poem "fixes" the speaker—whether she means something by it or is merely flirting, or whether he is a romantic sentimentalist who has imagined the entire episode. The "depth and passion of the earnest glance" in the portrait of "My Last Duchess" is so striking that the Duke is obliged to give an explanation, and he attributes it to some idle compliment made by Fra Pandulph or perhaps to the bough of cherries "some officious fool" brought her from the orchard. One wonders whether one of them was supposed to play the role of her rescuer but failed. For it is notable that Browning often gives this role not to proper knights but to irregular troops—a scapegrace canon, for instance, who operates quite outside the institution of the church. In "The Flight of the Duchess" the rescuer is an old gypsy woman, who seems to come up out of the earth itself and whose "glance of recognition" is the very process of hypnotism by which she mesmerizes the lady and draws her out of the world of death into that of life. But perhaps the most interesting of the glances is that in "The Glove," where it comes not from the youth loitering in the wings but from the lion, the very spirit of wildness, who, as he leaps into the arena and imagines that he is already leagues distant, driving the flocks up the mountain, exchanges with the lady a spiritual "glance of recognition." Each feels a kinship with the other as a wild thing caught, or about to be caught, in the toils of society, and the lady drinks from his eyes the spirit of freedom. To avoid the fate of the Duchess she "runs to meet the approaching evil," and it is the lion with his mane "vast and heapy," somewhat analogous to the shaggy mane of the old gypsy woman, who rescues her from her courtly dragon.

Browning gives "The Glove" a definite historical setting, in the court of Francis I during the short period (about 1542–1547) when the careers of the two poets Clément Marot and Pierre Ronsard overlapped. Marot, who in *Pauline* represented the just emerging spirit of the Renaissance, is here a generation older than Ronsard and embodies the still medieval interest in versifying the Psalms. Ronsard, on the other hand, represents the new naturalistic poetry of the Renaissance, and so, while Marot joins the court in hooting down the lady's behavior, Ronsard more thoughtfully stays behind to inquire into her motive. " 'Human nature,—behoves that I know it!' " He is the new psychological poet succeeding upon the older moralistic one, and since Leigh Hunt had versified this traditional tale a few years earlier with the conventional "Marot" ending, one may think that Browning is setting up an analogy: as Ronsard to Marot, so stand I to Leigh Hunt and the previous generation of poets. It is one more example of the "succession of the poets" to add to those of Aprile and Paracelsus, Eglamor and Sordello.

It is notable that, despite the classical origin of the Perseus myth, Browning never gave it a classical form but seems to have thought of it almost entirely in chivalric terms. Most of the poems embodying it are vaguely medieval or Renaissance in setting. Occasionally, as in the case of Guido Franceschini, the dragon takes on metaphysical dimensions and becomes incarnate evil—the very embodiment of hate, pride, violence, and spiritual death. But he still manifests himself through social forms, and in the case of most of these poems his being is coextensive with these forms. The Duke lives in his "nine-hundred-years-old name," Guido in the decaying house of his ancestors. Indeed, it is partly because they are nothing in themselves that they initially envy and then hate the joyous vitality of the ladies whom the law has placed within their power. Such creatures are to be found everywhere, but it is significant that Browning has made them all members of the aristocracy and placed them within the feudal system established in the Middle Ages and lingering on into the Renaissance. For in his view, though the spirit of chivalry occasionally provided a rescuer, the system itself encouraged husbands to regard their wives as pieces of private property whom they might incarcerate or even kill. By 1698, the date of the action of *The Ring and the Book,* it has become a question, as the court brief says, "if, and when, / Husbands may kill adulterous wives, yet 'scape / The customary forfeit" (I, 129–31). Guido feels deeply aggrieved that this is

so, complaining that only a generation before no one would have ques-
tioned his right (XI, 110–20). Certainly no one questions that of the
Duke (thought to be modelled on the Duke of Ferrara in the sixteenth
century) or of the nearly contemporaneous scion of the Riccardi family
in "The Statue and the Bust." It is likely that the Duchess in "The Flight
of the Duchess" is able to escape only because she lives in the nineteenth
century, and the effort by her husband to revive medieval manners is
regarded by Browning as comic and grotesque. But Browning is not
only laughing at things like the Eglinton tournament, he is also saying
quite seriously to Carlyle, Pugin, and Ruskin that feudalism was not a
system of mutual interdependence and responsibility. It was a system of
domestic and social tyranny.

Browning's religious faith presents a striking analogy with his doctrine
of love, for just as the Perseus and Andromeda legend taught him that
"some god / To save will come in thunder from the stars," so the doctrine
of the Incarnation lay at the very center of his faith. This faith, though
falling generally within the liberal or Broad Church tradition, was by
no means an easy or comfortable thing. On the contrary, it was electric
with excitement. For if it was true that the Almighty God had clothed
himself in human form and come down and lived among men, then this
was certainly the most momentous fact in human history. Everything
else paled in comparison to it. It meant that one's religious faith depended on one's ability to realize this fact, to bring it before one as a
vivid and present reality, and that depended in turn on whether one
lived before it had occurred, or shortly after the event, or so long after
that it had faded away into the mists of incredulity. Thus, the proper
order in which to read Browning's religious poems is not the order of
their composition but the order of history; for, taken all together, they
form a dramatic narrative leading up to and falling away from that great
event.

   Not that living at the time of Christ was the best condition to be
in. Lazarus, in the "Epistle of Karshish, the Arab Physician," who was
actually raised from the dead by Christ, whom he believed to be the
very God, was so dazzled by this fact that he was absolutely incapacitated
for human life. No contingent matter was of any importance to him,
and in Browning's view this would be the case with anyone who looked
on God direct. Far better to see him through the mists of history, from
a thousand years before or a thousand years after, and so be under the
necessity of realizing the Incarnation within oneself. David, from a

thousand years before Christ, was able, through the great love he bore to Saul, to rise through the grades of Physical and Natural Theology to the conception of a God of Love and so, for one trembling moment, to recreate—or rather precreate—the Incarnation. Euripides five hundred years later was not able to go so far. In the monologue of the Pope he complains that though he had virtually anticipated all the teachings of Paul, yet by the doctrine of the Church he was not to be accorded salvation.

> Pope, dost thou dare pretend to punish me
> For not descrying sunshine at midnight,
> Me who crept all-fours, found my way so far—
> While thou rewardest teachers of the truth,
> Who miss the plain way in the blaze of noon . . . ?   (X, 1780–84)

Still, there must have been something wanting in Euripides, for, unlike David, he was unable to rise above the conception of Natural Law and the pagan gods, various or one.

Even less satisfactory was Cleon, who, though living at the time of Christ and having, with his fine mind, reasoned out the necessity for a further revelation, was unable to accept it when it came because it was offered by a barbarian Jew. Cleon, of course, was blinded by pride. He had made a religion out of his own mind, a religion of culture and civilization, of a purely anthropomorphic humanism. Ironically, his humanism was not even very good. Unlike the great natural geniuses of the fifth century and the Heroic Age, he lacked the joy of spontaneous creativity and had been reduced to a mere Alexandrianism, almost an academicism. He represented what Newman called the "religion of philosophy," universal in his culture but at a dreadfully low level. Like Matthew Arnold's France, he was "famed in all great arts, in none supreme." Some have thought that in Cleon Browning was alluding to Arnold,[17] but in 1855 the prose works which would make Arnold known as the "Apostle of Culture" were still unwritten. It is far more likely that his model was Goethe, who in Victorian times was widely criticized for having sacrificed depth and height of religious feeling for universality of culture. In Emerson's *Representative Men,* for instance, which the Brownings were reading in 1851, Goethe is presented as one who "appears at a time when a general culture has spread itself, and has smoothed down all sharp individual traits; when . . . there is no poet, but scores of poetic writers; no Columbus, but hundreds of post-captains. . . . Goethe was the philosopher of this multiplicity. . . . He is the type of culture, the amateur of all arts, and sciences, and events; artistic, but not artist; spiritual, but not spiritualist." "He was the soul of his century."[18] In a similar manner Cleon was the soul of the universal culture of his own day.

Karshish, Cleon's contemporary, was neither blind like Cleon nor dazzled by excess of light like Lazarus; rather he greeted the possibility of the new religion as a "wild surmise."

> The very God! think, Abib; dost thou think?
> So, the All-Great, were the All-Loving too—

Whether it is that the scientific mind is more open to new truth than the humanist, or that humanism partly satisfies the spiritual craving whereas Karshish's materialism left his soul empty and craving for spiritual food, Browning does not say; but the Arab's reaction, of wonder mixed with incredulity and desire, is more satisfactory to Browning than any other. Karshish gets all the facts wrong and desperately offers naturalistic explanations of the Lazarus miracle, but the central meaning of the Incarnation he has seized—the God of Power and Wisdom is also a God of Love.

In "A Death in the Desert" Browning moves on to about 98 A.D. and imagines that John, the author of the fourth Gospel and the Book of Revelation, who has lived to a vast old age, is now dying, surrounded by a few followers, in a cave near Ephesus. He focuses upon the fact that John is the last human being who actually saw and spoke with Jesus and that once he is gone doubt is sure to creep in. Indeed, John can foresee the time when men may doubt his very existence, let alone the truth of the works he is purported to have written. That time, indeed, came with the writings of Strauss and Renan, which Browning was reading in the late 1840s and early 1860s, and Browning's attitude toward them is quite ambiguous. On the one hand, he attempts to turn the argument of the Higher Criticism against itself by asking, if the Gospel is a myth in which man has projected his love upon an objective figure, does not that very fact prove the existence of the Love which Revelation was designed to disclose? On the other hand, by the form of the poem he is more successful, and perhaps more interested, in reinforcing our sense of the tenuousness of tradition. For the poem consists in the text of a manuscript accompanied, in square brackets, by annotations and glosses, and by the time the reader has figured out that it was apparently dictated by one Pamphylax to one Phœbas just before Pamphylax was martyred and then came into the hands of one Xanthus, who passed it on to his niece, whence it came into the collection of her husband, an unknown Christian, having previously been read and annotated by Cerinthus, a heretic, and by another opposed to him—by the time the reader has figured all this out, he does indeed have a sense of the tenuousness of the written record and of the great likelihood that all may be corrupt.[19] Browning seems to have believed in the authenticity of the Gospel of John, but he had much greater faith in the experience of Christ which David had a thousand years before John wrote.

In one respect John did not prophesy correctly, for doubt did not immediately creep in and undermine the faith; rather that faith was established in an institution and a body of dogma which did more to destroy a living faith than all the skepticism of Strauss and Renan. In other words, Browning accepted Arnold's soon-to-be-developed conception of an *Aberglaube*—a fossilized faith in the externals of religion— which would substitute for meaningful religious experience all through the Middle Ages. "You'll say, once all believed, man, woman, child," says Bishop Blougram, "In that dear middle-age these noodles praise" (676– 77). So they did, yet they did not hesitate to "lie, kill, rob, fornicate / Full in belief's face" (691–92), as is made clear by "The Heretic's Tragedy," where the burning of Jacques du Bourg-Molay in 1314 is described in grotesque detail, or in "Holy Cross Day," where the enforced conversion of the Jews is attempted by a Pope less Christian than the Jews themselves, or in "Soliloquy of the Spanish Cloister," where the suppression of normal, healthy desires by monasticism had led the speaker to impute his own lecherous and murderous instincts to the one sane and healthy man in the cloister. Browning shared none of his contemporaries' admiration for the Middle Ages, which, in his view, was not an Age of Faith but of ignorance and dirt. In *Christmas-Eve,* while praising the impulse of Love that infused the early Church, he portrayed the Middle Ages as anti-intellectual—hostile to the poetry, eloquence, art, and music of pagan antiquity, knocking the noses off the statues of Aphrodite, tearing the pages out of the manuscripts of Sallust. Nor was the Renaissance much better, for with a respect for the art and literature of antiquity came a new worldliness, so that the Bishop ordering his tomb at Saint Praxed's church seemed to have forgotten the very meaning of the religion he professed.

As a result, when the Pope, in *The Ring and the Book,* sat in his darkened chamber looking back over the course of history and asked himself why it was the Church had so failed in its duty, he had to admit it was not through too much doubt but through too empty a faith. Euripides in the midnight of paganism had seen farther than his own archbishops in the full blaze of noon. "We have got too familiar with the light. / Shall I wish back once more that thrill of dawn?" (X, 1793–94). For in the early days of Christianity "how could saints and martyrs fail see truth / Streak the night's blackness?" (X, 1827–28)—whereas now we cannot distinguish heaven's white from the yellow torch of the world. Looking forward to the coming Age of Rationalism, the Pope declares,

> What if it be the mission of that age,
> My death will usher into life, to shake
> This torpor of assurance from our creed,
> Re-introduce the doubt discarded. . . .   (X, 1851–54)

As it is, people are breaking through the crumbling structure of religion and taking their stand upon "the next discoverable base," mere human nature, "the lust and pride of life" (X, 1889–91). There must be a new midnight before there can be a new dawn.

By Browning's day midnight had nearly come: "How very hard it is to be / A Christian!" laments the speaker of *Easter-Day*. Bishop Blougram agrees but adds that doubt is necessary to prove that faith exists. "The more of doubt, the stronger faith, I say / If faith o'ercomes doubt." Readers have been so preoccupied with the likeness of Blougram to Cardinal Wiseman that they have not always noticed his likeness, in all essentials, to Browning himself. Not in nonessentials. Browning has endowed his Bishop with a complex and baffling personality and has allowed him sophistical arguments with which to provoke and tease his opponent. To make him more paradoxical he has drawn elements of him from Emerson's portrait of "Montaigne; or the Skeptic"[20] and yet has made him a member of "the most . . . fixed, precise / And absolute form of faith in the whole world." He has confronted him with the "either-or" mentality of the shallow and jejune Gigadibs (either you believe, in which case you are a fool, or you don't believe, in which case you are a knave) and allowed him to offer a "both-and" reply which has baffled and irritated readers down to this time. Essentially his position is that to a finite human creature pure, naked belief in "God the Omnipotent, Omniscient, Omnipresent" is impossible. It would be to look on God direct and be, like Lazarus, blinded by the sun. Creation is meant to veil God, not to reveal him, and history veils him even more. This would be true at any time, but it is especially true in the nineteenth century. Blougram owes his position "on the dangerous edge of things" to his

> coming in the tail of time,
> Nicking the minute with a happy tact.
> Had I been born three hundred years ago
> They'd say, 'What's strange? Blougram of course believes;'
> And, seventy years since, 'disbelieves of course.'
> But now, 'He may believe; and yet, and yet
> How can he?'

Browning does not foresee, as Arnold did, a general revival of Christianity like that in the first age. Rather he believes in a continuing difficulty which will make the faith of those who do believe more lively and vital. In a novel version of the Perseus and Andromeda legend, he sees faith as the Archangel Michael standing upon the squirming snake of doubt and calm precisely *because* it squirms.

If we turn now to Browning's art poems, we find that in his view there is a striking analogy between art, love, and religion: all are versions of Love in the larger sense, the one being directed towards nature, the other towards man, and the third towards God. Hence, just as the "glance of recognition" constitutes a kind of revelation to the lover, comparable to the Christian revelation, so the artist, by his own "glance of recognition" at the natural world, is able to discern the Infinite in the Finite which is the subject of his art. His picture is a kind of embodiment or Incarnation, as is the descent of God to devotee or lover. This revelation is not easily attained, however, for just as doubt is essential to religious faith, and just as the little film of individuality which separates one human soul from another is essential to the exercise of love, so the limitation imposed by the artistic medium is essential to the striving and ultimate imperfection of the artist. By an act of faith which combines the human will with divine Grace, doubt, human individuality, and the medium are overcome for one "good moment"— the "moment, one and infinite" which David achieves in his vision of the Christ, which the lovers achieve in "By the Fire-side," and which Abt Vogler achieves in his improvisation. It would be folly, however, to attempt to perpetuate this moment, as theologians have done in their dead dogmas, as husbands do in the institution of marriage, and as artists do in their highly developed techniques and period styles. Indeed, the attempt to perpetuate it constitutes a kind of madness, as we see in the case of Johannes Agricola, who has an absolute belief in his own salvation, or Porphyria's lover, who strangles his beloved so as to perpetuate her in her perfect moment, or the Bishop at St. Praxed's, who hopes to take his art with him into the next world. Browning has no use for the connoisseur, whether of women or of pictures, but only for the creative artist, who can sometimes, in rare and unforseen conditions, experience the revelation of beauty for one tremendous moment.

This philosophy of art is turned by Browning into a historical myth as he applies it to the various periods of art in his dramatic monologues. Greek art, even of the greatest period, he had little use for, for it represented perfection within a limited mode; whereas Christian art, by its very imperfection, expressed the high ideals to which it aspired. This "philosophy of the imperfect," which Browning developed in "Old Pictures in Florence" and "Andrea del Sarto," was being voiced by Ruskin at exactly the same moment in "The Nature of Gothic." It would appear that neither man could have influenced the other, for it is thought that Browning's painter poems were written in the winter and spring of 1853 and the second volume of *The Stones of Venice,* containing "The Nature of Gothic," was published on July 28, 1853.[21] One would suspect a common source for both except that the view is so characteristic of the era that one is hardly necessary. It is, indeed, implicit in the contrast between the age's conceptions of Greek and Christian art. The first was voiced in its classic form by Winckelmann in his *History of Ancient Art* (1764), of which an English translation of the second (Greek) volume was published in 1850. The aim of Greek art, according to Winckelmann, was to depict the ideal beauty of the human form by combining various individual beauties into one harmonious whole. Its heroes were idealized human beings and its gods were idealized heroes. But, as Browning noted, it is a purely human ideal, and thus the perfection achieved by Phidias and others is a limited perfection. When, with the introduction of Christianity, man discovered that he had a soul as well as a body, then growth became possible, and self-transcendence, and the glories of "imperfection."

In "Old Pictures in Florence" Browning symbolizes the two ideals in the contrast between Giotto's soaring but unfinished campanile and the perfect circle which Giotto drew freehand at the request of a Pope who wanted a "sample" of his work. The point of the latter episode, which Browning tells rather too cryptically, is explained by Vasari:[22] it gave rise to the proverb, "Tu sei più tondo che l'O di Giotto," where the word *tondo* in Tuscan carries the double meaning "round" and "stupid." ("You are more stupid than Giotto's O was round.") Presumably, a Pope who was stupid enough to require a sample of Giotto's work was also stupid enough to be impressed by perfection. On the other hand, Lord Lindsay in his *Sketches of the History of Christian Art* (1847) tells a story, repeated by Ruskin in his *Lectures on Architecture and Painting* (1854), about the building of the campanile.

> The republic [of Florence] passed a decree in the spring of 1334, that "the Campanile should be built so as to exceed in magnificence, height, and excellence of workmanship whatever in that kind had been achieved of old by the Greeks and Romans in the time of their utmost power and greatness. . . ." The first stone was laid accordingly, with great pomp . . . , and the work prosecuted with such vigour and with such costliness and utter disregard of expense, that a citizen of Verona, looking on, exclaimed that the republic was taxing her strength too far . . . ; a criticism which the Signoria resented by confining him for two months in prison, and afterwards conducting him through the public treasury, to teach him that the Florentines could build their whole city of marble, and not one poor steeple only, were they so inclined.[23]

Such was the spirit in which men worked in the ancient days of the republic, for the tower's incompleteness signifies to Browning not only the aspiration to greatness but also modern Italy's inability to achieve greatness under the political domination of Austria. That is why, in the beginning of the poem, as he looks out over the familiar scene of Florence, he is "startled" by the sight of Giotto's tower, for in his mind's eye he sees it as completed. He has a prophetic vision, that is, of the recovery by Florence of political freedom and the recovery of great art along with it. Freedom was lost when Sordello failed to fulfill his responsibilities, but the poet now ponders the question, "once Freedom restored to Florence, / How Art may return that departed with her." For as he meditates on "art and history" and contrasts the "fructuous and sterile eras," he declares that it is not monarchy that fosters artists: "Pure Art's birth is still the republic's." Hence his cry, "Bring us the days of Orgagna hither!" He would go back to the glorious days of the thirteenth to fifteenth centuries, when art had its

> spring-birth so dim and dewy;
> My sculptor is Nicolo the Pisan,
> My painter—who but Cimabue?

Nicolo the Pisan is the artist mentioned in *Sordello* to typify the heady new movement in art when Sordello was alive, and these artists too are presented as precursors of the Renaissance, not the last of the Middle Ages.

Give these, I exhort you, their guerdon and glory
   For daring so much, before they well did it.
The first of the new, in our race's story,
   Beats the last of the old; 't is no idle quiddit.
The worthies began a revolution.

It may have been Christianity that first taught the painter he had a soul, but it is astonishing how little there is in this rollicking and boisterous poem about Christianity. It is the power of the artist's imagination as fostered by political freedom that produced the great art so prized by Browning in "Old Pictures in Florence."

Browning's tastes did not always lie in this direction. As a young man he had shared the predilections of the average Englishman for the "divine" Raphael and his contemporaries, but he also thought that in some respects they might have been surpassed by the later Bolognese school—the Carracci, Domenichino, Guido Reni, and Guercino. His father's tastes lay toward the Dutch school, in which the nearby Dulwich Gallery was especially strong. He himself, however, had been introduced to painting by Gerard de Lairesse's *The Art of Painting in All Its Branches* (1707), which opposed to the realism of the Dutch the classicism of Raphael, Correggio, and especially Poussin. That Browning tended in that direction is apparent from his letter to Elizabeth Barrett in 1846, in which he singled out for especial praise from the Dulwich collection "those two Guidos, the wonderful Rembrandt of Jacob's vision, such a Watteau, the triumphant three Murillo pictures, a Giorgione music-lesson group, all the Poussins with the 'Armida' and 'Jupiter's nursing.' "[24] After he went to Italy, however, he began to study and read about painting more intensively, and in 1850 he made a lucky purchase in a corn-shop outside Florence of five paintings which some said were by Cimabue, Giottino, and Ghirlandaio. Rossetti, on visiting the Louvre with him in 1855, declared, "I found his knowledge of early Italian Art beyond that of anyone I ever met,—*encyclopædically* beyond that of Ruskin himself."[25]

The shift in European taste away from Raphael and the later Mannerists and Eclectics toward the pre-Raphaelite painters was the work of nearly half a century, and the prime impetus came from the Catholic reaction.[26] Wackenroder's *Confessions from the Heart of an Art-Loving Friar* (1797) was a sentimental effusion which did not turn away from the 'divine' Raphael but did establish the central principle of the movement that great art was inseparable from the spirit of religion. This principle was reinforced by Friedrich von Schlegel, who, writing from the vantage point of Paris, issued his widely read *Description of Paintings in Paris and the Netherlands* (1802–04; English translation 1849). He declared frankly, "I have little taste except for the earlier schools of Christian art" and asserted that by the time of Guido and Domenichino "the genius of painting had lost its early splendour." Indeed, this distinction between "the devout, pious deeply significant style" of the old school and the "florid pomp" of the new was the most important that could be made, and it affected even the career of Raphael. At the end of his work Schlegel issued a call to the young painters of the day to recapture the spirit of religion, for "every effort will be fruitless, unless the painter be endowed with earnest religious feeling, genuine devotion, and immortal faith."[27]

As if in answer to this call there arose in Germany a group of young painters, of whom Friedrich Overbeck and Peter Cornelius were the most important, who migrated to Rome and there, in 1810, established a monastic community in which they attempted to wed art with religion in the manner of the old masters. Their official name was the Brotherhood of St. Luke, but they were popularly known as the Nazarenes. They will be mentioned again in connection with the English Pre-Raphaelites. Of perhaps more lasting importance was the work of an art historian, Karl Friedrich von Rumohr, who, though also a Catholic, did not attempt to identify so closely artistic excellence with the spirit of piety. Unlike Schlegel, he did not censure Raphael for his use of antique materials in his later years, and he attributed the decline of art in the sixteenth century to social and cultural causes. It was his aim to do for Christian art what Winckelmann had done for the art of antiquity, and his *Italienische Forschungen* (Berlin, 1827–31) was the first critical investigation of Italian art based on wide and sound scholarship.

Three volumes of sound German scholarship were not likely to become popular in England in the 1830s, and so as usual it remained for a young Frenchman to reap the fruit of this investigation. Alexis François Rio, a young professor of history at the Lycée Louis-le-Grand, follower of Montalembert and uneasy associate of Lamennais, found himself powerfully drawn to the paintings of Botticelli, Fra Angelico, and the early Raphael. He was totally ignorant of the work that had already been done in this field, but on going to Munich he was introduced simultaneously to German mysticism and the work of Rumohr. The latter wrought a revolution in his life, and drawing upon Rumohr's materials but going back in spirit to Schlegel and Wackenroder, he undertook a work of which the first volume appeared in 1836 under the misleading title, *De la poésie chrétienne: forme de l'art.* By *poésie* he meant the poetic or imaginative element in every art, a point which Schlegel had made before him and Ruskin would make after, and he intended to study this element as it manifested itself not only in Christian painting but also in sculpture, architecture, and music. Unfortunately, five months after the publication of his book only twelve copies had been sold, and so the project was never completed. What France spurned, however, England accepted, for Rio had married into a wealthy Catholic family in the north of England, and partly through his social connections, partly through his own very great charm, and partly through England's need to sublimate its Tractarian worries in the form of art, he became a "hit." He was introduced into English society by Richard Monckton Milnes, later Lord Houghton, and was invited by Samuel Rogers to his famous breakfasts. Through these people and others he met Henry Hallam, Macaulay, Carlyle, Thomas Moore, Thomas Campbell, John Kenyon, Henry Crabb Robinson, Tennyson, Landor, Lady Blessington, Lord Holland, Gladstone, and many others. Gladstone said he was the most remarkable Frenchman he had ever met, and carried his book with him to Italy to view the paintings by its light. For four years, from 1837 to 1841, he lived in England and moved easily in the elegant Whig circles of Lansdowne House and Holland House.[28]

What Rio's book would have told Gladstone was that the progressive view of Italian painting taken by Vasari in his *Lives of the Most Eminent Painters, Sculptors, and Architects* was wrong. Vasari had traced the evolution of painting from its rude beginnings in the thirteenth century through its increasing technical accomplishments to its culminating triumph in the great masters of his own day. But, asked Rio, of what avail is this if the heart of the painter meanwhile has become corrupt? Unlike Schlegel, Rio did not simply distinguish between early and late. With the information supplied by Rumohr he realized that there were different tendencies in different schools, and he made the tension between technical accomplishment and moral purity the central principle of his work. "Ce germe de décadence," he said, referring to the revival of paganism, "se développera lentement et presque invisiblement, pendant que, sous d'autres rapports, la peinture marchera rapidement vers sa perfection."[29] With his view that the Medici were a great source of evil the Florentines do not come off well; he tends to favor the softer Siennese and Umbrian schools, though the later work of Raphael is sharply denounced.

Rio's work was not anti-Protestant: the source of corruption was the Renaissance paganism within the Church, not a heresy from without. Nonetheless, it was well that he had someone to reinterpret and modify his views for a wider English public. That person was Anna Jameson, the gifted daughter of an Irish miniaturist. Serving as a governess in Italy, she had had an opportunity to educate herself about art and was now acting as a kind of middle-class Ruskin, informing the people what they ought to think about art. "Poor Mr. Babcock," wrote Henry James in *The American,* "was extremely fond of pictures and churches, and carried Mrs. Jameson's works about in his trunk; he delighted in aesthetic analysis, and received peculiar impressions from everything he saw."[30] Despite the irony, Mrs. Jameson was far from an inconsiderable person; she taught herself German, went to Germany and became intimate with A. W. von Schlegel, and read Rumohr. In 1841 the "great *event*" of her life was her meeting with Rio,[31] and thenceforth her books were infused with his spirit. She wrote a series of *Memoirs of the Early Italian Painters,* a kind of updated Vasari, which appeared originally in the columns of *The Penny Magazine* and then was republished in book form in 1845. She then went on to her great work, *Sacred and Legendary Art,* originally called *The Poetry of Sacred and Legendary Art* in accordance with Rio's usage, which was published in six volumes over the years 1848–1852. Her aim in these volumes was to provide the reader with the knowledge of sacred legends and subjects necessary for appreciating medieval Christian art, which he would normally have of classical myths. She ranged widely over the entire field, from galleries to churches, from painting to sculpture, from Ravenna mosaics to High Renaissance art, explaining the saints' legends, the doctrines of the Church, Christian emblems and iconography. This orientation towards the subject—she has sections on Angels and Archangels, the Four Evangelists, the Twelve Apostles, the Doctors of the Church, and Saints and Martyrs—necessarily gave to her work a pietistic cast. Nonetheless, her pleasant and soothing style, the wealth of information without pedantry, and the general sense of spiritual uplift made her work appealing to many, some of them more intelligent than Mr. Babcock.

Mrs. Jameson first met Browning, "a poet whom I like much," at a dinner given by John Kenyon, a friend of Browning's father, in June, 1842. Two years later she became acquainted with Elizabeth Barrett and soon was one of the few admitted to the sacred chamber. So intimate, indeed, were the three of them that the lovers contemplated taking her into their confidence on their elopement plans but ultimately, for prudential reasons, did not. Nonetheless, they joined her in Paris immediately after their marriage, traveled with her to Pisa and Florence, and remained friendly with her for many years. Thus, Browning knew

Mrs. Jameson well during the period when she was writing and publishing her art books, and these works, together with Rio's, with which
he was undoubtedly acquainted, constitute the background against
which his painterly poems must be read.[32]

They explain, for one thing, the tone of "Old Pictures in Florence."
Many readers are puzzled by the casual and informal air of the poem,
by its conversational, even slangy language, and particularly by its comic
and grotesque rhymes. Why rhyme "Giotto" with "(was it not not?)
'O!' " "Ghirlandajo" with "heigh ho!" and "Frà Angelico's" with "bel-
licose" if you really love these painters and want to do them honor?
Why refer to a "scrap" of Fra Angelico's work, which Rio would have
considered almost a sacred relic, or invoke Margheritone of Arezzo as
"You bald old saturnine poll-clawed parrot"? The answer, of course, is
that Browning is deliberately adopting an anti-sanctimonious tone in
order to indicate that although he prizes the early masters above "The
Michaels and Rafaels, you hum and buzz / Round the works of, you of
the little wit!" he does not prize them for their religious unction. So
much is clear from his comment on the work of another woman who
had been deeply influenced by Rio, Mary Shelley's *Rambles in Germany
and Italy* (1844).

> Oh that book [he wrote to Elizabeth Barrett]—does one wake or
> sleep? . . . Once she travelled the country with Shelley on arm; now
> she plods it, Rogers in hand [Samuel Rogers' *Italy* (1822)]—to such
> things & uses may we come at last! Her remarks on art, once she lets
> go of Rio's skirts, are amazing—Fra Angelico, for instance, only
> painted Martyrs, Virgins &c.—she had no eyes for the divine *bon-bour-
> geoisie* of his pictures; the dear common folk of his crowds, those who
> sit and listen (spectacle at nose and bent into a comfortable heap to
> hear better) at the sermon of the Saint—and the children, and
> women,—divinely pure they all are, but fresh from the streets and
> market place—but she is wrong every where, that is, not right, not
> seeing what is to see, speaking what one expects to hear—I quarrel
> with her, for ever, I think.[33]

Even in the sainted Fra Angelico, Browning perceives elements of the
naturalism of Fra Lippo Lippi.

In "Pictor Ignotus" (1845) Browning chose to depict, not one of
the early religious painters like Fra Angelico, who had never known
corruption, but a later artist who lived on the verge of the new naturalistic age but who, through timidity, shrank back into an archaic style.
In order to make this clear he has added to the title of the poem the
place and date, "Florence, 15—." Thanks to the researches of J. B. Bullen,[34] we can make this more precise and say it was 1504–1517. For

Browning has drawn upon the career of Fra Bartolommeo di San Marco (1472–1517) as told by Vasari and Mrs. Jameson, in order to construct his imaginary painter. Fra Bartolommeo lived just at the time when Florence, under the sway of Lorenzo de' Medici and his sons, became "one of the most magnificent, but also one of the most dissolute of cities."[35] It was also a time when painters were beginning to move out of the church into the world. Francis Turner Palgrave tells us in his *Handbook for Travellers in Northern Italy* (1842), which Browning knew, "Before the sixteenth century, it may be doubted whether any cabinet pictures, that is to say, movable pictures, intended merely to hang upon the wall and be looked at as ornaments . . . , ever existed."[36] Once they did, once pictures could be taken out of the churches into the homes of the wealthy bourgeoisie, moved about, bought and sold, and exhibited to vast throngs, the painter had the new and powerful motive of worldly fame. Vasari and Mrs. Jameson tell a "well-known anecdote" of a Madonna of Cimabue which excited so much curiosity that when it was uncovered on the occasion of a visit of Charles of Anjou to Florence, "the people in joyous crowds hurried thither to look upon it, rending the air with exclamations of delight and astonishment, whence this quarter of the city obtained and has kept ever since the name of the Borgo Allegri."[37] It is to this episode that Pictor Ignotus is alluding when he dreams of his own paintings being carried "Through old streets named afresh from the event." Indeed, he so lusts after fame that, as he peers into his own soul, he feels like one looking through a door at some obscene feast of idols, or like a nun about to be raped by a band of soldiers. But "a voice" changed all that. The uninstructed reader would take the voice to be that of his own puritanical conscience which would not allow him to satisfy the normal desires for fame in a normal way but, by repression, had enlarged them into these fantastic monsters. And so it is, for Browning has given to his poem a psychological depth not present in his source. But from Vasari and Mrs. Jameson we learn that the voice is also that of Savonarola, who was at this moment preaching against the vanities and sins of Florence and calling upon the people to fling their books and manuscripts, their paintings and musical instruments into the fire. Bartolommeo, caught up in the enthusiasm, brought all his designs and studies made from the undraped human figure, and, consigning them to the flames, became a follower of Savonarola. A short time later, when the enemies of Savonarola rose against him, Bartolommeo was one of five hundred supporters who shut themselves up in San Marco, but, being "of a timid and even cowardly disposition," he became terrified and made a vow, that if he escaped from this evil, he would assume the religious habit of the Dominicans.[38] That he did in July 1500, and for the next four years he abandoned art and gave himself to his devotions.

In 1504, however, there occurred an incident which "reawakened all his genius and enthusiasm." Young Raphael, then in his twenty-first year and already celebrated, arrived in Florence eager to study with Fra Bartolommeo. He taught the friar the new science of perspective and learned from him the secret of his coloring. Each profited from the other, and we are told by Jonathan Richardson, whom Mrs. Jameson quotes, that "at this time Fra Bartolomeo seems to have been the greater man, and might have been *the* Raphael, had not Fortune been determined in favor of the other." Raphael, then, is the "youth" alluded to in the opening lines of the poem, and Pictor's claim, "I could have painted pictures like that youth's / Ye praise so," is not vain boasting. Raphael's famed ability to represent the passions was Pictor's too, and he was again tempted to try his fate in the world. He followed Raphael back to Rome and watched the great stir of activity around him and Michelangelo in the Vatican and the Sistine Chapel. But he knew he could not compete, "a cloud fell upon his spirits," and he retreated to his convent where he accompanied "the labour of his hands with the uninterrupted contemplation of death."[39] Browning shows him in his last years, painting endless rows of saints and virgins while, with sinking heart, he rationalizes his choice.

The distinction between what Pictor Ignotus was and what he might have been is the distinction between the Purist (or Idealist) and the Naturalist schools in Italian painting. We have already met this distinction in Ruskin, but he was not the first to have made it. Rumohr emphasized it and made Masaccio the representative of the latter and Fra Angelico of the former. Mrs. Jameson, however, chose to contrast Fra Angelico with Fra Lippo Lippi and to emphasize the opposition by treating them together in a single Memoir which she opened with this general statement:

> Contemporary with Masaccio lived two painters, both gifted with surpassing genius, both of a religious order, being professed monks; in all other respects the very antipodes of each other; and we find the very opposite impulses given by these remarkable men prevailing through the rest of the century at Florence and elsewhere. From this period we date the great schism in modern art. . . . We now find, on the one side, a race of painters who cultivated with astonishing success all the mental and mechanical aids that could be brought to bear on their profession; profoundly versed in the knowledge of the human form, and intent on studying and imitating the various effects of nature

in color and in light and shade, without any other aspiration than the representation of beauty for its own sake, and the pleasure and the triumph of difficulties overcome: on the other hand, we find a race of painters to whom the cultivation of art was a sacred vocation—the representation of beauty a means, not an end; by whom Nature in her various aspects was studied and deeply studied, but only for the purpose of embodying whatever we can conceive or reverence as highest, holiest, purest in heaven and earth, in such forms as should best connect them with our intelligence and with our sympathies.

The two classes of painters who devoted their genius to these very diverse aims have long been distinguished in German and Italian criticism as the *Naturalists* and the *Idealists* or *Mystics*.[40]

Rio, of course, exalted the Idealists, and one of his most serious criticisms of the Naturalists was that they introduced portraits of themselves and their contemporaries into the sacred subjects. This was not objectionable in the early days when a donor was presented kneeling in adoration among the wise men and shepherds, for that merely enhanced the feeling of devotion. But soon they were represented as indifferent to the sacred scene, and some painters even introduced their own mistresses on the throne of the Madonna. Fra Lippo Lippi, says Mrs. Jameson, was the first to be guilty of this outrage, and he went even further by seducing a young novice who was sitting to him as a model of the Madonna and making her his mistress. "This libertine monk," she declares, "was undoubtedly a man of extraordinary genius, but his talent was degraded by his immorality."[41]

Fra Angelico, on the other hand, is described by Mrs. Jameson in an unctuous and sentimental manner as a man with whom the practice of art was a perpetual "hymn of praise, and every creation of his pencil an act of piety and charity." "His long life of seventy years presents only one unbroken tranquil stream of placid contentment and pious labors."[42] As we have already seen, Browning did not agree with this view of Fra Angelico, but neither did he agree with the condemnation of Fra Lippo Lippi. Indeed, his poem of that name is a direct reply to Mrs. Jameson, whose voice may be heard in the words of Browning's Prior, lecturing to Fra Lippo: " 'It's art's decline, my son! / You're not of the true painters, great and old; / Brother Angelico's the man, you'll find.' " Browning's problem is to rescue Fra Lippo from any serious imputation of immorality, which he does by portraying him as one who from eight years old has been made to "renounce the world" and who now, at carnival time, has been locked up, like Pictor Ignotus, "A-painting for the great man, saints and saints / And saints again." Being only flesh and blood, it is natural that he should break out into certain freaks and pranks, especially when it becomes apparent that the Prior and his whole religious system are one gigantic hypocrisy. For Browning transforms the episode of the little novice into the story of the Prior's "niece" who comes to minister to his "asthma" and presumably to other physical needs as well. All Fra Lippo wants to know is whether nature *is* evil and so to be repressed, or whether it was created by God, so that the painting of it, in all its beauty and wonder, is about the best hymn of praise that one can offer. By the end of the poem Fra Lippo has been so "rehabilitated" that when he describes the "Coronation of the Virgin" which he plans to paint for Saint Ambrogio's by way of compensation, he almost slips into Heaven himself by way of his own portrait—fortunately in an attitude of worship, not indifference, though whether of Saint Lucy or the Prior's niece is uncertain.

Indeed, if Fra Lippo has a fault, in Browning's view, it is not his bold naturalism but rather his not being bold enough in behalf of his new creed. For, as he acknowledges, "The old schooling sticks, the old grave eyes / Are peeping o'er my shoulder as I work." Indeed, as he describes his intended "Coronation," in the rather sugary style of Mrs. Jameson,

> God in the midst, Madonna and her babe,
> Ringed by a bowery flowery angel-brood,
> Lilies and vestments and white faces, sweet
> As puff on puff of grated orris-root,

it is evident he has compromised too much. Though leading into the art of the new age, he has not entirely shaken off the shadow of the old.

His excuse is that he thinks he has founded a new school. A youngster known as Hulking Tom comes to the convent, soaks up his practice, and doesn't mind the monks. He's sure to "paint apace, / I hope so— though I never live so long, / I know what's sure to follow." The youngster is Masaccio, and after the poem was published Edward Dowden wrote to Browning to ask if he hadn't made a mistake in saying Masaccio was a disciple of Fra Lippo Lippi since all the authorities said it was the other way around. Browning replied that he had gone into the matter very thoroughly at the time and was sure Fra Lippo was "the elder practitioner of Art, if not, as I believe, the earlier born."[43] Johnstone Parr has shown that Browning was misled on this matter, not by Filippo Baldinucci's *Notizie de' Professori del Disegno,* as DeVane thought, but by two footnotes in Gaetano Milanesi's edition of Vasari's *Vite* (1846–47), which Browning was using.[44] That Browning *was* misled seems clear, for all the other authorities—Vasari, Rio, Rumohr, Mrs. Jameson, and even Baldinucci himself—agree that Masaccio was the earlier man, and so the question arises why Browning wanted it the other way around. Possibly it was partly that Mrs. Jameson had set Fra Lippo up as the representative of Naturalism in her Memoir, but more generally it was that Browning wanted Fra Lippo's career to have not merely individual significance but to be representative of a new movement in art history. There was nothing in Masaccio's life that would dramatize that change, and therefore the change was associated with Fra Lippo. To Fra Lippo Browning also gave the trait assigned by Mrs. Jameson to Masaccio: "it was said of him that he painted souls as well as bodies."[45]

Andrea del Sarto, whom Rio classes among the Naturalists, lived almost a hundred years later than Fra Lippo Lippi, and the style which in Fra Lippo was just being hammered out had reached in Andrea its full perfection. In fact, Mrs. Jameson notes, "he was called in his own time 'Andrea senze errori,' that is, Andrea the *Faultless*." That, for Browning, was the very trouble, for it was an article of faith with him that whenever a literary, artistic, or musical style reached perfection it had better be abandoned. Mrs. Jameson attributes Andrea's deficiencies to moral reasons: he "would have been a far greater artist had he been a better man."[46] Rio, who agrees about the immorality, emphasizes rather the lack of religious feeling; and Vasari, who is tenderer to his friend than either Rio or Mrs. Jameson, posits merely "a certain timidity of mind, a sort of diffidence and want of force in his nature."[47] In Browning's complex and evasive monologue it is almost impossible to tell what part is played, and whether as cause or effect, by lack of faith, by moral obliquity, by mere uxoriousness, and by timidity of soul, but the thing that is emphasized is the paradox of technical perfection coupled with lack of grandeur and exaltation. To some degree the two things must be causally related, for in a painting of Raphael we are told that an arm is wrongly put and yet the "soul is right," and we feel the soul is right partly *because* the arm is wrongly put. "He means right—that, a child may understand." Since there is no way a viewer, child or adult, could tell whether an artist "means right" unless he had in fact rendered his meaning, it may be that putting the arm wrong is the right way of drawing the soul. As with El Greco, imperfect anatomy may be the perfect technique for expressing the soul. More probably, however, Browning means simply that most artists are "half-men" and cannot focus on body while they are thinking about soul, on technique while they are creating their conception. Raphael and Michelangelo focused upon the great conception—so great that their reach exceeded their grasp—whereas Andrea was so intent on grasping that he forgot to reach. But it was only partly an individual fault; it was partly that he was a little man who lived in "the golden age of painting."

The Grammarian, whose funeral took place "shortly after the Revival of Learning in Europe," seems at first to be a Raphaelesque figure whose reach exceeded his grasp, but in the end we perceive that it exceeded it so completely that he died grasping nothing at all. He is "famous calm and dead," and was half dead during much of his life. He is an example of the fact that even an idea like the "glory of the imperfect," if pursued too relentlessly and in the wrong way, can itself become a mechanical formula and destructive of the very life it would foster. The Grammarian began as a poet, a "Lyric Apollo," descended to a student of literature, then to a scholiast, and finally to a mere grammarian, grubbing among the detritus of corrupt texts. He is like the philologist who declared, "All my life has been spent in the study of the dative and ablative of Horace's odes. Woe is me! I attempted too much. I should have confined myself to the dative alone!" The Grammarian did not pursue the Infinite and fail; he pursued the infinitesimal and succeeded. Moreover, he pursued it in the wrong field—in knowledge rather than life. He is not to be classed among the creative artists but among the connoisseurs and collectors—those who, like the Duke of Ferrara and the Bishop at St. Praxed's engross and control objects to the neglect of life itself. Though presented with wonderful ambiguity and complexity, he ultimately represents the perversion and misapplication of an essentially good and true idea.

The proper application of the idea is seen in the career of Jules in the Jules/Phene episode in *Pippa Passes*. At the opening of the drama Jules is a sterile imitator of the neoclassical sculptor Canova (1757–1822). The only element in Canova's technique he has not mastered is "a certain method of using the drill in the articulation of the knee-joint." He has tried to "improve" nature by seeking out the abstract human archetype, ideal beauty, and his subjects are the approved classical subjects of Tydeus, Psyche, Hippolyta, Hipparchus, and an Almaign Kaiser. The Hipparchus, indeed, was done at the prompting of his enemy Lutwyche, writing as Phene, and so was the fulfillment of a deliberate hoax. He knows neither himself nor the true nature of art or life. Once Pippa sings, however, and Jules realizes that all his values have been wrong—that Art exists for Life, not Life for Art—he then transforms himself from a neoclassical sculptor into a romantic painter. The Monsignor, commenting on his decision, observes that it probably takes some dramatic break like this to strike out a new school, whether in painting, poetry, or music. Otherwise, the practiced hand "will pursue its prescribed course of old years, and will reproduce with a fatal expertness the ancient types, let the novel one appear never so palpably to his spirit." That is why, in "One Word More," Browning prefers Raphael's sonnets and Dante's picture and why he imagines that when the great painters go to heaven they turn to poetry.

When Browning sent "The Bishop Orders His Tomb" to the editor of *Hood's Magazine* on February 18, 1845, he added, "I pick it out as being a pet of mine, just the thing for the time—what with the Oxford business, and Camden society and other embroilments."[48] The "Oxford business," as Robert Greenberg has pointed out, was the culminating phase of the Oxford movement, particularly the public condemnation, on February 13, of W. G. Ward's *Ideal of a Christian Church* and the stripping Ward of his Oxford degrees.[49] As for the Camden Society, there were two societies which had taken William Camden as their patron, one at London, the other at Oxford. Both were concerned with the accurate revival of ecclesiastical architecture, and both in 1844 were involved in "embroilments," the one with its own Catholic members and the other with an external attack by a Protestant. Beyond this Browning's poem might be said to reflect the views of Pugin in the second edition (1841) of *Contrasts*. In the first edition Pugin had attributed the Reformation to an external attack on the Church by the Protestant heresy, but then in 1841, having in the meantime read Rio and Montalembert, he drastically revised his views and declared that the Church had initially been weakened by internal corruption through imbibing the pagan spirit of the Renaissance. Both Pugin and Montalembert in his *De l'état actuel de l'art religieux en France* (1839) had given many examples of the incongrous mixture of pagan and religious motifs such as the Bishop orders for his tomb. Browning's poem, then, had considerable topicality, not in the sense that its protagonist "represents" the Tractarians or the Camden Society or Pugin, which he in no sense does, but in the sense that it presents a picture of the Italian Renaissance that would have been widely accepted in 1845 by both Catholics and Protestants as historically accurate.

This, indeed, was Browning's genius. Whereas his friend Walter Savage Landor wrote *Imaginary Conversations* in which Scipio and Queen Elizabeth, Lady Godiva and Cromwell all discuss nineteenth-century issues in polished Landorean prose, Browning had a genius for projecting himself back into the past and condensing the essence of an age

into a representative figure. "He has an admirable capacity," wrote Swinburne, "of compressing as with a vice or screw into the limit of some
small monodrame or monologue the representative quality or spiritual
essence of a period."[50] That Browning himself was conscious of this as
the goal of his art is evident from the number of times he appends a
date and place to his titles, so as to locate the poem in a particular age
and culture: "My Last Duchess: Ferrara," "Count Gismond: Aix in Pro-
vence," "How They Brought the Good news from Ghent to Aix (16—),"
"Pictor Ignotus: Florence, 15—," "The Bishop Orders His Tomb at
Saint Praxed's Church: Rome, 15—," "The Laboratory: Ancien Régime," and so on. There are, in addition, the many poems that provide
in their text the means of a fairly exact dating. The person who has paid
the greatest tribute to Browning, however, for his ability to seize upon
the essence of an age is Ruskin. Writing in *Modern Painters* IV, Ruskin
declares that Shakespeare was incapable of entering into the spirit of the
Middle Ages—he always wrote as an Elizabethan—but "Robert Browning is unerring in every sentence he writes of the Middle Ages; always
vital, right, and profound." Shakespeare praises Giulio Romano, but
Browning, "living much in Italy, and quit of the Renaissance influence,
is able fully to enter into the Italian feeling, and to see the evil of the
Renaissance tendency." Ruskin then quotes "The Bishop Orders His
Tomb" and adds, "I know no other piece of modern English prose or
poetry, in which there is so much told, as in these lines, of the Renaissance spirit,—its worldliness, inconsistency, pride, hypocrisy, ignorance
of itself, love of art, of luxury, and of good Latin. It is nearly all that I
said of the central Renaissance in thirty pages of the *Stones of Venice* put
into as many lines, Browning's being also the antecedent work."[51]

Ruskin, of course, could not be more wrong. Initially, he is wrong
in his interpretation of "The Bishop Orders His Tomb," for although
the Bishop is certainly an old rapscallion, deeply confused about the
relation of this world and the next, we would hardly admire the poem
as much as we do if we did not strongly sympathize with his powerful
lust for life. It is in this, as much as in his worldliness, that he represents
the spirit of the Renaissance. Further, Ruskin is wrong in characterizing
the total range and tendency of Browning's work. Despite a remarkable
agreement on the "doctrine of the imperfect," the two men differed
radically on where, historically, that imperfect was to be found, Ruskin
finding it in the art and architecture of the Middle Ages, Browning in
the new spirit of the Renaissance. Both men's view of both periods was
complex and ambiguous, and Browning, like Kingsley, distinguished
between the medieval institutions of monasticism, which he detested,

and of chivalry, which he admired. But, by and large, Browning found the vitality of life smothered by the dogmatism of that faith which, for Ruskin, was the leaven of the Middle Ages. And though Browning acknowledged the pride and evil of the Renaissance, he found in it a vitality which Ruskin (in his unconverted moments) could not but acknowledge too. Moreover, the evil and the pride were primarily in the late Renaissance, and it was the early period, from the thirteenth through the fifteenth century, that Browning mainly prized. He is remarkably consistent in this respect. From the time he chose the epigraphs for *Pauline,* through *Paracelsus* and *Sordello* to the great art poems of 1855, it is the incubation of the new, not the spent perfection of the old, that he desires. Undoubtedly he felt there was an analogy between that period and his own day, the new "open" art of the Romantic poets emerging out of the "closed" art of the neoclassical period in the same way that the "openness" of the Renaissance emerged out of the "closure" of the Middle Ages. In the religiosity and conventional moralism of his own day there was, in Browning's view, a kind of "Victorian Middle Ages," often on the part of the very people, like Ruskin and Mrs. Jameson, who used the Middle Ages as their central metaphor, and so he tried to create in opposition to it a "Victorian Renaissance." In his day this Renaissance had not yet come: it was the fourteenth or fifteenth century, not the sixteenth, but that was all the better. He preferred a transitional age. Writing to Elizabeth Barrett, he declared, "the cant is, that 'an age of transition' is the melancholy thing to contemplate and delineate—whereas the worst things of all to look back on are times of comparative standing still, rounded in their impotent completeness."[52]

9

The English Pre-Raphaelites: Rossetti and Morris

*I*T IS FAIRLY CERTAIN that the Pre-Raphaelite Brotherhood would never have given themselves that name if they had had any idea of the trouble it was going to bring upon them. The accounts of the origin of the name are all very light-hearted. The most plausible is that of Holman Hunt, who says the name came about as a result of an incident in the Royal Academy Schools in 1847. He and Millais had been criticizing Raphael's *Transfiguration* for its "pompous posturing" and "unspiritual attitudinising" and had declared that it was "a signal step in the decadence of Italian art." "Then you are Pre-Raphaelite," said their fellow-students, more or less as a *reductio ad absurdum*—to which Millais and Hunt laughingly agreed.[1] Their remarks seemed absurd because it was widely agreed that the painters before Raphael were ignorant of those technicalities in the art of painting—the laws of perspective, chiaroscuro, proper composition—which it was the purpose of young art students in an academy to learn. As Dickens would say later in his savage review of the P.R.B., it was as if young scientists were to form a "Pre-Newton" or "Pre-Galileo Brotherhood." Thus, when Rossetti indiscreetly let out the secret of the initials with which the group had been signing their paintings, and when the reviewers, under the impression that a conspiracy was afoot, began furiously attacking, some members were willing to backtrack. In January 1851 William Michael Rossetti, secretary of the group, recorded in the P.R.B. Journal, "Millais having raised a doubt as to the propriety of our continuing to call ourselves P.R.B.s, considering the misapprehension which the name excites, it was determined that each of us should write a manifesto declaring the sense in which he accepts the name."[2] These manifestoes, if they were ever written, seem not to have survived, but the Brotherhood was soon provided with one by John Ruskin, who, in a letter to *The Times,* undertook to instruct them in what they ought to mean. While he could not compliment them, he said, on their "common sense in choice of a *nom de guerre,*" it was nonetheless accurate. "They intend to return to early days in this one point only—that, as far as in them lies, they will draw either what they see, or what they suppose might have been the actual facts of the scene they desire to represent, irrespective of any conventional rules of picture-making; and they have chosen their unfortunate though not inaccurate name because all artists did this before Raphael's time, and after Raphael's time did *not* this, but sought to paint fair pictures, rather than represent stern facts."[3] William Michael, copying this passage into the P.R.B. Journal, observes, somewhat with the air of a man who has spoken more wisely than he knew, that Ruskin's explanation of the name is "very sensible."[4] From that time forward there was no further talk of abandoning their nom de guerre.

For nom de guerre it was, and its true meaning was that they had declared war on the Art Establishment and particularly on their teachers in the Royal Academy Schools. Not that they were totally ignorant of the early Italian and Flemish painters and did not sincerely admire them. By August 1848 Rossetti knew enough about them so that, reading Monckton Milnes' *Life and Letters of Keats* (1848), he was overjoyed to discover that Keats, his poetic idol of the moment, was also a Pre-Raphaelite! "He seems to have been a glorious fellow," he wrote to his brother, "and says in one place (to my great delight) that, having just looked over a folio of the first and second schools of Italian painting, he had come to the conclusion that the early men surpassed even Raphael himself!"[5] A few weeks later the P.R.B. were assembled at Millais's studio poring over a borrowed copy of Carlo Lasinio's engravings of the frescoes in the Campo Santo at Pisa (apparently the very volume Keats had examined thirty years earlier, though he thought the church was in Milan), and they were charmed and delighted by the fresh naiveté and natural vigor of these drawings. A year later Hunt and Rossetti, on a trip to Paris, Antwerp, and Bruges, were excoriating Rubens and Correggio ("*Non noi pittori!* God of Nature's truth, / If these, not we!")[6] and were reveling in the work of Memling and Van Eyck. Finally, in February 1850 in a *Germ* article on "The Purpose and Tendency of Early Italian Art" F. G. Stephens, one of the lesser of the seven, makes mention of Benozzo Gozzoli, Ghiberti, Fra Angelico, Masaccio, Ghirlandaio, Baccio della Porta, Orcagna, Giotto, and Dürer, and acknowledges the histories of D'Agincourt, Rosini, and Ottley as the sources of his information.

In truth, the Pre-Raphaelites were not revolutionaries in this area. For fifty years there had been a growing interest, both in England and on the continent, in early Italian art.[7] It was in the 1780s in France that Séroux d'Agincourt began collecting materials for his great *Histoire de l'art d'après les monuments* (1811–23) which, for the first time, gave a prominent place to painting in the centuries before Raphael. A little later William Young Ottley, an amateur painter and writer on art, went to Italy to study trecento and quattrocento paintings, many of which he reproduced in his *Italian School of Design* (1823). It is to him we owe that the word *primitive* took on a descriptive and no longer an abusive flavor. As a result of these and other investigations a Select Committee on the Arts reported in 1836 that the pictures sought for the national collections "should be those of the era of Raphael, or of the times just antecedent to it, such works being of a purer and more elevated style than the eminent works of the Caracci."[8] This was exactly the thesis of A. F. Rio's *De la poésie chrétienne,* published in 1836, and it was soon to be supported by the writings of Mrs. Jameson and Lord Lindsay, whose *Sketches of the History of Christian Art* came out in 1847. Lord Lindsay actually called for the formation of something like a Pre-Raphaelite Brotherhood.[9] As if to provide the means for this, in June 1848, at the very moment when the Brotherhood was being organized, an important exhibition was held in London at the British Institution which contained, as its Catalogue informs us, "as a novelty . . . a series of Pictures from the times of Giotto and Van Eyck."[10] There is no evidence that any one of the Pre-Raphaelite group attended the exhibition, but, given the smallness of the London art world, it is hard to believe that they did not.

There was, however, an additional precedent for a Brotherhood. In 1810 a group of young German artists, repelled by the training they had received in the Vienna Academy, migrated to Rome and established a semi-monastic community devoted to wedding art to the spirit of the Christian religion in the manner of the early medieval painters. They called themselves the Brotherhood of St. Luke, since Luke, according to legend, had been a painter and was the patron saint of the medieval artists' guilds, but they were popularly known as the Nazarenes.[11] The most prominent members were Johann Friedrich Overbeck, a Catholic convert, and Peter Cornelius, born a Catholic. Cornelius soon went back to Munich, where he acquired such a reputation that in 1841 he was invited over to England to consult about the proposed frescoes for the new House of Commons. His visit aroused so much interest that when Ruskin's father submitted to John Murray the manuscript of the first volume of *Modern Painters,* he was advised to tell his son to forget about Turner and write about "the German school."[12] Meanwhile, in Rome the studio of Overbeck and his associates had become virtually a required stopping-place for tourists and foreign visitors, especially the English. Nicholas Wiseman, the young rector of the English College, went there, and David Scott, the brother of Rossetti's friend William Bell Scott, visited their studio and was favorably impressed by their work. Another Scottish painter, William Dyce, studied with them in 1827–28, and since it was he who dragged Ruskin up to Millais's *Christ in the House of his Parents* in the Academy exhibition of 1850 and forced him to notice its merits, one may say that Ruskin was introduced to the P.R.B. by one who already understood its ideals. Finally, Ford Madox Brown studied under Overbeck in the autumn of 1845 and was still painting in the Overbeckian manner when Rossetti became his pupil in the early summer of 1848. Indeed, Brown declared that it was through him that the P.R.B. acquired its name. "When they [Rossetti and Hunt] began talking about the early Italian masters, I naturally told them of the German P.R.'s, and either it pleased them or not, I don't know, but they took it."[13] One should not conclude from this, however, that the P.R.B. were "English Nazarenes," for whereas the Germans were a deeply religious and closely knit group devoted to the study and revival of medieval Christian painting, the P.R.B. were a much more loosely organized and secular group whose knowledge of these masters was relatively superficial.

Nonetheless, if the Pre-Raphaelites were not pioneers in the rediscovery of early Italian art, they were at least using this body of more enlightened opinion as a means of attacking the system of education in the Academy Schools, which had not yet caught up with it.[14] For them Raphael was simply the analogue and ancestor of Sir Joshua Reynolds, first president of the Royal Academy, whose *Discourses* epitomized the tradition of art education over the past three hundred years and were still the reigning authority in the Schools. Ruskin tells us what this authority enjoined.

We begin, in all probability, by telling the youth of fifteen or sixteen, that Nature is full of faults, and that he is to improve her; but that Raphael is perfection, and that the more he copies Raphael the better; that after much copying of Raphael, he is to try what he can do himself in a Raphaelesque, but yet original manner: that is to say, he is to try to do something very clever, all out of his own head, but yet this clever something is to be properly subjected to Raphaelesque rules, is to have a principal light occupying one-seventh of its space, and a principal shadow occupying one-third of the same; that no two people's heads in the picture are to be turned the same way, and that all the personages represented are to possess ideal beauty of the highest order, which ideal beauty consists partly in a Greek outline of nose, partly in proportions expressible in decimal fractions between the lips and chin; but mostly in that degree of improvement which the youth of sixteen is to bestow upon God's work in general. This I say is the kind of teaching which through various channels, Royal Academy lecturings, press criticisms, public enthusiasm, and not least by solid weight of gold, we give to our young men.[15]

The student was taught to draw from plaster casts of antique sculpture in the British Museum and from paintings in the National Gallery. There was no concern with whether he had anything to say, whether he had a fresh vision of the world to communicate, or indeed whether he was capable of having significant visual experience. The academic tradition was pure neoclassical formalism, and the Pre-Raphaelite rebellion was a phase of the Romantic movement in behalf of Nature coming just fifty years after it had occurred in poetry. The reason it was so late is that the education of the artist, being partly technical, was entrusted to an institution, whereas the education of the poet was a purely individual affair conducted by each poet for himself. Hence, in the poetic phase of Pre-Raphaelitism we find no rebellion. Rossetti's early poetry is simply a continuation of the work of Coleridge, Keats, Poe, Tennyson, Browning, and the Gothic revival. But in art (except in landscape, which was well ahead of historical painting) it was necessary to rebel against the despotism of compositional formulae and reassert the importance of subject. That is why the first critical article in *The Germ* is J. L. Tupper's "The Subject in Art." Tupper's thesis is that "fine art delights us from its being the semblance of what in nature delights." But since, as we come to know and love nature, all things affect us with equal intensity, all things are a proper subject of art so long as they are represented sincerely and truly.[16] The essay is the P.R.B. equivalent of the Preface to the *Lyrical Ballads*.

Of that and the first volume of *Modern Painters*, which also emphasized Ideas of Truth. Ruskin had concluded this volume by declaring that the duty of the young artist is "neither to choose, nor compose, nor imagine, nor experimentalize; but to be humble and earnest in following the steps of nature, and tracing the finger of God. . . . They should . . . go to Nature in all singleness of heart, and walk with her laboriously and trustingly, having no other thoughts but how best to penetrate her meaning, and remember her instruction; rejecting nothing, selecting nothing, and scorning nothing; believing all things to be right and good, and rejoicing always in the truth."[17] Reynolds, of course, was also concerned with truth, but he approached it through the general, not the particular. "All the objects which are exhibited to our view by Nature," he declared in the third Discourse, "upon close examination will be found to have their blemishes and defects." The artist, by a long habit of observing and comparing objects of the same kind, "makes out an abstract idea of their forms more perfect than any one original." "The whole beauty and grandeur of the Art consists, in my opinion, in being able to get above all singular forms, local customs, particularities, and details of every kind."[18] Ruskin, on the other hand, declared that "all truths . . . are valuable in proportion as they are particular, and valueless in proportion as they are general."[19] The Pre-Raphaelites went even further. They declared roundly that "nature has no peculiarities or eccentricities,"[20] and to suppose that it does is to defame the handiwork of God. Though Reynolds had cautioned against misinterpreting his advice as countenancing "a careless or indetermined manner of painting," that is exactly what the P.R.B. thought it did, and they nicknamed him "Sir Sloshua," and anything done in his manner "sloshy."

How "medieval" the P.R.B. was, was a point at issue among the Brothers themselves. Hunt always thought the main point of their creed was fidelity to Nature and deplored the "Early Christian" influence of Brown and the Nazarenes. He agreed that the early Italian masters exemplified fidelity to Nature but thought that they had their own mannerisms and that one should not imitate them any more than those of the Renaissance painters. There was also the question of how far back one should go. William Michael Rossetti refers to John Orchard's "Dialogue on Art" in *The Germ* as "treating . . . chiefly of early Christian—or, as he terms it, Pre-Raffaelle—Art, and seeming to out-P.R. the P.R.B." What he apparently meant by this is explained by Hunt's dictum that "Pre-Raphaelitism is not Pre-Raphaelism"[21]—that is, one should go back before the followers of Raphael but not before Raphael himself. Ruskin, as we have already seen, placed the decay of art right in the middle of Raphael's career, and this had been the opinion of Rio and Schlegel before him. When Ruskin came to review the work of the Brotherhood in *The Times,* he took the view of Hunt that the P.R.B. went back to the painters before Raphael only for their manner of patient and detailed representation of Nature, and he indicated that "if their sympathies with the early artists lead them into mediævalism or Romanism, they will of course come to nothing!"[22] Rossetti was forced by this statement to modify his allegiance to Brown, and in September 1851 he urged his brother, who was preparing a defense of the P.R.B. against the attacks of the reviewers, "not [to] attempt to defend my mediævalisms, which *were* absurd, but rather say that there was enough good in the works to give assurance that these were merely superficial."[23] By "mediævalisms" Rossetti apparently meant the lack of perspective and chiaroscuro, hard-edge modeling, stiff and angular poses, emaciated figures, and other rejections of post-Renaissance technique which the reviewers took to be their principal crime.

As to the subjects of their paintings, though the P.R.B. did paint many "medieval" (i.e., early Christian) subjects, there was actually much more emphasis in their theory on the importance of the modern subject. Both F. G. Stephens and J. L. Tupper had articles on the question in *The Germ,* declaring that poets take their subjects from the past because past events come clothed with poetry and romance, but since the present is the real source of their inspiration, why should they not take them thence? They go to Greece and Rome for an example of charity, when they might use that of a friend helping an old woman across the street. "And there is something else we miss: there is the poetry of the things about us; our railways, factories, mines, roaring cities, steam vessels, and the endless novelties and wonders produced every day." William Michael Rossetti also praised Clough's *Bothie of Toper-na-fuosich* for its "recognition of every-day fact, and a willingness to believe it as capable of poetry as that which, but for having once been fact, would not now be tradition."[24] William Michael, indeed, had already written one of the most dryly factual poems in the language, *Mrs. Holmes Grey,* a story of marital infidelity couched in the flat, newspaper style of a coroner's report. This concern with the modern subject was not original with the Pre-Raphaelite Brotherhood. It first became a major issue in Victorian criticism about the time of the first Reform Bill, and its proponents were generally the "march-of-mind" men and the Spasmodics, though John Sterling probably made the classic statement of the "new poem" in his 1842 review of Tennyson.

Despite this long tradition, Dante Gabriel evidently thought the idea of the modern subject was original with him, for he complains in a letter to Ruskin that Hunt had anticipated him. Ruskin professed to believe that he was right, but went on to say that "it would have been impossible for men of such eyes and hearts as Millais and Hunt to walk the streets of London . . . and not to discover also what there was in them to be shown and painted." The painting of Rossetti which had been anticipated was *Found,* which Rossetti always spoke of simply as his "modern subject."[25] It depicts a young farmer from the country, who, driving his calf to market, recognizes in a prostitute on the pavement his former sweetheart. He tries to raise her from the ground, but she shrinks back and turns her face to the wall. Rossetti began this painting in 1851 and worked on it off and on for thirty years but never finished it, so uncongenial was the subject. Its poetic counterpart is "Jenny," the reflections of a self-conscious young man musing over a prostitute asleep on his knee. Would that it too had never been finished, for it is a prudish piece, thoroughly uncharacteristic of Rossetti's genius. The trouble with the modern subject for the Pre-Raphaelites was that they thought of it in sociological terms. It was to deal, as J. L. Tupper makes clear, with the fallen woman, the oppressor of workmen, the domestic fireside, the victim of ruinous taxation. The Pre-Raphaelite movement was not un-related to the other events of 1848, with which both Hunt and Rossetti felt a mild sympathy. But it was only mild, and what they apparently did not realize was that they were modern not by virtue of their subject but their sensibility.

Indeed, the early Pre-Raphaelite pictures were distinctly modern precisely *because* they were medieval. They rejected a tradition of three hundred years in favor of a new movement in art toward the "primitive." The hard-edged, decorative style with pure, clear colors and angular poses shocked and outraged their contemporaries because people were used to soft religious pictures that were bland and mellifluous in the post-Renaissance style. Ruskin was overwhelmed by the frescoes in the Campo Santo because they persuaded him, for the first time, that Job and the patriarchs were real people who had actually lived. Millais rep-resented Christ in the carpenter's shop to show that he had once been a little boy who might well have jabbed his hand with a chisel—however much typological significance that fact would have. Rossetti's *Girlhood of Mary Virgin* showed the Virgin as an ordinary English girl looking very much like his sister Christina, taking an embroidery lesson from someone looking very much like their mother. And *Ecce Ancilla Domini* gave a startling interpretation of the Annunciation by showing an un-dernourished girl shrinking back on her pallet bed from the awesome responsibility of being the Mother of Christ. In *Found* Rossetti devoted most of his attention to the calf and the brick wall, but in these "non-modern" pictures he focused on the central spiritual drama common to ancient and modern times. Recent scholarship has emphasized the typological interpretation of these pictures—that the homely details prefigure the larger spiritual events of Christ's life—but they are also typological in another way, that they foreshadow similar events in our own lives. Rossetti gave a sharp edge of authenticity to scenes that had been dulled by centuries of formulaic repetition.

The true Pre-Raphaelite program may be found in the story "Hand and Soul." This eminently modern piece, which anticipates Pater's *Imaginary Portraits* by forty years, tells of a young painter of Arezzo, Chiaro dell' Erma, who, after pursuing the false goals of fame, religious faith, and public service, finally had a vision of a woman clad in green and grey raiment, who spoke to him, saying, "I am an image, Chiaro, of thine own soul within thee. . . . Paint me thus, as I am, to know me. . . . so shall thy soul stand before thee always, and perplex thee no more."[26] The narrator of this story tells us that he was in Florence in the spring of 1847 and saw, in the Pitti Gallery, Chiaro dell' Erma's picture of a woman in green and grey raiment. In one corner was the legend *Manus Animam pinxit* and the date 1239. Needless to say, the art students were all busy copying and admiring the *Berrettino* of Raphael.

That the true subject of the Pre-Raphaelite painter is his own soul is further reinforced in Rossetti's other metaphysical story, "Saint Agnes of Intercession." It is the story of a modern English painter who, as a child, had seen a reproduction of a painting of St. Agnes by the fifteenth-century Italian painter, Angiolieri, and had been so penetrated by its beauty that, years later, when he had totally forgotten the picture, he unconsciously reproduced it while painting his fiancée, Mary Arden. What is more, he discovered that he himself exactly resembled a self-portrait of Angiolieri and that Angiolieri had painted his St. Agnes from his own fiancée, who was then dying. The story is unfinished, presumably because Rossetti could not figure out any way to rescue his hero from the difficulty of having already painted the portrait of his fiancée which he obviously should have deferred until she was dying. But despite the creaking Gothic machinery, the meaning of the story is clear: there is a deep spiritual affinity between the modern and the medieval painter. "Hand and Soul" told of a medieval painter in whom the narrator found his alter ego, "Saint Agnes" of a modern painter who is a reincarnation of the Middle Ages.

The artist, then, must depict his own soul, but the question is, how shall it be garbed? In "Hand and Soul" it takes the form of a woman clad in green and grey raiment, but in "St. Agnes of Intercession" the speaker's fiancée is in modern dress. "The subject was a modern one," he says, "and indeed it has often seemed to me that all work, to be truly worthy, should be wrought out of the age itself, as well as out of the soul of its producer, which must needs be a soul of the age."[27] This is undoubtedly Rossetti's aesthetic creed: the artist is a distinctly modern spirit who creates out of the spirit of his own age. And yet it was in the garb of the fifteenth century that the speaker first fell in love with Mary Arden, and it was in that garb that he saw himself reflected. The question of costume is important, for both Ruskin and Morris tell us that it was partly because of the ugliness of nineteenth-century dress that artists fled to the Middle Ages. James Smetham, a minor Pre-Raphaelite painter, reminded Ruskin that when a medieval artist painted a religious or scriptural theme he dressed the figures in the normal clothes of his own time. Should not the modern artist do the same? Ruskin agreed that on his principles he should, adding that "if it would not look well, the times are wrong and their modes must be altered." Smetham replied that it would be a great deal easier for the painter, but "I could not do it for laughing."[28] Rossetti could not do it for tedium. Apropos of Ford Madox Brown's painting *Work* he wrote, "I am beginning to doubt more and more, I confess, whether that excessive elaboration is rightly bestowed on the materials of a modern subject—things so familiar to the eye that they can really be rendered thoroughly (I fancy) with much less labour; and things moreover which are often far from beautiful in themselves,—for instance the flowering waistcoat of a potboy on which Brown has lately been spending some weeks of his life."[29] Modern dress was ugly and irrelevant; the advantage of medieval or renaissance or even ancient dress was that it did not distract from the central drama of the soul. It could, indeed, be so conceived as to be the objective correlative of that psychological reality which it was Rossetti's main concern to paint.

For Rossetti was primarily a psychological artist. In a very perceptive essay Nicolette Gray observes that Rossetti's subjects are "all of people at some moment of psychological awareness."[30] More specifically, they are of people caught in a moment of expectation or dread, for Rossetti's characters are typically looking to the future rather than the past. They are waiting for something to happen which does not happen or is infinitely deferred, and they are feeling a sense of anxiety, strain, and frustration. The Blessed Damozel leans over the gold bar of Heaven scrutinizing the thin flames of mounting spirits to see if her lover is among them. In "My Sister's Sleep" the brother waits in dread and expectation for his sister's death. "The Staff and Scrip" is told not from the point of view of the knight who fights but of the Queen who waits till his body is brought back upon its bier. Sister Helen and her little brother wait while her waxen man slowly melts, and in "The Bride's Prelude" Amelotte waits in anguish while her sister slowly reveals her shame. "The Last Confession" is not so much a confession as the deferral of a confession as long as may be, and "The Stream's Secret" is not so much told as withheld, in agonizingly frustrating detail. "Ave," like *Ecce Ancilla Domini,* explores the question whether the Blessed Virgin did not from the very first feel the foreboding of the crucifixion. *The House of Life* is much more a House of Death than of Life, for it tells the story of lovers who find little fulfillment but wander ceaselessly in the wanwood of their own desire.

This typical situation, of strained and anxious waiting, might be called the "Mariana syndrome," after a poem by Tennyson which was very important to the P.R.B. and which several of them illustrated. It will be rememberd that the striking thing about Tennyson's Mariana is the way her mind, as she waits for the lover who will not come, fastens on minute details in her environment—the mouse shrieking in the wainscot, the motes of dust suspended in the sunlight, the rusted nails in the gable wall. Indeed, there is a sense in which the moated grange *is* Mariana's mind, and thus Tennyson may be said to have anticipated the P.R.B. in the use of minute details for psychological purposes.[31] Ruskin's interest in detail was generally to enable the artist to represent God's creation accurately, but even he acknowledged that an obsessive overelaboration of detail might have a subjective purpose. In interpreting Hunt's *The Awakening Conscience,* he comments on the minute rendering of inferior details in the picture and justifies these by saying, "Nothing is more notable than the way in which even the most trivial objects force themselves upon the attention of a mind which has been fevered by violent and distressful excitement. They thrust themselves forward with a ghastly and unendurable distinctness, as if they would compel the sufferer to count, or measure, or learn them by heart."[32]

This is Rossetti's technique in "My Sister's Sleep," where the brother's mind, exhausted from his long vigil in the sickroom, magnifies the minute sights and sounds—the light clicking of his mother's knitting needles, the pushing back of chairs in the room overhead—until they assume a greater prominence in his consciousness than the overwhelming fact of his sister's death. The poem has been criticized by some readers as religiously insincere, while others have found in the (presumably) crossed knitting needles a symbol of the crucifixion. But surely the focus of the poem is on mere phenomena—on the psychological experience of the sickroom, not its transcendental meaning. So in "A Last Confession" the thing that is etched most deeply into the speaker's mind is the way the girl's stiff bodice, as she fell, "scooped the sand / Into her bosom." And Amelotte, in the oppressive heat of the chamber in "The Bride's Prelude," is less acutely conscious of her sister's shame than of the sound, far beneath, of a hound plunging into a moat. Rossetti has summarized and symbolized this technique in the little poem "Woodspurge," where the poet, in a moment of intense grief, notes that the European woodspurge "has a cup of three," and stubbornly refuses to rise from that fact to any wisdom or deepened understanding. These poems are not ironic or reductive or deconstructive—they are the poems of one who feels that in his day the best way to convey intense emotional experience is not to appeal to outworn humanistic or religious symbols but rather to mere phenomena, on which the mind fastens in such a moment.

This technique bears on the way in which Rossetti is at once medieval and modern. "The Blessed Damozel" is obviously both. It could not have been written without Dante, but it deliberately reverses the Dantesque situation by having the lady in heaven longing for her lover on earth instead of the other way around. The situation is potentially blasphemous and scandalous, and it is not helped by the fact that the lady seems to have left none of her fleshly attributes behind. Her bosom makes the bar she leans on warm. Moreover, her idea of Heaven is

> Only to live as once on earth
>   With Love,—only to be,
> As then awhile, for ever now
>   Together, I and he.

Though she is conscious of her sexuality, she is quite unconscious that there is anything wrong with it, and one does not know whether love is thereby sacramentalized or religion eroticized. One is only sure that the mingling of the two elements is absolutely essential to Rossetti's purpose. If these are "Dantesque heavens," as Leigh Hunt suggested, they are put to a use at which Dante would have been scandalized, for the poem is not medieval but modern. And it could not be so modern if it were not also medieval.

The question of the degree to which Rossetti's poetry is religious or secular is a matter which has been much debated in recent years. The older humanistic view, stated by Harold Weatherby, Graham Hough, and others, is that Rossetti's extensive use of traditional religious symbolism is not supported by an inner core of belief, so that this material becomes at best decorative and at worst insincere. To this Jerome McGann has replied that transforming the traditional Christian imagery is precisely Rossetti's purpose.[33] He wants to empty it of its traditional content and give it a new, naturalistic meaning that will be consonant with the modern world. More recently a new group of scholars, George

Landow, Herbert L. Sussman, and D. M. R. Bentley, have emphasized the typological and iconographic content of the very early poems and paintings and so have taken us back to a position prior to Weatherby and Hough (which they claim is the historical one), in which the religious imagery is not decorative or insincere but constitutes the almost forgotten language of works that are "unequivocally religious."[34] For the most part their claims are limited to the early versions of "My Sister's Sleep," "The Blessed Damozel," "Ave," and the early P.R.B. paintings, and there is no question but that they have illuminated the typological language of these works. Still, it is not clear that McGann is not right after all about the use to which that language is put. One might say that there is simply more Christian imagery in these works than one had realized, to be transformed by Rossetti to his novel purpose. The fact that he did transform it so quickly suggests that his Christian phase was, at the very least, a passing one.

Indeed, all the biographical evidence suggests that Rossetti was not very religious. Professor Bentley notes that from 1843 to 1853 Rossetti attended with members of his family and his P.R.B. associates Christ Church, Albany Street, and then St. Andrew's, Wells Street, both renowned for their High Church ritual and Catholic appearance. One may concede that Rossetti was affected by the Tractarian movement and that he learned about Christian symbolism and ritual not only from books but also from institutions. But William Michael Rossetti, who knew his brother intimately and is a dependable reporter, says that although Rossetti had "a certain propensity" towards religion, he "had not at this time [1855] (nor at others) much religion of a definable kind." "Of all Rossetti's poems," he says, "['Ave'] is the one which seems most to indicate definite Christian belief, and of a strongly Roman Catholic kind. Such inference would, however, be erroneous; his training was not in the Roman but the Anglican Church, and by the time when he wrote 'Ave' he was more than vague in point of religious faith. That time was very early, 1847." Rossetti himself noted of the poem in 1869 that he had adopted "an inner [i.e., psychological] standing-point"[35] in writing it. Unlike the Nazarenes, the P.R.B. as a group clearly was not religious. In a meeting of November 6, 1849 they discussed whether they should admit "anything at all referring to politics or religion into our magazine," and in point of fact nothing on either subject was admitted. The following July, James Collinson, a Catholic, resigned from the Brotherhood because "I love and reverence God's faith, and I love His holy Saints; and I cannot bear any longer the self-accusation that, to gratify a little vanity, I am helping to dishonor them, and lower their merits, if not absolutely to bring their sanctity into ridicule." It is uncertain just what was troubling him, but it is difficult to see how anyone who was religious could have subscribed to the "List of Immortals" which Dante Gabriel drew up in August 1848. It consisted of the names of fifty-seven famous men and declared that "the following list of Immortals constitutes the whole of our Creed, and that there exists no other Immortality than what is centered in their names."[36] Jesus Christ comes first and has four stars (the only one who does), but the startling thing is that he is in the same list with Chaucer, Shakespeare, and Boccaccio. Indeed, Rossetti was generally cavalier in his references to religion. His *Ecce Ancilla Domini* was regularly referred to as the "blessed white daub," which hardly suggests he considered it a sacred object, and of "The Sacrament Hymn," which Professor Bentley considers "unequivocally religious," Rossetti says that it "was written merely to see if I could do [i.e., imitate] Wesley, and copied, I believe, to enrage my friends."[37]

Rossetti's medieval world, then, was not the age of faith envisioned by Ruskin, nor was it the simpler organic society dreamed of by Carlyle. It was essentially a decadent society preoccupied with love. The three bodies of medieval material which most deeply influenced Rossetti were Dante, Malory's *Morte D'Arthur,* and the English and Scottish popular ballads. But the Dante whom Rossetti affected was Dante the lover rather than the theologian—the author of the *Vita Nuova* rather than the *Commedia*—and when he turned to Malory it was not to the knightly quests but to the great adulterous love story at the center of that book. With two exceptions his imitations of the English and Scottish popular ballads also deal with love, particularly the destructive power of sexual passion. It is perhaps too much to say, with Richard L. Stein, that Rossetti's volume of translations, *The Early Italian Poets,* is "an almost self-conscious counterargument" to Ruskin's *Stones of Venice,* published a decade before, but it does present a strikingly different view of the Middle Ages. Rossetti's preliminary design for the titlepage shows a pair of lovers lightly kissing in a garden. The drawing, as Professor Stein notes, presents Rossetti's view of the true "nature of Gothic."[38]

The Gothic for Rossetti is not a harmonious cathedral which happy workmen have created as the expression of their hierarchical view of society, but a dark wood or an oppressive chamber in which pale-faced lovers speak wanly of their frustrated passions. Nicolette Gray notes how, in Rossetti's drawings and watercolors,

> with very few exceptions the setting to the figures is an enclosed space, in many cases so confined that there is no room for them to stand

upright. In the majority of designs the setting is a small room, in the
others the space is enclosed by a curtain, a high hedge, dense foliage,
or an architectural arrangement of walls or steps. The effect is a sense
of airlessness. . . . In almost all these rooms, there is a window looking
out on to a quite different world; outside the tense atmosphere the sun
is shining and the air is fresh, ordinary people are pursuing the normal
routine of life.[39]

It would be too much to say that the world outside this window is the
Renaissance, for, apart from the name Pre-Raphaelite, Rossetti hardly
distinguishes between the Middle Ages and the Renaissance. His world
includes medievalized versions of Greek and Biblical themes and also
the "modern Gothic" of the English and German romantics. It is a
timeless world which stands in no historical relation to his own because
it is a metaphor for his own. One cannot agree, then, with those critics
who say that Rossetti's medievalism is "essentially decorative" or that
it has no direct contemporary relevance.[40] One would rather say that
Rossetti's relation to the past is figured in his poem "The Mirror," where
a person in a crowded room, who thinks he discerns his own reflection
in a mirror, shakes his head but, finding that the image does not shake
back, knows he must look elsewhere for his image. Rossetti, looking
into the mirror of history, found he got no response from the classical
world or the eighteenth century, but he did from the medievalized or
Gothic world wherever he found it. It was both medieval and modern.
No one would mistake Rossetti's ballads for their originals, for they are,
as Rossetti said, "modern-antique." They are modern not in dealing
with modern social problems but in dealing with a modern sensibility.
They are also modern in their belatedness, for like Tennyson, Rossetti
gives us a medieval world that is already in decline. The Dante whom
Ruskin took to represent the height of the Middle Ages is already in
exile in Rossetti and waiting out his end, subject to the insults of little
men. It is not a simple and organic world that he inhabits but a bitter
and complex one.

Perhaps the best image, however, for Rossetti's relation to the past
is that provided by his drawing *How They Met Themselves,* in which a
pair of lovers in a dark wood encounter their own image and shrink
back in amaze. To see one's own doppelgänger is supposed to be an
omen of death, but it is the startling encounter with selfhood that is in
question here. Rossetti was fascinated with mirrors, reflections, echoes,
shadows, images—all things that suggest the self but do not constitute
it—for he was aware that it was often by means of the other that one
can best explore the self. One feels that the Victorian Age was peculiarly

blind in thinking that the modern subject means "our railways, factories, mines, and roaring cities." For Rossetti, as for many of the best artists, it meant the soul of modern man.

William Morris shared Rossetti's opinion about the intimate relation between medieval and modern art. By "modern art," he declared, he meant the art which arose about the time of Justinian, reached its height in the Middle Ages, and declined in the age of Charles V. The Renaissance and subsequent neoclassical period was simply an interruption of this natural, organic style which, if it had been allowed to continue, would have developed down to the present. "As an epoch of art [the Renaissance] can teach us nothing; so the nearest possible period to our own days must stand for modern art."[41] "Those only among our painters do work worth considering, whose minds have managed to leap back across the intervening years, across the waste of gathering commercialism, into the later Middle Ages; they are steeped through and through with the manner and ideas of the great Italian painters and their forerunners, and it is through this alone that they are able to produce their beautiful and, paradox as it may seem, *original* works. Anyone who wants beauty to be produced at the present day in any branch of the fine arts, I care not what, must be always crying out 'Look back! look back!' "[42]

The question is, in what sense or with what purpose does one look back, that of pure antiquarianism, of high adventure and romance, of idle regret and nostalgia, or, as Morris says, "with humility, hope, and courage; not in striving to bring the dead to life again, but to enrich the present and the future"?[43] Morris embodied most of these attitudes at some period of his life and, indeed, is almost an epitome of the development of nineteenth-century medievalism. As a boy he had read through all the Waverley novels by the age of seven and used to ride about the park on his pony in a suit of toy armor. Then, at Oxford, he fell under the influence of Puseyism and, with Burne-Jones, contemplated founding a monastic order which would have had as its patron Tennyson's Sir Galahad: "My strength is as the strength of ten, / Because my heart is pure." Even before arriving at Oxford he had read Ruskin's first two volumes, and soon thereafter he added Carlyle's *Past and Present* and Ruskin's *Stones of Venice,* whose chapter on "The Nature of Gothic" became his central text. Ruskin, he wrote, was "my master," and "I cannot help saying . . . how deadly dull the world would have been twenty years ago but for Ruskin!" (XXIII, 279). Also at Oxford he read Chaucer, Froissart, and Malory, his favorite medieval authors, and began the study of illuminated manuscripts in the Bodleian. Then, in 1856 he came under the influence of Rossetti, painted with him the murals in the Oxford Union on subjects drawn from Malory, and began to write poems in "a medieval volume with a large clasp." The result was *The Defence of Guenevere, and Other Poems* (1858), the first proper Pre-Raphaelite volume, "exceedingly young also and very mediæval."[44]

Pater, in his review of Morris's poems, notes that the medievalism of the nineteenth century went through three phases, first, a superficial phase of mere adventure and romance as represented by Scott's novels, then a more refined and imaginative phase which reproduced the mystic religion of Dante and Saint Louis, the mystic passion of Abelard and Lancelot. This is found in Victor Hugo in France, in Heine in Germany. Morris's medievalism, according to Pater, was a refinement upon this refinement. His poetry "is neither a mere reproduction of Greek or mediæval life or poetry, nor a disguised reflex of modern sentiment. . . . It is a finer ideal, extracted from what in relation to any actual world is already an ideal. Like some strange second flowering after date, it renews on a more delicate type the poetry of a past age, but must not be confounded with it."[45] Pater explains his meaning by comparing Morris's poems with the Hellenism of the late Middle Ages; it is the reflex of one civilization through another. We cannot recreate a past age, for we cannot obliterate the subsequent experience that has modified us; but we can isolate some part of that age, throw it into relief, and be divided against ourselves in our zeal for it. This light of the late Middle Ages or early Renaissance is, says Pater, to some choice spirits more exquisite than the Renaissance itself, and so Morris's subtle mingling of the Christian and the pagan, the sensuous and the spiritual, makes him a figure of reverie, illusion, and delirium—at once medieval and modern.[46]

The poems of *The Defence of Guenevere,* indeed, are medieval in a curiously decadent sense. The title poem sounds like Baudelaire protesting against *Paradise Lost.* Whereas Tennyson had the adulterous Queen chided by the innocent voice of a little novice and then denounced by King Arthur, Morris represents Guenevere as a woman trapped in the unintelligible world of men and resting her case purely upon her beauty and her passion. It is tempting to read Morris's poem as an answer to Tennyson, but since Morris's "Defence" was published in March 1858 and Tennyson's "Guinevere" was not published till 1859 (though it was written in January to March 1858), it is clear that neither poem could have influenced the other. Nevertheless, they are opposition pieces, and Morris's "Sir Galahad: A Christmas Mystery" undoubtedly was written in opposition to Tennyson's "Sir Galahad," whom Morris had come by this time to consider "rather a mild youth."[47] Gone are the thoughts of a celibate monastic order, for it is clear that Galahad's celibacy has been arduously attained and he rather envies Lancelot and Sir Palomydes their worldly loves. Moreover, the quest for the Holy Grail is a bitter failure: "Sir Lionel / And Gauwaine have come back . . . / Just merely shamed." Lauvaine is perhaps dead, and "everywhere / The knights come foil'd from the great quest." The other major body of poems derive from Froissart and deal with the bitter failure of the Hundred Years War. Sir Peter Harpdon's end is to be hanged, and John of Castel Neuf tells of finding the skeletons of two lovers in a wood, which evokes boyhood memories of seeing a group of women burned to death in a church. Jehane is dragged to the "haystack in the floods" only to see her lover's head bashed in under the iron heels of Godmar's men. All the characters in Morris's volume are in impossible situations. It is a world of rude violence and brutal passion that has no relation to Carlyle's or Ruskin's ideal. It is, in a way, a more masculine version of Rossetti's late, decadent world of frustration and delay. It has, in great measure, the Pre-Raphaelite quality of intensity, and one may think that, just as Wordsworth chose to write of simple people because in them the passions were more transparent and overt, so Morris chose the Middle Ages for a similar reason.

In Morris's *The Life and Death of Jason,* published nine years after *The Defence of Guenevere,* Pater professes to see a change of manner so fundamental that it is "almost a revolt." "Here there is no delirium or illusion . . . ; but rather the great primary passions under broad daylight as of the pagan Veronese. This simplification interests us not merely for the sake of an individual poet—full of charm as he is—but chiefly because it explains through him a transition which, under many forms, is one law of the life of the human spirit, and of which what we call the Renaissance is only a supreme instance." Pater asserts this not because of the Greek subject of the poem, for he notes its many "medievalisms," but because he thinks Morris has moved from dreamlight to daylight— to "the simple elementary passions . . . and what corresponds to them in the sensuous world."[48] In other words, he thinks that Morris in *The Life and Death of Jason* has made a personal transition from the Middle Ages to the Renaissance, and that is perhaps why he felt free to reprint the entire last part of his review as the Conclusion to *The Renaissance.* When we read this famous utterance in its present place, with its advice "to burn always with this hard, gemlike flame," we assume that Pater arrived at this conclusion as a result of his study of Botticelli, Michelangelo, Leonardo da Vinci, and Giorgione; but it was not so. It was as a result of reading a modern poet who was infatuated with the Middle Ages. Whether Morris was wrong in his choice of period or Pater was doing him a wrong in assigning him to the Renaissance may well be a question, but one does feel that Morris's medievalism, like Rossetti's, was fundamentally different from that of many of his older contemporaries. He was using an ancient period in behalf of an outlook that was revolutionary and modern.

Morris, indeed, began to differentiate himself from some elements in the Gothic revival when, in 1877, horrified by the wanton destruction of ancient buildings in the name of their "restoration," he formed the Society for the Protection of Ancient Buildings, known as Anti-Scrape. It was his view that one literally could not restore a Gothic building because the quality of its stonework, the texture of its surface, was so deeply imbued by the mind and spirit of the workmen who had produced it that, no matter how much antiquarian knowledge one might assemble, the reproduction would be all wrong. A Victorian workman could no more recreate a Gothic building than a Gothic workman could recreate the Parthenon, and if one says that the twelfth-century building has been added to in the fifteenth and sixteenth centuries, Morris replies that these were living styles and part of its organic growth. But now the nineteenth century, by its very antiquarianism and eclecticism, has deprived itself of any living style and would simply falsify the past in Wardour Street stone. No one would think of attempting to restore an entire system of medieval thought, but medieval buildings are so much a part of that system that one cannot restore the one without the other. We may use history as a mirror, but we cannot recreate the past, for "history never returns on itself" (XXIII, 230).

From his earliest days Morris had "a passion" for history, and he speaks repeatedly of the "new sense" which history has given man in the nineteenth century. He is referring to the revolution in historiography which occurred in the Romantic period and which rejected the older academic view that "there were but two periods of continuous order," that of Greek and Roman classical civilization and the period from the Renaissance to the present day. All else was "mere accidental confusion." But then the historians turned away from the books of their predecessors to the actual relics of the past and found a totally different picture: "inchoate order in the remotest times, . . . moving forward ever towards something that seems the very opposite of that which it started from, and yet the earlier order never dead but living in the new. . . . How different a spirit such a view of history must create it is not difficult to see. No longer shallow mockery at the failures and follies of the past, from a standpoint of so-called civilization, but deep sympathy with its half-conscious aims . . . ; that is the new spirit of history."[49] Since Morris had acquired, along with his passion for the past, a hatred of modern civilization, the question arose, where was it all to end? "Think of it!" he declared. "Was it all to end in a counting-house on the top of a cinder-heap, with Podsnap's drawing-room in the offing, and a Whig committee dealing out champagne to the rich and margarine to the poor in such convenient proportions as would make all men contented to-gether, though the pleasure of the eyes was gone from the world, and the place of Homer was to be taken by Huxley?" Such an end "would turn history into inconsequent nonsense, and make art a collection of the curiosities of the past" (XXIII, 280).

Nevertheless, this was the conclusion at which Morris had nearly arrived during the period when, in *The Earthly Paradise,* he cast himself as "the idle singer of an empty day."

> Dreamer of dreams, born out of my due time,
> Why should I strive to set the crooked straight?
> Let it suffice me that my murmuring rhyme
> Beats with light wing against the ivory gate.   (III, 1)

In the late 1870s, however, through his increasing engagement in public life, his travels to Iceland, where he saw a heroic people struggling with a harsh environment, through the practice of his craft and the further study of history he put this despair behind him and transferred the ideal with which Ruskin had furnished him from the past to the future.[50] In 1883 he joined the Democratic Federation, and "the meaning of my joining that body was that I had conceived a hope of the realization of my ideal." He read the first volume of Marx's *Capital,* and, though he "suffered agonies of confusion of the brain over reading the pure eco-nomics of that great work," he "thoroughly enjoyed the historical part" (XXIII, 278). In the historical part Marx not only explained how the present situation had come about but also gave Morris hope that change would not stop there, but would continue into the future.

The disturbing thing about Marx was that he introduced an element of conflict with Morris's previous master, Ruskin. For whereas Ruskin had presented the feudal system as an integrated, harmonious society in which every individual had his place, Marx showed that the class struggle was present even there and was responsible for the ultimate dissolution of the system. The great change had come with the Tudors in the first quarter of the sixteenth century, when the feudal lords, greedy for the profits to be made in the wool trade, forcibly drove the peasantry from the land, which they converted from agriculture to grazing. Through these forcible evictions, the spoliation of the Church estates, and the enclosing of common lands, there was created a vast proletariat of landless men who flocked to the towns and became ripe for exploitation by the new class of masters. For here too the old system of handicrafts and guilds was changing. Whereas the independent artisan had made his product from beginning to end and sold it directly to the user for his livelihood not for profit, now a number of journeymen who had nothing to sell but their labor were gathered together in one place, the task was divided among them so that each performed only one minute portion, and the product was sold by the master for his profit. Thus, out of the feudal system, through the intermediary system of the guilds, was born the eighteenth-century workshop, which, with the vast increase of machinery in the nineteenth century, became the full-blown commercial system.[51]

Morris's growing recognition of the imperfection of the Middle Ages led him to hesitate whether the workman was in all respects better off then than now; it also led him to compromise in his language about that period. The serf was "in theory at least" at liberty to earn his living as best he could, and the artisan was "in some sense, at least, free." Also, the Renaissance was, on the social, political, religious, and scientific side, "a necessary instrument for the development of freedom of thought and the capacities of man." In this respect it was "a genuine new birth," though it was "bound to the dead corpse of a past art" (XXIII, 59–60, 203). Even that art was not entirely dead, for "in the early days of the Renaissance there were artists possessed of the highest qualities," though they were "really but the fruit of the blossoming-time, the Gothic period."[52] Morris deeply believed that art and society were inextricably bound together, that the one grew out of and was the expression of the other, but in point of fact he more and more often noted a discrepancy. In the fourteenth-century England depicted in "A Dream of John Ball" the houses and clothing of the people have the same beauty and neatness that they have in the utopian *News from Nowhere,* yet the people are so oppressed by their feudal lords that they are rising in revolt against them. And though Morris hated modern civilization, that hatred did not include the poetry of Keats, Tennyson, and the Pre-Raphaelites, the paintings of Burne-Jones, and the writings of Carlyle and Ruskin. In truth, as John Goode has noted, there had been in Morris from the beginning the concept of alienation, the idea that civilization has bred in the artist desires which it refuses to satisfy.[53] The question is whether the artist will allow those desires to make him into a mere railer against the present or whether, by focusing upon history, he will socialize those desires and make them into an instrument of revolutionary change.

In both "A Dream of John Ball" and *News from Nowhere* the alienation of the dreamer is suggested by his feeling of strangeness as he awakens in the strange land, and by the recognition on the part of others that he is not one of them but occupies a special status in reality. Thus, Morris cannot dream himself back into the Middle Ages or forward into the twenty-first century, but he can use both history and vision to gain an understanding of dialectical change. The academic historians of Morris's own day—William Stubbs, J. R. Green, Thorold Rogers, and C. Edmund Maurice—were much interested in Wat Tyler's rebellion of 1381 as an articulate uprising with a real socialist ideology which did in fact bring about the end of serfdom in England.[54] "A Dream of John Ball" is based upon that insurrection, but Morris did not overemphasize the parallels. Indeed, his dreamer had to inform John Ball that his effort, though it would be successful in putting an end to villeinage, would only bring into being a system of commercial slavery far worse than that which it displaced, and that the hope lay in the fact that men would continue to struggle for freedom as they had in the past. Indeed, Morris returned to the rebellion of Wat Tyler less for a historical parallel than for a sense of fellowship with the past. "You must not suppose," he wrote in a lecture, "that the revolutionary struggle of to-day . . . is paralleled by the insurrections of past times. A rising of the slaves of the ancient period, or of the serfs of the mediæval times, could not have been permanently successful, because the time was not ripe for such success, since the growth of the new order of things was not sufficiently developed" (XXIII, 230). Similarly, though the revolution in *News from Nowhere* is modelled upon the Bloody Sunday conflict of 1887, it took a different turn, and Morris regarded it as "one of the signs of the genuineness and steadfastness" of the working man's movement that "there is nothing in it of conscious and pedantic imitation of former changes—the French Revolution for instance."[55]

The society envisioned in *News from Nowhere* is not, of course, medieval. The two principal medieval institutions of feudalism and the Church are simply gone, being replaced by equality among men, the abolition of private property, and a joyous humanism in which all labor is converted into art. As to the houses and clothing of the inhabitants, though they are very like those of the fourteenth century, Morris is

careful to say they are not identical. The dress of the young women at
the Guest House was "somewhat between that of the ancient classical
costume and the simpler forms of the fourteenth-century garments,
though it was clearly not an imitation of either" (XVI, 14). The architecture of the great hall in the market place "seemed to me to embrace
the best qualities of the Gothic of northern Europe with those of the
Saracenic and Byzantine, though there was no copying of any one of
these styles" (XVI, 24). In truth, Morris did not know what the art of
the future would be like. He thought that the form as well as the spirit
of its architecture must be Gothic, but that was only because the Gothic
was an "organic" style, capable of indefinite change. He rather thought
that the high art of the past would disappear as a product of aristocratic
culture, and that "the new art will come to birth amidst the handicrafts:
that the longings of simple people will take up the chain where it fell
from the hands of the craft-guilds of the fifteenth century."[56] But he did
not really know—he only knew there would be continuous change. Indeed, Old Hammond's account in *News from Nowhere* of "How the
Change Came" has a kind of authenticity and reality about it not possessed by the description of the pastoral society that resulted, so that
one must think it was change, more than the "Epoch of Rest," that
Morris wanted. Indeed, the very term "Epoch of Rest" suggests that
further change is to follow, but it is to be change within continuity. Just
as Morris has no wish to take society back to the Middle Ages, so he
has no wish to divorce it from that period. History is concerned with
the past, the present, and the future. "I love art," he says, "and I love
history; but it is living art and living history that I love. If we have no
hope for the future, I do not see how we can look back on the past with
pleasure" (XXII, 233). He notes that at the present time it is those
people who take pleasure in the life of the Middle Ages who are most
deeply pledged to the forward movement of modern life. He has heard
such people called "romantic," but "what romance means is the capacity
for a true conception of history, a power of making the past part of the
present." "In short, history, the new sense of modern times, the great
compensation for the losses of the centuries, is now teaching us wor-
thily, and making us feel that the past is not dead, but is living in us,
and will be alive in the future which we are now helping to make."[57]

10

The Victorian Renaissance:
Walter Pater

WALTER PATER, sitting in a chair that once belonged to George Eliot in the home of Richard Jackson, the supposed original of Marius, said that "he preferred to all the rest of her works her only historical novel, *Romola*." On another occasion, when asked which is the most remarkable passage in George Eliot, Pater replied, "The words put into Piero di Cosimo's mouth in *Romola*—'The only passionate life is in form and colour.'"[1] Piero di Cosimo's words are hardly central to the meaning of George Eliot's novel, but they do express admirably the philosophy of Pater's Conclusion to *The Renaissance*. One may assume, then, that Pater admired *Romola* not for its moral theme but for its vivid picture of fifteenth-century Florence—and for its portrait of Savonarola.

For Savonarola had become at this time a symbolic figure. After the great fame of his own day he had fallen into oblivion, and in the eighteenth century he was almost a comic figure. But then in the nineteenth century, with the renewed interest in the Middle Ages, he was rediscovered, initially by the Germans, who saw him as a precursor of the Reformation. Two biographies, one by A. G. Rudelbach and a more learned work by Karl Meier, came out almost simultaneously in 1835 and 1836. Both noted that Luther himself had canonized the friar as a Protestant martyr. Stung by this claim, a member of Savonarola's own order, Father Vincenzo Marchese, came to his defense, claiming that he was not an Italian Luther but a sincere Catholic and had been persecuted only for his republican opinions. In 1853 a French scholar, F. T. Perrens, published a more complete and dispassionate biography but one which hedged on the central issue, and from this point on everyone interpreted Savonarola according to his own opinions. Rio praised him for having opposed the New Naturalism in Italian art. Ruskin contrasted him with the Reformers of the North as having gone about his work reverently but not carried it through. Mill accepted the view of Rudelbach and

Meier. So too did J. A. Heraud, a friend of Carlyle, whose biography
of Savonarola (1843), the first in English, was designed to support the
views of Thomas Arnold on church reform and to counter those of
Newman. Newman, the patron of whose Order, St. Philip Neri, regarded Savonarola as a saint, preached a sermon on him in 1850 which
showed a certain English reserve. F. D. Maurice in his *Modern Philosophy*
(1862) wrote that Savonarola was trying to bring back the Kingdom of
Christ, but Kingsley declared he could not agree: Savonarola represented mere monkish superstition. Henry Hart Milman, the liberal Anglican historian, opened his review (1856) of a number of these volumes
with a series of questions: "Savonarola!—Was he hypocritical impostor?
self-deluded fanatic? holy, single-minded Christian preacher? heaven-
commissioned prophet? wonder-working saint? martyr, only wanting
the canonization which was his due? Was he the turbulent, priestly dem-
agogue . . . , or a courageous and enlightened lover of liberty? . . . Was
he the forerunner of Luther or of Loyola, of Knox or of S. Philippo
Neri?" Milman's answer was that he was pure in his moral character but
that "it was a monkish reformation which he endeavoured to work, and
therefore a reformation which could not have satisfied the expanding
mind of man." Michelet in his work on the Renaissance agreed, but
Pasquale Villari, who was also a liberal and whose classic biography of
Savonarola appeared in 1859–1861, said not. True, the past and the
future contended fiercely in Savonarola, as in all men of that age, but
he could not be properly understood unless he was placed at the head
of the new era. "He was the first to raise up, and display before the
world, the standard of that epoch which many call the *Renaissance*. He
was the first, in the fifteenth century, to make men feel that a new life
had penetrated to and had awakened the human race; and hence he may
justly be called the prophet of a new civilization."[2]

It was in 1860, just as Villari's biography was being published, that
George Eliot, then in Florence with George Henry Lewes, decided to
turn to Savonarola as the subject of her next novel.[3] Unfortunately, she
did not grapple with the problem of his meaning in history. Lewes had
said that all one needed to do to write a historical romance was to read
Scott and "cram up" on the facts. George Eliot did both, but she did
not follow Scott's formula of making historical change one of the actual
forces in the novel. She commented in one of her notebooks on the
"jocose light character of the XV. century," and we are aware in the novel
that the first flush of enthusiasm of the early Renaissance has passed. It
is now the age of scholiasts and grammarians who write endless comments on a barren text. That, indeed, was the task of Romola's father—

"that laborious erudition, at once minute and copious, which was the chief intellectual task of the age"—and it is partly because this misguided humanism arouses no ardor in the breast of Romola that she turns to the antithetical ideal of Savonarola, a deeper spiritual life in the service of others. It is only when she finds that Savonarola's spiritual ideal is inextricably mixed with a low political aim, with irrational superstitions, and with a narrow sectarianism that cannot encompass her godfather that she rejects his creed in favor of her own Religion of Humanity. One might possibly consider this Religion the result of the dialectical conflict between Bardo's and Tito's corrupt humanism on the one hand, and the narrow Christianity of Savonarola on the other, except that George Eliot gives us no sense of this as something that might actually have developed in the sixteenth century. Instead, we are precipitated abruptly into the nineteenth century, with analogies to Comte and George Eliot herself, and so wonder retrospectively how much of Carlyle's prophetic denunciations and Newman's attempt to renew an outworn Church are included in Savonarola. "The great artistic purpose of the story," wrote R. H. Hutton, "is to trace out the conflict between liberal culture and the more passionate form of the Christian faith in that strange era, which has so many points of resemblance with the present."[4]

In a very youthful essay, "Diaphaneitè," dated July 1864, Pater drew on George Eliot's conception of Savonarola to define a new type of "diaphanous" character whose simplicity or integrity was distinguished from that of the saint, the artist, and the speculative thinker in that it was achieved without a struggle, by a happy gift of nature. Savonarola, according to Pater, aspired toward this simplicity, though his aspiration, as the author of *Romola* had noted, struggled with "a lower practical aim."[5] Eleven more times in the essays in *The Renaissance* Pater alluded to Savonarola, on one occasion seeing him, along with Winckelmann, as one who had sacrificed breadth of culture in favor of intensity on his own line. He and other forms of the "diaphanous" character looked toward the Conclusion to *The Renaissance,* but ultimately it was Piero di Cosimo, not Savonarola, who expressed for Pater the spirit of that era. Both Savonarola and George Eliot were far too "medieval" for Pater to be interested in them permanently.

There were other "medieval" characters in the Victorian scene with whom Pater would have to deal if he were to make his transition to the Renaissance. One of them was Matthew Arnold. Pater never named names, but no contemporary would have been unaware, when he read in the Preface to Pater's *Studies in the History of the Renaissance* (1873), " 'To see the object as in itself it really is,' has been justly said to be the aim of all true criticism whatever," that the allusion was to Arnold, for Arnold had said it not once, but twice, in lectures delivered as Professor of Poetry at Oxford.[6] But perhaps only the more alert would have realized that, when Pater went on to say, "and in æsthetic criticism the first step towards seeing one's object as it really is, is to know one's own impression as it really is" (R, viii), that he was subtly subverting Arnold's position, for the whole thrust of Arnold's lectures, both *On Translating Homer* and "The Function of Criticism at the Present Time," was to get away from the subjectivity, the individualism, the eccentricity of provincial England toward some more universal and objective ideal. On the other hand, when Pater goes on to elaborate, "What is this song or picture . . . to *me*?" he seems to be echoing Arnold's praise of Goethe's "profound, imperturbable naturalism" which "puts the standard, once for all, inside every man instead of outside him," which asks, in the face of some venerable custom or authority, "But *is* it so? is it so to *me*?"[7] Arnold's only concern is that it should be so to the "best self," not to some "ordinary self," to a self formed in harmony with a wide and universal culture—and with this Pater would agree. His revisionism, then, was not a fundamental subversion of Arnold but a change of venue; and yet, for a young man in relation to an older a change of venue can be the most important thing in the world.

A second shadow lurking behind the opening pages of the Preface was John Ruskin. When Pater said in the opening sentence, "Many attempts have been made by writers on art and poetry to define beauty in the abstract, to express it in the most general terms, to find a universal formula for it," his remark might have been applied to many writers on aesthetics, but the best known person in England writing on art was the then Slade Professor of Fine Art at Oxford who, in *Modern Painters* II (1846), had offered highly abstract definitions of "vital beauty" and "typical beauty" of which one might say, with Pater, that the most valuable element lay in "the suggestive and penetrating things said by the way" (R, vii). Pater had read Ruskin from the age of nineteen, but whereas he admired the cool "impudence" of Arnold, he read Ruskin with increasing irritation and a sense of rivalry. "I cannot believe that Ruskin saw more in the Church of St Mark than I do," he declared.[8] Several of his essays were written consciously against Ruskin's, and in 1885 he hoped to succeed Ruskin as the Slade Professor of Fine Art. He was disappointed, but in late editions of *The Renaissance* he firmly added the date of the original publication of his essay on Botticelli (1870) to show that it was he, and not Ruskin, who had "discovered" that artist in England.[9] The ten slender volumes of his wide-margined prose stand as a silent rebuke to the thirty-eight fat volumes of Ruskin's hectoring works. Two more divergent personalities one can hardly imagine—the one an aesthetic moralist, the other a highly moral aesthete.

Pater's philosophic difference with his two older contemporaries had a historic dimension. In "Pagan and Mediæval Religious Sentiment" Arnold gave his most comprehensive account of his historic scheme, contrasting the "religion of pleasure" of late paganism, which was fine when all was going well but which provided no "stay" when one was "sick or sorry," with the "religion of sorrow" of the Middle Ages, which did provide such a stay for the mass of mankind, whose lives are full of trouble. The former he illustrated by the fifteenth Idyl of Theocritus, the latter by St. Francis's "Canticle of the Sun," and he concluded: "The poetry of later paganism lived by the senses and understanding; the poetry of mediæval Christianity lived by the heart and imagination. But the main element of the modern spirit's life is neither the senses and understanding, nor the heart and imagination; it is the imaginative reason." At this point the reader expects Arnold's dialectic of history to cast the Renaissance in the role of the "imaginative reason," but instead he finds that period dismissed in a single sentence as being "in part, a return towards the pagan spirit . . . , towards the life of the senses and the understanding," and the role of the imaginative reason is given to fifth-century Greece. "There is a century in Greek life," says Arnold, "the century preceding the Peloponnesian war, from about the year 530 to the year 430 B.C.,—in which poetry made, it seems to me, the noblest, the most successful effort she has ever made as the priestess of the imaginative reason, of the element by which the modern spirit, if it would live right, has chiefly to live."[10]

The concept of the imaginative reason had a deep influence on Pater, who used it several times in "The School of Giorgione," but he could not accept Arnold's characterization of any of the three periods. Far from agreeing that the Middle Ages ministered to the heart and imagination, he spoke in the Preface to *The Renaissance* of "those *limits* which the religious system of the middle age imposed on the heart and the imagination" (R, xii; my italics), and which were broken down by the Renaissance. And in his essay "The Myth of Demeter and Persephone" he repudiated the idea that the religion of paganism was gay and cheerful. The religion of the Greeks, he says—again with no mention of Arnold—"has been represented as a religion of mere cheerfulness." It

served to keep the Greeks from peering "too curiously into certain shadowy places, appropriate enough to the gloomy imagination of the middle age; and it hardly proposed to itself to give consolation to people
who, in truth, were never 'sick or sorry.' But this familiar view of Greek
religion is based on a consideration of a part only of what is known
concerning it" (GS, 110–11). It leaves out of account the dark chthon-
ian element of primitive Greek religion, its ritual and myth. And then,
just as Arnold translated St. Francis's "Canticle of the Sun" and the Idyl
of Theocritus to illustrate his views, so Pater translated the "Hymn to
Demeter" to illustrate that "worship of sorrow" which he asserted was
a part of Greek religion. Pater was perhaps a little unjust to Arnold,
who was speaking only of the Alexandrian period of late paganism and
who found in Homer and the great tragedians a highly fortifying stay
for those who were "sick or sorry." But it is true that Arnold neglected
the irrational, Dionysian element in Greek culture to which Pater was
so powerfully drawn—perhaps in corresponding neglect of the Apollonian element of the classic period.

As for Ruskin, Richard Ellmann has said that Pater is "Ruskin inverted," by which he means not merely that Pater inverted the values
which Ruskin placed upon the Middle Ages and the Renaissance, but
also that Pater is "all blend" whereas Ruskin is "all severance."[11] Ruskin,
it will be remembered, had dated the "fall" of Venice from May 8, 1418,
the date of the death of Carlo Zeno, and had declared that the Renaissance began for Venice on March 27, 1424, when the first hammer was
lifted up against the old palace of Ziani. Pater, on the other hand, deplored these "trenchant and absolute divisions." Alluding to Rio as well
as to Ruskin, he declared, "Pagan and Christian art are sometimes
harshly opposed, and the Renaissance is represented as a fashion which
set in at a definite period. That is the superficial view: the deeper view
is that which preserves the identity of European culture. The two are
really continuous; and there is a sense in which it may be said that the
Renaissance was an uninterrupted effort of the middle age, that it was
ever taking place" (R, 225–26). This was in the final essay in *The Renaissance*. In the first essay, speaking of the efflorescence of French culture in the twelfth century, Pater declared that "this theory of a
Renaissance within the middle age," connecting the characteristic work
of one period with that of the other, would heal "that rupture between
the middle age and the Renaissance which has so often been exaggerated" (R, 3). Whereas Ruskin rigidly separates ages into tight com-
partments, Pater sees one culture as running imperceptibly into another
and the interest of each enhanced by the presence of the other.

This is particularly apparent in the two men's treatment of Raphael. In his lectures on Pre-Raphaelitism (1853) Ruskin had dated the crisis in European art from the moment, in 1509–10, when Raphael walked across the Stanza del Segnatura, from where he had painted the World or Kingdom of Theology, presided over by Christ, and on another wall painted the World or Kingdom of Poetry, presided over by Apollo. By thus equating the objects of fancy on the one wall with the objects of faith on the other Raphael had ensured the degradation of Italian painting. "The doom of the arts of Europe went forth from that chamber."[12] Not so, said Pater. In his lecture on Raphael delivered some forty years later he took as the "*formula*" of Raphael's art "genius by accumulation" (MS, 39). It was precisely because Raphael, in moving from Urbino to Perugia to Sienna to Florence to Rome, and associating with a series of great artists at each place, was able to learn from each something new without forgetting the old, that he was able, in the Stanza del Segnatura, to depict with perfect harmony the grace of pagan poetry and of religious faith. In his "synoptic intellectual power" he was the Lessing, the Herder, the Hegel of his age, and he did not move forward from the Middle Ages into the Renaissance without bringing with him the Catholic faith. Moreover, it was not as a mere "after-glow" but as a living ideal. He was, in his cosmopolitan intelligence, "conterminous with the genius of the Renaissance" (MS, 56–58; R, 197–98).

Why did Pater find in the culture of the Renaissance his intellectual home as Arnold found his in fifth-century Greece and Ruskin in the Middle Ages? Undoubtedly it was associated with his loss of religious faith and the efflorescence of his nature into a new humanism. As a boy at the King's School, Canterbury, he was deeply drawn to the High Church views of Keble and Isaac Williams and, living in the shadow of the great cathedral, thought of himself as a kind of religious acolyte. But even before leaving school he had begun to have doubts about religion, and during his first year at Queen's College, Oxford, which he entered as an Exhibitioner in 1858, he completely cut himself off from Christianity. As a result, he also alienated his two closest friends, Henry Dombrain and John Ranier McQueen, whom he deeply offended by his "Mephistophilean sneers" at their faith. He read Darwin's *Origin of Species* shortly after it came out and in 1860 burned his early poems, which were chiefly religious, and disposed of his overtly religious books. Strangely enough, he continued to attend High Church services, chiefly for their ritual and music, and did not think it inconsistent with his position to plan to take orders. Apparently he considered the Church a social and historical institution which one might join for aesthetic reasons, independently of one's attitude toward its creed. His two friends, horrified at the idea of an agnostic priest, denounced him to the Bishop of London and effectively prevented his ordination. After twice failing to secure a clerical fellowship, he was elected in 1864 to a non-clerical fellowship at Brasenose, where we find one of his pupils, the young Gerard Manley Hopkins, writing in his journal for May 31, 1866: "Pater talking two hours against Xtianity."[13]

According to Pater's tutor, W. W. Capes, and a slightly younger contemporary, T. H. S. Escott, Pater showed no interest in or knowledge of art while he was an undergraduate at Queen's. His interests were philosophic, scientific, and literary. During the Long Vacation of 1860, while visiting his aunt and two sisters at Heidelberg, he began to learn German, and on his return to Oxford he subjected himself to a severe course of reading in English and German philosophy. His borrowings from the Queen's College Library for 1860–62 include Goethe, Fichte, Heinrich Ritter's *History of Ancient Philosophy*, Kant, Schleiermacher, and Hegel; and in English, Hobbes, Hume, Berkeley, Bacon, and Locke—the whole empirical and skeptical tradition. One would like to know what first turned Pater's attention to art. The aesthetic movement, which was just then beginning at Oxford, had as its primary sources the Pre-Raphaelites and French writers, but Pater at that date could not read French. Goethe was doubtless a factor and perhaps also *Romola*, for Pater must have read it on its first publication in 1862–63, and in February 1863 he took out of the Queen's College Library Humphrey Hody's *De Græcis illustribus* (1742), the first systematic account of those Greeks who, like Tito Melema, brought their language and culture to Italy. At the same time he borrowed Henry Hallam's *Introduction to the Literature of Europe in the Fifteenth, Sixteenth, and Seventeenth Centuries* (2d ed., 1843), and from that point on he was reading regularly in works that would contribute to his *Studies in the History of the Renaissance*.[14]

That book, however, did not emerge simply out of other books. It emerged out of the trip which Pater took to Italy in the summer of 1865 with his close friend, C. L. Shadwell. What it meant in Victorian times for an Englishman who had suffered repression in the "moral north" to go over the Alps and descend into sunny, pagan Italy may be best learned from Samuel Butler's account of his emancipation from his harsh clerical father. He went to Italy twice in his youth and experienced such a sense of freedom and relief that he afterwards represented the descent into

Erewhon as a descent into Alpine valleys, with only this difference that the wayside shrines were of young, healthy figures instead of the emaciated Christ. To enter Erewhon was also to travel back in time, for the clothing and machinery of the country are those of twelfth- and thirteenth-century Europe, the medieval metaphor having triumphed, in Butler's case, over the more appropriate one of the Renaissance. It is no accident that Butler's book was published just a year before Pater's, for its frank, healthy naturalism, though different in temper from Pater's aesthetic relativism, represents the same impulse to throw off the incubus of Christianity in favor of the freedom of one's own nature. What freedom Pater asserted we do not know but suspect that in Italy he must have experienced a sexual as well as an aesthetic awakening, for he associates the Renaissance, as in the figures of Winckelmann, Leonardo, and Michelangelo, with the Hellenic ideal of male friendship, and his companion was renowned in Oxford for his extreme beauty. In any case, there was the "lust of the eye" to be experienced in art, and as Pater went to Pisa, Florence, and Ravenna, examining their treasures, a whole new world must have opened before him. By the loss of his religious faith and the efflorescence of his nature into a new humanism he reenacted in his own person the transition from the Middle Ages to the Renaissance.

Pater was not alone in making this transition, for during the last half of the nineteenth century the Renaissance gradually replaced the Middle Ages as the dominant post-antique era in people's consciousness. It was defined at this time as a distinct period in the history of civilization, and it was given a name of its own. The metaphor of rebirth, of course, was as old as the Renaissance itself, having been used by Vasari, but it was the French form of the word which established itself during the eighteenth century as an accepted term in art history. It was admitted into Furetière's *Dictionary* in 1701 and into that of the Academy in 1718. Usually it was followed by a qualifying phrase, as in *la renaissance des beaux arts* or *la renaissance des lettres,* but by the 1830s it was used absolutely, either as an adjective to describe the art and architecture of the period or as a noun to denote the period itself. In this form it spread to Germany and England by the 1840s.[15] The first recorded use of the word *renaissance* in English is that of T. A. Trollope in 1840: "That heaviest and least graceful of all possible styles, the 'renaissance' as the French choose to term it" (*OED*). It is clear that for several decades English writers were conscious of the foreignness and novelty of the term. Ruskin speaks in the *Stones of Venice* (1851) of "the art commonly called Renaissance" (IX, 45), and in 1869 in *Culture and Anarchy* Arnold, speaking of "the great movement which goes by the name of the Renaissance," asks "but why should we not give to this foreign word . . . a more English form, and say Renascence?" In the edition of 1875 he ventured to do so, declaring in a note that the word is "destined to become of more common use amongst us as the movement which it denotes comes, as it will come, increasingly to interest us."[16] Possibly this note was prompted by the appearance in 1873 of Pater's book, for he too opened his first essay with a comment on the meaning of the word: "The word *Renaissance,* indeed, is now generally used to denote not merely the revival of classical antiquity which took place in the fifteenth century, and to which the word was first applied, but a whole complex movement, of which that revival of classical antiquity was but one element or symptom" (R, 1–2).

If by 1873 the word *Renaissance* had taken on this enlarged sense, it was due primarily to Jules Michelet, the seventh volume of whose *Histoire de France* was published in 1855 under the title *Renaissance.* What is the Renaissance? he asks in his Introduction. Those who think it is limited to a new style in art and the renewed study of antiquity have forgotten two things: "the discovery of the world and the discovery of man. The sixteenth century, in its large and legitimate extension, goes from Columbus to Copernicus, from Copernicus to Galileo, from the discovery of the earth to that of the heavens. Man there found himself again. While Vesalius and Servetus revealed his physical life, by Luther and by Calvin, by Dumoulin and Cujas, by Rabelais, Montaigne, Shakespeare, and Cervantes he penetrated the mysteries of his own soul. He has sounded the depths of his nature."[17] This view of the Renaissance, now a commonplace of intellectual history, was in 1855 a new interpretation. In the view which had prevailed during the Romantic era and which found expression in the dramas of Byron and Hugo, the Renaissance was a period of sinister beauty and unnatural passion. Unmitigated pride, irreligion, bloodlust, and secret intrigue were its common elements, and not Columbus and Galileo, but Machiavelli and Cesare Borgia, were its representative men. Hegel, of course, presented a different view. To him the Renaissance was the return of the human spirit to the consciousness of freedom, but Hegel was not on everyone's shelves, and Michelet took essentially his view and presented it in vivid and rhetorical phrases. Moreover, he was repudiating his own earlier view, expressed in volume VI of his History in 1833, that the Middle Ages was an age of faith. Now, writing after the failure of the Revolution of 1848, he saw that age as the dead hand of the past, and in the Renaissance he saw a symbol of human freedom—of an age in which the human spirit had once triumphed and by whose guidance it might triumph again.

Jacob Burckhardt, whose *Civilization of the Renaissance in Italy* was published five years after Michelet's volume, had also been disillusioned by the failure of the Revolution of 1848 and had withdrawn into the Renaissance as a golden interlude between two gray eras, the Middle Ages, which oppressed by its establishment of religion, and the nineteenth century, which oppressed by the establishment of the state. Burckhardt repeated Michelet's famous phrase, "the discovery of the world and of man," but he emphasized individualism as the hallmark of the Renaissance, both for good and evil. Abandoning the narrative for the topical method, he attempted to capture the spirit of the age as arising from the genius of the Italian people and their particular moment in history. To him the Renaissance was a work of art which he regarded with ironic detachment, for unlike Michelet he did not expect its repetition in the future any more than he expected another Veronese. His account of the period is tinged with melancholy and a Schopenhauerian pessimism.

Not so the account of John Addington Symonds, whose *Renaissance in Italy* (1875–86) is the third great work in the tradition. Symonds acknowledges indebtedness to both Burckhardt and Michelet, deriving from the former his scheme of organization and from the latter his faith in humanity and progress. Struggling against consumption, he poured into his work on the Renaissance the vitality he felt ebbing from his own body. In his view the Renaissance is

> the history of the attainment of self-conscious freedom by the human spirit manifested in the European races. It is no mere political mutation, no new fashion of art, no restoration of classical standards of taste. The arts and the inventions, the knowledge and the books, which suddenly became vital at the time of the Renaissance, had long lain neglected on the shores of the Dead Sea which we call the Middle Ages. It was not their discovery which caused the Renaissance. But it was the intellectual energy, the spontaneous outburst of intelligence, which enabled mankind at that moment to make use of them. The force then generated still continues, vital and expansive, in the spirit of the modern world.[18]

Symonds was seeking the origins of a continuing spirit of liberty rather than its revival in the modern world, and his thesis proved so attractive that, coupled with his vivid dramatization of the period, it was chiefly responsible for the "Renaissance complex" which, according to one historian, dominated England and America for the next fifty years.[19]

Pater and Symonds knew each other at Oxford, but neither was very sympathetic to the other. Pater is said to have referred habitually to Symonds as "poor Symonds," and Symonds once described Pater as "well-dressed and ghastly." Of Pater's *Renaissance* Symonds said, "There is a kind of Death clinging to the man, which makes his Music (but heavens! how sweet that is!) a little faint and sickly."[20] Pater, on the other hand, said that Symonds lacked "the quality of reserve." Had he known, when he wrote this in his review of Symonds's first volume, that there were six more to follow, he might have phrased his criticism even more emphatically, but what he chiefly objected to was Symonds's return to something like the sensationalism of the Romantic era. Perhaps it was inevitable given the subject of that volume ("The Age of the Despots"), but Pater noted that "the spirit of the Renaissance proper, of the Renaissance as a humanistic movement," is not that of Francesco Sforza and Alexander VI. "The Renaissance is an assertion of liberty indeed, but of liberty to see and feel those things the seeing and feeling of which generate not the 'barbarous ferocity of temper, the savage and coarse tastes,' of the Renaissance Popes, but a sympathy with life everywhere, even in its weakest and most frail manifestations."[21]

Pater belongs to the tradition of Michelet, Burckhardt, and Symonds, but he is clearly the odd man out.[22] The chief difference between him and his contemporaries is that he thought of the Renaissance less as a period than as a process—a process of spiritual and cultural rebirth that could occur at any time. Thus, in his opening essay, after acknowledging that the meaning of the word has been enlarged beyond the mere revival of classical antiquity to denote "a whole complex movement, of which that revival . . . was but one element or symptom," he indicates that he would enlarge it further. "For us the Renaissance is the name of a many-sided but yet united movement, in which the love of the things of the intellect for their own sake, the desire for a more liberal and comely way of conceiving life, make themselves felt, urging those who experience this desire to search out first one and then another means of intellectual or imaginative enjoyment, and directing them not only to the discovery of old and forgotten sources of this enjoyment, but to the divination of fresh sources thereof—new experiences, new subjects of poetry, new forms of art" (R, 2). Such a feeling there was in the end of the twelfth and the beginning of the thirteenth century, and it is with that "Renaissance within the limits of the middle age itself" (R, 1) that he begins. Even more strikingly, he extends the process to Winckelmann in the eighteenth century, not really, one would think, because Winckelmann "belongs in spirit to an earlier age" (R, xiv), but because he personally experienced a rebirth in his own lifetime. Further, there is strong evidence that Pater intended at one time to include in *The Renaissance* his essay on Wordsworth (later published in *Appreciations*), which would have indicated that he thought of the Romantic movement as a Renaissance.[23] And when one remembers that the Conclusion to *The Renaissance* was originally part of a review of William Morris's poetry, which was seen as "renew[ing] on a more delicate type the poetry of a past age,"[24] one could say that the Renaissance is extended into the 1860s. There are, of course, periods when it is easier to experience this rebirth than it is at others. It was easier in the fifteenth century than it was in the tenth or the eighteenth, and that is presumably why Pater is writing about that period. But his purpose is to assist in a Victorian Renaissance—to achieve by a revival of the Renaissance what the Renaissance achieved by a revival of antiquity.

If the Renaissance is a process, it follows that Pater will not be primarily interested in the High Renaissance. Unlike Burckhardt he does not care to seize the spirit of the age, for that would be to reduce it to a stereotype—to those fixities and definites which tend to stifle and extinguish the "hard gem-like flame." "The choice life of the human spirit," he writes, "is always under mixed lights, and in mixed situations; when it is not too sure of itself, is still expectant, girt up to leap forward to the promise."[25] As a result, all of his essays in *The Renaissance* are fraught with this sense of cultural or artistic transition. In "Two Early French Stories" we are told that "the Renaissance has not only the sweetness [an Arnoldian term] which it derives from the classical world, but also that curious strength [a Ruskinian term] of which there are great resources in the true middle age" (R, 15). The twelfth century is the moment when "the rude strength of the middle age turns to sweetness" (R, 2). Pico della Mirandola, who spent all his life trying to reconcile Christianity and paganism, is shown "lying down to rest in the Dominican habit, yet amid thoughts of the older gods" (R, 44). Botticelli's sad and dejected figures occupy "that middle world in which men take no side in great conflicts, and decide no great causes, and make great refusals." They are "neither for Jehovah nor for His enemies" and have "the shadow upon them of the great things from which they shrink" (R, 55–57). The bas-reliefs of Luca della Robbia and the Tuscan sculptors are likewise midway between two sculptural systems, the broad generality of the Greeks and the puzzling "incompleteness" of Michelangelo. It is so that they achieve *expression*, the passing of the smile over the face, the ripple of the air on a still day. The poetry of Michelangelo (his painting Pater avoids, for the same reason that Browning preferred

Dante's drawing and Raphael's sonnets) also involves "that strange in-
terfusion of sweetness and strength" (R, 97) which was to be found in
the twelfth century. Leonardo da Vinci, part artist and part scientist,
has as the two elements in his genius "curiosity" and the "desire of
beauty," the one looking back to antiquity, the other forward to the
modern spirit (R, 109). The paintings of the school of Giorgione are
characterized by that *Anders-streben,* that striving to transcend the lim-
itations of their own medium, which is characteristic of the Renaissance.
And finally, even in mid-sixteenth-century France, when one would
think the Renaissance triumphant everywhere, there comes a "new and
peculiar phase of taste," not imported ready-made from Italy but rather
"the finest and subtlest phase of the middle age itself, its last fleeting
splendour and temperate Saint Martin's summer" (R, 156). Generally,
Pater prefers the exquisite "early light" of the Renaissance, for afterwards the period "takes its side, becomes exaggerated and facile."[26]

Finally, it is not merely a process that constitutes the Renaissance
for Pater but the experience of that process by a particular temperament.
This temperament is defined for us in the Conclusion to *The Renaissance,*
but Pater had already made a sketch of it in his essay "Diaphaneitè,"
written for the Old Mortality Society in July 1864. He is concerned
with defining a cultural ideal that is quieter and more inward than the
standard conception of the artist, the saint, or the speculative thinker.
He calls it the "diaphanous" man because its clear, crystal nature allows
the light from within to pass forth unimpeded by any veil of the purely
practical life. Its connection with the Conclusion is indicated by the
phrase, "it is that fine edge of light, where the elements of our moral
nature refine themselves to the burning point" (MS, 248), but there is
more emphasis here upon the unity, the simplicity, and the repose
achieved, without struggle, as by a happy gift of nature. Thus, the type
is exemplified not by Luther or Spinoza, whom Carlyle or Arnold would
have named, but by Raphael, "who in the midst of the Reformation and
Renaissance, himself lighted up by them, yielded himself to neither, but
stood still to live upon himself, even in outward form a youth, almost
an infant, yet surprising all the world." "A majority of such," we are
told, "would be the regeneration of the world" (MS, 253–54).

The most remarkable passage in "Diaphaneitè" is a short one alluding to the Platonic doctrine of reminiscence and the Renaissance revival
of antiquity which Pater later applies to Winckelmann, implying that he
too is a type of the "diaphanous" man and that that character has a
historical and cultural dimension. Winckelmann is in some ways the
most important figure in the book because he experiences the whole

process of the Renaissance. Brought up in the dusty world of eighteenth-century German theology, he ultimately escaped from that world, though at the cost of renouncing his faith for that of his Roman Catholic patrons, to the world of antique beauty as then being unearthed in Italy. "Filled as our culture is with the classical spirit," says Pater, "we can hardly imagine how deeply the human mind was moved, when, at the Renaissance, in the midst of a frozen world, the buried fire of ancient art rose up from under the soil. Winckelmann here reproduces for us the earlier sentiment of the Renaissance. On a sudden the imagination feels itself free. How facile and direct, it seems to say, is this life of the senses and the understanding, when once we have apprehended it! Here, surely, is that more liberal mode of life we have been seeking so long, so near to us all the while. How mistaken and roundabout have been our efforts to reach it by mystic passion, and monastic reverie; how they have deflowered the flesh; how little have they really emancipated us!" (R, 184). "Hellenism," says Pater, "has always been most effectively conceived by those who have crept into it out of an intellectual world in which the sombre elements predominate. So it had been in the ages of the Renaissance" (R, 190). So it was with Winckelmann, and so it was with Pater. Even in Winckelmann's slight loss of religious sincerity Pater saw a parallel with himself, and he makes a short digression in order to justify them both. The ideal is that our culture should be both intense and complete, but often both are not possible and it may be necessary to renounce perfection on one line in order to achieve it on another. "Which is better?—to lay open a new sense, to initiate a new organ for the human spirit," as Hegel said that Winckelmann did, "or to cultivate many types of perfection up to a point?" (R, 188). Pater can have no doubt that it is better to live intensely on the one line indicated by one's own nature than to sacrifice purity and clarity for catholicity.

Not Winckelmann, however, but Goethe is the hero of Pater's *Renaissance*. For though Winckelmann initiated a new organ for the human spirit, he was too distant from the modern world to use it properly. As a result, his actual analysis of Greek art in terms of breadth and generality does not greatly interest Pater. Winckelmann is of interest primarily as having prepared the way for Goethe by providing him with the ideal of balance and centrality which he needed before proceeding into the modern world. That Goethe had so to proceed was clear to Pater, for Pater agreed with Hegel that each phase of the human spirit generates its opposite, so that, by the dialectic of history, it moves forward to greater self-consciousness and freedom. In particular, he is alluding to Hegel's division of art, according to its mode of embodying

the Idea in sensuous form, into Symbolic, which embodies it imperfectly
(the primitive art of the East); Classical, which embodies it perfectly in
the physical human form; and Romantic, which again embodies it imperfectly but on the higher level of the soul. Architecture is the typical
Symbolic art, sculpture the typical Classical art, and painting, music,
and poetry are the typical Romantic arts. The fault of Winckelmann was
that he focused exclusively upon, and rested in, sculpture and so could
not pass beyond the classical into modern times. Goethe, however, combined Helena with Faust in a poetry that was distinctively modern. It
may appear to us, says Pater, as we look back upon the Hellenic ideal,
in which man was at harmony with himself, that he never should have
passed beyond it. "But if he was to be saved from the *ennui* which ever
attaches itself to realisation, even the realisation of the perfect life, it
was necessary that a conflict should come, that some sharper note should
grieve the existing harmony, and the spirit chafed by it beat out at last
only a larger and profounder music" (R, 222–23). The recovery of any
past ideal must always be from the vantage point of the modern.

Modernity is certainly the keynote of *The Renaissance*. Just as Arnold
delivered a series of lectures (attended by Pater) on "The Modern Element in Literature," beginning with Augustan Rome, so Pater wrote a
similar series of essays on the Renaissance. Not every figure, of course,
was distinctly modern. Pico della Mirandola failed in his effort to reconcile Christianity and paganism because the fifteenth century "lacked
the very rudiments of the historic sense" (R, 34). Nonetheless, Pico is
of interest to the modern mind because he discerned a modern problem,
and it is this quality of modernity in each of his subjects that Pater is
trying to define. "What is this song or picture, this engaging personality
presented in life or in a book, to *me?*" (R, viii). In the Preface Pater
says that the aesthetic critic regards all works of art as "powers or forces
producing pleasurable sensations, each of a more or less peculiar or
unique kind." They are like the "virtues" of an herb, a wine, or a gem;
and "the function of the aesthetic critic is to distinguish . . . the virtue"
by which each work of art or object "produces this special impression
of beauty or pleasure" (R, ix). Its virtue is due to its having been produced by a unique temperament at a particular moment in history, and
therefore when Pater asks, in the Conclusion, how we can "be present
always at the focus where the greatest number of vital forces unite in
their purest energy?" (R, 236) the answer is to live in the art and culture
of the past as discriminated by a modern sensibility.

Pater gave his fullest definition of the modern spirit in his first published essay, on Coleridge. "Modern thought," he says, "is distinguished

from ancient by its cultivation of the 'relative' spirit in place of the 'absolute.' Ancient philosophy sought to arrest every object in an eternal outline, to fix thought in a necessary formula, and the varieties of life in a classification by 'kinds,' or genera. To the modern spirit nothing is, or can be rightly known, except relatively and under conditions" (Ap, 66). This view of the modern spirit is repeated in the opening pages of the Conclusion and there forms the basis for the aesthetic philosophy that follows. But what is relativistic in philosophy and aesthetic in art is historicist in the broader reaches of human culture. The aesthetic critic who enters into each work of art or experience to savor its peculiar quality and then withdraws is doing precisely what the world-spirit did with reference to creeds, religions, systems of thought. It moves from one to another as the critic moves past the pictures in a gallery. It is in this way, says Pater, that one achieves Goethe's ideal of living *im Ganzen*—in the whole—not by a continuous, synthesizing activity but by a successive, discriminating activity, by withdrawing, over and over again, from what was once precious but has become indifferent. "With a kind of passionate coldness, such natures rejoice to be away from and past their former selves" (R, 229), so that their new self can remain intellectually alive. Where Arnold distinguished between the "ordinary self" and the "best self," Pater distinguished between the old self and the new. Or rather he attempts to keep the self perpetually new by a series of rebirths. He emphasizes this not merely by the metaphor of the Renaissance but also by the myth of palingenesis or the transmigration of souls.

In the essay "Diaphaneitè" Pater asserts that the diaphanous man is "like the reminiscence of a forgotten culture that once adorned the mind; as if the mind of one φιλοσοφήσας ποτε μετ' ἔρωτος, fallen into a new cycle, were beginning its spiritual progress over again, but with a certain power of anticipating its stages. . . . Such a character is like a relic from the classical age, laid open by accident to our alien modern atmosphere" (MS, 250–51). It is clear that the diaphanous man lives in two different cultural ages. If he has a kind of serenity, it is because he has been here before and knows his way around. If he is otherworldly, it is because he is not of this world but is a relic of former ages. He is both antique and modern. As a part of the world-soul, he has a racial as well as a personal consciousness, and if he reverts to the past it is to recover there a portion of his own nature. Pater regarded Wordsworth's "Immortality Ode" as a modern version of Plato's doctrine of reminiscence, and he constantly asserted that we come "trailing clouds of glory," clad in the vesture of a past (PP, 72–73). Our birth, however, is not "a sleep and a forgetting;" rather it is an effort, through recollection, to recover a portion of our own nature. Or to vary the metaphor, we are "a palimpsest, a tapestry of which the actual threads have served before, or like the animal frame itself, every particle of which has already lived and died many times over" (PP, 8). Given the diaphanous quality of Pater's cultural ideal, it is doubtful if the mirror is the best image to express his relation to history. It may be that he looks down through the clarity of his own nature into a many-layered past, each layer of which is stained with the tincture of that through which it is perceived. The image which he himself employs for the world-soul, which is also the soul of modern man, is Leonardo's painting of Mona Lisa. For one thing, it shows immediately what is lacking in Greek art.

> Set it for a moment beside one of those white Greek goddesses or beautiful women of antiquity, and how would they be troubled by this beauty, into which the soul with all its maladies has passed! All the thoughts and experience of the world have etched and moulded there, in that which they have of power to refine and make expressive the outward form, the animalism of Greece, the lust of Rome, the mysticism of the middle age with its spiritual ambition and imaginative loves, the return of the Pagan world, the sins of the Borgias. . . . The fancy of a perpetual life, sweeping together ten thousand experiences, is an old one; and modern philosophy has conceived the idea of humanity as wrought upon by, and summing up in itself, all modes of thought and life. Certainly Lady Lisa might stand as the embodiment of the old fancy, the symbol of the modern idea. (R, 125–26)

If this many-layered picture is Pater's deepest image of man's relation to the past, he did not limit himself to that. In *Marius the Epicurean* he retreated to an earlier and simpler mode in order to explore a no less fundamental analogy.

Clive Bell wrote on the eve of World War I, "To compare Victorian England with Imperial Rome has been the pastime of the half-educated these fifty years. . . . To similise the state superstitions and observances of Rome with our official devotions and ministration, the precise busts in the British Museum with the 'speaking likenesses' in the National Portrait Gallery, the academic republicanism of the cultivated patricians with English Liberalism, and the thrills of the arena with those of the playing-field, would be pretty sport for any little German boy."[27] Actually, the comparison with Rome had been going on for much longer than fifty years, as these pages have made clear, but Bell is right that it was just about fifty years before, in the 1860s, that the power and opulence of the British Empire had become such that the comparison was inevitable. "The analogy between the present age," wrote Leslie Stephen, the father-in-law of Clive Bell, "and that which witnessed the introduction of Christianity is too striking to have been missed by very many observers. The most superficial acquaintance with the general facts shows how close a parallel might be drawn by a competent historian."[28]

T. H. S. Escott was certainly a competent historian, at least of the Victorian scene, which he described in 1880 in a notable volume, but in 1875 he published an article in *Macmillan's Magazine* entitled "Two Cities and Two Seasons—Rome and London. A.D. 408–1875." As Escott was a private pupil of Pater's at Oxford, Pater is sure to have read it, and indeed, we know that he borrowed details from it in one chapter of *Marius the Epicurean*. The article is a comparison of the social life and manners, the morals and religious beliefs in Rome of 408 A.D. and contemporary London. The author draws chiefly on Ammianus Marcellinus and the Christian fathers, and the emphasis is on the opulence and vanity of the two societies—the carriages on Rotten Row and the Appian Way, the dress of fashionable ladies and beaux, the yachts on the Solent and the Lucrine Lake. There was also a nearly identical religious situation. "In the Rome of Ammianus Marcellinus, one system of thought and of religion had decayed without another having yet completely taken its place. It was a period of transition, and like all periods of transition it was one in which conviction was weak, and superstition and scepticism strong." Escott then asks, "Are we not, too, passing through a period of transition—of transition political, social, religious, philosophical? Is not our lot cast also amid the conflict of creeds and the fierce antagonism of ideas? Are we beset by no perils of political infidelity and national selfishness? If this is the case, then the contrast which in these pages it has been attempted to draw cannot be otherwise than seasonable and suggestive." Escott ends by reminding the reader that in A.D. 408 the Goth was at the gates, and in a few years "Roman civilization received its death-blow from the hands of Attila and his hosts."[29]

It was not apparent, however, that the Goth was at the gates in 1875. True, there was the beginning of a world-wide depression and the Franco-Prussian War and Paris Commune had been a severe shock. But most Englishmen would have considered their country to be at the height of prosperity and felicity, and since Gibbon had declared, "If a man were called to fix the period in the history of the world during which the condition of the human race was most happy and prosperous, he would, without hesitation, name that which elapsed from the death of Domitian to the accession of Commodus,"[30] it was probably that age, the Age of the Antonines, that furnished the more appropriate parallel. This was reinforced by a great interest in Marcus Aurelius. A new translation of his *Thoughts* had been published by George Long in 1862, and Matthew Arnold took the occasion to speak of Marcus Aurelius as "perhaps the most beautiful figure in history. . . . Besides him, history presents one or two other sovereigns eminent for their goodness, such as Saint Louis or Alfred. But Marcus Aurelius has, for us moderns, this great superiority in interest over Saint Louis or Alfred, that he lived and acted in a state of society modern by its essential characteristics, in an epoch akin to our own, in a brilliant civilisation. . . . Marcus Aurelius thus becomes for us a man like ourselves, a man in all things tempted as we are."[31] Arnold had earlier, in his lecture on "The Modern Element in Literature," described the Augustan Age as eminently modern but as inadequate in its literature to deliver us from the complexity which a modern age, then or now, imposes upon us. But now Marcus Aurelius is more adequate, or, if not quite adequate, at least he is more touching in his inadequacy. "It is because he too yearns as [we] do for something unattained by him." What if he had become a Christian? "Vain question! yet the greatest charm of Marcus Aurelius is that he makes us ask it. We see him wise, just, self-governed, tender, thankful, blameless; yet, with all this, agitated, stretching out his arms for something beyond."[32] As Arnold yearned backward for a time before the Sea of Faith had withdrawn, so he sees his counterpart yearning forward for a time when its tide was at the full.

Arnold's essay was to some degree a reply to John Stuart Mill's essay *On Liberty* (1859), for Mill had criticized Marcus Aurelius for persecuting the Christians. Not that he had a lower opinion of Aurelius than Arnold had. On the contrary, he regarded him as "the gentlest and most amiable of philosophers and rulers," and thought it a paradox that "this man, a better Christian in all but the dogmatic sense of the word, than almost any of the ostensibly Christian sovereigns who have since reigned, persecuted Christianity."[33] On the character of the man, then, Arnold and Mill agreed, and the fact that a modern Epicurean could admire Marcus Aurelius almost as much as a modern Stoic, that Christian and non-Christian alike could salute him as the highest type of humanity, made him a key figure of the age. In him was embodied the question whether Christianity was a desirable or necessary addition to the natural attributes of man.

Some scholars have thought that it was Arnold's essay on Marcus Aurelius which suggested to Pater that he should write a novel in which

the Emperor was a leading figure, but the interval of twenty years between the two works is a long time and there were other more immediate
sources.[34] In 1876 Pater's former tutor, W. W. Capes, published *The
Roman Empire of the Second Century; or, The Age of the Antonines*, which
would have provided Pater with most of the facts he needed had he
cared to consult so popular a volume. Then, in 1880 the Society for
Promoting Christian Knowledge published two volumes, *Stoicism* by
Capes and *Epicureanism* by William Wallace, a former member of Old
Mortality. Far more important than these, however, was the appearance
in London, in the spring of 1880, of Ernest Renan to deliver the Hib-
bert Lectures on "Rome and Christianity" and, at the Royal Institution,
an additional lecture on Marcus Aurelius, which was immediately published in *The Nineteenth Century*.[35] It was drawn from Renan's forth-
coming book, *Marc-Aurèle et la fin du monde antique* (1881), the seventh
volume of the *Histoire des origines du Christianisme*, which had begun
in 1863 with the *Vie de Jésus*. Pater had read the *Vie de Jésus* by 1865,
and indeed Capes reported that even as an undergraduate Pater was
"drawn to Renan." Billie Andrew Inman, who has made a study of Pater's
reading, notes that the *Histoire des origines* was not included among his
library borrowings but only, in all likelihood, because he owned his own
copy, reading each volume as it came out. Since he began work on
Marius in 1881–82, it seems virtually certain that his primary inspiration came from Renan's lecture and his final volume. That was the opinion of Mary Duclaux, a friend of both Renan and Pater.[36]

Despite all this interest in Marcus Aurelius and the analogy with
Rome, it is a little surprising to find Pater, who had made his spiritual
home in the Renaissance, turning away to an age which was really the
property of quite a different group of people, the conservative humanists of the two universities. It is even more surprising to find him writing
a novel. Curtis Dahl and Doris B. Kelly have noted that *Marius the Epicurean* belongs to a distinct subgenre of the historical novel—that with
an early Christian setting—which rose into prominence in the 1820s
with Lockhart's *Valerius, a Roman Story* (1821) and Thomas Moore's
The Epicurean (1827), gained great popularity with *The Last Days of
Pompeii* (1834) by Bulwer-Lytton, became religio-didactic with Kingsley's *Hypatia*, Newman's *Callista*, and Wiseman's *Fabiola* in the 1850s,
wandered into the paths of sentimentality and sensationalism in the
work of various lesser novelists, and then flared up into melodrama in
General Lew Wallace's *Ben Hur, a Tale of the Christ* (1880), one of the
most popular novels ever published in America. Altogether there were
over eighty "early Christian" novels written during the nineteenth cen-

tury.[37] Pater's was one of the last of these, and thus one has to say that
his work, which many people think looks forward in technique to Mann
and Proust, utilized an old-fashioned and popular form, which he completely transcended for modernist and elitist purposes. But why did he,
a Renaissance Epicurean, want to write in that genre about an age dominated by the great Stoic?

One reason was certainly his desire to correct the false impression
created by the Conclusion to *The Renaissance*. When that piece was first
published anonymously in a periodical, as part of a review of William
Morris's poems, it did not have any great impact, but when it was republished in book form, as the deliberately formulated "Conclusion" of
an Oxford tutor, it created a furor. Not only did the bishop of the
diocese preach against it, but so too did Pater's own former tutor. His
younger colleague at Brasenose, John Wordsworth, remonstrated with
him in a stiff letter and suggested that he give up his share in the Divinity examination at Collections.[38] He was passed over for the proc-
torship, Jowett avoided him, and W. H. Mallock satirized him in *The
New Republic*. "I wish they wouldn't call me 'a hedonist,'" Pater complained; "it produces such a bad effect on the minds of people who
don't know Greek."[39] One function, then, of the novel was to take people
back to the actual followers of Heraclitus, Epicurus, and Aristippus of
Cyrene and show them what the word *hedonism* meant in its original
setting and what, making some distinctions, it could mean in the modern world. For one of Pater's most insistent ideas is that the actual
bearing of an abstract philosophy is determined by the particular temperament in which it happens to be lodged (ME, I, 135–36, 144–45;
II, 90, 218). "It is better," said Mill, "to be . . . Socrates dissatisfied
than a fool satisfied." In the case of so vague a term as hedonism it is
obvious that everything depends on what the individual takes pleasure
in—whether in gross sensual pleasures or the refined pleasures of art or
even of altruism. Every sensitive reader of *The Renaissance* should have
been able to deduce the temperament that Pater had in mind, but it is
true he did not specify it. Thus, in this "corrective" book it would not
do merely to write a series of essays on the "Religion of Numa," Apuleius, the *Pervigilium Veneris,* Epicureanism, the humanism of Fronto,
Marcus Aurelius, Lucian, and the emerging Christian sects. It was necessary to depict the temperament on which these various influences
played, to write about Marius, "His Sensations and Ideas." So much
Pater had learned from a short work which he had published in 1878,
"The Child in the House." "The Child in the House," being translated,
is "a temperament in an environment," and Pater declared that from this

work came everything original which he had subsequently done. Certainly, from it came the *Imaginary Portraits,* of which it is a first instance and of which *Marius* is a larger development.

In the temperament of Marius we see the hidden nature of Pater himself: a vague fear of evil, a feeling that the world is full of sacred presences and that he has an office of priesthood toward them, an ideal of bodily health, a certain inward tacitness of mind. Even before he met any Epicureans Marius had a "natural epicureanism" (ME, I, 49, 128) in his delight in the capacity of the eye, but he also shrank from excess in any kind. It is this temperament, "this feeling of a responsibility towards the world of men and things," which kept him serious and dignified amid the Epicurean speculations of later years and made him anticipate "some great occasion of self-devotion" (ME, I, 22) such as actually came. Thus, he was also an "anima naturaliter Christiana" even before he met any Christians.

It is not the Roman story, however, but the English analogy we are interested in. Only once, well along in the novel, does Pater comment overtly upon it. "That age and our own," he says, "have much in common—many difficulties and hopes. Let the reader pardon me if here and there I seem to be passing from Marius to his modern representatives—from Rome, to Paris or London" (ME, II, 16). For the most part he does not force it upon our attention. Certain modern phrases in inverted commas—" 'subjective immortality,' to use a modern phrase" (ME, I, 24), "an 'aesthetic' education, as it might now be termed" (ME, I, 151)—keep it hovering before our eyes. Occasionally, there will be more explicit comparisons: "That late world, amid many curiously vivid modern traits, had this spectacle, so familiar to ourselves, of the public lecturer or essayist" (ME, I, 157). "The long shows of the amphitheatre were, so to speak, the novel-reading of that age" (ME, I, 243)—though the chapter title, "Manly Amusement," might rather suggest a comparison to the blood sports of the English aristocracy. Without ever deforming the structure of his novel or turning it into a one-to-one allegory Pater, by his images and allusions, his metaphors and general reflective language, gives us the sense of a second world, with which we are more familiar and to which the actions and attributes of the first might apply. This is true of each one of the major phases of thought and feeling through which Marius passes.

An allusion to Wordsworth, for example, to the value which he placed on the superstitious awe of the northern peasantry, helps to associate "that old, staid, conservative religion" (ME, I, 51) of Marius's childhood, "a religion of usages and sentiment rather than of facts and beliefs" (ME, I, 8), with the traditional Anglicanism of the English countryside, also conservative and patriarchal, linked with festivals and domestic life, a religion of natural piety rather than dogmatic creeds. This religion, initially so important a stay in Marius's childhood, is ultimately felt to be constricting and is put from him with less trouble than Pater had in putting away Christianity.

It was generally accepted in nineteenth-century England that Utilitarianism was the modern counterpart of Epicureanism, the "greatest happiness of the greatest number" being the modern democratic or universalistic version of ancient hedonism. The scientific and metaphysical assumptions of positivism also seemed in harmony with the atomism and evolutionary thought of Lucretius and Heraclitus. In *Plato and Platonism* Pater said of the Heraclitean flux, "It is the burden of Hegel on the one hand, to whom nature, and art, and polity, and philosophy, aye, and religion too, each in its long historic series, are but so many conscious movements in the secular process of the eternal mind; and on the other hand of Darwin and Darwinism, for which 'type' itself properly *is* not but is only always *becoming*" (PP, 19). Even the Pythagorean doctrine of the transmigration of souls, which Plato applied to the individual, is now seen to apply to humanity. "It is humanity itself now—abstract humanity—that figures as the transmigrating soul, accumulating into its 'colossal manhood' the experience of ages" (PP, 72–73). Pater also emphasized the general philosophic implications of the doctrine of flux in the Conclusion and the essay on Coleridge, but in *Marius,* in harmony with the different turn given to that doctrine by the temperament of Marius, he emphasizes the aesthetic movement in France and England.

In Marius's friend Flavian, in the "Golden Book" of Apuleius's *Metamorphoses,* and in the *Pervigilium Veneris,* which Flavian is supposed to have composed, Pater describes a Roman "Euphuism" which has its counterpart in all ages dedicated to restoring the power of the word but which, in his view, had its special equivalent in Flaubert's search for le mot juste, in Gautier's penchant for the macabre, in Swinburne's neopaganism, and especially in the work of Rossetti. Rossetti's *Poems* and *Ballads and Sonnets* had just been published in 1881, and Pater in 1883 was writing his essay on Rossetti which emphasized many things parallel to Flavian: his desire to be the leader of a "new literary school" (ME, I, 100), his effort to find an expression which was the exact equivalent of the data within, his search for an ideal love of imaginative intensity like the love in "Cupid and Psyche," his ransacking of the older literature for archaic phrases, his self-conscious relation to the past, his revival of the ballad form and the refrain, and, one might add, his death immediately after he had published his two volumes. Flavian was not Rossetti, but the Victorian conception of Rossetti was nearer to Flavian than our own. In the *Edinburgh Review* for 1882 the Pre-Raphaelite movement was actually called "a kind of modern euphuism."[40]

In the "New Cyrenaicism" Pater attempted to correct the impression left by the Conclusion to *The Renaissance* that he was a "hedonist" and had made pleasure the end of life. "Not pleasure, but fulness of life, and 'insight' as conducting to that fulness—energy, variety, and choice of experience, including noble pain and sorrow even . . . —whatever form of human life, in short, might be heroic, impassioned, ideal: from these the 'new Cyrenaicism' of Marius took its criterion of values" (ME, I, 155–56). It is not immediately apparent what is "new" about the Cyrenaicism of Marius, for Marius says that in turning from the abstract doctrine of Heraclitus to the "subtly practical world-wisdom" of Aristippus of Cyrene he was turning from "an ancient thinker generally" to "a modern man of the world" (ME, I, 138–39). In other words, Aristippus himself was modern. "The most discerning judges saw in him something like the graceful 'humanities' of the later Roman, and our modern 'culture,' as it is termed" (ME, I, 141). Presumably, Marius's Cyrenaicism was even more refined than that of Aristippus, but in truth the addition of the epithet "New" to every form of "-ism" was so much the habit of the late nineteenth and early twentieth century—one thinks of the New Liberalism and the New Realism, of Shaw's New Man and New Woman—that one suspects the newness was more a matter of Pater's age than of Marius's. The word *culture* makes Arnold a partner in this crime, for we must remember that to the Victorians Arnold seemed far more Epicurean than he does to us.

Nonetheless, Pater could hardly help associating Arnold with Marcus Aurelius, and his distinctly cool and even unfriendly assessment of the Emperor must reflect his attitude toward that element in Arnold— also in Carlyle, Goethe, and all the other humanists who preached "renunciation." Even the enthusiasm of Renan he could not share, for he finds the *Thoughts* marked by mediocrity, though "a mediocrity for once really golden" (ME, I, 233). When Marius sees the Emperor sit impassively through the gladiatorial contests, he could not but believe that the great philosopher was his inferior. His famous impassivity "amounted to a tolerance of evil" (ME, II, 53). His asceticism was "hardly the expression of 'the healthy mind in the healthy body,' but rather of the sacrifice of the body to the soul" (ME, I, 195). The true descendant of the imperial Stoic, declared Pater, was the hermit of the Middle Ages (ME, I, 205; II, 52).

Thus, one may say that Pater transferred to Marius himself the unction (to use a Victorian word) which Renan felt in the Emperor. It was he, not Marcus Aurelius, who had come so close to being a Christian. The question is, how close? Mrs. Humphry Ward said of Pater, "He never returned to Christianity in the orthodox or intellectual sense. But his heart returned to it."[41] That return is charted in *Marius the Epicurean,* which differs from *The Renaissance* less in fundamentals than in the matter of tone. *The Renaissance* is a young man's book, provocative, daring, skirting the dangerous edge of things, deliberately courting scandal by the indecent mixture of paganism and Christianity. Its favorite fancy is Heine's notion that after the fall of paganism the old gods, in order to maintain themselves, took up employment in the new religion—a deliberate reversal of the orthodox idea that the fallen angels, after their expulsion from heaven, took up employment as the gods of paganism. In *Marius* all that youthful effervescence is gone. As a result of his contact with Stoicism, Marius is led to "Second Thoughts" about even the New Cyrenaicism. He perceives that it is a philosophy characteristic of youth, that it is antinomian, and that it has its own exclusiveness and negation which have cut him off from a thousand sympathies. There is "a venerable system of sentiment and idea," the product of the world's mind operating over generations, which is rich in experience and from which he, in his carefully cultivated solipsism, has been cut off. Cornelius Fronto, the Emperor's tutor, had spoken of "a universal commonwealth of mind," and the Emperor himself of an "other" with whom he held converse, but to Marius these seem like mere abstractions. Yet on one summer evening in the Campagna he has a vision of a divine companion who seemed to have accompanied him through life and, perceiving that a life-sustaining vision might have its ground in itself, he arrives at the idea of the will as an organ of knowledge. But on another occasion, meeting in the house of a friend with Apuleius, the superstitious Platonist who believes in a whole class of divine beings midway between gods and men, he concludes that "for himself, he must still hold by what his eyes really saw" (ME, II, 92). Then, at another house, that of the Christian Cecilia, he is taken by his friend Cornelius to witness the celebration of the Eucharist, and finds it the most beautiful act of worship he has ever seen. But it also speaks obscurely of "some fact, or series of facts, in which the old puzzle of life had found its solution" (ME, II, 106), and in a dialogue between his friend Lucian and a young student of philosophy, Hermotimus, he learns once again to distrust those who pretend to have found solutions. Thus, Marius moves backwards and forwards between skepticism and belief, and when he and Cornelius are seized in an outbreak of violence against the Christians and Marius saves Cornelius's life rather than his own—dying, however, not at the hands of the soldiers but simply from fever—it is not certain in what sense or to what degree he is a Christian. His Christian friends administer extreme unction, calling out *Anima Christiana!* and after his death, "according to their generous view in this matter" (ME, II, 224), they regard him as a martyr. But the chapter title is "Anima Naturaliter Christiana,"—a soul *naturally* Christian, or Christian by nature—and we recall that the idea of "some great occasion of self-devotion" had been with him from the first. Even as he lies waiting for death he thinks that his condition of Epicurean receptivity is the best to be in, in case the Christian doctrine of immortality should be true and there is any further revelation, after death, to be made. If Marius does in any sense die a Christian, he does not cease for that reason to be an Epicurean. It is but the last and highest phase of a life ever open to new experience.

Pater wrote to Violet Paget (Vernon Lee) in July 1883, while he was engaged upon the composition of *Marius,* that he regarded the writing of this work as a kind of "duty." "For, you know, I think there is a . . . sort of religious phase possible for the modern mind . . . , the conditions of which phase it is the main object of my design to convey."[42] That phase must have been one which accepts the morality, the sentiment, the poetry, and the ritual of Christianity without its dogma, for it is notable that in Marius's encounter with the Christians in the house of Cecilia there is no mention of any creed or dogma or system of theology. Three times Pater mentions as implied by the service of the Eucharist a "fact, or series of facts, to be ascertained by those who would" (ME, II, 113; cf. II, 106, 134), almost as if a belief in Christ's life and death were optional. Somewhat later these facts are described as "supposed facts" and even as a "legend" (ME, II, 139). Certainly they are never presented to Marius as essential to the Christian religion. What is essential, in his view, is a community of noble persons living together as a family in order and peace, presided over by women and pervaded by the ideal of chastity. Their lives are dedicated to fruitful labor and animated by a spirit which is at once gravely serious and deeply cheerful. For although Arnold had said it was the late pagan world that was "blithe and debonair" and that Christianity was a "religion of sorrow," Pater says that in this early period "the tables in fact were turned: the prize of a cheerful temper on a candid survey of life was no longer with the pagan world" but with the Church (ME, II, 124; cf. II, 112, 115). For one brief moment "there was no forced opposition between the soul and the body, the world and the spirit" (ME, II, 122), and one could speak of "the naturalness of Christianity," of its "humanism" (ME, II, 123, 116). Pater called this moment, in the second century A.D., "The Minor Peace of the Church" in contrast to the "Greater Peace" under Constantine. But by that time there had been two centuries of persecution, reinitiated by Marcus Aurelius. The Church had been driven in upon itself; it had become grim, militant, exclusive, at war with itself and the world. It had adopted the second of the two ideals which are a part of its history, the "ideal of asceticism" rather than the "ideal of culture," which alone was in harmony with the gracious spirit of its Founder. Under the Antonines, however, there was not this conflict between the Church and the world. Marius "had lighted, by one of the peculiar intellectual good-fortunes of his life, upon a period when, even more than in the days of austere *ascêsis* which had preceded and were to follow it, the church was true for a moment, truer perhaps than she would ever be again, to that element of profound serenity in the soul of her Founder, which reflected the eternal goodwill of God to man" (ME, II, 118).

Pater called this moment a Renaissance. In describing the early Christian sanctuary in the house of Cecilia, he says it consisted almost exclusively of "the remains of older art" combined and harmonized in accordance with some finer taste than was available to the ancient world. "It was the old way of true *Renaissance*— . . . conceiving the new organism by no sudden and abrupt creation, but rather by the action of a new principle upon elements, all of which had in truth already lived and died many times" (ME, II, 96–97). So too with the music of divine service: drawing upon the old, it also, like Flavian's poetry, seemed to foreshadow the new. "As if in anticipation of the sixteenth century, the church [in its music] was becoming 'humanistic,' in an earlier, and unimpeachable *Renaissance*" (ME, II, 126). In truth, Pater now thought that it was not the classical world but the early Christian world which the early Renaissance had tried to recover. In the second century Marius saw, "in all its primitive freshness and amid the lively facts of its actual coming into the world, as a reality of experience, that regenerate type of humanity, which, centuries later, Giotto and his successors, down to the best and purest days of the young Raphael, . . . were to conceive as an artistic ideal" (ME, II, 110–11). Their ideal had been a reality in the second century. Indeed, the analogy that Pater would now make was

not between Antonine Rome and Victorian England but between Antonine Rome and early Renaissance Italy. Whereas before he apologized
to the reader for passing from Rome to London, now he declared that
the reader may think that Marius, by a kind of inversion of the Platonic
doctrine of reminiscence, has "descended, by *foresight,* upon a later age
than his own," namely, that of St. Francis of Assisi. For St. Francis,
Dante, and Giotto had reestablished a continuity, only partly broken
during the Middle Ages, with "the gracious spirit of the primitive
church, as manifested in that first early springtide of her success" (ME,
II, 118–19).

It is now apparent why Pater turned in *Marius* from the Renaissance
to the early Christian period. It too was a Renaissance—a birth of a
Christian humanism out of a dying paganism, as the other was the birth
of a Christian *humanism* out of a dying asceticism. They were alike in
the combination of their elements and in their sense of newness, different only in their emphasis and in the ruins out of which they sprang.
Only by a novel set in this period could Pater accomplish his double
purpose of explaining his former position in *The Renaissance* and also
the new position that he now occupied. For by the analogy between the
religion of Marius's childhood and that of his own he could present his
break with orthodox Christianity, and by analogy he could explain the
various forms of Epicureanism in his own day. But when it came to his
new position, to the religious phase possible to the modern mind, that
could be presented only by the thing itself—by an emerging Christianity
which had no real counterpart in his own day. Of course, there were
others working towards it. In a sense, Pater was saying what Arnold had
said in 1867 in "Obermann Once More." Reviewing the parallels between the outworn Roman Empire and his own day, and the regeneration accomplished by the birth of Christ, Arnold cried,

> 'Oh, had I lived in that great day,
> How had its glory new
> Fill'd earth and heaven, and caught away
> My ravish'd spirit too!'

But then Arnold was diverted into asceticism.

> 'No cloister-floor of humid stone
> Had been too cold for me.
> For me no Eastern desert lone
> Had been too far to flee.'

Pater could not follow him there, but he could follow him in much that he said in *Literature and Dogma* (1873) and *God and the Bible* (1875). The vision of a New Christianity, without metaphysics and without dogma, was shared by Pater with Arnold, Renan, and a few others, and to that extent there was a parallel between the Christianity of the second century and that of 1885.

Pater wrote to an American correspondent: "I may add that 'Marius' is designed to be the first of a kind of trilogy, or triplet, of works of a similar character; dealing with the same problems, under altered historical conditions. The period of the second of the series would be at the end of the 16th century, and the place France: of the third, the time, probably the end of the last century—and the scene England."[43] There is no trace of the third novel, but the second was published after Pater's death in fragmentary form under the title *Gaston de Latour.* Pater's literary executor, C. L. Shadwell, explains in the Preface that the work would have been parallel to *Marius* but with "the scene shifted to another age of transition, when the old fabric of belief was breaking up, and when the problem of man's destiny and his relations to the unseen was undergoing a new solution" (GL, vi). It was, in fact, the same scene as that with which *The Renaissance* had ended, but with Joachim du Bellay replaced by another member of the Pléiade, Ronsard, who represents for the young Gaston the same kind of "modern" poetry that Flavian and Apuleius had represented for Marius. The fact that there were "flowers of evil" among his poems suggests the connection Pater intended to make, but he also describes his work in terms of the particularity and sensuous immediacy of Browning and the Pre-Raphaelites, and we recall that Rossetti had translated early French poetry and Browning had used Ronsard in "The Glove" as the type of the modern poet. Montaigne, who figures as the Skeptic in Emerson's *Representative Men,* replaces Epicurus and Aristippus as the new philosophy that dissolves old beliefs, but since the novel is unfinished we do not know in what form of transcendent philosophy Gaston was to end. Presumably, he would have bridged the excessive spirituality of the Reformation and the sensuality of the Renaissance so as to lead into the modern world.

It is not in his trilogy, however, but in the *Imaginary Portraits,* to which Pater turned after completing *Marius,* that he presents most clearly and impressively his conception of a series of cultural Renaissances extending from the Middle Ages to his own day. Gerald Monsman has interpreted these Portraits, very perceptively, in terms of the myths of Apollo and Dionysus, but they may also be interpreted in terms of history. Indeed, they were often written in connection with Pater's historical investigations of a particular culture or region. The essay "Art-Notes in North Italy," for example, was written, as Pater told Arthur Symons, "by way of prologue to an Imaginary Portrait with Brescia for background." The portrait in question is undoubtedly the fragmentary "Gaudioso, the Second," which begins with a discussion of a painting by Romanino in the National Gallery to which Pater had made reference at the end of his "Art-Notes in North Italy." Pater said that he called his pieces "portraits" intending readers, "as they might do on seeing a portrait, to begin speculating—what came of him?"[44] Similarly, on looking at a work of art, he allowed his imagination to rove, turning the details of a painting into a story and imagining the peculiar conditions out of which it arose. It is this rather old-fashioned literary device, indeed, which provides the *entrée en sujet* of most of the portraits. In "Denys l'Auxerrois," for instance, the narrator-as-tourist arrives in Auxerre and is struck by a peculiarly brilliant piece of stained glass which he finds in the shop of an antique dealer. He is impressed by the curious figures it depicts, is directed to a priest who has a tapestry with the same figures, and finally reconstructs the story of Denys, which explains not only the tapestry and the glass but also the entire cathedral, its rich heritage of organ music, and even the riant character of the Burgundian countryside. Denys is, of course, a French Dionysus, but he is also the center of an etiological myth which embodies both the spirit of the age and, to some degree, the spirit of place. In the thirteenth century, Pater tells us, "Auxerre had its turn in that political movement which broke out sympathetically, first in one, then in another of the towns of France, turning their narrow, feudal institutions into a free, communistic life— a movement of which . . . the French cathedrals are in many instances the monument" (IP, 55). Denys is the "genius" of that movement. He is also the genius loci, for the narrator notes that on certain days, "when the trace of the Middle Age comes out, like old marks in the stones in rainy weather" (IP, 77), he may actually be seen haunting the narrow streets.

Similarly, in "Apollo in Picardy" a visitor to the region, seeing a thirteenth-century stone barn which begins in a heavy Gothic manner and ends in a lighter, more pliant style, wonders how this came about. By the aid of an old manuscript found at the time of the Revolution he is able to reconstruct the story of Prior Saint-Jean, who had spent all his life within the high forbidding walls of a monastery but, on being sent to a country retreat for his health, finds his soul opening up under

the genial influences of earth and sky. A strange gypsy-like figure, who
seems to be the very "embodiment of all those genial influences of earth
and sky" (MS, 155), arrives to dwell with and serve the Prior. To the
classically minded he seems, with his harp and bow, to be a medieval
Apollo, but the local people mishear his name as Apollyon. It is under
his influence that the great monastic barn is completed and given its
strange twist towards lightness and the sun. "Yes!" says the narrator, "it
must have so happened often in the Middle Age. . . . Style must have
changed under the very hands of men who were no wilful innovators"
(MS, 153). Lest we think this a mere fancy, placed immediately before
"Apollo in Picardy" in *Miscellaneous Studies* are two essays, on the abbey
church at Vézelay and the cathedral of Amiens, in which Pater actually
traces the opening up of the dark, monastic churches of the Cluniac
order into the lighter Gothic style of the secular communes. For in
defiance of Ruskin he asserts,

> The greatest and purest of Gothic churches, Notre-Dame d'Amiens,
> illustrates, by its fine qualities, a characteristically secular movement of
> the beginning of the thirteenth century. Philosophic writers of French
> history have explained how, in that and the two preceding centuries, a
> great number of the more important towns in eastern and northern
> France rose against the feudal establishment, and developed severally
> the local and municipal life of the commune. . . . Over against monastic
> interests . . . they pushed forward the local, and, so to call it, secular
> authority of their bishops. . . . [They] promoted there the new, revo-
> lutionary Gothic manner. . . . Nay, those grand and beautiful *people's*
> churches of the thirteenth century . . . concurred also with certain
> novel humanistic movements of religion itself at that period. (MS,
> 109–10)

What they sought, by the admission of light into their buildings, was
"an immense cheerfulness" (MS, 118). The disappearance of the wall
into windows, which Ruskin considered the beginning of the end of
medieval architecture, Pater considered the beginning of its glory. The
very barn built by Prior Saint-Jean to the sound of Apollyon's music
seems to allude to the abbey church of Pontigny, itself a "reaction against
monasticism" and, in the long unbroken line of its roof, looking like "a
great farm-building" (MS, 126–27) amid the fields. Apollo/Apollyon,
then, is the spirit of cultural change which was abroad in the twelfth
and thirteenth century and turned people away from darkness to light.
It even affected the crabbed treatise which Prior Saint-Jean had been
writing, on mathematics as applied to music and astronomy, and turned
it into an anticipation of the Copernican theory. The admission of the

sun into medieval churches was a precursor of the heliocentric theory of the Renaissance.

No such cultural Renaissance is found by Pater in seventeenth-century Flanders when, in "Sebastian van Storck," he turns his attention to that era. Sebastian is the scion of a wealthy Dutch family living in the midst of the material surroundings which have been made familiar to us in Dutch genre painting. On the other hand, he shrank from these surroundings, withdrawing to a lonely tower where he meditated on the abstract essence of life in the manner of Spinoza, to whose philosophy he was strongly drawn. Ultimately, he spurns the marriage that would have led him back into life and finds the death he apparently had been seeking in a lonely house by the sea. In his death he saves the life of a little child, and although we are told that he is not one of those who deduce from the pantheistic philosophy that every particle of the concrete world is divine, he must at the last moment have had some inkling of that idea. He is clearly one of those who, in the austere tradition of Parmenides, Plato, and Spinoza, seem to Pater to be oriented towards death rather than life. And yet, says Pater, "extremes meeting, [Sebastian's] cold and dispassionate detachment from all that is most attractive to ordinary minds came to have the impressiveness of a great passion" (IP, 99). Pater is puzzled as to how something so immersed in the material world as Dutch genre painting and something so removed from it as Spinoza's *Ethics* could emerge from the same intellectual world.

The next two Imaginary Portraits are both set in the early eighteenth century, the one in France on the border of Flanders, the other in Germany. The Grand-duchy of Rosenmold was one of those tiny German principalities in which, at the beginning of the eighteenth century, time seemed almost to have stood still since the Middle Ages. One day, however, the young Duke Carl, wandering through the vast Gothic lumber-room of a palace, came upon a book printed in 1486, by one Conrad Celtes, containing an ode "To Apollo, praying that he would come to us from Italy, bringing his lyre with him," and thenceforth to bring the God of light to hyperborean Germany became Carl's object. Unfortunately, he attempted to do this in "the somewhat questionable form" of importing French art and literature from the court of Louis XIV. The seventeenth-century rococo imitations of the Renaissance called forth in him the same enthusiasm that the true Renaissance had evoked in France two centuries before, and the reason for this was that he found in these false rosettes some portion of himself. Thus, it was only when he suffered a symbolic death and rebirth that he could decide, not traveling south to Hellas but wandering in his own native Germany, that

"America is here or nowhere!" "For you, France, Italy, Hellas, is here!" Recognizing the untried spiritual possibilities of meek Germany, he "transferred the ideal land out of space beyond the Alps or the Rhine, into future time," and he believed that he must be the leader. The *Aufklärung* (he had already found the name for the thing) would come only through the development of a native poetry, a national art and literature, a German philosophy. " 'Only,' he thought, 'if I had coadjutors! If these thoughts would awake in but one other mind!' " (IP, 143–45). They did awake in the minds of Lessing and Herder, and Pater says it is the aspirations of a thousand other precursors of Goethe that he has tried to embody in Duke Carl.

Just as "Duke Carl of Rosenmold" is an interpretation of those baroque palaces verging towards rococo which Pater might have seen on visiting his sisters in Germany, so "A Prince of Court Painters" is a sensitive reading of the paintings of Antony Watteau and his contemporary, Jean-Baptiste Pater. Wright says that the Portrait was occasioned by a visit to the Dulwich Gallery, which was the only public gallery in England where paintings by Watteau were to be seen during Pater's lifetime. But he must have seen others as well, perhaps, as Monsman suggests, at the municipal museum at Valenciennes, where Jean-Baptiste Pater's *Portrait de la Soeur de Pater* is to be found. For it is through the eyes of this sister and in the words of her journal that the story of Watteau is told. She dearly loves the young painter, who grew up with her in the severe Spanish-Flemish atmosphere of Valenciennes and then went off to Paris, where he has developed a new manner of painting, light and gay, which represents all the world as if it were an eternal fête champêtre. She cannot but think he would have been happier if he had remained at home, and yet, she admits, he has revealed a light, a beauty, in those scenes which we would not have seen if he had not painted them. Still, "methinks Antony Watteau reproduces that gallant world, those patched and powdered ladies and fine cavaliers, so much to its own satisfaction, partly because he despises it" (IP, 33). She notices there is always a cloud upon his horizon, the sign of a storm before night. It is because he foresees the French Revolution, because he understands the delicacy and fragility of this world, that he is able to make his pictures of it so poignant and so moving. Had he really been a part of it he could not have done so. But, being of "the old time—that serious old time which is passing away," he dignifies by a profound melancholy the essential insignificance of what he touches. He does for eighteenth-century France what Browning's "Tocatta of Galuppi" did for Italy.

If Pater had attempted the third part of his projected trilogy, which was to have been set in England at the end of the eighteenth century, it seems likely he would have treated the Romantic movement as yet another Renaissance, for in the unfinished Imaginary Portrait "An English Poet" he describes the awakening of the artistic vision of a Wordsworthian youth in the austere beauty of the Cumberland mountains. The youth actually is of mixed ancestry, the illegitimate offspring of an English girl and a Dionysian figure from the south of France—a kind of Annette Vallon in reverse—and his art mingles the classic with the romantic. Pater seems generally to have been impressed with the mixed inheritance of the English as a source of their strength, for in another Portrait, "Emerald Uthwart," set at the time of the Napoleonic Wars, he emphasizes the "old-English" inheritance of Uthwart and the fact that, attending a school like Pater's own at Canterbury, he was taught the classics in a medieval setting. "By one of our wise English compromises, we still teach our so modern boys the Classics. . . . Nay! by a double compromise, . . . we teach them their pagan Latin and Greek under the shadow of medieval church-towers, amid the haunts and traditions, and with something of the discipline, of monasticism" (MS, 205). The French have done away with this, but there is some value in the older English method. "It is of such diagonal influences, through complication of influence, that expression comes, in life, in our culture, in the very faces of men and boys" (MS, 205).

Such is the "history" of that elusive spirit of cultural change which Pater gives us in his Imaginary Portraits. As he explored the Hellenic origins of this spirit in the lectures and essays which were gathered together in *Greek Studies* and *Plato and Platonism* he attempted to be more precise as to the mechanism of this change. It operated through a conflict between two antithetical tendencies or influences which Pater, borrowing his terms from Jowett, called the "centrifugal" and the "centripetal." The centrifugal tendency was Asiatic in origin, was associated with the Ionian people, and was embodied in the Athenian democracy. The centripetal tendency was broadly European, Doric, and Lacedaemonian. The one emphasized variety, change, individualism; the other unity, stability, order. Heraclitus was the philosopher of the one, Parmenides of the other. In the world of Greek myth, Apollo, as Nietzsche had noted just a few years earlier, was the *principium individuationis,* the limiting human tendency, whereas Dionysus was the tendency of nature to be unlimited. In Pater, however, the matter was complicated by Dionysus's being divided into a summer and a winter god, so that in himself he represents the death and rebirth of human cultures. On all levels and in all developments of human thought one finds this alternating and self-correcting tendency between the closed and the open society, authority and liberty, the One and the Many, objective and subjective, form and matter, the abstract and the concrete, realism and nominalism, the classic and the romantic. "The whole of Pater's world view," says Gerald Monsman, "is structured around this tension between the Heraclitean centrifugal tendency and the Parmenidean centripetal tendency."[46]

Though Pater traces the dialectic of human culture through many modes and many periods, it is obvious he considers the Renaissance to be the model or paradigm of how an artistic culture develops. Thus, in his studies of Greek art he continually draws parallels between Greek civilization and the Italian Renaissance. Several times he complains that Pausanias in his travels did not collect the same kind of detailed information about the early art in the Greek demes that Vasari collected in the provincial cities of Italy. If he had, we would not only have a knowledge of works of art valuable in themselves but would also have a better understanding of later developments. Those who would understand Phidias without a knowledge of earlier Greek sculpture are "like people criticising Michelangelo, without knowledge of the earlier Tuscan school—of the works of Donatello and Mino da Fiesole" (GS, 157, 214). Cicero, for example, undervalued Canachus in the same way that critics of the last century undervalued early Tuscan sculpture. Now, however, that we understand the value of early Italian art we can also understand that of the earliest phase in the development of Greek art and religion. For the religion of Dionysus as depicted on Greek vases reminds us of the frescoes of Benozzo Gozzoli in the Campo Santo at Pisa. Giotto's symbolism at Assisi arises out of the same mood and temper as that which gave rise to the earliest versions of the myth of Demeter. Euripides' *Bacchanals* suggests the existence of sculptured reliefs like those of Luca della Robbia in the organ loft at Florence. The chest of Cypselus, which Pausanias did describe, must have impressed him much as the ancient bronze doors impressed later observers at Pisa. The Marbles of Aegina have the stiffness of early Flemish painters and so "remind us of the Middle Age where it passes into the early Renaissance." Their creator is "as it were the Chaucer of Greek sculpture" (GS, 268–69). A more primitive work, a Hermes bearing a ram upon his shoulders in the Museum of Athens, seems so Gothic in its style that we can easily imagine it set into the front of Auxerre or Wells cathedral. For "the connoisseur assures us"—and this is the generalization to which Pater has come from all these instances—"that all good art, at its respective stages of development, is in essential qualities everywhere alike" (GS, 270).

The naive art in the first phase of a culture, the classic art at its full development, and the decadent art as it deliquesces into something else are, in their best examples, the same in their essential qualities all over the world. Pater pays lip service to the Phidiases, the Michelangeloes— the art of the Imaginative Reason which Arnold prefers—but it is the art which is coming into being and passing away which he really admires. "For as art which has passed its prime has sometimes the charm of an absolute refinement in taste and workmanship, so immature art also, as we now see, has its own attractiveness in the *naïveté*, the freshness of spirit, which finds power and interest in simple motives of feeling, and in the freshness of hand" (GS, 267). Of the two it is the birth of the new rather than the decay of the old that really fascinates him— "the budding of new art" amid "the survival of old religion" (GS, 158), whether it occurs in early Greece, in the early Renaissance, or in the Victorian Renaissance of his own day. For it is here, amid the tensions of a new freedom and an old bondage, that one lives at "the focus where the greatest number of vital forces" have their play (R, 236).

The thing that Pater discovered in his travels from the Renaissance to the early Christian period, then through the Middle Ages and the seventeenth and eighteenth centuries, and back to ancient Greece is that there are Renaissances everywhere. In the first place, there is no defining the spirit of the age without specifying the spirit of place, for the Renaissance is a ripple which moves from Greece to Italy, across France to Germany and England, and then washes back over those same countries. There are Renaissances everywhere. In the Preface to his first book Pater had said, "The ages are all equal." To the true critic "all periods, types, schools of taste, are in themselves equal" (R, x). Not quite equal, one thinks, for if there were no valleys there would not be hills. If there were no Middle Ages, there could not be Renaissances. But it is true that in Pater the periods so merge into one another that the very concept of periodicity comes into question. It is not eliminated entirely, for though Pater prizes the particular, the individual, he notes that we are made more intensely conscious of the particularity of individual things (a seashell, for instance) by being aware of the type to which they belong. Examples of a Renaissance "within the Middle Ages" would not be so piquant if there were not a Middle Ages all around. Centrifugality could not exist without centripetality, the ecstasy of self-indulgence without the discipline of *ascêsis*. It is at the tension between the two that Pater lives.

Hence Pater accepts as a "valuable suggestion" Stendhal's theory that "all good art was romantic in its day" (Ap, 258, 255). "It is the addition of strangeness to beauty, that constitutes the romantic character in art" (Ap, 246), and thus if the art of the past was good—if it had the sharp edge of modernity about it—it must always have appeared strange. It will not cease to appear strange simply because it is passé. For history does not simply unroll objectively through time. In Pater's world it is gathered up subjectively in the human consciousness as one discovers it. One can, therefore, create one's own Renaissance by moving constantly from culture to culture. The Romantic movement may have been a Renaissance as it succeeded upon neoclassical poetry, but neoclassical poetry would be a Renaissance to one sated upon Romantic poetry. Greek poetry was "classic," but the Renaissance recovery of Greek poetry was, in Pater's sense, "romantic." The Middle Ages in Pater's conception was overwhelmingly a centripetal age, but the nineteenth century found "in the overcharged atmosphere of the Middle Age . . . , unworked sources of romantic effect, of a strange beauty" (Ap, 248), and so created a centrifugal age. All things are new to him who discovers them, and that is why Pater finds a place in the "House Beautiful" for every form and style of art. *Nihil humani a me alienum puto* is for Pater literally true, because he thinks himself a part of the world-spirit that went through all these phases of culture in the first place. Thus, in unearthing the artifacts of the past he is recovering a portion of his own nature—a portion, perhaps, with which he has previously been unacquainted. In order to become a complete human being he has to recover them all. He is really just "remembering" what he once knew, but this application of the Platonic doctrine of reminiscence to Hegel's concept of the evolving consciousness of the race gives to his vision a curious complexity. Everything that he recovers is at once old and new. In returning to the past, says Pater, "anything in the way of an actual revival must always be impossible. . . . The composite experience of all the ages is part of each one of us; to deduct from that experience, to obliterate any part of it, to come face to face with the people of a past age, as if the middle age, the Renaissance, the eighteenth century had not been, is as impossible as to become a little child, or enter again into the womb and be born." We are ineluctably modern and adult. "But though it is not possible to repress a single phase of that humanity . . . , it is possible to isolate such a phase, to throw it into relief, to be divided against ourselves in zeal for it."[47] With one eye we see ourselves as we are now, with the other as we were at some time in the past. The mirror of history for Pater is a stereoptic glass which reflects the self truly but with the added dimension of the past.

Conclusion

ONE COULD CARRY THIS STORY on down through the twentieth century to the latest practitioner of "pragmatic history," Barbara W. Tuchman, whose *A Distant Mirror* looks at modern life through the glass of the fourteenth century and whose *March of Folly* finds analogies between events as distant as the Trojan War and the Vietnam War. But perhaps it is better simply to ask ourselves what patterns emerge from the materials we have already covered. There are two large questions to consider: first, in what way does the concept of a Victorian mirror of history add to our understanding of the thought and culture of the period? and, second, did the Victorians' use of this mirror assist them in understanding and dealing with their own problems?

In reply to the first, we have already noted that it was primarily during the crises surrounding the passage of the first Reform Bill and the Revolution of 1848 and perhaps in the years immediately following the Franco-Prussian War that we find the greatest inclination to look to the past for guidance. What William Morris said is true: "It is mostly in periods of turmoil and strife and confusion that people care much about history."[1] This is partly because, as J. H. Plumb has noted, history has always been used to justify authority, and thus when writers argued about the earlier history of England, especially the Civil War and the Glorious Revolution, the very rights and privileges of their own day were at stake.[2] But even when they were dealing with another culture, the power of analogy and the developmental idea which had become so central to modern thought meant that history had largely replaced the Christian idea of Providence. G. H. Lewes wrote in 1844: "[Ours is] an age of universal anarchy of thought. . . . The desire of belief is strong; convictions are wanting: there is neither spiritual nor moral union. In this plight we may hope for the future, but can *cling* only to the past:

that alone is secure, well-grounded."[3] History, then, was the Delphic oracle of the nineteenth century, and it was dutifully consulted, however cryptic its answers. As Sir Lewis Namier used to say, the nineteenth century consulted history somewhat in the spirit of the man who sold earthquake pills, because there was absolutely nothing to take its place.[4]

We have also noted that those who looked back to the past tended to be those whose youth or young manhood fell upon these moments of crisis, and that they not unreasonably found a pattern in the past which corresponded very closely to the pattern in their own lives. The "conversions" of Carlyle, Mill, and Arnold, the slow development of Newman, and the flip-flops of Ruskin correspond too closely to their visions of history for us to think the relation is accidental. By far the most pervasive paradigm in the nineteenth century is the parallel between the life of the individual and the life-cycle of civilizations. Both were expressions of the deep-seated organicism of the age, and the discovery of the parallel was often the means whereby the individual overcame his alienation and reconciled himself with the world. As Northrop Frye once wrote, borrowing a metaphor from Matthew Arnold, "The culture of the past is not only the memory of mankind, but our own buried life, and study of it leads to a recognition scene, a discovery in which we see, not our past lives, but the total cultural form of our present life."[5]

This element of subjectivity in the individual's vision of the past did not prevent his using that vision as a means of imputing objectivity to his own views. One thinks of the writer in *Blackwood's* in 1830 who complained that he was being forced to give up all his most cherished reactionary ideas simply because they were out of phase with the "Spirit of the Age." Who was it, he asked, who had decided what the Spirit of the Age was? Similarly, there is no question but that the Zeitgeist was a club which Matthew Arnold used to hit his opponents over the head when they would not accept his word that more Hellenism (or perhaps more Hebraism) was what the nation needed. The rhetorical use of "history" is a main feature of the great Victorian debate, but it need not invalidate that debate any more than any other appeal to "external" authority. The thing we need to be aware of is that the arguments over science, religion, politics, culture, and art almost always had a historical dimension. When Oscar Wilde says, "Whatever . . . is modern in our life we owe to the Greeks. Whatever is anachronism is due to mediævalism,"[6] he is sending a message to Ruskin which he also sent in other terms. All the interlocking, overlapping, and contradictory visions of history which we find in the Victorian Age constitute one large, elaborate system of discourse, a structure of symbolism or fabric of meaning, which we need to know in order to read the poems, dramas, novels, essays, histories, and biographies of the age aright. We need to know that many individual figures—Cromwell, Savonarola, Marcus Aurelius, Lucretius, Raphael, King Arthur, Montaigne—are "representative men" who stand in a symbolic relation to their age, and to the Victorian Age as well.

The second question, as to whether the Victorians' use of the mirror of history assisted them in understanding and dealing with their problems, is much more difficult, for it involves the whole question of the validity of pragmatic history. This question has been vigorously debated by professional historians over the past hundred years, and, like all vital and important questions, remains essentially unresolved. Most of the great historians, from Thucydides and Polybius down through the eighteenth century, believed that history was directly useful: it provided a storehouse of examples to instruct the individual in the conduct of his life and the prince in the conduct of the state. It provided the materials of moral and civil maxims. The main change in the nineteenth century was that with the introduction of the historicist outlook historians began to focus more upon the larger evolution of civilization. They noted that history fell into periods and that each of these had its special characteristics, determined perhaps by the Spirit of the Age. They then sought to discover whether these periods succeeded each other according to any set pattern, either alternating back and forth, or repeating themselves in cycles, or moving upward *en ligne spirale,* or following some organic pattern of growth and decay. Mill looked forward to the day when history would become a science, with definite laws which would facilitate prediction, and Taine and Buckle thought that day had arrived. Apart from these positivistic historians, however, faith in periodic patterns faded somewhat after the middle years of the century, and it is probably no accident that in our chapters there is a gradual shift from political to aesthetic history. With the professionalization of historical study in the universities after the 1870s there was a greater and greater inclination simply to ascertain the true character of the past (insofar as one could) without reference to the present. Geoffrey Elton, President of the Royal Historical Society, declared that he could not be persuaded "that a minister of foreign affairs is better able to discharge his office because he once investigated the career of Metternich." And S. R. Gardiner declared shortly, "He who studies the history of the past will be of greater service to the society of the present in proportion as he leaves it out of account."[7]

Against the clear and cool wisdom of this remark one has to place the fact that when Hume, Macaulay, Carlyle, Froude, and others were writing their multivolume and highly tendentious histories, almost every educated person read them, whereas now the professional historians are not so widely read. Indeed, history as a guide to the future has now been replaced by the social sciences. "In Western societies," says J. H. Plumb, "we no longer prophesy the future by brooding over the past; it offers so little guidance. We limit the problem in time and use the computer, and get alternative answers."[8] This development was foreseen even by the Victorians, for the social sciences took their rise among the thinkers of the Benthamite and positivistic school, and the historically oriented members of this group believed that a major function of history was to furnish materials for the social sciences. G. H. Lewes declared in 1844 that "for the first time a mission is assigned to the study of the past, worthy of fulfillment: this mission is, to exhibit the evolution of humanity, and to form thereby a social science."[9] At the end of the century J. B. Bury also asserted that the truth which Cicero had expressed by calling history *magister vitae* and Dionysius by calling it "Philosophy teaching by examples" should now be expressed "by saying that history supplies the material for political and social science."[10] It did provide those materials to Comte, Marx, and others, but it has now largely ceased to provide them—or, more exactly, the social sciences have largely dispensed with its services. One would not wish, of course, to be without the exact picture of the present moment which modern statistical data provide. The shift from a diachronic to a synchronic frame has its advantages, but there are also disadvantages. In the first place, time *is* one of the dimensions of human life, and in the second, even if the economic indicators were refined to the point where they really would tell us where the economy was leading, they still do not tell us what to do about it. The numbers are value-free, whereas history is impregnated with human experience and hence with some degree of wisdom.

If one were to ask, however, whether any of the great Victorians received a helpful answer to a current problem by looking into the mirror of history, one would have to reply that probably he did not. It probably did not help England in dealing with the problems of the 1830s to be told by Thomas Arnold that it stood at the same point in its history as Greece had stood at the revolution of Corcyra. It probably did not help the nation in its drift toward secularization to be told by Ruskin that just such a drift had resulted in the fall of Venice. It is not simply that history is a Cassandra who never is listened to or believed;

it is rather that every situation is unique, the parallels are not really parallel, and the causes of events are multiple and complex. All the great Victorians understood this, for if there is one thing that is notable about them it is that, if in their young manhood they adopted a scheme of history involving alternating periods, or Viconian cycles, or irreversible falls from grace, they soon relaxed those schemes, no longer applied them so rigorously, moved out from their chosen period into other areas, and ended up in the general humanization of knowledge. This is true of Carlyle, Mill, Newman, Arnold, Ruskin, and Pater. Pater is perhaps the best example, for, beginning narrowly in the Renaissance, he ended in the realization that there are "renaissances" everywhere, and, finding in the evolution of the world-spirit a model for his own evolution, he kept himself perpetually alive by cultivating a tolerance, a sympathy, an understanding of all things. It is perhaps a main virtue of historical study that it does beget breadth of understanding and tolerance.

Ultimately, those who have thought most deeply about the subject agree that the historian must serve two masters: the past and the present. If he writes with his eye too exclusively upon the present, he will deform the past and produce nothing of value at all. But if he writes with his eye too exclusively upon the past, he will become a mere antiquarian, will lose the very life of his subject, which derives, paradoxically, from his life in the present. "An objective knowledge of the past," wrote Hajo Holborn, "can only be attained through the subjective experience of the scholar."[11] Thus, the scholar must focus exclusively on the past and yet know, in the back of his mind, that it is exclusively for the present he is writing. "The understanding of the present," wrote Ernst Troeltsch, "is always the final goal of all history."[12]

Precisely this paradox lies at the heart of the Victorian Age. Newman assigned to the university the task of teaching "liberal" knowledge, by which he meant knowledge whose sole value lies in enlarging, developing, and perfecting the mind that possesses it. But he knew that knowledge would not have that value unless it were also true. Mill believed that happiness was the end of life but also that one could not achieve happiness by pursuing it directly. One must act as if something else were the end of life and one would then attain happiness by the way. This "as if" philosophy became a central Victorian mode for handling the problem of science and religion. T. H. Huxley said that the Ten Commandments certainly were not divine, but that he could think of ten good human reasons for obeying them, i.e., for acting "as if" they were divine. So through this philosophy, which Mill calls the anti-

self-conscious philosophy of Carlyle, the Victorian Age attained a double vision, balancing the religious and the secular, the objective and the
subjective, the past and the present. In looking into the mirror of history it saw not merely itself reflected but also the whole panorama of
the past. It read history for its bearing upon the present, but in the
course of reading history it educated itself and so was better prepared
to offer new, creative solutions of its own. Indeed, in the course of
looking to the past it became conscious of the distinctive characteristics
of the present. We have already noted that it was in the early nineteenth
century, in conjunction with the emergence of the new historicist outlook, that the idea of "modernity" in its current meaning arose. It was
by the process of searching through the past for analogies to its own
situation and becoming aware that there was a certain sense in which
Thucydides, Lucretius, and Botticelli were "modern," whereas Herodotus, Cicero, and Raphael were not, that the Victorians became conscious of the true meaning of modernity and of the characteristics of
their own age. "It seems to me," wrote Wilde, "that with the development of the critical spirit we shall be able to realise, not merely our own
lives, but the collective life of the race, and so to make ourselves absolutely modern, in the true meaning of the word modernity. For he to
whom the present is the only thing that is present, knows nothing of
the age in which he lives. To realise the nineteenth century, one must
realise every century that has preceded it and that has contributed to
its making."[13]

Notes

INTRODUCTION

1 J. H. Newman, *Apologia pro Vita Sua: Being a History of His Religious Opinions,* ed. Martin J. Svaglic (Oxford: Clarendon Press, 1967), pp. 108–09.
2 Ibid., pp. 110–11.
3 Thomas Arnold, "The Oxford Malignants and Dr. Hampden," *Edinburgh Review* 63 (April 1836): 234, reprinted in the American edition of Arnold's *Miscellaneous Works* (New York, 1845), pp. 131–45. For a full account of the Hampden episode see Owen Chadwick, *The Victorian Church* (London: A. & C. Black, 1971), I, 112–21. Chadwick notes that the title of Arnold's article was supplied by the editor of the *Review.*
4 Arnold, "Oxford Malignants and Dr. Hampden," p. 236.
5 Newman, *Apologia,* p. 109.
6 Thomas Carlyle, *Critical and Miscellaneous Essays,* vol. 3, in *Works,* Centenary ed. (London, 1899), XXVIII, 43; Tennyson, "The Passing of Arthur," ll. 98–101; A. H. Clough, *The Bothie of Tober-na-Vuolich,* IX, 48–54; J. H. Newman, *Sermons, Chiefly on the Theory of Religious Belief* (Oxford, 1843), p. 193. Mary Schneider, "Plutarch's Night Battle in Arnold, Clough, and Tennyson," *The Arnoldian* 9 (Spring 1982): 32–38, notes that the description of the battle occurs in Plutarch's *Life of Nicias* as well as in Thucydides.
7 Richard Grafton, cited in E. M. W. Tillyard, *Shakespeare's History Plays* (London: Chatto & Windus, 1951), pp. 57–58; G. W. Leibnitz, *Philosophische Schriften,* ed. Gerhardt, VI, 198, cited in Giambattista Vico, *Autobiography,* trans. Max H. Fisch and Thomas G. Bergin (Ithaca: Cornell University Press, 1944), p. 23. See also David Bevington, *Tudor Drama and Politics: A Critical Approach to Topical Meaning* (Cambridge: Harvard University Press, 1968), p. 6; M. M. Reese, *The Cease of Majesty: A Study of Shakespeare's History Plays* (London: E. Arnold, 1961), pp. 1–19; Lily B. Campbell, *Shakespeare's Histories: Mirrors of Elizabethan Policy* (San Marino: Huntington Library, 1958), pp. 107–09.
8 Dionysius of Halicarnassus, *Ars Rhet.* xi. 2; Henry St. John Bolingbroke, *Letters on the Study and Use of History* (London, 1752), p. 14 (letter 2).
9 David Hume, *Enquiry concerning Human Understanding* (1748), in *Enquiries,* ed. L. A. Selby-Bigge, 3d ed. (Oxford: Clarendon Press, 1975), p. 83

[sec. 8]. For a general discussion of the eighteenth-century view of the uniformity of human nature see Paul Fussell, *The Rhetorical World of Augustan Humanism* (Oxford: Clarendon Press, 1965), chap. 3.

10 Bolingbroke, *Study and Use of History,* pp. 18, 55.

11 Henry Hallam, *View of the State of Europe during the Middle Ages* (London, 1846; 1st ed., 1818), II, 333.

12 Matthew Arnold, *Complete Prose Works,* ed. R. H. Super (Ann Arbor: University of Michigan Press, 1960), I, 135.

13 Friedrich Meinecke, *Historism: The Rise of a New Historical Outlook,* trans. J. E. Anderson (London: Routledge & Kegan Paul, 1972), pp. 122–26. See also Maurice Mandelbaum, *History, Man, and Reason: A Study in Nineteenth Century Thought* (Baltimore: Johns Hopkins University Press, 1971), pt. 2; Peter Hanns Reill, *The German Enlightenment and the Rise of Historicism* (Berkeley: University of California Press, 1975).

14 Johann Wolfgang von Goethe, *Französisches Haupttheatre,* 1828; see also *Dichtung und Wahrheit,* bk. 14, cited by Meinecke, *Historism,* pp. 411–12, 388; Percy Bysshe Shelley, *Hellas,* ll. 805–06.

15 Geoffrey Tillotson, *A View of Victorian Literature* (Oxford: Clarendon Press, 1978), p. v.

16 Walter Houghton, *The Victorian Frame of Mind* (New Haven: Yale University Press, 1957), p. 1. The quotation from Lord Holland and the list of names at the end of the paragraph are also from Houghton, p. 1n. The term *transition,* in the sense of "a passage from an earlier to a later stage of development," was new in the 1810s, and since the first three instances cited by the *OED* (1813–23) are geological, it may be that its introduction at this time was due to the German geologist Abraham Gottlob Werner, who gave that name to a stratum of rocks laid down "when the world was passing from an uninhabitable to a habitable state."

17 J. S. Mill, *Autobiography* (New York: Columbia University Press, 1924), p. 1; cf. pp. 116, 118.

18 Matthew Arnold, "Stanzas from the Grande Chartreuse," ll. 85–86; Thomas Arnold, letter of April 17, 1847, cited in Park Honan, *Matthew Arnold: A Life* (New York: McGraw-Hill, 1981), p. 121.

19 Elizabeth Barrett Browning, *Aurora Leigh,* V, 163–65.

20 Hallam Tennyson, *Alfred Lord Tennyson: A Memoir* (New York, 1897), II, 337.

21 I refer of course to Hayden White's *Metahistory: The Historical Imagination in Nineteenth-Century Europe* (Baltimore: Johns Hopkins University Press, 1973)—a work which I admire but do not find wholly applicable to this study.

22 Carlyle, "The Nibelungen Lied," *Works,* Centenary ed., XXVII, 220.

CHAPTER I: ENGLAND'S AUGUSTAN AGE

1 G. W. Trompf, *The Idea of Historical Recurrence in Western Thought from Antiquity to the Reformation* (Berkeley: University of California Press, 1979).

2 For a discussion of Typology, see Erich Auerbach, "Figura," *Scenes from the Drama of European Literature* (Gloucester, Mass.: Peter Smith, 1973); Jean Daniélou, *From Shadows to Reality: Studies in the Biblical Typology of the Fathers,* trans. W. Hibberd (London: Burns & Oates, 1960); Patrick Fairburn, *The Typology of Scripture,* 4th ed. (Grand Rapids, Mich.: Baker Book House, 1975); George P. Landow, *William Holman Hunt and Typological Symbolism* (New Haven: Yale University Press, 1979); Earl Miner, ed., *Literary Uses of Typology from the Late Middle Ages to the Present* (Princeton: Princeton University Press, 1977); Linda H. Peterson, "Biblical Typology and the Self-Portrait of the Poet in Robert Browning," in *Approaches to Victorian Autobiography,* ed. George P. Landow (Athens: Ohio University Press, 1979); Herbert L. Sussman, *Fact into Figure: Typology in Carlyle, Ruskin, and the Pre-Raphaelite Brotherhood* (Columbus: Ohio State University Press, 1979).

3 Wallace K. Ferguson, *The Renaissance in Historical Thought: Five Centuries of Interpretation* (Cambridge: Houghton Mifflin, 1948), pp. 1–3, 6, 8, 65, 73.

4 J. E. Spingarn, ed., *Critical Essays of the Seventeenth Century* (Oxford: Clarendon Press, 1909), III, 50.

5 Peter Gay, *The Enlightenment: An Interpretation* (New York: A. A. Knopf, 1967), I, 34–35.

6 Christopher Dawson, "Edward Gibbon," *Proceedings of the British Academy* 20 (1934)): 162–63. From the time of Elizabeth I there was also a widespread belief that Britain was a "second Israel." See William Haller, *The Elect Nation* (New York: Harper and Row, 1963); and Harold Fisch, *Jerusalem and Albion* (New York: Schocken Books, 1964).

7 For the concept of the "Augustan Age" in the eighteenth century see J. C. Maxwell, "Demigods and Pickpockets: The Augustan Myth in Swift and Rousseau," *Scrutiny* 11 (Summer 1943): 34–39; James W. Johnson, "The Meaning of 'Augustan,' " *Journal of the History of Ideas* 19 (1958): 507–22; Herbert Davis, "The Augustan Conception of History," in *Reason and the Imagination: Studies in the History of Ideas,* ed. J. A. Mazzeo (New York: Columbia University Press, 1962), pp. 213–29; Addison Ward, "The Tory View of Roman History," *Studies in English Literature* 4 (1964): 413–56; James W. Johnson, *The Formation of English Neo-Classical Thought* (Princeton: Princeton University Press, 1967); Howard Erskine-Hill, "Augustans on Augustanism: England, 1655–1759," *Renaissance and Modern Studies* 11 (1967): 55–83; Ian Watt, ed., *The Augustan Age: Approaches to Its Literature, Life, and Thought* (Greenwich, Conn.: Fawcett, 1968), pp. 11–19; Howard D. Weinbrot, *Augustus Caesar in 'Augustan' England: The Decline of a Classical Norm* (Princeton: Princeton University Press, 1978).

8 Reed Browning, *Political and Constitutional Ideas of the Court Whigs* (Baton Rouge: Louisiana State University Press, 1982), p. 227. My account of the Cato–Cicero episode is based largely on Browning's excellent analysis, pp. 1–10, 210–30. See T. B. Macaulay, *The Works of Lord Macaulay Complete,* ed. Lady Trevelyan (London: Longmans, Green, 1866), VI, 133; VII, 100–01.

9 Browning, *Ideas of the Court Whigs,* p. 9n, says, "in politics at least, *no one*

thought that Britain should be Augustan. Augustus had completed the destruction of the republic."

10   John Dryden, Preface to the *Fables* (1700), in *Essays,* ed. W. P. Ker (Oxford: Clarendon Press, 1926), II, 259. For the "English Ennius" see Samuel Cobb, *Of Poetry: Its Progress* (1700), cited by René Wellek, *The Rise of English Literary History* (Chapel Hill: University of North Carolina Press, 1941), p. 133.

11   Francis Atterbury (attr.), "Preface to the Second Part of Mr. Waller's Poems," in Edmund Waller, *Poems,* ed. G. Thorn Drury (London, 1893), I, xix.

12   John Oldmixon, *Reflections on Dr. Swift's Letter to the Earl of Oxford, about the English Tongue* (London, 1712), p. 19; Samuel Johnson, *Lives of the English Poets,* ed. G. B. Hill (Oxford: Clarendon Press, 1905), I, 469; Suetonius, ii. 29.

13   Jonathan Swift, "Thoughts on Various Subjects," in *A Proposal for Correcting the English Tongue . . . ,* ed. H. Davis with L. Landa (London: Basil Blackwell, 1957), p. 249; cf. pp. 9–10.

14   David Hume, *History of Great Britain* (London, 1757), II, 453.

15   Joseph Warton, *Essay on the Genius and Writings of Pope,* 3d ed. (London, 1772), I, 161–62.

16   Oliver Goldsmith, *Collected Works,* ed. Arthur Friedman (Oxford: Clarendon Press, 1966), I, 498.

17   Leonard Welsted, cited by Wellek, *Rise of English Literary History,* p. 58.

18   John Pinkerton, cited by Weinbrot, *Augustus Caesar in 'Augustan' England,* p. 78 and n.

19   George Saintsbury, *The Peace of the Augustans* (London: G. Bell, 1916), pp. v–vi.

20   Augustine Birrell, "Pope," in *Collected Essays and Addresses* (1922), cited by Henry K. Miller, "The 'Whig Interpretation' of Literary History," *Eighteenth-Century Studies* 6 (1972): 61–62. Arnold wrote in 1880: "There are many signs to show that the eighteenth century and its judgments are coming into favour again." *Complete Prose Works,* ed. R. H. Super (Ann Arbor: University of Michigan Press, 1960–77), IX, 178.

21   Mark Van Doren, *John Dryden,* 3d ed. (New York, 1946), p. 9; see also Oliver Elton, *A Survey of English Literature, 1730–1780* (New York, 1928), I, 1.

22   Hugh Kenner, "The Urban Apocalypse," *Eliot in his Time,* ed. A. Walton Litz (Princeton: Princeton University Press, 1973), pp. 25–27.

23   Horace Walpole, *Selected Letters,* ed. W. S. Lewis (New Haven: Yale University Press, 1973), p. xv.

24   See Johnson, *Formation of English Neo-Classical Thought,* pp. 69–90; M. L. Clarke, *Greek Studies in England, 1700–1830* (Cambridge: Cambridge University Press, 1945); J. E. Sandys, *A History of Classical Scholarship* (Cambridge: Cambridge University Press, 1903–08), vol. II.

25   E. M. Butler, *The Tyranny of Greece over Germany* (Cambridge: Cambridge University Press, 1935; Clarke, *Greek Studies in England*; Stephen A. Larrabee, *English Bards and Grecian Marbles: The Relationship between Sculpture and Poetry Especially in the Romantic Period* (New York: Columbia University

Press, 1943); Richard Jenkyns, *The Victorians and Ancient Greece* (Cambridge: Harvard University Press, 1980); Harry Levin, *The Broken Column: A Study in Romantic Hellenism* (Cambridge: Harvard University Press, 1931); Gayle Stanley Smith, *Romantic Hellenism in England: A Facet of the Romantic Revolution of the Past* (Ann Arbor: University Microfilms, 1958); Terence Spencer, *Fair Greece, Sad Relic: Literary Philhellenism from Shakespeare to Byron* (London: Weidenfeld & Nicolson, 1954); Bernhard Herbert Stern, *The Rise of Romantic Hellenism in English Literature, 1732–1786* (New York: Octagon Books, 1969); Frank Turner, *The Greek Heritage in Victorian Britain* (New Haven: Yale University Press, 1981); David Watkin, *Thomas Hope, 1769–1831, and the Neo-Classical Idea* (London: Murray, 1968).

26 Wood, *Essay on Homer* (London, 1775), p. 341.

27 David Watkin, *Athenian Stuart: Pioneer of the Greek Revival* (London: George Allen & Unwin, 1982).

28 John Keats, "On Seeing the Elgin Marbles" and "To Haydon"; *The Diary of Benjamin Robert Haydon,* ed. W. B. Pope (Cambridge: Harvard University Press, 1960), II, 76. For a full account of the Elgin Marbles see William St. Clair, *Lord Elgin and the Marbles* (London: Oxford University Press, 1967).

29 Thomas Paine, *Rights of Man: Part the Second* (London, 1792), chap. 3, p. 24; Turner, *Greek Heritage in Victorian Britain,* pp. 194–95; see Turner's authoritative account of the entire debate, pp. 187–263.

30 Macaulay, "On Mitford's History of Greece," *Works,* VII, 689; Byron, *Don Juan,* Canto XII, st. 19, note.

31 William St. Clair, *"That Greece Might Still Be Free": The Philhellenes in the War of Independence* (London: Oxford University Press, 1972), pp. 1–65.

32 J. S. Mill, "Grote's *History of Greece,*" *Edinburgh Review* 84 (1846): 343.

33 Joseph Mordaunt Crook, *The Greek Revival: Neo-classical Attitudes in British Architecture, 1760–1870* (London: J. Murray, 1972), pp. 104–07.

CHAPTER 2: SCOTT, MACAULAY, AND THE PROGRESS OF SOCIETY

1 T. B. Macaulay, *The History of England from the Accession of James the Second,* ed. C. H. Firth (London: Macmillan, 1913), I, 272.

2 Harold Perkin, *The Origins of Modern English Society, 1780–1880* (London: Routledge & Kegan Paul, 1969), p. 4.

3 David Daiches, "Scott and Scotland," in *Scott Bicentenary Essays,* ed. Alan Bell (Edinburgh: Scottish Academic Press, 1973), pp. 49–51.

4 Walter Scott, Introduction to *Minstrelsy of the Scottish Border,* 4th ed. (Edinburgh, 1810), I, cxxxi.

5 Excellent accounts of Scott's relation to the philosophic historians may be found in the following: Duncan Forbes, "The Rationalism of Sir Walter Scott," *Cambridge Journal* 7 (1953): 20–35; and " 'Scientific Whiggism': Adam Smith and John Millar," *Cambridge Journal* 7 (1954): 643–70; Peter D. Garside, "Scott and the 'Philosophical' Historians," *Journal of the History of Ideas* 36 (1975): 497–512; and "Scott, the Romantic Past and

the Nineteenth Century," *Review of English Studies* 23 (1972): 147–61; and Graham McMaster, *Scott and Society* (Cambridge: Cambridge University Press, 1981), pp. 49–77. See also David Daiches, *Sir Walter Scott and His World* (New York: Viking Press, 1971), pp. 36, 45–46; and David D. Brown, *Walter Scott and the Historical Imagination* (London: Routledge & Kegan Paul, 1979), pp. 173–209.

6   The text of Scott's novels used here is that of the Dryburgh Edition (Edinburgh and New York, 1892–99), 25 vols. References, when significant, hereafter cited parenthetically in the text.

7   See Francis R. Hart, *Scott's Novels: The Plotting of Historic Survival* (Charlottesville: University Press of Virginia, 1966), pp. 182–86.

8   The original insight into the nature of Scott's historical fiction by Georg Lukács in *The Historical Novel* (1937), trans. H. and S. Mitchell (Boston: Beacon Press, 1963) has been extended and corrected by Daiches, Forbes, Garside, McMaster, and Brown in the works cited above. See also Daiches, "Sir Walter Scott and History," *Études Anglaises* 24 (1971), 458–77; Avrom Fleishman, *The English Historical Novel: Walter Scott to Virginia Woolf* (Baltimore, 1971); Robert C. Gordon, *Under Which King? A Study of the Scottish Waverley Novels* (Edinburgh: Oliver & Boyd, 1969); Hart, *Scott's Novels*; H. R. Trevor-Roper, *The Romantic Movement and the Study of History* (London: Athlone Press, 1969); Alexander Welsh, *The Hero of the Waverley Novels* (New Haven: Yale University Press, 1963); and the essays by Daiches, Joseph E. Duncan, P. F. Fisher, and Robert C. Gordon in *Walter Scott: Modern Judgments,* ed. D. D. Devlin (Nashville: Aurora Publishers, 1970).

9   Scott, *Poetical Works* (1900), cited by Forbes, "Rationalism of Sir Walter Scott," p. 28.

10   Hart, *Scott's Novels,* pp. 16ff.

11   Walter Scott, *The Prefaces to the Waverley Novels,* ed. Mark A. Weinstein (Lincoln: University of Nebraska Press, 1978), pp. 138, 147, 179.

12   Brown, *Scott and the Historical Imagination,* pp. 185–86.

13   Augustin Thierry, "Autobiographical Preface," *The Historical Essays* (Philadelphia, 1845), p. xi. See also J. S. Mill, *Dissertations and Discussions* (London, 1859), II, 130.

14   E. A. Freeman, *History of the Norman Conquest of England* (Oxford, 1876), V, appendix, note W.

15   Macaulay, *History of England,* I, 18, 12.

16   Matthew Arnold, *Complete Prose Works,* ed. R. H. Super (Ann Arbor: University of Michigan Press, 1960–77), III, 273.

17   Macaulay, *History of England,* I, 87–88.

18   Samuel Taylor Coleridge, *Miscellaneous Criticism,* ed. T. M. Raysor (London, 1936), pp. 341–42.

19   *The Letters of Thomas Babington Macaulay,* ed. Thomas Pinney (Cambridge: Cambridge University Press, 1974), I, 132–34.

20   T. B. Macaulay, *The Works of Lord Macaulay Complete,* ed. Lady Trevelyan (London: Longmans, Green, 1866), VII, 687. Hereafter cited parenthetically in the text.

21   Harold T. Parker, *The Cult of Antiquity and the French Revolutionaries* (Chicago: University of Chicago Press, 1937); Elizabeth Rawson, *The Spartan*

Tradition in European Thought (Oxford: Clarendon Press, 1969), chaps. 15–17.

22 Macaulay, *History of England,* III, 1352.
23 T. B. Macaulay, *Speeches* (New York, 1866), I, 143.
24 John Clive, *Macaulay: The Shaping of the Historian* (New York: Random House, 1975), p. 263.
25 Macaulay, *Speeches,* I, 35, 102.
26 Clive, *Macaulay,* pp. 65–67, 90–91, 206–08.
27 Ibid., pp. 85–90. Trevor-Roper's comment, cited by Clive, is from his edition of Macaulay's *Critical and Historical Essays* (London, 1965), p. 12.
28 Macaulay, *History of England,* I, 22.
29 Cited by J. W. Burrow, *A Liberal Descent: Victorian Historians and the English Past* (Cambridge: Cambridge University Press, 1982), p. 14.
30 T. B. Macaulay, "Essay on the Life and Character of King William III," ed. A. N. L. Munby, in *TLS,* May 1, 1969, pp. 468–69; see also Macaulay, *Works,* VI, 97–98.
31 Joseph Hamburger, *Macaulay and the Whig Tradition* (Chicago: University of Chicago Press, 1976), pp. x, 89–91. I am indebted to Professor Hamburger's careful analysis for several points. The quotations by and about Halifax are cited by him.
32 Macaulay, *Speeches,* I, 143.
33 Ibid., I, 91.
34 Ibid., I, 82.
35 George Otto Trevelyan, *Life and Letters of Lord Macaulay* (London, 1876), II, 13–14.
36 Macaulay, *History of England,* III, 1312.

CHAPTER 3: MILL, CARLYLE, AND THE SPIRIT OF THE AGE

1 J. S. Mill, *The Spirit of the Age* (Chicago: University of Chicago Press, 1942), p. 1.
2 Friedrich Meinecke, *Historism: The Rise of a New Historical Outlook,* trans. J. E. Anderson (London: Routledge & Kegan Paul, 1972), pp. 77–80, 121–22; see also René Wellek, *The Rise of English Literary History* (Chapel Hill: University of North Carolina Press, 1941), pp. 12, 29–30.
3 *The Letters of Percy Bysshe Shelley,* ed. F. L. Jones (Oxford: Clarendon Press, 1964), II, 189 (see also 180); Shelley, *A Philosophical View of Reform,* in *Shelley's Prose,* ed. David Lee Clark (Albuquerque: University of New Mexico Press, 1954), p. 240; Henry Crabb Robinson, *Diary, Reminiscences, and Correspondence,* ed. T. Sadler (Boston, 1869), I, 482; Walter Savage Landor, *Imaginary Conversations* (London, 1824), II, 85; Macaulay, "Milton," *Historical and Critical Essays* (1860), I, 211; *Letters and Diaries of John Henry Newman,* ed. Ian Ker and Thomas Gornall (Oxford: Clarendon Press, 1979), II, 185; Carlyle, *Works,* Centenary ed. (London, 1898–99), XXVI, 66; XXVII, 91; XXVIII, 18; *Blackwood's Magazine* 28 (December 1830): 900–04; Edward Lytton Bulwer, *England and the English* (1833), bk. IV.
4 Jacob and Wilhelm Grimm, *Deutsches Wörterbuch* (Leipzig, 1956), XV, 558.

5 *Matt.* 16: 3–4.
6 Mill, *Spirit of the Age,* pp. 4, 1, 2.
7 Carlyle, *Works,* XXVII, 57–58. Hereafter cited parenthetically in the text.
8 Carlyle, *Two Notebooks,* ed. C. E. Norton (New York: Grolier Club, 1898), p. 223.
9 John Stuart Mill, *Autobiography* (New York: Columbia University Press, 1924), p. 30. Hereafter cited parenthetically in the text.
10 *The Love Letters of Thomas Carlyle and Jane Welsh,* ed. A. Carlyle (London, 1909), II, 380–81.
11 Carlyle, *Two Notebooks,* p. 100.
12 Ibid., pp. 61, 124.
13 Ibid., pp. 71, 214–15; James Anthony Froude, *Thomas Carlyle: A History of the First Forty Years of His Life, 1795–1835* (London, 1882), II, 310.
14 Carlyle, *Two Notebooks,* p. 132. For the element of periodicity in Carlyle's philosophy of history see René Wellek, "Carlyle and the Philosophy of History," *Philological Quarterly* 23 (1944): 55–76; C. F. Harrold, *Carlyle and German Thought: 1819–1834* (Hamden: Archon Books, 1963), pp. 171–73.
15 Jean François Marmontel, *Memoirs, Written by Himself* (London, 1830), I, 51, 52.
16 Saint-Simon, *Oeuvres* (Paris: Éditions Anthropos, 1966), I, 247–48. On the Saint-Simonians see Frank E. Manuel, *The New World of Saint-Simon* (Cambridge: Harvard University Press, 1956); Richard K. P. Pankhurst, *The Saint-Simonians, Mill and Carlyle: A Preface to Modern Thought* (London: Sidgwick & Jackson, n.d.); Hill Shine, *Carlyle and the Saint-Simonians: The Concept of Historical Periodicity* (Baltimore: Johns Hopkins University Press, 1941); F. A. von Hayek, Introductory Essay to Mill's *Spirit of the Age* (1942).
17 [Saint-Armand Bazard], *The Doctrine of Saint-Simon: An Exposition: First Year, 1828–1829,* trans. Georg G. Iggers (Boston: Beacon Press, 1958), p. 16.
18 Mill, *Spirit of the Age,* pp. 6, 33, 35–36, 76; Mill, *Earlier Letters, 1812–1848,* ed. Francis E. Mineka, in *Collected Works of John Stuart Mill* (Toronto: University of Toronto Press, 1963), XII, 71, 88–89.
19 Carlyle, *Two Notebooks,* p. 158; *The Collected Letters of Thomas and Jane Welsh Carlyle,* ed. C. R. Sanders et al., Duke-Edinburgh ed. (Durham: Duke University Press, 1970–77), V, 136, 222; *Correspondence between Goethe and Carlyle,* ed. C. E. Norton (London, 1887), p. 225.
20 Mill, *Autobiography,* p. 122; Carlyle, *Collected Letters,* V, 398; Mill, *Earlier Letters,* in *Collected Works,* XII, 153, 204–05; Carlyle, *Two Notebooks,* p. 248.
21 Mill, "Coleridge," *Dissertations and Discussions* (London, 1859), I, 394; Mill, *Earlier Letters,* in *Collected Works,* XII, 41–43.
22 Mill, *Spirit of the Age,* p. 6.
23 Mill, *Dissertations and Discussions,* II, 125, 127.
24 Ibid., II, 127.
25 Ibid., I, 235–36.
26 Ibid., II, 129, 130.
27 Ibid., II, 232, 237.

28 Mill, *On Liberty,* in *Utilitarianism, On Liberty, and Representative Government,* Everyman ed. (London: Dent, 1947), pp. 95, 115, 119, 120.
29 *Carlyle's Unfinished History of German Literature,* ed. Hill Shine (Lexington: University of Kentucky Press, 1951); Shine, *Carlyle and the Saint-Simonians,* pp. 9–10.
30 Carlyle, *Collected Letters,* V, 106.
31 Carlyle, *Lectures on the History of Literature, or the Successive Periods of European Culture, Delivered in 1838,* ed. R. P. Karkaria (Bombay: Curwen, Kane, 1892), pp. 45, 48, 147.
32 J. S. Mill, *Literary Essays,* ed. Edward Alexander (New York: Bobbs-Merrill, 1967), p. 143.
33 Carlyle, *Collected Letters,* II, 94.
34 Carlyle, *Two Notebooks,* pp. 17, 20, 93, 139–40, 142.
35 Carlyle, *Lectures on the History of Literature,* pp. 53–54.
36 Grace J. Calder, in *The Writing of Past and Present: A Study of Carlyle's Manuscripts* (New Haven: Yale University Press, 1949), held that Carlyle followed his medieval source very closely. This view has been challenged by Linda Georgiana, "Carlyle and Jocelin of Brakelond: A Chronicle Rechronicled," *Browning Institute Studies* 8 (1980): 103–27.
37 Wilbur C. Abbott, "The Fame of Cromwell," *Yale Review* n.s. 2 (January 1913): 345, 348–49.
38 Carlyle, *Two Notebooks,* p. 184.

CHAPTER 4: THOMAS ARNOLD AND THE IDEA OF MODERNITY

1 Lowell is cited in the *OED*; Emerson, *Representative Men,* in *Works* (New York: Tudor Publishing, n.d.), II, 252. See Raymond Williams, *Keywords: A Vocabulary of Culture and Society* (New York: Oxford University Press, 1976), p. 174.
2 Duncan Forbes, *The Liberal Anglican Idea of History* (Cambridge: Cambridge University Press, 1952). I am much indebted to this work in the present chapter.
3 Charles R. Sanders, *Coleridge and the Broad Church Movement* (Durham: Duke University Press, 1942), pp. 7–8, 14–15. For the term *Broad Church* see the *OED* and *Memorials of William Charles Lake,* ed. Katherine Lake (London, 1901), p. 35.
4 Arthur P. Stanley, *The Life and Correspondence of Thomas Arnold, D.D.,* 2d ed. (London, 1844), I, 4, 27, 18, 200, 17.
5 Ibid., I, 55.
6 Ibid., I, 132.
7 Ibid., I, 142, 136–37; Thomas Arnold, *Miscellaneous Works,* 1st American ed. (New York, 1845), p. 348.
8 Arnold, *Miscellaneous Works,* 1st American ed., pp. 341–44, 354.
9 Stanley, *Thomas Arnold,* I, 49, 264, 268–69, 280–81; II, 196.
10 Ibid., I, 301–02.
11 Ibid., I, 40.
12 MS at Rugby School, cited by Forbes, *Liberal Anglican Idea of History,* p. 14.

13 A full account of Vico's reputation and influence has been given by Max
Harold Fisch and Thomas Goddard Bergin, eds., *The Autobiography of
Giambattista Vico* (Ithaca: Cornell University Press, 1963), pp. 61–108. It
has been corrected and supplemented by René Wellek, "The Supposed Influence of Vico on England and Scotland in the Eighteenth Century," in
Giambattista Vico: An International Symposium, ed. Giorgio Tagliacozzo
and Hayden V. White (Baltimore: Johns Hopkins University Press, 1969),
pp. 215–24; and George Whalley, "Coleridge and Vico," ibid., pp. 225–
44. Michelet's translation was first published under the title *Principes de la
philosophie de l'histoire, traduits de la Scienza nuova de J. B. Vico, précédés
d'un Discours sur la système et la vie de l'auteur* (1827). That Arnold may
have become acquainted with Vico in 1825 (and hence through the Italian)
is suggested by the Vichonan phrase, "when society was in its second infancy, in the Middle ages," in his *Quarterly Review* article for June 1825
(XXXII, 78). I see no reason to suppose, as Forbes does (p. 157, note 25),
that this phrase was inserted in the article by J. T. Coleridge.

14 Vico, *New Science,* trans. T. G. Bergin and M. H. Fisch, rev. ed. (Ithaca:
Cornell University Press, 1968), sec. 349.

15 Arnold, "Essay on the Social Progress of States," *Miscellaneous Works* (London, 1845), pp. 79–111; 1st American ed. (New York, 1845), pp. 306–
27. This essay was first published as an Appendix to Thucydides, *History
of the Peloponnesian War,* ed. Thomas Arnold (London, 1830). References
are to the 4th ed. (Oxford, 1857), I, 503–24 (for this quotation, I, 504).

16 Arnold, "Social Progress of States," in Thucydides, *History,* ed. Arnold
(1857), I, 503, 519, 521.

17 Republished as *History of the Later Roman Commonwealth, from the End of
the Second Punic War to the Death of Julius Caesar; and of the Reign of Augustus: with a Life of Trajan* (New York, 1846). The articles were written
between 1821 and 1827.

18 [Thomas Arnold], "Review of Henry Bankes' *Civil and Constitutional History of Rome,*" *Quarterly Review* 27 (July 1822): 280–81. Arnold identified
himself as the author of this article in the *Quarterly Review* 32 (June 1825):
67.

19 B. G. Niebuhr, *The History of Rome,* trans. Julius Charles Hare and Connop
Thirlwall (Cambridge, 1828–32), I, 216–21; H. R. Trevor-Roper, *The Romantic Movement and the Study of History* (London, 1969), pp. 10–12.

20 Stanley, *Thomas Arnold,* II, 101–02.

21 Thomas Arnold, *History of Rome,* 2d ed. (London, 1840–45), I, 156–57;
II, 32–61; Niebuhr, *History of Rome,* II, 129–73.

22 Mill, *Autobiography* (New York: Columbia University Press, 1924), pp. 9–
10.

23 Arnold, *History of the Later Roman Commonwealth,* pp. 43, 49; Arnold,
"Review of Henry Bankes," 302.

24 [Thomas Arnold], "Review of Niebuhr's *History of Rome,*" *Quarterly Review*
32 (June 1825): 73, 75, 76; reprinted as "Early Roman History," *Miscellaneous Works,* 1st American ed. (1845), pp. 384, 386, 387. See also Arnold, "The Social Progress of States," in Thucydides, *History,* ed. Arnold
(1857), I, 521. In Arnold's 1832 letters to the *Sheffield Courant* he evi-

dently thinks there is not much suitable waste land to be divided in England and suggests emigration. (*Miscellaneous Works,* 1st American ed. (1845), pp. 422–25).

25 Arthur P. Stanley, *Whether States, like individuals* . . . , *inevitably tend to decay* (Oxford, 1840), pp. 8, 9, cited by Forbes, *Liberal Anglican Idea of History,* p. 47.

26 Arthur P. Stanley, cited by Forbes, *Liberal Anglican Idea of History,* pp. 44–46.

27 Julius and Augustus Hare, *Guesses at Truth* (London, 1867), p. 309.

28 Florus, *Epitome of Roman History,* trans. E. S. Forster. Loeb Classical Library (London, 1929), pp. 9–17; see also pp. 25, 69, 77, 157, 213 for further uses of the metaphor.

29 [Bazard], *Doctrine of Saint-Simon,* p. 34; Karl Löwith, *Meaning in History* (Chicago: University of Chicago Press, 1949), pp. 56, 69, 171; Friedrich Meinecke, *Historism: The Rise of a New Historical Outlook,* trans. J. E. Anderson (London: Routledge & Kegan Paul, 1972), pp. 308, 327.

30 Forbes, *Liberal Anglican Idea of History,* pp. 57–58.

31 Hare, *Guesses at Truth,* p. 338.

32 Thomas Arnold, *Introductory Lectures on Modern History, delivered in Lent Term, MDCCCXLII,* 2d ed. (London: 1843), pp. 28–31.

33 Arnold, "The Social Progress of States," in Thucydides, *History,* ed. Arnold (1857), I, 522.

34 Stanley, *Thomas Arnold,* II, 281, 295; Arnold, *Introductory Lectures,* p. 92.

35 Stanley, *Thomas Arnold,* I, 401–02.

36 Arnold, *Miscellaneous Works,* 1st American ed., pp. 337–38.

37 Mill, "Michelet's History of France," *Dissertations and Discussions* (London, 1869), II, 130; cf. II, 222.

38 Matthew Arnold, *Letters, 1848–1888,* ed. G. W. E. Russell (New York, 1895), II, 5.

CHAPTER 5: NEWMAN AND THE OXFORD COUNTER-REFORMATION

1 Thomas Arnold, *Sermons,* new ed. (London, 1878), IV, xx; A. P. Stanley, *Life and Correspondence of Thomas Arnold,* 2d ed. (London, 1844), II, 14.

2 Stanley, *Thomas Arnold,* I, 206, 245, 51–52; II, 250; Arnold, *History of Rome* (1838), I, viii–ix.

3 *Letters and Correspondence of John Henry Newman,* ed. Anne Mozley (London, 1891), I, 22.

4 J. H. Newman, *Apologia pro Vita Sua,* ed. Martin J. Svaglic (Oxford: Clarendon Press, 1967), pp. 17, 18. Hereafter cited parenthetically in the text.

5 J. H. Newman, *Autobiographical Writings,* ed. Henry Tristram (London: Sheed & Ward, 1955), p. 150.

6 J. H. Newman, *Idea of a University,* 4th ed. (London, 1875), p. 36.

7 Newman, *Letters and Correspondence,* I, 169; *Letters and Diaries of John Henry Newman,* ed. Charles Stephen Dessain, Ian Ker, and others (Oxford: Clarendon Press, 1961–   ), II, 30, 369; Newman, *Autobiographical Writings,* p. 83.

8   Arnold, *Sermons,* IV, xx–xxi; *Miscellaneous Works* (New York, 1845), p. 244.

9   J. H. Newman, *Historical Sketches* (London, 1872), II, ix.

10 J. H. Newman, *Lectures on the Prophetical Office of the Church* (London, 1837), p. 30.

11 Newman, *Prophetical Office,* p. 63; *Historical Sketches,* I, 380–81.

12 J. H. Newman, *An Essay on the Development of Christian Doctrine,* new ed. (London, 1878), pp. 279–316.

13 J. H. Newman, *Lectures on Certain Difficulties Felt by Anglicans,* 2d ed. (London, 1850), pp. 304–05.

14 [Nicholas Wiseman], "Anglican Claim of Apostolical Succession," *Dublin Review* 7 (1839): 154.

15 Newman, *Letters and Diaries,* II, 319–20; cf. Henry P. Liddon, *Life of Edward Bouverie Pusey, D.D.,* 4th ed. (London, 1894), I, 213.

16 Newman, *Historical Sketches,* I, 159–60.

17 Ibid., I, 162, 178.

18 J. H. Newman, *The Via Media of the Anglican Church* (London, 1877), I, 212.

19 Owen Chadwick, *From Bossuet to Newman: The Idea of Doctrinal Development* (Cambridge: Cambridge University Press, 1957), pp. 4–13, 17.

20 Charles Smyth, *Dean Milman* (London, 1849), p. 19, quoted in Duncan Forbes, *Liberal Anglican Idea of History* (Cambridge: Cambridge University Press, 1952), p. 2.

21 [Henry Hart Milman], *The History of the Jews* (London, 1829), I, 9, 16, 36–37, 90; III, iv–v.

22 Godfrey Faussett, *Jewish History Vindicated from the Unscriptural View of It Displayed in the History of the Jews* (Oxford, 1830); [Richard Mant], *A Letter to the Rev. Henry Hart Milman, M.A.* (Oxford, 1830) and *A Second Letter to the Rev. Henry Hart Milman, M.A.* (Oxford, 1830). This paragraph and the next are taken from my *Imperial Intellect: A Study of Newman's Educational Ideal* (New Haven: Yale University Press, 1955), pp. 249–50.

23 Newman, *Letters and Diaries,* II, 299.

24 J. H. Newman, "Milman's View of Christianity," *British Critic* 29 (1841), 71–114, reprinted in J. H. Newman, *Essays, Critical and Historical* (London, 1890), II, 186–248.

25 Newman, *Development of Christian Doctrine* (1878), p. 10; J. H. Newman, *The Arians of the Fourth Century,* 6th ed. (London, 1890), pp. 77–78.

26 Newman, *Difficulties Felt by Anglicans,* p. 321.

27 Newman, *Arians of the Fourth Century,* pp. 42–79; see also William E. Addis and Thomas Arnold, *A Catholic Dictionary* (London, 1884), p. 266.

28 Newman, *Arians of the Fourth Century,* p. 71; J. H. Newman, *Fifteen Sermons Preached before the University of Oxford* (London, 1906), pp. 340–42.

29 Newman, *Development of Christian Doctrine* (1878), p. 151; *Difficulties Felt by Anglicans,* pp. 320–21.

30 J. H. Walgrave, O.P., *Newman the Theologian,* trans. A. V. Littledale (New York: Sheed & Ward, 1960), p. 14; Jaroslav Pelikan, *Development of Christian Doctrine: Some Historical Prolegomena* (New Haven: Yale University Press, 1969), p. 2.

31 Newman, *Development of Christian Doctrine,* 2d ed. (1846), p. 44. Note

that I have used two different editions; the work was extensively revised for the edition of 1878.

32 Robert Chambers, *Vestiges of the Natural History of Creation,* 2d ed. (London, 1844), p. 362.

33 Newman, *Essays, Critical and Historical,* II, 193–95.

34 MS Sundries, Unconnected, p. 83 verso (Birmingham Oratory); JHN to Dr. David Brown, 1874 (Oriel Library).

35 Mark Pattison, quoted in Chadwick, *From Boussuet to Newman,* p. x.

36 *Charles Kingsley: His Letters and Memories of his Life,* ed. Frances Kingsley (London, 1877), I, 325, 255–57.

37 Ibid., I, 264.

38 There are good analyses of *Hypatia* in Allan J. Hartley, *The Novels of Charles Kingsley* (Folkestone, Eng.: Hour-Glass Press, 1977), pp. 84–103; and David A. Downes, *The Temper of Victorian Belief: Studies in the Religious Novels of Pater, Kingsley, and Newman* (New York: Twayne, 1972), pp. 48–81.

39 Charles Kingsley, *Hypatia* (London: Macmillan, 1902), pp. xv, xiii.

40 Guy Kendall, *Charles Kingsley and His Ideas* (London: Hutchinson, 1947), p. 115.

41 Charles Kingsley, *Alexandria and Her Schools* (Cambridge, 1854), pp. x–xi.

42 Newman, *Letters and Diaries,* XIII, 69; XIV, 343. For an authoritative account of the background of *Callista,* including Newman's use of his sources, see Sister Mary Paton Ryan, "Newman's Callista: A Critical Edition" (Ph.D. diss., Yale University, 1967). See also Susann Dorman, "Hypatia and Callista: The Initial Skirmish between Kingsley and Newman," *Nineteenth-Century Fiction* 35 (1980): 173–93.

43 Newman, *Letters and Diaries,* XVI, 7, 368; cf. Charlotte E. Crawford, "Newman's *Callista* and the Catholic Popular Library," *Modern Language Review* 45 (1950): 219–22.

44 Newman, *Letters and Correspondence,* I, 18; Newman, *Letters and Diaries,* I, 72, 107. Among other Early Christian or classical novels which Newman and Kingsley may have known are Thomas Moore, *The Epicureans* (1827), Bulwer-Lytton, *The Last Days of Pompeii* (1834), G. P. R. James, *Attila* (1837), and Wilkie Collins, *Antonina; or the Fall of Rome* (1850). W. A. Becker's *Gallus: or Roman Scenes of the Time of Augustus* (1838), trans. F. Metcalfe (1844), which Newman did consult, consists of a brief narrative and an extensive appendix on various aspects of Roman life.

45 Waldo H. Dunn, *James Anthony Froude: A Biography* (Oxford: Clarendon Press, 1861), pp. 40, 41–42, 48; J. A. Froude, *Short Studies on Great Subjects* (London, 1917), IV, 247–48.

46 Newman, *Apologia,* pp. 190–92; Dunn, *Froude,* pp. 78–79; [Newman et al.], *Lives of the English Saints* (London, 1844), IV, 72, 3–4.

47 Dunn, *Froude,* p. 93.

48 J. A. Froude, *The Nemesis of Faith* (London: Scott Library, n.d.), p. 197; Dunn, *Froude,* p. 170.

49 Dunn, *Froude,* p. 166.

50 Newman, *Apologia,* p. 201; Liddon, *Life of Pusey,* II, 65–76, 260–68; Mat-

thew Arnold, *Poems,* ed. K. Allott (New York: Barnes & Noble, 1965), p. 13.

51   Dunn, *Froude,* pp. 174, 267, 280, 313, 574.

52   J. A. Froude, *History of England from the Fall of Wolsey to the Defeat of the Spanish Armada* (New York, 1870), XII, 361, 468.

53   Susan Chitty, *The Beast and the Monk: A Life of Charles Kingsley* (London: Hodder & Stoughton, 1974), pp. 172–74.

54   Charles Kingsley, "Froude's History of England, Vols. VII & VIII," *Macmillan's Magazine* 9 (January 1864), 217.

55   Dunn, *Froude,* p. 505.

CHAPTER 6: MATTHEW ARNOLD AND THE ZEITGEIST

1   Matthew Arnold, *Unpublished Letters,* ed. Arnold Whitridge (New Haven: Yale University Press, 1923), pp. 56, 65–66.

2   Matthew Arnold, *Complete Prose Works,* ed. R. H. Super (Ann Arbor: University of Michigan Press, 1960–77), X, 165. Hereafter cited parenthetically in the text.

3   A full account of Arnold's myth is given in my book *Imaginative Reason: The Poetry of Matthew Arnold* (New Haven: Yale University Press, 1966). See also Francine B. Malder, "Matthew Arnold and the Circle of Recurrence," *Victorian Poetry* 14 (1976): 293–307.

4   In the next few paragraphs I have drawn upon my essay, "Arnold on Etna," *Victorian Essays,* ed. Warren D. Anderson and Thomas D. Clareson (Kent: Kent State University Press, 1967), pp. 44–59.

5   Park Honan, *Matthew Arnold: A Life* (New York: McGraw-Hill, 1981), pp. 124, 146, 150–68.

6   "Obermann Once More," l. 39; *The Letters of Matthew Arnold to Arthur Hugh Clough,* ed. Howard Foster Lowry (London: Oxford University Press, 1932), p. 95.

7   C. B. Tinker and H. F. Lowry, *The Poetry of Matthew Arnold: A Commentary* (London: Oxford University Press, 1940), p. 287.

8   Arnold, *Letters to Clough,* p. 110.

9   Tinker and Lowry, *Poetry of Arnold,* p. 271.

10 Arnold, *Letters to Clough,* p. 140.

11 R. L. Lowe, "Two Arnold Letters," *Modern Philology* 52 (May 1955): 262–63.

12 I have ventured to substitute the Lang, Leaf, and Myers translation since it was deliberately done in accordance with Arnold's principles.

13 Matthew Arnold, *Letters, 1848–1888,* ed. G. W. E. Russell (New York, 1895), I, 68.

14 William E. Buckler, *Matthew Arnold's Books: Towards a Publishing Diary* (Geneva: Librairie E. Droz, 1958), p. 67. In the next few paragraphs I have drawn upon my article, " 'No Arnold Could Ever Write a Novel,' " *Victorian Newsletter* 29 (Spring 1966): 1–5.

15 Carlyle, *Works,* Centenary Edition (London: Chapman & Hall, 1898–1902), I, 69, 155; XXVIII, 34.

16   Arnold, *Letters to Clough*, p. 86; cf. Arnold, *Complete Prose Works*, IX, 225–26.
17   Arnold, *Letters to Clough*, p. 65.
18   Fraser Neiman, "The Zeitgeist of Matthew Arnold," *PMLA* 72 (December 1957): 979. See David J. DeLaura's comment in his excellent article, "Matthew Arnold and the Nightmare of History," *Victorian Poetry*, ed. Malcolm Bradbury and David Palmer (London: Edward Arnold, 1972), pp. 53–54.
19   Arnold, *Letters, 1848–1888*, I, 73.
20   Peter Allan Dale, *The Victorian Critic and the Idea of History: Carlyle, Arnold, Pater* (Cambridge: Harvard University Press, 1977), pp. 105–06, 108–09; Paul W. Day, *Matthew Arnold and the Philosophy of Vico*, University of Auckland Bulletin 70, English Series 12 (Auckland, N.Z.: Pelorus Press, 1964).
21   Arnold, *Letters, 1848–1888*, I, 10.
22   Arnold, *Unpublished Letters*, p. 48.
23   Arnold, *Letters, 1848–1888*, II, 192.
24   Arnold, *Letters to Clough*, pp. 142–43.
25   Ibid., p. 123. There was great interest in Lucretius in the latter half of the nineteenth century. W. Y. Sellar published "Lucretius and the Poetic Characteristics of his Age" in *Oxford Essays* (1855). In 1860 H. A. J. Munro of Trinity College, Cambridge, published a critical edition of the *De rerum natura*, which he supplemented four years later with further commentary and an English translation. In 1868 Tennyson's "Lucretius" suggested subtle parallels between Lucretian and modern atomism, and from that time forth there was extensive discussion of the degree to which Lucretius anticipated nineteenth-century scientific views. See Frank M. Turner, "Lucretius among the Victorians," *Victorian Studies* 16 (March 1973): 329–48.
26   Arnold, *Unpublished Letters*, p. 44.
27   Yale MS, 69r; cf. Tinker and Lowry, *Poetry of Arnold*, p. 270.
28   Arnold, *Letters, 1848–1888*, I, 147. See John P. Farrell, "Matthew Arnold and the Middle Ages: The Uses of the Past," *Victorian Studies* 13 (1969–70), 319–38.
29   Matthew Arnold, *Note-books*, ed. H. F. Lowry, K. Young, and W. H. Dunn (London: Oxford University Press, 1952), pp. 32, 35, 47.
30   Arnold, *Letters to Clough*, pp. 124, 64–65.
31   Arnold, *Letters, 1848–1888*, II, 217.
32   G. W. E. Russell, *Matthew Arnold* (London: Scribner's, 1904), p. 168.
33   Arnold, *Letters, 1848–1888*, II, 55.
34   Ibid., I, 240.

CHAPTER 7: RUSKIN AND VICTORIAN MEDIEVALISM

1   Edmund Burke, *Works* (1866–67); Sir Walter Scott, *Complete Works* (1833); both cited by Alice Chandler, *A Dream of Order: The Medieval Ideal in Nineteenth-Century English Literature* (Lincoln: University of Nebraska Press, 1970), pp. 28–29.

2   Nick Shrimpton, " 'Rust and Dust': Ruskin's Pivotal Work," in *New Approaches to Ruskin,* ed. Robert Hewison (London: Routledge & Kegan Paul, 1981), p. 52.

3   David Hume, *The History of England from the Invasion of Julius Caesar* (London, 1841), I, 1; William Robertson, *Works* (Oxford, 1825), I, 3; Henry Hallam, *View of the State of Europe during the Middle Ages,* 10th ed. (London, 1853), I, iii.

4   Richard Hurd, *Letters on Chivalry and Romance,* ed. Edith J. Morley (London: Henry Frowde, 1911), pp. 80, 94–95, 115, 154.

5   Rosemary Jann, "Democratic Myths in Victorian Medievalism," *Browning Institute Studies,* ed. William S. Peterson (New York: Browning Institute and Graduate School of City University of New York, 1980), VIII, 129–49.

6   William Cobbett, *A History of the Protestant "Reformation"* (London, 1827), para. 111.

7   G. D. H. Cole, *The Life of William Cobbett* (London: Collins, 1924), pp. 286–94; W. Baring Pemberton, *William Cobbett* (Penguin Books, 1949), pp. 129–35.

8   Robert Southey, *Sir Thomas More: Or, Colloquies on the Progress and Prospects of Society* (London, 1829), I, 18, 19, 45, 62, 93–94, 32.

9   This is the wording of the title page of the second edition (1841).

10 Benjamin Disraeli, *Sybil,* chap. 11, in *Works,* Empire Edition (New York and London: M. Walter Dunne, 1904), XIV, 91.

11 For an account of both Kenelm Digby and the Eglinton tournament see Mark Girouard, *The Return to Camelot* (New Haven: Yale University Press, 1981), chaps. 5, 7.

12 Carlyle, *Past and Present,* bk. II, chaps. 1, 2.

13 Oscar Wilde, Preface to *The Picture of Dorian Gray.*

14 John Ruskin, *Works,* ed. E. T. Cook and Alexander Wedderburn (London: George Allen, 1903–12), XXXIX, 352. Hereafter cited parenthetically in the text.

15 Patrick Conner, "Ruskin and the 'Ancient Masters' in *Modern Painters,*" in Hewison, *New Approaches to Ruskin,* pp. 17–32.

16 *Ruskin in Italy: Letters to his Parents, 1845,* ed. Harold I. Shapiro (Oxford: Clarendon Press, 1972), p. 168.

17 A. F. Rio, *De la poésie chrétienne* (Paris, 1836), p. 2.

18 *Ruskin in Italy,* p. 142.

19 Robert Hewison, "Notes on the Construction of *The Stones of Venice,*" in *Studies in Ruskin: Essays in Honor of Van Akin Burd,* ed. Robert Rhodes and Del Ivan Janik (Athens: Ohio University Press, 1982), pp. 131–36.

20 P. Daru, whose *Histoire de la république de Venise,* 4th ed. (Paris, 1853), Ruskin was generally following, makes nothing of it (II, 198–99). Richard Ellmann, aware of the sexual themes in Ruskin's book, speculates that Ruskin chose the date because it was four hundred years to the very day before the presumed date of his own conception—a delightful idea, but perhaps not intended to be taken seriously. Ellmann, *Golden Codgers: Biographical Speculations* (New York: Oxford University Press, 1973), p. 48.

21 R. G. Collingwood, *Ruskin's Philosophy* (1971); W. G. Collingwood, *The*

Art Teaching of John Ruskin (1891); both cited by Robert Hewison, *John Ruskin: The Argument of the Eye* (Princeton: Princeton University Press, 1976), pp. 204–05.

22 *Ruskin in Italy,* pp. 96–97.
23 Ibid., pp. 144–45.
24 Ibid., p. 207.
25 Ibid., pp. 210, 212.
26 Ibid., p. 210.
27 George P. Landow, *The Aesthetic and Critical Theories of John Ruskin* (Princeton: Princeton University Press, 1971), pp. 281–85; Hewison, *John Ruskin,* p. 124.
28 Hewison, *John Ruskin,* pp. 41–46; Ruskin, *Diaries,* ed. Joan Evans and J. H. Whitehouse (Oxford: Clarendon Press, 1956), I, 223.
29 *Letters of John Ruskin to Charles Eliot Norton* (Boston: Houghton, Mifflin, 1904), I, 67; John Ruskin, *Letters from the Continent,* ed. John Hayman (Toronto: University of Toronto Press, 1982), pp. xxi, 92–120.
30 J. A. Froude, *Short Studies on Great Subjects* (London, 1867), I, 1.

CHAPTER 8: BROWNING AND THE VICTORIAN RENAISSANCE

1 The quotation is from the epigram "De Soy Mesme," which Browning could have found in *Oeuvres choisies de Clément Marot,* ed. M. Desprès (Paris, 1826), p. 384.
2 Robert Browning, *The Poems,* ed. John Pettigrew (New Haven: Yale University Press, 1981), I, 1021.
3 Ibid.
4 Mrs. Sutherland Orr, *Life and Letters of Robert Browning* (London, 1891), pp. 71–72.
5 Browning, *Poems,* I, 143n.
6 Ibid., I, 145.
7 See Michael Mason, "The Importance of *Sordello,*" in *The Major Victorian Poets: Reconsiderations,* ed. Isobel Armstrong (Lincoln: University of Nebraska Press, 1969), pp. 145–48.
8 Alan P. Johnson, "*Sordello*: Apollo, Bacchus, and the Pattern of Italian History," *Victorian Poetry* 7 (1969): 321–23.
9 Ibid., p. 324.
10 Jules Michelet, *Histoire de France* (Paris, 1855), VII, cxxxv.
11 Herbert F. Tucker, Jr., *Browning's Beginnings: The Art of Disclosure* (Minneapolis: University of Minnesota Press, 1980), pp. 17–18.
12 J. C. L. Simonde de Sismondi, *Histoire des républiques Italiennes du moyen âge,* new ed. (Paris, 1826), III, 7–8. See also Stewart W. Holmes, "The Sources of Browning's *Sordello,*" *Studies in Philology* 34 (1937): 487–88.
13 Johnson, "*Sordello*: The Pattern of Italian History," pp. 321–38.
14 D. G. Rossetti, *Works,* ed. William M. Rossetti (London, 1911), pp. 180, 268.
15 W. C. DeVane, "The Virgin and the Dragon," *Yale Review* 37 (Autumn 1947): 33–46.

16 John Maynard, *Browning's Youth* (Cambridge: Harvard University Press, 1977), pp. 150–51, 160–61, 425.

17 A. W. Crawford, "Browning's 'Cleon,'" *Journal of English and Germanic Philology* 26 (October 1927): 485–90; W. C. DeVane, *A Browning Handbook* (New York: Appleton-Century-Crofts, 1955), p. 264.

18 R. W. Emerson, *Works* (New York: Tudor Publishing, n.d.), II, 400, 402, 410. For Browning's reading of *Representative Men* see Theresa Coolidge, "A Letter by Elizabeth Barrett Browning," *More Books* 21 (1946): 179; cited by C. E. Tanzy, "Browning, Emerson, and Bishop Blougram," *Victorian Studies* 1 (March 1958): 256, who persuasively argues for the influence of Emerson's essay on Montaigne on "Bishop Blougram's Apology."

19 See E. S. Shaffer's treatment of the poem in *"Kubla Khan" and the Fall of Jerusalem: The Mythological School in Biblical Criticism and Secular Literature, 1770–1880* (Cambridge: Cambridge University Press, 1975), chap. 5.

20 Tanzy, "Browning, Emerson, and Bishop Blougram," p. 256.

21 John Ruskin, *Works,* ed. E. T. Cook and Alexander Wedderburn (London, 1903–12), X, lxvii. The point has been made by David J. DeLaura, "The Context of Browning's Painter Poems: Aesthetics, Polemics, Historics," *PMLA* 95 (May 1980): 374.

22 Giorgio Vasari, *Lives of the Most Eminent Painters, Sculptors, and Architects,* trans. Mrs. Jonathan Foster (London: Bohn, 1855–64), I, 103.

23 Alexander W. C. Lindsay, *Sketches of the History of Christian Art,* 2d ed. (London, 1885), II, 57–58; Ruskin, *Works,* XII, 8. Vasari says the campanile was left unfinished because the later architects thought it looked better without the Gothic steeple Giotto had provided (Vasari, *Lives,* I, 114).

24 *The Letters of Robert Browning and Elizabeth Barrett Barrett, 1845–46,* ed. Elvan Kintner (Cambridge: Belknap Press, 1969), I, 509.

25 *Letters of Dante Gabriel Rossetti,* ed. Oswald Doughty and J. R. Wahl (Oxford: Oxford University Press, 1965–67), I, 280.

26 DeLaura, "Context of Browning's Painter Poems," gives an excellent account of the background of Browning's painter poems.

27 Friedrich von Schlegel, *The Aesthetic and Miscellaneous Works,* trans. E. J. Millington (London: Bohn, 1849), pp. 5, 49, 145.

28 For an account of Rio see Mary Camille Bowe, *François Rio* (Paris: Boivin, 1938).

29 A. F. Rio, *De la poésie chrétienne dans son principe, dans sa matière et dans ses formes; Forme de l'art* (Paris, 1836), p. 90.

30 Henry James, *The American* (1877), quoted by Clara Thomas, *Love and Work Enough: The Life of Anna Jameson* (London: Macdonald, 1967), p. 176.

31 Mrs. Steuart Erskine, ed., *Anna Jameson: Letters and Friendships (1812–1860)* (London: T. Fisher Unwin, 1915), pp. 203–04.

32 G. H. Needler, ed., *Letters of Anna Jameson to Ottilie von Goethe* (London: Oxford University Press, 1939), p. 136. See also Gerardine MacPherson, *Memoirs of the Life of Anna Jameson* (Boston, 1878), pp. 190, 229–31.

33 *Letters of Robert Browning and Elizabeth Barrett Barrett,* I, 189–90. Mary Shelley's comments on Fra Angelico are in vol. II, pp. 144–45.

34 J. B. Bullen, "Browning's 'Pictor Ignotus' and Vasari's 'Life of Fra Barto-
    lommeo di San Marco,'" *Review of English Studies*, n.s. 23 (1972): 313–
    19. Bullen's thesis has been attacked by Michael Bright in *English Language
    Notes* 13 (1976): 192–94, 209–15, and again in *Studies in Browning and
    His Circle* 4, i (1976): 53–61. Bullen replied in *English Language Notes* 13
    (1976): 206–09.

35 Anna Jameson, *Memoirs of the Early Italian Painters* (Boston, 1859), p. 161.

36 Quoted by Bullen in "Browning's 'Pictor Ignotus,'" 314n.

37 Jameson, *Memoirs of the Italian Painters*, p. 18; cf. Vasari, *Lives*, I, 41–42.

38 Vasari, *Lives*, II, 449.

39 Jameson, *Memoirs of the Italian Painters*, pp. 163–65; Vasari, *Lives*, II, 457.

40 Jameson, *Memoirs of the Italian Painters*, pp. 84–85.

41 Ibid., pp. 87–88.

42 Ibid., pp. 89–90.

43 *The Letters of Robert Browning*, ed. Thurman L. Hood (New Haven: Yale
    University Press, 1933), p. 104.

44 Johnstone Parr, "Browning's *Fra Lippo Lippi*, Baldinucci, and the Milanesi
    Edition of *Vasari*," *English Language Notes* 3 (March 1966): 197–201; see
    also "Browning's *Fra Lippo Lippi*, Vasari's Masaccio, and Mrs. Jameson,"
    English Language Notes 5 (June 1968): 277–83.

45 Jameson, *Memoirs of the Italian Painters*, p. 81.

46 Ibid., pp. 222–23.

47 Rio, *De la poésie chrétienne*, pp. 406–26; Vasari, *Lives*, III, 181.

48 *New Letters of Robert Browning*, ed. W. C. DeVane and K. L. Knickerbocker
    (New Haven: Yale University Press, 1950), pp. 35–36.

49 Robert A. Greenberg, "Ruskin, Pugin, and the Contemporary Context of
    'The Bishop Orders His Tomb,'" *PMLA* 84 (1969): 1590.

50 A. C. Swinburne, *New Writings*, ed. Cecil Y. Lang (Syracuse: Syracuse Uni-
    versity Press, 1964), pp. 42–43.

51 Ruskin, *Works*, VI, 446–49.

52 *Letters of Robert Browning and Elizabeth Barrett Barrett*, II, 710.

CHAPTER 9: THE ENGLISH PRE-RAPHAELITES: ROSSETTI AND MORRIS

1 W. Holman Hunt, *Pre-Raphaelitism and the Pre-Raphaelite Brotherhood*
   (New York: AMS Press, 1967), I, 100–01.

2 William Michael Rossetti, *The P.R.B. Journal*, ed. William E. Fredeman
   (Oxford: Clarendon Press, 1975), p. 87.

3 John Ruskin, *Works*, ed. E. T. Cook and Alexander Wedderburn (London,
   1903–12), XII, 322.

4 W. M. Rossetti, *P.R.B. Journal*, pp. 93–94.

5 D. G. Rossetti, *Letters*, ed. O. Doughty and J. R. Wahl (Oxford: Clarendon
   Press, 1965), I, 40; cf. Milnes, *Life, Letters, and Literary Remains of John
   Keats* (London, 1848), I, 255. Hyder Rollins, in *The Letters of John Keats,
   1814–1821*, ed. H. E. Rollins (Cambridge: Harvard University Press,
   1958), II, 19, identifies the volume Keats looked at as Carlo Lasinio's
   Pitture a fresco del Campo Santo di Pisa (Florence, 1812). Leigh Hunt has

four pages of enthusiastic comment on the frescoes in the Campo Santo in his *Autobiography*, first published in 1850 (ed. J. E. Morpurgo, London: Cresset Press, 1949), pp. 340–43.

6 Hunt, *Pre-Raphaelitism and the Pre-Raphaelite Brotherhood*, I, 130–31; D. G. Rossetti, *Letters*, I, 73.

7 Camillo von Klenze, "The Growth of Interest in Early Italian Masters from Tischbein to Ruskin," *Modern Philology* 4 (October 1906): 207–74; Robyn Cooper, "The Relationship between the Pre-Raphaelite Brotherhood and Painters before Raphael in English Criticism of the Late 1840s and 1850s," *Victorian Studies* 24 (Summer 1981): 405–38.

8 *The Architectural Magazine* 3 (December 1836): 554; cited, though with rather culpable inaccuracy, by Sir Kenneth Clark in *The Gothic Revival: An Essay in the History of Taste,* rev. ed. (London: Constable, 1950), p. 147.

9 Alexander W. C. Lindsay, *Sketches of the History of Christian Art* (London, 1847), III, 422.

10 Keith Andrews, *The Nazarenes: A Brotherhood of German Painters in Rome* (Oxford: Clarendon Press, 1964), p. 79.

11 The best account of the Nazarenes is that of Keith Andrews cited above, note 10.

12 Joan Abse, *John Ruskin: The Passionate Moralist* (London: Quartet Books, 1980), pp. 61–62.

13 Ford Madox Ford, *Ford Madox Brown: A Record of His Life and Works* (London: Longmans, Green, 1896), p. 63. This anecdote, which was dictated to Ford Madox Ford by Brown just before his death in 1893, cannot be literally true, since there is no evidence the Nazarenes were ever called "Pre-Raphaelites."

14 Rossetti wrote to Hall Caine: "We had at that time a phenomenal antipathy to the Academy, and in sheer love of being outlawed signed our pictures with the well-known initials" (Hall Caine, *Recollections of Rossetti*, London, 1928, p. 59). In 1891 William Morris described the Pre-Raphaelite movement as "a really audacious attempt; a definite revolt against the Academical Art which brooded over all the Schools of civilized Europe at the time. . . . One must look upon it as a portion of the general revolt against Academicism in Literature as well as in Art. In Literature the revolt had taken place much earlier." May Morris, *William Morris: Artist, Writer, Socialist* (Oxford: Blackwell, 1936), I, 297.

15 Ruskin, *Works*, XII, 353–54.

16 *The Germ: Thoughts towards Nature in Poetry, Literature, and Art* (Portland, Maine: Thomas B. Mosher, 1898), pp. 14, 18–19.

17 Ruskin, *Works*, III, 623–24.

18 Sir Joshua Reynolds, *Discourses* (London, 1842), pp. 40–41.

19 Ruskin, *Works*, III, 154.

20 *The Germ*, p. 65.

21 W. M. Rossetti, *The P.R.B. Journal*, p. 64; Hunt, *Pre-Raphaelitism and the Pre-Raphaelite Brotherhood*, I, 135.

22 Ruskin, *Works*, XII, 357–58n.

23 D. G. Rossetti, *Letters*, I, 104.

24 F. G. Stephens, "Modern Giants," *The Germ*, p. 189; see also J. L. Tupper,

"The Subject in Art," ibid., pp. 11–18, 131–38; W. M. Rossetti, Review, ibid., p. 47.

25 W. M. Rossetti, *Ruskin: Rossetti: PreRaphaelitism* (London, 1899), pp. 11–12; D. G. Rossetti, *Letters,* I, 226, 283.

26 D. G. Rossetti, "Hand and Soul," *The Germ,* pp. 31–33; D. G. Rossetti, *Works,* ed. William M. Rossetti (London, 1911), pp. 553–55.

27 D. G. Rossetti, *Works,* p. 558.

28 Humphrey House, "Pre-Raphaelite Poetry," in *Pre-Raphaelitism: A Collection of Critical Essays,* ed. James Sambrook (Chicago: University of Chicago Press, 1974), p. 128.

29 D. G. Rossetti, *Letters,* I, 335.

30 Nicolette Gray, *Rossetti, Dante, and Ourselves* (London: Faber & Faber, 1947), pp. 23–24.

31 Carol Christ, *The Finer Optic: The Aesthetic of Particularity in Victorian Poetry* (New Haven: Yale University Press, 1975), pp. 18–20.

32 Ruskin, *Works,* XII, 334.

33 Jerome J. McGann, "Rossetti's Significant Details," *Victorian Poetry* 7 (Spring 1969): 41–54.

34 D. M. R. Bentley, "The *Belle Assemblée* Version of 'My Sister's Sleep,'" *Victorian Poetry* 12 (Winter 1974): 321–34; and "Rossetti's 'Ave' and Related Pictures," *Victorian Poetry* 15 (Spring 1977): 21–35; George P. Landow, *William Holman Hunt and Typological Symbolism* (New Haven: Yale University Press, 1979); Herbert L. Sussman, *Fact into Figure: Typology in Carlyle, Ruskin, and the Pre-Raphaelite Brotherhood* (Columbus: Ohio State University Press, 1979).

35 W. M. Rossetti, *Ruskin: Rossetti: PreRaphaelitism,* p. 40n; D. G. Rossetti, *Works,* p. 661.

36 W. M. Rossetti, *The P.R.B. Journal,* pp. 23, 71, 107; Hunt, *Pre-Raphaelitism and the Pre-Raphaelite Brotherhood,* I, 159.

37 D. G. Rossetti, *Works,* p. 666.

38 Richard L. Stein, *The Ritual of Interpretation* (Cambridge: Harvard University Press, 1975), pp. 127–28.

39 Gray, *Rossetti, Dante, and Ourselves,* pp. 20–21.

40 Alice Chandler, *A Dream of Order* (Lincoln: University of Nebraska Press, 1970), p. 194; Jerome Buckley, "Pre-Raphaelite Past and Present: The Poetry of the Rossettis," *Victorian Poetry* (London: E. Arnold, 1972), p. 134.

41 William Morris, *Collected Works* (London: Longmans, Green, 1910–15), XXII, 208. Hereafter cited parenthetically in the text.

42 May Morris, *William Morris,* I, 239–40.

43 Ibid., I, 121.

44 E. P. Thompson, *William Morris: Romantic to Revolutionary* (New York: Pantheon Books, 1977), p. 48; William Morris, *Letters to his Family and Friends,* ed. Philip Henderson (London: Longmans, Green, 1950), p. 186.

45 Walter Pater, "Poems by William Morris," *Westminster Review,* n.s. 90 (October 1868): 300.

46 Ibid., p. 307.

47 J. W. Mackail, *The Life of William Morris* (London, 1899), I, 45.

48 Pater, "Poems by Morris," p. 305.

49　May Morris, *William Morris,* I, 125–26.
50　Thompson, *William Morris,* p. 240.
51　Karl Marx, *Capital,* pt. VIII, chaps. 26–28. Morris would have found a similar account in H. M. Hyndman, *The Historical Basis of Socialism in England* (London, 1883), chaps. 1–3.
52　May Morris, *William Morris,* I, 131, 134, 281, 282.
53　John Goode, "William Morris and the Dream of Revolution," in *Literature and Politics in the Nineteenth Century,* ed. John Lucas (London: Methuen, 1971), p. 236.
54　Ibid., pp. 247–49.
55　Thompson, *William Morris,* p. 611.
56　May Morris, *William Morris,* I, 285, 241.
57　Ibid., I, 148, 287–88.

CHAPTER 10: THE VICTORIAN RENAISSANCE: WALTER PATER

1　Thomas Wright, *The Life of Walter Pater* (London, 1907), II, 179, 180; William Sharp, "Some Personal Reminiscences of Walter Pater," *Atlantic Monthly* 74 (December 1894): 810. Cf. David J. DeLaura, "*Romola* and the Origin of the Paterian View of Life," *Nineteenth-Century Fiction* 21 (December 1966): 225–33; Donald L. Hill, "Pater's Debt to *Romola,*" *Nineteenth-Century Fiction* 22 (March 1968): 361–77.
2　A. F. Rio, *De la poésie chrétienne* (Paris, 1836), chap. 8; John Ruskin, *Works,* ed. E. T. Cook and Alexander Wedderburn (London, 1903–12), XXII, 436; Mill, *On Liberty,* chap. 2; J. H. Newman, *Sermons on Various Occasions* (London, 1857), pp. 247–55; F. D. Maurice, *Modern Philosophy* (London, 1862), pp. 83–95; Charles Kingsley, *Letters and Memories* (London, 1877), II, 219; Henry Hart Milman, *Savonarola, Erasmus and Other Essays* (London, 1870), p. 73; Jules Michelet, *Renaissance; Histoire de France,* vol. VII (Paris, 1855), pp. 21–24; Pasquale Villari, *The History of Girolamo Savonarola and of His Times,* trans. Leonard Horner (London, 1863), I, 315–16; II, 372. Villari's Preface gives a full account of the history of Savonarola's reputation.
3　Gordon Haight, *George Eliot: A Biography* (Oxford: Oxford University Press, 1968), p. 326. Lewes first suggested the subject to George Eliot as a result of reading an account of Savonarola in a guidebook.
4　R. H. Hutton, *George Eliot: The Critical Heritage,* ed. David Carroll (London, 1971), p. 200.
5　Pater, *Miscellaneous Studies,* in *Works,* New Library Edition (London: Macmillan, 1910), p. 253. Hereafter cited parenthetically in the text with the following abbreviations to denote the individual volumes: R (*The Renaissance*), ME (*Marius the Epicurean*), IP (*Imaginary Portraits*), Ap (*Appreciations*), PP (*Plato and Platonism*), GS (*Greek Studies*), MS (*Miscellaneous Studies*), GL (*Gaston de Latour*), EG (*Essays from the "Guardian"*).
6　Arnold, *Complete Prose Works,* ed. R. H. Super (Ann Arbor: University of Michigan Press, 1960–77), I, 140; III, 258.
7　Ibid., III, 110. For a full account of Pater's relation to Arnold see David J.

DeLaura, *Hebrew and Hellene in Victorian England* (Austin: University of Texas Press, 1969), chaps. 10–17.

8 Michael Levey, *The Case of Water Pater* (London: Thames and Hudson, 1978), p. 116.

9 Ibid., pp. 123–25, 173, 137–38.

10 Arnold, *Complete Prose Works,* III, 230, 226.

11 Richard Ellmann, *Golden Codgers: Biographical Speculations* (London: Oxford University Press, 1973), p. 51.

12 Ruskin, *Works,* XII, 148–50.

13 Gerard Manley Hopkins, *Journals and Papers,* ed. Humphrey House and Graham Storey (London: Oxford University Press, 1959), p. 138.

14 Billie Andrew Inman, *Walter Pater's Reading: A Bibliography of His Library Borrowings and Literary References* (New York: Garland Publishing, 1981), pp. 37–38. I am much indebted to this modestly titled work, which is really a history of Pater's intellectual development.

15 Wallace K. Ferguson, *The Renaissance in Historical Thought* (Cambridge: Houghton Mifflin, 1948), pp. 69, 144–45. Ferguson notes that about this same time, in the 1830s, the word *humanism* (from the German *Humanismus*) was generally adopted to denote the intellectual movement associated with the revival of the classics (pp. 154–55).

16 Arnold, *Complete Prose Works,* V, 172, 438, 515.

17 Jules Michelet, *Renaissance* (1855), pp. 1–3 (my translation).

18 John Addington Symonds, *The Renaissance in Italy: The Age of the Despots* (London, 1897), p. 3.

19 Ferguson, *The Renaissance in Historical Thought,* pp. 204–05; Ernest Samuels, *Bernard Berenson: The Making of a Connoisseur* (Cambridge: Belknap Press, 1979), p. 36.

20 Wright, *Walter Pater,* I, 194; II, 115; Phyllis Grosskurth, *John Addington Symonds: A Biography* (London: Longmans, 1964), p. 157.

21 Walter Pater, "Review of Symonds, *Renaissance in Italy,*" reprinted in Walter Pater, *The Renaissance: Studies in Art and Poetry,* ed. Donald L. Hill (Berkeley: University of California Press, 1980), p. 198.

22 Professor Inman thinks Pater read Michelet by 1868 but says there is no evidence he read Burckhardt, whose work was not well known in the early years (*Pater's Reading,* pp. 175–76, 221).

23 Inman, *Pater's Reading,* pp. 264–66.

24 Walter Pater, *Westminster Review* 90 (1868): 300.

25 Ibid., p. 307.

26 Ibid.

27 Clive Bell, *Art* (New York: Capricorn Books, 1958), p. 137.

28 Leslie Stephen, "The Religion of All Sensible Men," *An Agnostic's Apology, and Other Essays* (London, 1893), p. 353.

29 T. H. S. Escott, "Two Cities and Two Seasons," *Macmillan's Magazine* 32 (July 1875): 257–58. R. V. Osbourn drew attention to Escott's article in "Marius the Epicurean," *Essays in Criticism* 1 (1951): 387–403.

30 Edward Gibbon, *The History of the Decline and Fall of the Roman Empire* (New York: Harpers, n.d.), I, 316.

31 Arnold, *Complete Prose Works,* III, 140–41.

32   Ibid., III, 156–57.

33   J. S. Mill, *Collected Works,* ed. J. M. Robson et al. (Toronto: University of Toronto Press, 1963–81), XVIII, 236–37.

34   Louise M. Rosenblatt, "The Genesis of *Marius the Epicurean,*" *Comparative Literature* 14 (Summer 1962): 242–60.

35   Ernest Renan, *Conférences d'Angleterre: Rome et le Christianisme; Marc-Aurèle,* 5th ed. (Paris, 1897); and "Marc-Aurèle," *The Nineteenth Century* 7 (May 1880): 742–55.

36   Inman, *Pater's Reading,* p. 88; Wright, *Walter Pater,* I, 156; Mary Duclaux, "Souvenirs sur Walter Pater," *La Revue de Paris* 32 (January 1925): 351.

37   Curtis Dahl, "Pater's *Marius* and Historical Novels on Early Christian Times," *Nineteenth-Century Fiction* 28 (June 1973): 1–24; Doris B. Kelly, "A Checklist of Nineteenth-Century English Fiction about the Decline of Rome," *Bulletin of the New York Public Library* 72 (1968): 400–13.

38   *Letters of Walter Pater,* ed. Lawrence Evans (Oxford: Clarendon Press, 1970), Letter 20.

39   Edmund Gosse, *Critical Kit-Kats* (1896), cited by Donald L. Hill in his excellent account of the reception of the Conclusion (Pater, *The Renaissance,* ed. Hill, pp. 443–51).

40   *Edinburgh Review* (April 1882), cited by Osbourne, *Essays in Criticism* 1 (1951): 401.

41   Mrs. Humphry Ward, *A Writer's Recollections* (London, 1918), p. 121.

42   *Letters of Walter Pater,* Letter 78.

43   Gerald C. Monsman, *Pater's Portraits: Mythic Pattern in the Fiction of Walter Pater* (Baltimore: Johns Hopkins University Press, 1967), p. 140.

44   *Letters of Walter Pater,* Letters 189, 47; cf. Monsman, *Pater's Portraits,* p. 198.

45   Wright, *Walter Pater,* II, 92; Monsman, *Pater's Portraits,* p. 103n. Pater's interest in Watteau was possibly stimulated by Edmond de Goncourt's *Catalogue raisonné d'oeuvre peint, dessiné et gravé d'Antoine Watteau* (Paris, 1875).

46   Monsman, *Pater's Portraits,* p. 9.

47   Pater, "Poems by William Morris," *Westminster Review* 90 (October 1868): 307.

CONCLUSION

1   William Morris, *News from Nowhere,* in *Collected Works* (London: Longmans, Green, 1910–15), XVI, 30.

2   J. H. Plumb, *The Death of the Past* (London: Macmillan, 1969), pp. 39–40.

3   G. H. Lewes, "The State of Historical Science in France," *British and Foreign Review* 16 (1844): 73.

4   Quoted in John Kenyon, *The History Men: The Historical Profession in England since the Renaissance* (London: Weidenfeld & Nicolson, 1983), p. 267.

5   Northrop Frye, *The Anatomy of Criticism: Four Essays* (Princeton: Princeton University Press, 1957), p. 346.

6   Oscar Wilde, *The Critic as Artist,* in *Works,* Sunflower Edition (New York: Lamb, 1909), X, 132.

7   Geoffrey Elton, "The Historian's Social Function," *Transactions of the Royal Historical Society,* 5th ser., 27 (1977): 199; S. R. Gardiner, *History of England, 1603–42* (London, 1884), I, viii; both quoted in Kenyon, *The History Men,* p. 286.

8   Plumb, *Death of the Past,* p. 100.

9   Lewes, "State of Historical Science in France," p. 73.

10 J. B. Bury, "The Science of History," in *The Varieties of History: From Voltaire to the Present,* ed. Fritz Stern (Cleveland: World Publishing, 1956), pp. 213–14.

11 Hajo Holborn, cited by Stern, *Varieties of History,* p. 25.

12 Ernst Troeltsch, *Protestantism and Progress,* trans. W. Montgomery (Boston: Beacon Press, 1958), p. 3.

13 Wilde, *The Critic as Artist,* in *Works,* X, 190–91.

Index